*Resolving*_____
Childhood Trauma

Dedication

To the unnamed women who are my coauthors, proud of who they are and all they have accomplished. This volume celebrates their commitment and courage.

To Stuart Oskamp—my colleague, husband, and lover, who has been with me all the way.

To our children and grandchildren, grown and growing, strong and whole, confident of their own worth, giving and receiving, loving and beloved—our hope for a better world.

Catherine Cameron

Resolving
Childhood Trauma

A Long-Term Study of Abuse Survivors

Sage Publications, Inc.
International Educational and Professional Publisher
Thousand Oaks ■ London ■ New Delhi

For information:

Sage Publications, Inc.
2455 Teller Road
Thousand Oaks, California 91320
E-mail: order@sagepub.com

Sage Publications Ltd.
6 Bonhill Street
London EC2A 4PU
United Kingdom

Sage Publications India Pvt. Ltd.
M-32 Market
Greater Kailash I
New Delhi 110 048 India

Printed in the United States of America

Library of Congress Cataloging-in-Publication Data

Cameron, Catherine.
    Resolving childhood trauma: A long-term study of abuse survivors / by Catherine Cameron.
        p.   cm.
Includes bibliographical references and index.
    ISBN 0-7619-2128-1
    ISBN 0-7619-2129-X
    1. Adult child sexual abuse victims—Longitudinal studies.
2. Recovered memory.   I. Title.
    RC569.5.A28   C35   2000
    616.85'8369—dc21   99-050448

This book is printed on acid-free paper.

00   01   02   03   04   05   10   9   8   7   6   5   4   3   2   1

Acquiring Editor:	Kassie Gavrilis
Editorial Assistant:	Anna Howland
Production Editor:	Denise Santoyo
Editorial Assistant:	Victoria Cheng
Designer/Typesetter:	Janelle LeMaster
Cover Designer:	Candice Harman

Contents

Preface

> *Healing from trauma depends upon . . . being able to safely tell the story to someone who is listening and who can be trusted to retell it truthfully to others in the community. So before analyzing, before classifying, before thinking, before trying to do anything, we should listen. . . . The singularity of each story is sacred stuff.*
> —Jonathan Shay (1994, pp. 4-5)

A DUTY TO LISTEN

Shay's admonition launches this preface and this book, *Resolving Childhood Trauma*. Shay challenges all professionals, whether researchers or therapists, who plumb the depths of traumatized lives, to really *listen*. I believe that Shay's message also applies to concerned laypersons whose lives touch those of trauma survivors. He calls on all of us to listen without prejudgment to those who, perhaps for the first time, reveal their profound and secret pain to another human being. He also challenges us to share what they teach us about human trauma with the larger social community.

As I apply Shay's admonition to my own 12-year study of child sexual abuse survivors, I feel affirmed in my research role of objective humanist. I was *not* my respondents' therapist; yet, by "listening" respectfully (through successive surveys over many years) to their struggles and their triumphs, I probably contributed to the healing process that was taking place during that same time period. Moreover, by consistently seeking *their* viewpoint in interviews, I encouraged the women to *shape my understanding* of trauma, rather than imposing my own viewpoint. In addition, I have faithfully retold their stories—of childhood betrayal, adult crisis, and dizzying cycles of struggle and healing—to audiences in a dozen countries of Europe and Asia as well as here at home. Yet, Shay's admonition *chastened*, as well as affirmed, me. I had promised respondents that their stories would be told in a *book*. They believed that such a book would promote both greater understanding of the crippling impact of child sexual abuse and the realistic hope for a better life through confronting that trauma. I was greatly delayed in fulfilling that commitment to my respondents. In these pages, at last, the promise is fulfilled.

To continue Shay's emphasis on responsible listening, the longitudinal surveys that elicited the data for this volume also provided a forum where adult survivors of child sexual abuse could safely tell their stories. As child victims, they had been ordered "not to tell." During silent decades of denial, they guarded their secret even from themselves. Following their crisis of recall as adults, their own families typically refused to listen. Some of these women were fortunate enough to have a caring friend or partner. Others shared their returning memories only with a concerned therapist. But for each one, there was, at last, someone who cared enough to listen, and their healing could begin.

However, *Resolving Childhood Trauma* is not only a forum for survivors. It also invites *you* to be their audience. This book was written for all persons who are willing to listen, who want to better understand the subjective experience of severe child sexual abuse, its long-term repercussions, and its potential resolution. Readers of this volume may come from various fields of trauma research, or they may be clinicians working with traumatized children or adults. Others will be family members devastated by the memories of a sibling or a child, or media persons caught up in the acrimonious debate, or trauma survivors struggling to put together the puzzle pieces of their life. Perpetrators may choose to be among the readers. Whatever your own motives for joining this audience of readers, you share with all the others a willingness to *listen*. The voices of scores of survivors speak from these pages, describing the pain they experienced and the progress they made in the dozen years between 1986 and 1998. Their openness will contribute significantly to a clearer understanding of the impact of child sexual abuse, and especially of incest.

A COMMON CONTEXT FOR ALL
TRAUMAS OF HUMAN ORIGIN

Why have I prefaced this book about *women survivors of child sexual abuse* with Shay's quotation from his study of *male Vietnam combat veterans*? The simple answer is that I believe Shay's words apply equally well to *both*. A fuller answer is that stories drawn from other traumatized populations have helped me to step outside the specific realm of child sexual abuse. I then began to see child sexual abuse within the context of three broad and inexorably linked issues: (a) All traumas of human origin are (b) violations of human rights and (c) of social justice. These overarching issues provide a common context for *any* study of trauma of human origin. Moreover, studying particular traumas can contribute to an understanding of all of them. As this book unfolds, you will find occasional statements about the relevance of the survivors' stories to the broader context of human rights violations and of atrocities that are recognized in the international system of justice. In making these links to larger human rights concerns, I hope to provide a deeper and broader perspective on childhood sexual abuse.

Resolving Childhood Trauma expands dialogue among therapists and researchers concerned with a wide variety of trauma settings. Professionals working with sexual abuse survivors have learned much from those who deal with survivors of other atrocities and human rights violations (for example, genocide, terrorist bombings, torture, or sexual enslavement). Similarly, their intense study of child sexual abuse and its aftermath is advancing the entire field of trauma study and treatment. *Labeling a problem* calls it to attention. *Naming a wrong* demands changed attitudes and corrective measures. "Child battering," "date rape," and "elder abuse" became visible as severe and prevalent wrongs when they were named. Similarly, if we recognize that sexual abuse can produce profound and long-lasting *amnesia*, we can no longer minimize damage by saying "children forget these things." Various sources of amnesia, along with delayed recall, are being increasingly recognized and acknowledged in the trauma literature (e.g., Arrigo & Pezdek, 1997; Elliott & Briere, 1995; Herman, 1992; Pope & Brown, 1996; van der Kolk, McFarlane, & Weisaeth, 1996).[1] The label has allowed us to see the problem.

There are many valuable books today that focus on a *particular* theme and readership—therapists, academicians, researchers, survivors, or laypersons. This book—perhaps because it was so long in its birthing—is different. It took on a shape and direction of its own. Layer on layer, it *became* a longitudinal study, it *transcended* child sexual abuse, it *demanded* comparison with other forms of trauma. And now it *requires* of readers, whatever their background, that they find for themselves whatever is most meaningful in these pages.

ANATOMY OF THIS BOOK

In this book, *Resolving Childhood Trauma*, the women respondents make a unique contribution to an exchange of ideas by teaching us about the life history of traumatic amnesia—its origin, its impact over time, and its eventual dissipation. Amnesia was both an outcome of their trauma and an influence on it for many years to come. The nature of their abuse (Chapter 4) helped to determine the kind of amnesia that sprang from it. In personal terms, their memory loss expressed itself across a *continuum* from full recall to obliteration of *all* traumatic incidents. In research terms, their "memory of abuse" ranged from no amnesia, through partial amnesia, to full amnesia. Yet, as this book went to press, over half of the women who originally believed that they had "no amnesia" regarding their abuse had also recalled important lost elements. And some amnesic women realized that there had been elements of awareness beneath their "not knowing." In the study, the women were assigned to their memory group in accordance with the way that they first presented themselves to their counselors and to me.

This volume is divided into five sections, briefly described here. In Part I, three introductory chapters provide an orientation to the various contexts that frame this study of survivors. The first explains the general background of this longitudinal study. The second reveals the societal context—during this period, for the first time in human history, serious attention was paid to child sexual abuse. It also briefly summarizes the research procedures and groups of participants. The third introductory chapter describes the respondents' early personal and family life.

Through the course of this book, beginning with Part II, the survivors unfold their stories sequentially—from childhood abuse to adult resolution—a real-life journey of anywhere from 35 to 65 years. They describe the early part of that journey (up until 1986, when this study began) *retrospectively*. They share their healing experience (from 1986 to the present) *concurrently*. As a reader, you can walk with them, witnessing their struggles and recognizing their remarkable growth. Chapter 4 introduces the original group of 72 women respondents and describes their personal histories of childhood sexual abuse and the family settings where most of it took place. Chapter 5 gives evidence of the cumulative developmental damage that followed in the wake of their trauma. Chapter 6 examines amnesia as a key issue—why it is linked to *many* forms of trauma (not just to sexual abuse) and how it both facilitates and disrupts the lives of victims. For many centuries, society had virtually denied the existence of incest and minimized the prevalence and impact of other forms of sexual abuse. This idealized "construction of social reality" dominated world opinion until the latter part of the 20th century. Behavioral patterns of amnesia, dissociation, and posttraumatic stress disorder (PTSD) became means to psychic survival for respondents until they could safely address their trauma in adulthood.

In Part III, Chapter 7 focuses on the interim years between abuse and recall. It spans a period that typically stretched over three decades of "secrecy and silence" in the women's lives—a period of time when they denied their past abuse in whatever way they could. Their stories recount the public behavior, private feelings, and the means of coping that they used to avoid dealing with the past. In Chapter 8, the (formerly) amnesic women describe the triggering of lost memories, and the nonamnesic women share their reevaluation of past trauma. The meaning and impact of what they then recalled ended the long silence of the interim years.

Part IV (Chapters 9 through 12) begins with the disruptive "crisis of recall" as survivors faced the past, frequently through flashbacks, and recognized the wrongs they had suffered. It follows them through the roller-coaster process of remembering past traumas that still held power over them—a journey that took many months or even years, depending on the severity of what they had to recall. Amnesic women, previously unable to remember, now faced a horror that they had not known existed. Nonamnesic women, who had been unable to forget, were forced at last to recognize the meaning and impact of abuse, which they had tried so long to ignore or minimize. Chapter 10 illuminates the survivor's personal responses to remembering and the nature of the long process of recall and recovery, whereas Chapter 11 summarizes the reactions of people close to them. Chapter 12 examines an issue faced by many of the survivors—whether to confront their past abuser(s) if they were still living, and if so, how, when, and where such a confrontation could best occur.

In Part V, Chapter 13, "Changed Lives," updates the reader on the women's recovery by 1992, 6 years after the original survey. It describes the momentous task faced by survivors of integrating the reality of abuse into their concept of the world, their life story, and their view of themselves. Important changes had taken place in the women over the span of this study. A major but seldom emphasized task of recovery was to recognize and overthrow destructive patterns of thought, feeling, and action, which may have helped them survive over the years but which now obstructed their recovery. This chapter describes the women's subjective struggle toward wholeness, as well as objective measures of their success. Most of these survivors had come to terms with the past, were dealing realistically with the present, and were feeling optimistic about the future. Chapter 14, the Epilogue, was written in late 1998 and 1999 to bring closure to the women's stories. As the book manuscript was being reviewed prior to publication, a final survey of the respondents revealed still further personal and interpersonal growth. Letting go of the past, the women had moved well beyond mere "recovery." They were embarking on a new way of living—with strength, compassion, and even joy. Trauma was no longer the driving force in their lives.

NOTE

1. Of course, evidence of amnesia (and memory loss) was not *absent* from earlier trauma literature. However, it was typically *assumed* to be common in the aftermath of trauma, without being *examined* as a key variable in its own right.

PART I

About This Book

Andrea, *age 38, began in 1986 to remember sexual abuse at the hands of her father and her uncle when she was a child. She was in crisis. Memories, like ghosts from the past, haunted her by day, and distressing dreams disturbed her sleep at night. A week before our first interview, she dreamed of finding a small band of sexually abused children, disconsolate and wandering the streets. In her dream, Andrea shepherded them into a court of justice, choosing the oldest, a 10-year-old girl, to tell their story to a judge. However, peering down at the child from his high bench, the judge frowned, pounded his gavel, and announced impatiently, "Case dismissed. This girl cannot give evidence. She has no mouth."*

This book provides a mouth for Andrea's silenced child. It is the voice of all the women who entrusted me with their experiences of childhood sexual abuse. It tells the story of their courage to remember and to re-solve trauma experienced decades before. They have told their stories to promote a greater understanding of the impact of childhood sexual abuse and of the challenge involved in overcoming it. Their hope, and mine, is that such understanding will help to provide a climate in which this kind of exploitation of children will become unthinkable.

CHAPTER 1

Background

*Being one of the women who help you with your book makes me feel
less alone. You "connect me" to the others, and we are working this
through together.*

—Pamela, 1988

In the past two decades, more people of all ages have been working
through the sexual traumas of childhood than ever before in the history
of humankind. This book could not have been written 20 years ago. Its focus on amnesia would have been premature. Back then, mental health
workers and researchers were only beginning to recognize and document
the prevalence of sexual abuse and its position among the most serious
forms of trauma. Now, they are far more knowledgeable. They have created a burgeoning literature of increasingly refined information about
the prevalence and consequences of sexual abuse as well as its treatment.
These pioneers have mapped out the terrain. Now it is time to specialize
and to ask questions that remain unanswered. We need research-based
books that investigate particular aspects of child sexual abuse. This
book's contribution is to relate traumatic amnesia to survivors' experiences over time and to describe to others the meaning of abuse, its aftermath, and its healing in their lives.

As professionals pursuing specialized knowledge, we also need to relate our work to the overall context of trauma. In this, the most violent
century ever, there have been many forms of trauma to study. Two general types of trauma are differentiated by their origin. The first is unin-

tended trauma, such as major accidents (e.g., the crash of TWA Flight 800) and calamities of nature (e.g., the Northridge earthquake); these are called *disasters*. The other is traumas of deliberate human origin (e.g., the bombing of the Oklahoma City Federal Building, barbaric hate crimes); these are called *atrocities*. This second form of trauma ruptures basic personal and societal assumptions about human bonding. The closer the relationship that is betrayed, the greater is the psychological damage. This is true whether trauma occurs on a battlefield or in a small child's bedroom (American Psychiatric Association, 1994; Freyd, 1996; Shay, 1994).

Research into one form of trauma can benefit another. The study of posttraumatic stress disorder (PTSD) in combat veterans was valuable later for understanding the more personal trauma of child sexual abuse. Similarly, the concept of "amnesia and recovered memories," when applied to survivors, called attention to the fact that amnesia (and other memory deficits) follow many kinds of trauma. Examples of amnesia that have been well documented in the trauma literature involve survivors of natural catastrophes such as earthquakes and floods, witnesses to murder and other violent crimes, and victims of torture or concentration camps (Arrigo & Pezdek, 1997; Pope & Brown, 1996; van der Kolk, 1987). Naming the occurrence of amnesia permitted it to be recognized more easily, and finding amnesia in many traumatic contexts has underscored its importance.

The years that I have spent completing this book allowed me to maintain contact with most of the research participants, to recognize the enormous complexity of their healing process, and to bear witness to their painful but gratifying growth. In trying to understand why some survivors of sexual abuse became amnesic, how this affected their growing-up years, and what caused their confrontation with the past as adults, I familiarized myself with multidisciplinary studies of memory. As a result, I find myself advocating cooperation among *all* professionals interested in memory, and especially between experimental and clinical psychologists. It is common knowledge that these fields diverge in method and focus. It is less often recognized that, with cooperation instead of antagonism, both disciplines could be enriched.

In writing about *women* sexually assaulted as children, I am fully aware that many men have also been traumatized. Their story is being written by others (e.g., Hunter, 1990; Lew, 1988), as adult male survivors also begin to deal with the past. Such accounts reveal trauma and consequences similar to (but also different from) those that the women survivors describe. And among the husbands of my respondents, some of the most supportive were men who had themselves endured child sexual abuse, sometimes at the hands of women.

Resolving Childhood Trauma is based on longitudinal survey research that spanned the years between 1986 and 1998. As I look back over these two decades, I note that society's attitude toward "survivors"[1] of child sexual abuse has shown a great deal of fluctuation. Around 1980, several highly respected authors helped to establish public recognition of child sexual abuse as a serious problem with long-lasting consequences for survivors (cf. Finkelhor, 1979; Herman, 1981; Meiselman, 1978; Rush, 1980). In contrast, around 1990, following several years of concern and attention to survivors from professionals, laypersons, and the media, a backlash against them became evident. They began to be viewed by some authors as attention-seeking, self-pitying and whiny, and egocentric (cf. Loftus & Ketcham, 1994; Nethaway, 1993; Tavris, 1993).

Meanwhile, as I continued to gather information for this volume, I found my respondents deeply committed to the project. By 1992, they were filling out the third full survey in 6 years. Whatever they were asked—questions about the past, descriptions of their current situation and concerns, or hopes for the future—they were consistently patient and helpful, and often hopeful. Such a response was not congruent with the then-current negative image of survivors.

In the 1990s, television and radio talk shows were increasingly featuring survivors who were emotional exhibitionists. But were my research respondents attention seekers? If that label means wanting the limelight, the answer is an unequivocal no. Their silence about abuse had endured for an average of 30 years, and it was followed by such a severe crisis of recall that many, especially the formerly amnesic women, were suicidal. Then, entering therapy, they alternated for many months between reluctant admission and desperate denial of their abuse. However, although these women were not seeking the limelight, they *did* want to be heard. They had waited from childhood for that, and it gave them a sense of grounding to explore their own grief and fear with other human beings for the first time.

Were they self-pitying? One respondent was for awhile. She described a desolate childhood of total rejection. As a teenager, she was institutionalized for several years. At 38, she was on full medical disability and could scarcely leave her bed. More generally, most respondents did *not* pity themselves (nor did they solicit the pity of others). However, they did have to work through profound grief at the many losses of their lives. Many had felt orphaned as children, having "lost" a father through incest and a mother through the secrecy that separated them. And there was heartbreak in the present also, when they tried to share their story with angry adult siblings. But their grief should not be equated with self-pity.

Were the research respondents egocentric, uninterested in social wrongs, concerned only with what was happening to themselves? Again, my considered answer is no. Certainly, these survivors were forced to focus inwardly when memories brought on florid symptoms of PTSD. Like soldiers returning from combat duty, they were overwhelmed by flashbacks, nightmares, and intrusive memories. But meanwhile, they managed to carry out their responsibilities to jobs, homes, families, and relatives. In the limited ways that their strength allowed, some also became social activists, speaking out so that other children might be spared. Many viewed this book as a podium, allowing them to tell professionals and the general public what "fondling, stroking, and caressing" really meant to a child. Some of the women also invested time in helping others to survive. For example, **NANCY** opened her home to weekly meetings of survivors. **Pam** regularly drove child victims to their therapy groups for help, befriending them as well. **Audrey** volunteered on a rape crisis line. As for mutual caring (in therapy groups I visited), none surpassed what I witnessed among the imprisoned women.

Books are often born of personal as well as professional interest. As a social psychologist in the area of family life—a professor, survey researcher, and author—I found myself increasingly concerned with the issue of violence in society, communities, and families. In 1984, I began to remember childhood sexual assault. I had been amnesic to it for half a century. As I pursued my own recovery and became increasingly capable of objectivity, I realized that my personal and professional background would enable me to conduct sensitive interviews with other survivors. I was trained in research and was an "insider" as well.[2] Getting to know the women who participated in this research as respondents has been a unique privilege. Their commitment to understanding and recovery has been unfaltering. This is their story, their message, their book.

NOTES

1. In this book, for simplicity of exposition, the terms *survivor, abuser,* and *sexual abuse* are used with recognition that these are claims made by the respondents. *Amnesia, partial amnesia,* and *nonamnesia* are classifications assigned to participants on the basis of the extent to which they had (previously) remembered their abuse.

2. Of course, the research positions of insider or outsider present unique risks that must be considered, as well as particular advantages. It is especially important for a researcher (a) to reveal his or her relationship to the research topic, (b) to allow for the rejection of expectations through the testing of hypotheses, and (c) to avoid interpreting ambiguous findings as proof of a hypothesis.

CHAPTER 2

A Study of Sexual Abuse Survivors

Mine was the last home where one might suspect incest. My world shifted off its axis when I remembered, and I had no place to stand to put it right again.

—**Amy,** 1986

A my had grown up in a family that was "privileged in every way." Or so she had told herself. She was 43 when I first interviewed her and had remembered incest a year earlier. Her feelings of desperation exploded in the words quoted above. In the past, she had always found life difficult, and she had faulted herself for not coping better. (Other troubled people came from troubled homes, she thought, so *their* inadequacies were more understandable than hers.) Gradually, over time, Amy had managed to improve her living situation through a happy second marriage and a better job. She was feeling more confident and secure and, for the first time, it was personally "safe to remember." And it was not by chance that she remembered in the 1980s, when social support became more available.

THE "DISCOVERY" OF CHILD SEXUAL ABUSE

In the 1980s, three factors—increasing public recognition of the exploitation of children, the demythologizing of Freud and Kinsey, and greater professional understanding of the nature and impact of trauma—created

8

an environment in which survivors of childhood sexual trauma could break through their past denial and find help.

Changing Social Attitudes

Although the sexual abuse of children is centuries old (Kahr, 1991), it had been denied, minimized, or ignored by society in recent times (Rush, 1980). Americans, especially, had clung to a "Norman Rockwell" view of childhood. Although parents dutifully warned their children about going off with strangers, they did not conceive of danger in the schoolroom or within the family. For most, incest was imaginable only in some ancient culture or, possibly, in someone else's neighborhood. As recently as 1976, an authoritative textbook of psychiatry cited the yearly incidence of incest in the United States as being between one and two cases per million population—which would translate into less than 500 cases per year (Freedman, Kaplan, & Sadock, 1976, p. 770). In contrast, a more recent edition of the same text estimated that 15 million U.S. women had experienced incestuous approaches (Kaplan & Sadock, 1988, p. 378) and stated the annual incident rate of reported child sexual abuse cases in the United States as being at least 125,000 per year (p. 635).

Abuse victims, as part of the larger society, absorbed the denial all around them. If they remembered what happened to them, they usually labeled it as normal, or as punishment, or something children had to put up with. If they were amnesic, their inner denial was reinforced by those who might have helped them. Likewise, sexual abuse perpetrators denied their actions to themselves and to their secret victims: They reasoned that they were "satisfying" the needs of seductive preschoolers, "educating" their school-age children in sexual matters, or "protecting" their teenage girls from predatory adolescent males by providing a "safe" sexual outlet at home. (All these rationalizations had been stated to the women who participated in this research.) How could anyone see a problem that no one believed existed?

Social awareness of the prevalence of abuse developed during the latter part of the 20th century. Decade by decade, the conscience of the nation awoke to new revelations of the exploitation of smaller and weaker members of society—children, women, and those disadvantaged by handicap or age. Evidence of family violence was increasingly met with social acknowledgment and intervention. In the 1960s, the prevalence and horror of child physical abuse was recognized. In the 1970s, the rape and battering of women began to concern society. During these years, volunteers working in safe houses for women and children were increasingly hearing tales of marital rape and family incest.

In the 1980s, the sexual misuse of children exploded as a major social issue. Suddenly, both mental health professionals and the general public began to face the reality and extent of current child sexual abuse. A rash of charges—against nursery schools, respected community leaders, and parents—was instrumental in creating this new awareness. Police exposure of documented evidence and frequent reports in the media kept this shocking "new" social problem in the public eye. Reluctantly, Americans accepted the notion that child sexual abuse was widespread in our society. Public outrage at the escalating evidence, as well as sympathy for the young victims, created a climate that demanded disclosure. Neighbors, teachers, and the children themselves began reporting sexual abuse offenses. Incest, which had previously been viewed as an arcane practice studied by anthropologists in primitive societies, was suddenly something that could happen down the street or next door. The public was finally recognizing sexual abuse as a current assault on childhood.

However, it soon became evident that the problem was not a new one. Survey researchers were finding noteworthy percentages of adults who remembered being sexually misused as children, and mental health professionals found an increasing number of women who were still affected by their childhood sexual exploitation. This group of victims, who had always remembered their childhood abuse, were sharing their burden with counselors, and many survivors of sexual abuse first knocked on the doors of therapists in the 1980s. Although many therapists had originally been trained to treat reports of childhood sexual abuse as "fantasies," they were now recognizing truth in such reports, whereas most victims' stories would probably not have been accepted earlier.

In the more enlightened setting of the 1980s, genuine social concern was expressed for both child victims and adult survivors of sexual abuse. In this safer, more understanding environment, molested children were speaking up, and women who had once been similarly traumatized were entering treatment to try to repair past damage to their lives. Gradually, adult male survivors added their voices. These men and women were the damaged children of yesterday, benefiting from concern for the children of today. A new acronym, AMACs (adults molested as children), was applied to those who were finally confronting sexual abuse decades after it occurred.

The Demythologizing of Freud and Kinsey

A hundred years ago, Freud and Janet concluded that the problems of most of their women patients stemmed from their seduction as children by adults (and especially by their fathers). In response, scathing criticism from their colleagues was heaped on this seduction theory. Janet held to his views steadfastly and lost status. Freud revamped his and won fame (see Herman, 1992, for a fuller description). In Freud's revised theory, memories of incest were viewed as fantasies arising from the child's sexual drive rather than from actual adult exploitation. For generations, this perspective shaped the beliefs of therapists toward child victims and adult survivors. Clients were frequently told that they themselves had been seductive children who had imagined or invited incest.

Later views about incest were shaped by Freud's cover-up of socially respected fathers whose molested daughters had been his patients. Over the decades, the "seductive child" was considered at least equally responsible for incestuous situations. In 1907, Abraham (1927) agreed with Freud's revised theory, advancing the notion of the child as a co-conspirator in her own abuse. In 1937, psychiatrists Bender and Blau described adult-child sexual relations as a "form of childhood sexuality" (p. 518), stated that the pre-pubescent children they had studied had usually cooperated or even initiated the contact, and suggested that "the child might have been the actual seducer rather than the one innocently seduced" (p. 514).

These psychiatric views that absolved men from culpability in child sexual abuse continued well into the 1970s and extended to blaming the wives as well as the abused daughters. In 1967, Raphling, Carpenter, and Davis described incest as frequently originating in the daughter as seducer, which they explained was due to a frustrating relationship with her mother that forced her to seek love and security from her father:

> This can lead to a confusing relationship in which paternal affection and sexuality merge. The father . . . may justify the sexual relationship as an expression of his own love for his daughter, or he may view himself as her protector and initiator into the mysteries of sexual experience. (p. 506)

As late as 1976, a major textbook of psychiatry proclaimed that the wives of incestuous fathers "promote the incestuous liaison by frustrating their husbands sexually or symbolically deserting them" and suggested that "conceivably, such wives identify with their daughters and gratify in fantasy their childhood incestuous wishes toward their own fathers" (Freedman et al., 1976, p. 771). Shortly thereafter, however, researchers such as Rush (1980), Masson (1984), and Herman (1981) persuasively documented that Freud's distortion of the evidence of sexual trauma in his female patients occurred after he had recognized that their problems were rooted in father-daughter incest.

The famous Kinsey studies of human sexuality (Kinsey, Pomeroy, & Martin, 1948; Kinsey, Pomeroy, Martin, & Gebhard, 1953) were shaped by the earlier psychiatric views and, in turn, reinforced them. Kinsey's huge tomes on male and female sexual behavior indexed *incest* only once (Kinsey et al., 1948, p. 558). That single paragraph began and ended as follows:

> Heterosexual incest occurs more frequently in the thinking of clinicians and social workers than it does in actual performance. . . . The most frequent incestuous contacts are between pre-adolescent children, but the number of such cases among adolescent or older males is very small.

Any preadolescent sexual contact with adult relatives that *did* exist, according to Kinsey et al. (1953), was initiated and prolonged because children, as sexual beings, wanted it (p. 118). Potential distress or harm to the child was downplayed: "It is difficult to understand why a child, except for cultural conditioning, should be disturbed at having its genitalia touched, or . . . even more specific sexual contacts" (p. 121). According to Kinsey and his colleagues, society's rigid attitude had led to "the current hysteria over sex offenders," which was likely to "disturb the child more seriously than the sexual contacts themselves" (p. 121).

Kinsey's work, like Freud's, has also fallen in reputation. Recently (e.g., Jones, 1997), there have been revelations of Kinsey's personal homosexual, masochistic, and nudist inclinations and of his preoccupation with sexual aberrations (e.g., videotaping the sexual interactions of staff members). He saw himself as liberating society from Victorian prudery. There is evidence that these private predispositions encroached on, or even governed, the direction of his research: His sampling did not represent a cross section of Americans, and his conclusions about the sexual behavior of Americans were slanted polemically. If Kinsey had informed readers of his personal stance, they would have been wiser consumers of his findings.

One of the most questionable aspects of Kinsey's research is the source of information for his sections on preadolescent orgasms (Kinsey et al., 1948, pp. 175-180; 1953, pp. 105, 127). There, several tables provide data such as the number and speed of orgasms that small children can have in a given time period. Questions have been raised as to the sources of such information—was it supplied by pedophiles, gained through observed experiments, or even fabricated? A recent television documentary (Tate, 1998) disclosed that Kinsey accepted information from men whom he knew were confirmed pedophiles and treated it as scientific proof that children are sexual from birth and enjoy sex with adults. One particular informant ("Mr. Green") apparently kept detailed records of his sexual encounters with hundreds of infants and children throughout the period when Kinsey was collecting data. Green even used a stopwatch to note his subjects' orgasms, data that are presented in Kinsey's tables.

The writings of Freud and Kinsey and their followers have permeated popular wisdom and shaped professional theories and attitudes, as evidenced by the experience of my research participants. **Alison** reported, "My uncle said that he could tell I was 'experienced.' At the time, I was 5 years old." **Chelsea** recalled, "I was 6 when the young man attacked me, and my first child-thought on remembering was 'I must have asked for it.' " And when **Adel** confronted her father, a retired therapist, about his abuse of her, his reaction astounded her: "He treated me like a client with a 1-hour appointment—trying to help me understand my fantasies and why I wanted what my mother had!"

Informed Professionals

About the same time that Freudian views began to be challenged, mental health professionals were becoming increasingly informed about psychological trauma. A major shift in professional understanding came with the recognition and labeling of a problem that affected many Vietnam War veterans—often long after their return home. They suffered from a delayed reaction termed *posttraumatic stress disorder* (PTSD)—which came to be recognized as a normal response to exceptional stress rather than as pathological.

Alert therapists began to notice, among women clients recalling child sexual abuse, symptoms that were similar to those of veterans—intrusive thoughts and flashbacks alternating with avoidance of reminders of the past; numbed affect alternating with hyperalertness—the cyclical symptoms of PTSD. Like combat veterans, these women were experiencing delayed PTSD. Those who had never forgotten their sexual abuse, but had survived by denying its impact, now felt compelled to deal with its effect on their lives. Others, stunned to remember early trauma for the first time, sought therapy. Like veterans who had forgotten particular wartime ordeals, these women had—to a greater or lesser extent—lost episodes of childhood abuse from consciousness.

Clinicians found that explaining away traumatic memories as "symbolic" or as childhood sexual fantasies no longer made sense. They saw before them survivors of a secret war, the walking wounded of our society, who had been unable to explain the fear and depression that shadowed their days (Cameron, 1994a). Some were making remarkable contributions to society at a cost known only to them; others, less fortunate, were in the psychiatric wards of hospitals.

These three factors—increasing public recognition of the reality of abuse, the demythologizing of Freud and Kinsey, and greater professional understanding of the nature and impact of trauma—promoted a safer and more caring atmosphere in which survivors of childhood sexual trauma could face the truth they had fled from and begin to find support. Increasingly, such survivors became the object of intensive study (e.g., Courtois, 1988; Forward & Buck, 1987; Gelinas, 1983; Herman, 1992; Meiselman, 1990). The next section describes my own longitudinal research study of sexual abuse survivors.

OVERVIEW OF THIS RESEARCH STUDY

The survivors whom you will meet in the pages of this book were among those who first sought help in the more informed and concerned social atmosphere of the 1980s. Their experiences may or may not be similar to those of the whole population of women who have been sexually abused as children. In survey research, it is useful to have a representative sample (of registered voters, for example) so that your findings can be generalized to the whole population. However, in my study this was impossible because a population of child sexual abuse survivors could not be identified. Moreover, because my goal was to target a specific topic in a particular way, a purposive sample offered me salient advantages.

I wanted to do in-depth interviews with women survivors who had been traumatized severely enough that they required intense counseling or psychotherapy many years later. I sought such women through private therapists, asking that they select clients who (a) had been amnesic to their abuse for at least 15 years and (b) had never before dealt with their trauma. I also requested women who had never forgotten their sexual abuse. This plan allowed me to compare two distinct memory groups —(formerly) amnesic and nonamnesic women. In examining respondents' questionnaires, I found an intermediate group of women who remembered part but not all of the key facts about their childhood abuse. Thus, these three groups differed in the extent of their amnesia—full, partial, or none. But in other respects, they were quite homogeneous, for they were all (a) in private therapy, (b) dealing with child sexual abuse that had occurred decades earlier, and (c) had never dealt with that trauma before. Because these groups were similar in these respects, differences (based on their memory of abuse) were expected to stand out.

Seeking research participants through their therapist, as I did, yielded humane benefits: A private therapist, who knew which clients had (or had not) experienced amnesia, was also likely to know who would be willing, and secure enough, to take part in the study. Having met me, she (or he) could reassure clients of the legitimacy and importance of the research project. Moreover, if the questionnaire or interview proved disturbing, the therapist could provide support.

Although this study's findings may not exactly represent the general survivor population, it contributes to the emerging literature in several unique ways: First, it documents the process of trauma resolution for a group of survivors over 12 years. During this period of time, intense research by other writers has enriched our knowledge about trauma, based on other kinds of samples. Second, the study adds to our understanding of different ways that dissociative amnesia manifests itself. And third, it allows parallels to be drawn between trauma within a family (e.g., incest) and trauma within a society (e.g., repressive dictatorships, or genocide).

Amnesia and Remembering

In adopting amnesia as my focus and a long-term series of surveys as my means, I was both planful and fortuitous. My purpose was to study

amnesia as both an effect and a cause. The questions that drove the research were:

- What was it about the childhood sexual abuse that led to amnesia?

And in turn,

- What impact did the amnesia have on long-term consequences and
  recovery?

The research plan was to relate amnesia (its presence or absence) to severity of trauma by comparing women at the polar ends of the memory
continuum. My general expectations, or hypotheses, were: Women who
had been amnesic to their childhood sexual abuse would have had more
extreme abuse (by criteria used in previous research) than women who
had never been amnesic; they would report more symptoms over the
years; and they would have a more difficult recovery.

To achieve a purposive sample, I had therapists ask survivor clients
who represented these extremes of memory if they would participate.
Those respondents who had (until recently) not remembered their abuse,
I termed *amnesic*; and those who had always remembered it, I termed
nonamnesic. Among the 60 questionnaires received, 25 women qualified
as amnesic but only 21 as nonamnesic. The other 14 had remembered
parts of their abuse and had been amnesic to the rest. Realizing that they
could serve as an intermediate memory subgroup, I termed them *partially
amnesic*.[1]

The opportunity also arose for me to meet with a therapy group at a
women's penitentiary. It was composed of 12 imprisoned women who
had been offered the opportunity of dealing with their child sexual abuse
in a group setting. I was impressed by the atmosphere of mutual concern
among these women, under the guidance of a therapist who volunteered
her time each week. When a later wave of questionnaires was sent out,
these imprisoned women proved as committed as any other participants
to helping with the research. Because individual interviews with them
were not feasible (with one exception), they were not assigned to a memory subgroup. But whenever the total sample is described in this book,
these imprisoned women are included, bringing the initial sample to 72.
These survivors provided a valued perspective on the aftermath of child

sexual abuse, although again they should not be considered representative of imprisoned survivors.

Like the amnesic, partially amnesic, and nonamnesic women, the imprisoned women are discussed as a separate subgroup from time to time throughout this book. These four categories of survivors are described more fully in Chapter 3. Meanwhile, the following brief discussion of the original survey will orient the reader to the research behind this book.

The Original Survey

The content of the questionnaire. The study was originally intended as a single survey, consisting of a seven-page questionnaire followed by intensive personal interviews with those women who provided information on how to contact them. The initial 1986 questionnaire solicited the women's subjective description of (a) their sexual abuse, (b) its impact during the years before they sought help as adults, (c) the triggering of old memories and the decision to seek therapy, and (d) the beginnings of therapeutic healing. (The information in Parts I and II of this book came mainly from this first survey.) An estimated 50% of those contacted by their therapists responded to the original seven-page questionnaire in 1986. Their ages ranged from 25 to 64. On average, 30 years had passed since their first sexual abuse (36 years for those who had been amnesic).

Benefits for respondents. Filling out the questionnaire provided interesting bonuses for many of the respondents. I provided a second copy of the questionnaire for each woman and carbon paper so that she could fill in both at the same time. Participating gave many of the women some objectivity about their distressing memories, and they felt less isolated in their shame and grief: "Writing it down made everything more real and manageable." Therapists appreciated the way the questionnaire helped to cue additional memories or clarified those previously recalled by clients. Some women shared their copy with the therapist, who reproduced it for the office file and used it during therapy. One small group of survivors held a "questionnaire day," bringing their copies to therapy to discuss key issues. Often, the women were later astonished to read what they had written. This was especially true for the sentence completions, (e.g., "I am angry when . . . ," "I am lonely when . . ."), which sometimes tapped into feelings unrecognized until a later reading.

Delayed responses. Return of the first questionnaire was occasionally delayed (even as long as 12 months) for a variety of reasons. First, the seven-page questionnaire, although composed mostly of checklists to lessen emotional pressure, was time-consuming. It covered (among other topics) the molestation, its impact at several points in time, and the healing process to date. Most women took time to write comments, some even adding extra pages. Second, respondents were dealing with an extremely personal and painful topic. Judging from comments in the margins, answering the questionnaire was a stop-and-go process for many, interrupted by headaches, abdominal pain, nausea, and flashbacks. **Nell** explained, "Usually, I deal with this problem in snatches. But answering these questions made me recognize what happened to me from beginning to end. It was hard to face everything at once." Third, other participants set the questionnaire aside until they could give fuller and more accurate answers: "My brother gave it to me a year ago, but I remembered almost nothing at that time." Several delayed responses occurred when participants, upset by the questionnaire, threw it away or "lost" it for a month or two. "Now I feel differently," said **Pam**, requesting another copy. In an intriguing variation, two women reported that they had discarded their own carbon copy but sent me the original.

Most delayed responses came from (formerly) amnesic women. Within days or weeks of their first memories, they were experiencing turbulent emotions, with bits of the past emerging and receding and new levels of traumatic response. Maintaining confidence in their memories was important when recurring doubts assailed them and essential when they faced the disbelief of friends and relatives. The amnesics, especially, brought a strong sense of responsibility to what they reported. Grasping the truth was essential to them. Many had grounded their values, their goals, their very lives, on a lie—that they had had a privileged and protected childhood—so they were careful not to commit uncertainties to paper. This led to underreporting memories, which they themselves found hard to credit. For example, **Alex** suggested that I not write about certain elements of her sadistic abuse that she worried might undermine the credibility of the book.

Interviews

Each woman filled out and returned her questionnaire, keeping the carbon copy for herself. I then conducted personal interviews with every survivor who gave her name and contact information[2] except for the imprisoned subgroup. These interviews were held at the woman's convenience and her choice of location. Although I could not talk separately with the imprisoned women, I was able to get official permission to attend one of their regular sessions in the prison, and this experience proved invaluable. These survivors valued their chance to be heard more than anyone on the outside could have imagined.

The interviews, which lasted from $1\frac{1}{2}$ to 6 hours, were not standardized but were geared to exploring unique aspects of each participant's experience that might clarify the nature of sexual abuse and its consequences. For example, some women offered insight into what role drinking or overeating had played in coping with their trauma. Or, if flashbacks involved smells, I requested examples. Before the interview was over, each woman had the opportunity to ask questions that were troubling her, for example, "Have you talked with anyone else whose mother abused her?" Before leaving, I affirmed the strengths I saw in each woman.

I will always treasure the gift of trust that I received from these interviewees. The following excerpt from **Alana**'s letter illustrates the costs and rewards of an interview from the survivor's point of view:

> The meeting with you was exhausting! Afterward, I cried and wished so much that none of this had ever happened. I felt like an empty shell, having given myself to a stranger. I felt that I had been a traitor to my family. I wanted to phone you and beg that you tell no one. Today I feel better, but my emotions are very close to the surface. I realize that you are not really a stranger. I can be open with you and other women who are in a position to understand.

The information in the questionnaires and interviews proved extraordinarily rich and complex. After 2 years of gathering, organizing, and analyzing the material from the first survey, I sent a follow-up questionnaire to participants. Thus was born a longitudinal study and the satisfaction of repeated contacts, formal and informal, over a 12-year period.

Follow-up

In 1988 and again in 1992, I sent 4-page follow-up questionnaires to participants. (In each of these years, there were 57 and 55 women, respectively, including imprisoned women, whose addresses I believed were accurate.) These surveys elicited 51 responses each time—a 90% and 93% response rate, respectively—with 74% of the original sample responding to at least one follow-up. I again conducted interviews with the women following receipt of these questionnaires, but this time usually by phone. The 1988 questionnaire asked about the women's support system, their family background, their experience in therapy, and their progress in healing. Part IV, "Remembering and Healing," is based on the first and second surveys.

The goal of the third questionnaire in 1992 was to secure a 6-year picture of personal change in the women. This third survey provided insight and information for Chapter 13, "Changed Lives." From 1992 through 1998, I continued to have contacts from some of the women, usually by telephone. In 1998, while the book's manuscript was being reviewed, I decided to write an epilogue, bringing the picture up-to-date after 12 years for all the women who could still be reached. By this time, at least 3 of the 51 follow-up women had died; however, 44 survivors were located (92%). Once more, they participated. I interviewed each woman personally, using the telephone to reach those living out of state. Twelve years had passed since our first contact, and I felt deeply honored by their continuing loyalty to our joint project.

Limitations and Advantages of the Study

The women who participated in this study belonged to the early surge of sexual abuse survivors who received help for the first time in the mid-1980s—a backlog of survivors who had been silent for the many years since their trauma. Those responding to the questionnaire were typically in private therapy for some time, so they were usually better educated and more financially secure than most survivors. Neither they nor their therapists were randomly selected; their level of abuse had been severe (see Chapter 4); and they were resolving its long-term consequences in the first era in recorded history that was supportive of sexual abuse survivors. Findings from this study are, therefore, more descriptive than broadly generalizable. However, if most of the women in the three memory groups were more privileged than many survivors, the imprisoned women were not. In addition to their disadvantaged backgrounds and long-term incarceration, they did not have private therapy, and prison regulations allowed most of them only brief group therapy (usually less than a year).

Today's survivors of child sexual abuse may be younger and closer in time to their abuse than the women in this study, so their problems and resolutions may differ. Also, as we enter the 21st century, laypersons and therapists are better informed, and the understanding of trauma is more widespread.

The nature and timing of this study provided major advantages for expanding the frontiers of knowledge. The women's stories of trauma and recovery were recorded in depth and longitudinally, yielding a wealth of important details concerning their experience. Also, the focus on comparing women who had experienced different amounts of forgetting, from total amnesia to none at all, may further clarify the debate about recovered memories. Findings from this study can help ground our understanding of recovered memories, especially when they involve abuses repeated over a long period of time. The results of this study dispute, for this group of survivors, the idea that "false memories" of sexual abuse were "created." Instead, the findings demonstrate that complex memories of repeated trauma, lost to amnesia for many years, can be recalled years later. And these memories return with enough accuracy and validation that survivors can change their lives.

This introduction has sketched the social and professional context that allowed these women, after decades of silence, to be heard in the mid-1980s. In the next chapter, you will meet individual women survivors who had experienced varying levels of amnesia to their sexual abuse during the years before they received help. You can follow their stories as they return to the past to reclaim their present and future, and you will better understand the part that amnesia played in that process.

NOTES

1. Note that the numbers in these subgroups (25, 21, and 14) may not represent a typical distribution of amnesia among survivors. However, in the mid-1980s, it was easier to find survivors with at least some amnesia than ones who had always remembered abuse.

2. Only 8 (13%) from the three memory groups did not. Consequently, they were unavailable for interview or follow-up.

CHAPTER 3

The Women
and Their Families

Many voices will speak from the pages of this book. Most will be like members of a large discussion group, offering bits and pieces of themselves when it is helpful to do so. They number over 100 women, if we include, in addition to the 72 original respondents, other survivors (outside of this study) who have shared their stories with me. In this book, all the women are identified by pseudonyms, the first letter of which identifies their subgroup (**A** for *amnesics*, **N** for *nonamnesics*, **P** for *partial* amnesics, and **I** for *imprisoned* women. Also, I use the letter **C** to identify *correspondents*—survivors who corresponded with me (or who introduced themselves) after a presentation of my work. Although not part of the study, they occasionally augment it with interesting insights.

You will not get to know most of the research participants as separate individuals (as you would in case studies) because each one is contributing to an overall picture of survivorship. (For example, the name Andrea may be used for many different women in the book.) However, four women will share their stories with you using the *same* pseudonym throughout the book. They are **ILENE, ANNE, PAULA,** and **NANCY.** You will meet them in this chapter, and as you read further you will get to know each of them well as a representative of her group. **ILENE** was in the imprisoned group. **ANNE, PAULA,** and **NANCY** were women from the three memory subgroups, who had been, respectively, amnesic, partially amnesic, or nonamnesic to their childhood abuse. They had assigned themselves to these subgroups by their answer to the following question:

To what extent had you forgotten that you were sexually abused?[1]

Amnesic

1a. I had *no* memory of sexual abuse—not even awareness of any
     memory gaps.
1b. I had no memory of sexual abuse, but I *was* aware of memory gaps.

The 25 amnesic women (those who checked statements 1a or 1b) had
had no conscious (extrinsic) recollection of childhood sexual abuse. Their
amnesia had resulted from trauma and was supported by a multitude of
emotional, cognitive, and behavioral defenses erected for psychic survival, as you will read in later chapters. Two thirds of them were not even
aware of memory gaps until their crisis of recall in the early 1980s.

Partially Amnesic

2a. I had some awareness, but no idea of the extent of the sexual abuse.
2b. I was aware of one sexual abuser, but not of another.

The 14 partially amnesic women (checking statements 2a or 2b) had
been selectively amnesic to their abuse rather than to all of it. They were
neither totally amnesic nor fully remembering. Six had been minimally
aware that they had been sexually abused but were ignorant of the severity of their abuse. The other eight had remembered one abuser but not another.

Nonamnesic

3a. I never forgot, but I hadn't labeled it as sexual abuse.
3b. I never forgot that I was sexually abused.

The 21 nonamnesic women (checking statements 3a or 3b) had been
unable to forget what had happened. Of these, 11 had not identified their
remembered experience as abuse, but 10 had. Almost all had denied its
impact on their lives.

It is important to recognize that the three memory subgroups were actually composed of six potential ones, and thus there were differences
within as well as between the subgroups. The amnesics differed among
themselves in their awareness of memory gaps, the partial amnesics dif-

fered on whether they had dissociated certain abuses or abusers, and the nonamnesics differed in their labeling of their abuse. Future research with larger samples will permit further discussion of such refined memory differences.

For this research to focus on the role played by amnesia in child sexual abuse, its consequences, and recovery, the two extreme memory subgroups (amnesics and nonamnesics) are compared throughout the book. Their characteristics will become more distinct as we continue to explore their experiences. Important findings for the other two groups are presented wherever they occur.

THE RESEARCH PARTICIPANTS

The Amnesic Women

First, let me introduce the 25 amnesic women. (**ANNE** will add to her story in many chapters, and **Angie** will briefly step forward in this one). The amnesic women reported that they had had no memory of their childhood sexual trauma—for a period that ranged from 15 to 54 years. Their amnesia may have obscured only episodes of abuse, or much of their childhood as well. They had (on average from their first abuse as young children) lost painful memories for 36 years. In the early 1980s, the first fragmentary memories of abuse burst into awareness, sending them into therapy before long. Most of the amnesic women had been molested by one or both parents. Many of them had a strong tendency to idealize their childhood, their "perfect" family, and, especially, an abusing parent. In many cases, the social status of the abuser made the idea of sexual abuse especially unbelievable—for those within the family as well as outsiders. In childhood, these women felt torn between their own experience of the abuser and the idealized image projected all around them. In analogy to the famous children's tale, they were expected to affirm the existence of the Emperor's clothes. Amnesia solved the problem, and idealization helped them to maintain the illusion.

Those unaware of memory gaps. Although the amnesics are treated here as a group, those who had been unaware of memory gaps were especially oblivious to their childhood trauma. **ANNE** explained it this way:

I had no memory of abuse of any kind and lived with an unreal image of a wonderful, happy family. Recently, I had begun to realize that my parents were not as perfect as I had thought. However, I was utterly unprepared for the truth when my job required that I help an abused teenager and my own memories began to surface.

ANNE's father was a physician and community leader. His family was enlisted in a scenario that promoted his image. He played the hero, but he had a strong supporting cast in his docile wife and the children whom she trained to be "better than good." Onlookers' heads turned in admiration as this handsome family entered a restaurant or a church pew. No matter what was going on backstage in the family, the adulation that ANNE's father won in the community made it difficult for her to question the script that she was expected to follow. She accepted it as truth until she remembered.

Those aware of memory gaps. The rest of the amnesic women had known that there were gaps in their memory long before they knew what lay hidden behind them. The gaps had taken various forms. For some, the blanks extended from birth to a particular age—8, 12, or even 14 years. For others, the gap came between (for example) age 6 and 9, with normal memory before and after that time span. One woman recalled certain childhood experiences at school, but recalled nothing of her home life. A few recognized "foggy periods" among their many memories of childhood. For others, it was the reverse—fragments of memory were scattered against a general backdrop of amnesia. If these survivors, as children and as adults, occasionally wondered about these memory gaps, they assumed that they were "normal" or at least unimportant.

Growing up in a struggling farm family, **Angie** had many early memories, but they started only after the age of 6. She did not wonder why. Angie's family had lived in emotional isolation from each other under the same roof. Her father was hard-working, taciturn, and withdrawn. Her mother went through the motions of living—depressed, emotionally unresponsive, and unsmiling. Her older brothers kept to themselves. Only her older sister smiled—always—but it was a smile that Angie had reason to distrust. It had been especially bright on the day that she enticed 6-year-old Angie into her teenaged brother's bedroom so that he could rape her. Afterward, as Angie struggled down the stairs, she saw her mother smiling up at her (one of only four times that she could remember her mother ever smiling). Young as she was, Angie sensed that her mother had acquiesced to her sexual initiation. Believing then that three family members had betrayed her, Angie survived by means of amnesia. When she was 14, another brother raped her, and she assigned that episode also to oblivion. Middle-aged when she recalled these traumatic events, Angie was well into her 60s before she realized that her father had been a perpetrator also. He had made an off-hand apology when she was 12: "Sorry about when you were younger, but I needed my sex."

The Partially Amnesic Group

Minimal memory. Six of the women had always recalled inappropriate treatment when they were children but had not known that there had also been serious sexual abuse. **Phyllis**, growing up in a middle-class family, had a stepfather who handled her body freely, tickled her mercilessly, and roared with laughter at her distress. By the age of 12, she was already saving money to leave home and to educate herself. She was burning with a deep rage, kindled by what she remembered and fueled by what she did not. After an unsuccessful first marriage, Phyllis found a man who loved and nurtured her. Feeling safe at last, she was gradually able to recall memories that had been scattered among multiple personalities. Her stepfather had not only raped her but, together with his friends, had made her the focus of organized abuse. One positive memory returned, however, that helped her understand how she had survived. From birth to age 5, Phyllis had been cared for by a foster mother who had given her appreciation, tenderness, and deep love. This good start may have been what enabled Phyllis to take charge of her life, to find a partner who saw and loved what her foster mother had nurtured in her, and to do the difficult therapeutic work required for emotional recovery.

Those who remembered one abuser. The other eight women among the partially amnesic group had always remembered one or more abusers but had forgotten one or more others. The forgetting seemed to be associated with early abuse, deep dissociation at the time, betrayal by someone loved, or special shame. **PAULA** was born to teenaged parents and into poverty. Her extended family was composed of domineering, lascivious men (who ignored sexual boundaries) and passive women (who tried to squelch this bright and feisty girl). Her parents did not protect her from either. Among the relatives, the emotional needs of girls went unrecognized, sexual boundaries were ignored, and it was every child for herself. PAULA escaped being raped, but she was constantly at the mercy of intrusive sexual advances. Moreover, she was assigned most of the household and child care chores. When PAULA received my questionnaire, she had recalled two sexual abusers, but as she filled it out, she remembered three others. (They had been forgotten but not dissociated from memory.) She had recently recalled her father's brother, who spent much time at her house. He had habitually made her sit on his knee so he could handle her whenever her parents glanced away. When she told on him, her father slapped her and called her a liar. PAULA "completely blotted it out," thinking she had dreamed it. Painful memories returned to her as an adult when a hysterectomy required her to take a period of rest.

The Nonamnesic Women

Memory without a label. Ten women had remembered their experiences but had not defined them as sexual abuse. Despite their unhappiness, they had believed what they had been told—that their treatment was a parental prerogative, a form of punishment, or somehow normal in families. Generally, they held themselves responsible. **Norene** hadn't realized, over the years, that *rape* and *battering* were the correct words for what she had experienced. Her stepfather, a skilled laborer, and her mother, a housewife, were both alcoholics. Norene's mother did not molest her sexually, but she was sadistic. When enraged, she would grab Norene by her hair and slam her head against the doorpost. Norene can also remember her mother strangling her until she dropped to the floor. Her stepfather provided the child with some protection from his wife as long as Norene did not fuss when he used her sexually. For 10 years, he exploited her in ways that ranged from fondling to violent rape and torture. Norene was 18 when her mother died. At first, she remained at home because she had done most of the parenting of her younger brothers, and her stepfather threatened their safety if she left. During this time, she bore a baby by him, which died. A priest to whom she told her story told her to flee. Since then, Norene has experienced much unhappiness and the breakup of several marriages.

Awareness of abuse and its meaning. In 1986, it was much easier to find survivors with some level of amnesia than those who had always remembered *and* who had accurately identified the sexual nature of their trauma. Among the 11 women who did have such accurate recall, their abuse had ranged from infrequent molestation by a nonrelative to long and regular abuse by a parent. **NANCY** was one of the latter. Her father was voted "most friendly" among 300 coworkers at his place of employment. But he was a different man when he walked through the front door of his home each evening. For him, females existed to gratify his wishes. While his daughters were still in elementary school, they were trained to be his personal bath attendants—scrubbing his back, cleaning his toenails, and grooming his genitals. He was physically abusive toward his wife and daughters, and he had regular sexual relations with the girls from preteen years until they left home. All of them witnessed his explosions of temper toward other family members, but each girl thought that she was the only one who endured his bedroom visits.

NANCY survived by living behind a protective facade. She was beautiful, perfectly mannered, and a popular teenager, but she was also hyper-alert to her father's presence. NANCY never became amnesic for two apparent reasons: First, her alertness sometimes helped her to escape him. Second, his ever-present anger and lust were constant reminders of grim reality. There was no tenderness to help her idealize this violent man. Instead, she clung to the idea that she had a loving, protective mother—not admitting to herself that it was she who looked after her mother and not the other way around.

ANNE and Angie were amnesic, PAULA and Phyllis were partially amnesic, and NANCY and Norene were nonamnesic to what had happened to them as children. Although each woman's case is unique, these women illustrate respondents who had experienced one of the three levels of amnesia to their child sexual abuse.

The Imprisoned Therapy Group

I met the imprisoned women survivors through their therapist, but **ILENE** was the only one whose progress I was personally able to follow. I talked to her twice in the prison and more frequently after she was discharged on completion of her 5-year sentence. She described her molestation, perpetrated by her stepfather and witnessed by her mother, as beginning at age 4 and extending until she left home to marry at age 16. When she was 13 and again at age 15, she bore a child by her stepfather, and her parents (declaring her promiscuous) arranged for the babies' adoptions. ILENE's marriage was abusive and ended in the death of her husband during a fight over a gun. Convicted of manslaughter, she served 5 years in prison and, while there, she completed her high school degree, took college-level classes, and joined the therapy group that turned her life around.

As the chapters of this book unfold, you will learn more about the women who represent the four main subgroups—**ANNE, PAULA, NANCY,** and **ILENE**. Their stories, recounted with their permission, can become complete in your minds, and this will help you to understand the common as well as different struggles of women who had experienced different levels of amnesia to child sexual abuse. However, the pseudonyms Angie, Phyllis, and Norene will no longer be reserved for the women who bore them in this chapter. Like other pseudonyms beginning with A, P, N, and I, they may represent *any* member of that subgroup of women. Collectively, and protected by anonymity, these respondents will contribute much to our knowledge of sexual abuse, its consequences, and its healing.

THE FAMILY BACKGROUND OF THE SURVIVORS

Now, let's look at the parents who gave these women birth and shaped their early lives. We will note some objective family characteristics, first for all survivors, and also comparing those who were amnesic and nonamnesic. Then, we will examine the respondents' subjective views of their family life.

Objective Characteristics of the Families

Most of the survivors in the three memory groups came from apparently stable, middle-class families. Sixty percent of their fathers were professional, managerial, or white-collar workers, and the rest were blue-collar workers. Their religious background was 60% Protestant, with the rest being Catholic, nonreligious, and Jewish (in that order). Almost all of these women were Caucasian. At the time of the study, the women themselves were upwardly mobile, with 90% in professional or white-collar work. This meant that these women could afford therapy and were therefore available for inclusion in this particular study. Selecting women in private therapy served my research goal, but it limited the generalizability of the findings to other less-privileged survivors. Note, however, that the imprisoned women were in group therapy only. Moreover, their families and they themselves had generally been less well established than was the case for the other three groups of women. Thus, they added breadth to the sample, and their findings can suggest how generalizable the findings of the other three groups may be.

Comparing the memory subgroups, we find that half of the amnesics and a third of the nonamnesics came from professional/managerial families and that this gap grew in the respondents' generation. Two thirds of the amnesic women were currently in professional or managerial occupations, whereas the upward mobility of nonamnesics had largely been from blue-collar into white-collar occupations. The partially amnesic women seemed most mobile of all, almost doubling their parents' proportion among professionals.

Most of the marriages of survivors' parents (80%) were intact at least until after their daughters graduated from high school. This marital longevity was slightly more true for amnesics' parents (85%)—reducing the possibility of stepfather abuse—than for nonamnesic's parents (73%). Among the survivors themselves, the amnesic and nonamnesic subgroups appeared similar in marital status (about half currently married, a quarter never married, and a quarter divorced), but amnesics were less likely to have had more than one divorce (0% vs. 22%). These findings suggest that the amnesic survivors had the advantage of a little more social and marital stability in both generations.[2]

In birth order, about half of the women were the oldest girls in their family, a quarter were the only girl, and the rest were middle or youngest girls. Amnesics and nonamnesics were almost identical in birth order, with most (about 80%) being the first-born or only girl. These findings do not mean that younger sisters were not molested. You will learn respondents' views on that topic later in this chapter.

Concerning their own childbearing, the respondents who had ever married had 3.5 children, on average. However, 20% of the amnesic women had none, and some cited fears of parenting.

Because this book is a forum for survivors, I turn now from objective comparisons to the women's subjective views of the families into which they were born. Their descriptions may make it easier to understand why they waited so long to deal with their childhood sexual abuse.

The Survivors' Subjective View of Their Families

Family Themes[3]

Given that most of the survivors participating in this research came from homes that were objectively stable in financial and marital terms, one might expect them to view their families in a positive light. However, when asked on Questionnaire 2 to characterize their early family life in two words, the women answered with descriptors that were almost entirely negative. (Some of that excessive negativity might be attributed to their mood, however, because the women were currently dealing with depressing memories of sexual abuse; cf. Bower, 1981.)

Six themes, listed here in descending order of frequency, summarized their retrospective view of family life:

1. Dangerous—frightening, destructive, nightmarish
2. Unstable—dysfunctional, chaotic, confusing
3. Lonely—disengaged, abandoned
4. Pathological—sick, weird, horrible
5. Phony—a sham, acted perfect, a fantasy
6. Uncaring—unavailable, indifferent, hurtful

Typically, several such themes were interwoven in their descriptors.

Danger was a commonplace experience. Safety, a primary life need, was frequently threatened in families where the women, as children, had lived in an atmosphere of apprehension or fear. Half of them reported fearing their fathers, and 18% feared their mothers. They expressed their anxiety in telling glimpses of family life: "I was afraid when Dad was home or Mother was smiling." Their bedrooms were special places of fear. Many, like **Pia**, were afraid to fall asleep. "My bedtime prayer was that this would be the night God would take me." And there was anxiety with the dawning of each new day: "I'd wake up with a feeling of impending disaster."

Instability, a subtler kind of danger, was also prevalent. **Polly**'s description of her home environment was "chaotic, unpredictable, confusing, and unhappy." For such children, family life lacked any sense of order and guidance. Breaches of generation roles were often unrecognized as being bizarre. For instance, half of the women felt that their mother had viewed them as an extension of herself and had expected them to take on her responsibilities. Excessive obligations toward younger siblings were often part of this role reversal, and quite a few daughters looked after their mother instead of the other way round. Some, like 11-year-old **NANCY**, had to take care of their father as well:

> Mother had to work that weekend, so I got the rest of the family ready for our camping trip. I packed the food and clothing for the younger children and finished sewing and ironing Mother's Sunday dress before we left. That night, my father unzipped my sleeping bag and told me that it was time for him to take my cherry. I was not to fuss and wake the younger children.

Loneliness, the third theme, was a feeling of separation from family members, peers, and even from self. As reported on their first questionnaire, most of the survivors had felt ill at ease with others (67%) and lonely (67%). With their peers, they felt different (72%) and didn't fit in (69%). **Penny** summed up the sense of isolation: "I had a fantasy of myself screaming inside a block of ice. People were walking right by, but no one saw or heard me. I wanted so much for *someone* to melt the ice."

Many were lonely within their families as well. Several women spoke of childhood dreams wherein they were separated from other family members, or deserted by them, and unable to find their way home:

> No matter how often I had this dream, it was always the same: I would go with my family to a deserted beach and they would disappear. Looking around, I'd see an empty house and go inside. There before me was a bureau with three drawers which I felt *compelled* to open one by one. In the last drawer, there was a little wooden doll, all in pieces. Looking at her, I was overwhelmed with terror.

This dream expressed **ANNE**'s isolation and fragmentation long before she recalled the truth about her father. Loneliness, for children like her, was a way of life. Two thirds of these women believed that their fathers, as well as their mothers, were emotionally unavailable. The mother who is viewed as "not there" for her children in a sexually abusive home has been well documented (e.g., Finkelhor et al., 1986). It is important to recognize that fathers, and especially abusive ones, may be similarly perceived.

Pathology was the fourth theme of family life, illustrated by **Anita's** pungent summary: "My parents were strange." Whereas abusive mothers were typically viewed as "sick" on a checklist of parental qualities, abusive fathers tended to be viewed as "bad." Comparing abusive parents with nonabusive ones, according to the respondents' descriptions of them, well over half of the abusive mothers (60%) had overused alcohol or other drugs, versus only 22% of nonabusive mothers. Similar proportions had suffered from mental problems such as deep depression (64% vs. 22%). About a third of the women's fathers—whether or not they were sexually abusive—overused alcohol or other drugs, but few were seen as emotionally disturbed. However, the daughters did view abusive fathers (much more than nonabusive ones) as having serious character defects. They saw their incestuous fathers as more dominating (89% vs. 39%), manipulative (78% vs. 35%), insistent on male rights (78% vs. 35%), and tending to "act like God" (56% vs. 17%). **April's** father, for example, would sit in his chair as if it were a throne, and he liked to say that his wife "waited on him hand and foot" (a phrase from the days of Roman slavery). At the dinner table, he never reached for anything—he simply let his eye fall on what he wanted and his ever-watchful wife would pass it to him.

Especially among those amnesic women who had remembered their childhood as quite trouble-free, this theme of distorted reality or phoniness was mentioned. Having lived with massive misperception, these women were horrified to recall a past they had never imagined being theirs. Suddenly, everything that they had lived by for decades was called into question. What was real and what was false concerning their parents? Their siblings? Themselves? What should they believe about values on which they had built their identity? **Audrey** said in dismay, "I might just as well have discovered that Jesus Christ was a pedophile."

Uncaring disregard of children's needs was present in all the themes listed above. Over half of the participants, looking back, rated the fathering they had received as poor (53%) and the mothering as simply fair (59%). About two thirds of *both* the abusive mothers (65%) and the nonabusive mothers (67%) were seen as emotionally unavailable by their daughters—a finding that fits with the past research literature on incestuous families. The respondents' fathers were seen as even more emotionally unavailable, especially those who were abusive (78%). Surprisingly,

Table 3.1 Percentage of Survivors Who Believed That Other Family Members Had
Also Experienced Child Sexual Abuse

Knowledge or Belief	Family Member			
	Father	Mother	Brother	Sister
Knowledge of the abuse	10	32	24	59
Strong suspicion of abuse	38	49	38	22
Total	48	81	62	81

the amnesic group (which had experienced the most parental incest) were the least likely to rate their parenting as poor but most likely to rate it as fair. In addition, they felt more love for their father than the other groups did *even* if they had been sexually abused by him. Apparently, it was hard to shake their idealization of father and family.

When asked about the emotions that they had experienced toward their parents, about a third of the total sample of respondents checked *love*. A quarter hated or disliked their fathers, and 14% felt that way toward their mothers. The others expressed painful ambivalence and, typically, an enduring longing for the kind of love and parenting that might have been theirs.

Other Victims of Sexual Abuse Among Family Members

The women were asked if they "knew" or "strongly suspected" that their parents and siblings had experienced sexual abuse themselves. Their responses indicated strong beliefs that other family members had also been victimized as children, and this was true even if their own abuse came from beyond the family circle. However, as shown in Table 3.1, this belief differed according to the gender of the family member. That is, more of the respondents judged their sisters and mothers to have been victims than their brothers and fathers. Furthermore, the generation of the family member influenced how certain the women were. They were more likely to know about their siblings' abuse and to strongly suspect the abuse of their parents.

If the women's sexual abuse had occurred within their family circle (rather than only beyond it), their estimates of past abuse rose for all family members. This was especially so if a brother or father had abused them; estimates soared for that person—to 86% for the brother and to 73% for the father. (Only three respondents were molested by sisters, and all of these sisters were thought to have been victims.)

Whether or not the research participants were accurate in their judgments about the past abuse of others in their family, their point of view raises an intriguing question. Believing what they know is understandable, but why would so many respondents strongly suspect other family members' abuse without confirmation? First, circumstances and symptoms may support that interpretation. Second, perceiving a family abuser as "also wounded" may make his or her acts more understandable. Third, beliefs or stereotypes that are prevalent in our society may have influenced the women's efforts to bring logic into an irrational situation. For example, commonly expressed views in our society include the following: "Sex abuse is intergenerational"; "Offenders usually have more than one victim"; "More girls than boys are sexually abused"; and "Abused boys become abusers, abused girls marry abusers."

Physical Abuse and Harsh Discipline

The survivors were also asked about severe forms of punishment in their families. Almost half reported that they had been battered, and even more had been severely disciplined. A quarter had experienced both kinds of treatment, but one third had experienced neither. (Siblings were usually thought to have been punished similarly.) Severe punishment was more commonly administered by fathers than by mothers, but in a third of the cases, both parents were punitive.

There was a good deal of difference among the subgroups, however. Battering was most often reported by amnesic and partially amnesic women. However, a third of the amnesic group had experienced no excessive punishment, and this group was especially likely to have adopted and maintained a fantasy of ideal parents and a privileged home life. By contrast, few nonamnesics had been battered, although most had been severely disciplined. The imprisoned women reported more punitive mothers, but half believed they had not experienced excessive punishment as children. (It seems possible that their definitions were less stringent.) Chapter 4 describes the sexual abuse experienced by respondents and expands on the topics just discussed. But before moving on, let me sum up what has been learned by comparing the family backgrounds of the survivors according to their level of amnesia.

Family Background and
Memories of Child Sexual Abuse

This study took an unusual approach by sorting survivors into subgroups according to their memory of abuse. Behind that choice lay the expectation that amnesia would both be a consequence of the abuse situation and have an impact on the results of that abuse over time. In other words, characteristics of the abuse situation would influence the level of amnesia that survivors experienced, and that amnesia, in turn, would influence the entire process of long-term consequences, recall, and recovery. The general expectations for this study were that the formerly amnesic women would have endured more severe abuse, that their consequences would be more grave, and that their recovery would be more difficult than that of the nonamnesics.

In this chapter, I have begun to look at the objective and subjective similarities and differences among the women who participated in this study, especially of those who were either amnesic or nonamnesic. First, let me sum up the objective similarities. Respondents were almost all Caucasian and currently middle class. About half of the two comparison groups were currently married, and the rest were divided equally between those who were always single and those who were divorced. Members of the amnesic and nonamnesic categories were highly similar in birth order, with about 80% having been the only or oldest girl.

To list objective differences, amnesic and partially amnesic women, in comparison to nonamnesic ones, were more likely to have come from professional- or managerial-level homes and to be more upwardly mobile than their parents' generation. Amnesics tended to come from somewhat longer-lasting parental marriages and to be less likely than nonamnesics to divorce more than once.

In examining subjective differences in the two key groups, I found that most of the amnesics had either been battered or raised with no harsh treatment, whereas the nonamnesics were more likely to have been strictly disciplined. Amnesic women more often believed that other family members had also been sexually abused. The family theme for amnesics tended to be "distorted reality," whereas for nonamnesics it was "uncaring disregard."[4]

This chapter has opened a window into the subjective world of adult survivors of child sexual trauma. Most important, you have met the women who will share their stories throughout the book. You have learned something of the families that gave them birth. The patterns that have begun to emerge will become clearer as we follow **ANNE, PAULA, NANCY,** and **ILENE.** In the next chapter, I examine the nature of the sexual trauma that so powerfully affected the rest of their lives.

NOTES

1. By the time this research began, *all* participants knew that they had been abused as children. The subgroups therefore divide the women according to their memory status during the interim period between being abused (as a child) and seeking help (as an adult)—as having memories that were newly recovered or never lost.

2. The objectively stable family situation of amnesic survivors closely resembles that of the accusing daughters of False Memory Syndrome Foundation parents (see Cameron, 1996). Both of these sets of survivors had private therapists. However, in contrast to the foundation's description of members' daughters, my respondents generally remembered abuse *prior* to entering therapy (73%) and had external verification of it (65%). They also gained strength through therapy, rather than deteriorating emotionally.

3. Most of the information for the remainder of this chapter came from responses to items in the second (1988) survey questionnaire.

4. Some of this variation between amnesic and nonamnesic respondents may have occurred because a few of my nonamnesic survivors came through therapists not in direct contact with me. They picked up questionnaires in response to my presentation at a conference on sexual abuse.

PART II

Sexual Abuse in Childhood

On October 14, 1987, tiny Jessica McClure tumbled 25 feet down an abandoned mineshaft in the backyard of her parents' home. For the next 58 hours, several hundred volunteer workers struggled to free her, and millions of concerned Americans watched television screens in their homes, workplaces, stores, and bars. Finally, she was freed, and a shout of joy went up across the nation. As I watched the report on evening television, an anchorwoman marveled at the "incredible stamina" of this 18-month-old child, who had cried and talked and sung her way through the long, long hours.

I found myself affirming the little girl's courage but not surprised by it. For several years, I had immersed myself in the lives of other victims of early childhood trauma. I had been awed at the amazing creativity and courage with which they had coped, both at the time of the trauma and in the ensuing years before help became available to them. As I thought about the massive outpouring of love and concern that went into freeing one small girl, I felt deep sadness for many thousands of other little children in our nation who were experiencing a different kind of trauma during the same time period as Jessica's. Where were the workers struggling to free them, the television cameras recording their anguish, the prayers and letters of support, the hundreds of stuffed animals to comfort them? Their ordeal did not end in 58 hours. For many, it is still going on as you read these words.

CHAPTER 4

Childhood Trauma

Please listen to us. Sexual abuse is far more devastating than anyone conceives. I can't even imagine who or what I'd be if it hadn't happened. It separated me from myself.

—**Inga**, 1988

Now that you have met the women who took part in this study, I take up (at their request) an unhappy topic—their experience of sexual abuse. I asked them what messages they wanted me to convey to readers. Above all else, their responses suggested the four themes of pain, struggle, courage, and victory. Part II, and especially this chapter, carries their message of pain, encapsulated in the words of Inga above. In the pages that follow, you will read about child sexual abuse from the point of view of women who have experienced it. It is they who defined what was done to them as sexual abuse and who labeled their abusers. I believe that their *subjective* perspectives on the sexual abuse experience are at least as important to understanding it as the *objective* measurements and theories of researchers. Throughout this chapter, the point of view presented is that of the children who underwent the abuse, as expressed by the adult survivors they became.

I begin with the children at the age of onset of their abuse—when, as adults looking back, they believed mistreatment had actually begun. Next, I focus on the survivors' accounts of who exploited them— among the relatives, neighbors, and strangers whose lives crossed theirs. Then you will hear about the abuse itself, gaining understanding of various re-actions evoked by noncontact abuse, contact without penetration, various forms of penetration, and the differing impact of sexual versus physical abuse. The survivors also describe a variety of distressing experiences that intensified an already abusive situation, including humiliation, threats, trickery, lack of dependable emotional support in the children's lives, and the secrecy that served the offender while sabotaging the child. Finally, I examine the time when the abuse ended, which often carried its own pain.

All study participants contributed to the discussion of childhood trauma that follows. However, special attention is given in the tables to comparing the two comparison groups of amnesic and nonamnesic women to understand how the presence or absence of amnesia relates to the abuse experience. In later chapters, you will learn how amnesia influences symptoms, recognition of past trauma, and the recovery process.

CHARACTERISTICS OF THEIR SEXUAL ABUSE

Age at Onset of Sexual Abuse

The pervasiveness of sexual abuse, its early onset, its varied indignities, and its lengthy duration have been generally unrecognized by lay-persons and researchers until recently. As late as 1976, the estimated annual occurrence rate of incest was 1 to 2 cases out of every 1 million children (Freedman et al., 1976) and the prototypical age group was considered to be teenagers. By 1986, Finkelhor et al.'s review of major studies of child sexual abuse reported that the annual occurrence rate of reported cases was close to 1 per 1,000 children, and that this was a "substantial underestimate" of the true rate (p. 18). In that era, on average, preteens (age 10 to 12) were considered to be the age group at highest risk. However, some reports from hospitals and social workers have indicated that 0- to 5-year-olds were the fastest growing group of sexual abuse victims (Kempe & Kempe, 1978). Some of my respondents, as children, were carefully warned to avoid "strangers" 5 or 10 years *after* people in their own family had begun to abuse them.

Why did public awareness of the early onset of sexual victimization take so long? There are several plausible explanations. The "sanctity of the family" made the topic of incest off limits to researchers for many years. The social myths were that strangers were the threat and that the

Table 4.1 Characteristics of Survivors' Sexual Abuse and Abuser, by Group

Characteristic	Amnesic	Partial Amnesic	Nonamnesic	Imprisoned	Total
Mean age at first abuse	3.7 years	4.1 years	7.0 years	6.8 years	5.3 years
Mean duration of primary abuse	5.7 years	7.4 years	4.4 years	6.1 years	5.7 years
Mean number of related abusers	1.9	2.0	1.6	1.4	1.7
Father was an abuser	75%	29%	24%	17%	41%
Mother was an abuser	33%	14%	14%	25%	22%
Stepfather or foster father was an abuser	8%	21%	19%	33%	18%
Abused by natural parent	88%	36%	38%	42%	55%
Abused by parent figure	92%	50%	52%	58%	66%
Abused by >1 parent figure	25%	14%	5%	25%	17%
Abused by nonparental relative	54%	64%	57%	33%	54%

predominant form of real sexual abuse was vaginal penetration of pubescent girls. Laypeople were reluctant to recognize the multitude of harmful sexual behaviors that can be perpetrated on children from infancy on. Together, ignorant adults and voiceless child victims allowed such abuse to flourish. In individual cases where sexual abuse was recognized, it might have gone on for years before the age at which it was recorded by a social agency.

In my study, 62% of the original group of respondents reported that their first abuse had occurred before their 7th birthday, and only one girl had been over 11 years of age. Moreover, comparison of the three memory groups showed that the level of amnesia varied inversely with the child's age at the onset of abuse. The average age at first molestation for amnesic, partially amnesic, and nonamnesic women was 3.7, 4.1, and 7.0 years (see Table 4.1). In other words, the younger the victim, the more likely amnesia was to develop. The imprisoned women were similar to the nonamnesics in their age at first abuse (6.8 years).

It was startling to hear interviewees describe flashbacks to some events that happened even before they were 3 years old. These flashbacks to very early years were fragmentary and experiential in nature (as were many of the flashbacks to later years), and they tended to feature a single component of memory—such as a powerful emotional or sensory experience—rather than a story line with a beginning, middle, and end. Researchers who equate personal memories with narratives that include elements of time, place, and sequence may ignore such elusive and incomplete memory components. However, survivors typically interpreted these fragments in connection with later, more complete memories. The fragments frequently fell into context because these same women also recovered memories of abuse from their later childhood. These memories from older ages were increasingly complex, and they integrated multiple components of memory—sensations, thoughts, emotions, meanings, and sequence. They demonstrated vividly the increasing awareness of the maturing child. (Issues concerning delayed recovery of early memories are addressed in Chapter 6, and flashbacks are discussed in Chapter 9.)

The Duration of Their Primary Abuse

Memories from toddlerhood to the teen years also helped survivors to estimate the duration of their primary (main) abuse experience. For the amnesic and partially amnesic women, their primary abuse lasted longer (5.7 and 7.4 years, respectively) than for the nonamnesics (4.4 years). As shown in Table 4.1, the imprisoned respondents also reported a relatively long period of primary abuse (6.1 years).

WHO WERE THE ABUSERS?

Findings on abuser characteristics typically show males as far more frequent abusers than females (e.g., Finkelhor et al., 1986; Russell, 1986). Father figures are the most common abusers of girls, followed by other male family members, such as uncles, brothers, and grandfathers. People casually known to the child, such as neighbors or family friends, are next most frequent, followed by strangers. Women perpetrators make up only 5% to 10% of girls' sexual contacts with adults, according to Finkelhor et al. (1986). This chapter focuses largely on family abusers because betrayal by someone who is emotionally close has especially serious consequences (Freyd, 1996). I look first at the abusers for the full original sample of 72 respondents (including the imprisoned women), and then, referring again to Table 4.1, examine the three memory subgroups to explore the relationship between the abuser's identity and amnesia.

For the full sample, parents were prominent among family perpetrators. Over half of the women (55%) had been abused by at least one natural parent, and the figure was two thirds (66%) if stepfathers were included. Many of the survivors had been abused by an uncle (24%), brother (23%), grandfather (17%), or more than one relative. Only 20 survivors had a single perpetrator but, in 11 cases, he was their natural father. The age distribution of the primary abusers was similar to that found in other studies (e.g., Finkelhor et al., 1986, p. 115). Respondents reported that about half of their primary abusers[1] were age 20 to 40, and the rest were equally divided between younger and older ages.

The percentage of all perpetrators who were women (13%) barely exceeded findings from other studies. However, because most respondents had two or more abusers (within or outside the family), a female as well as a male had molested many of them. In fact, although males far outnumbered females among offenders, nearly one quarter (22%) of the survivors named their mother as one of their abusers, and 7% had been molested by an aunt or a sister.

Table 4.1 shows the relationship of the abuser to the child for the three memory groups. The women in these groups were similar only in their proportion of abuse by nonparental relatives (roughly 60% of each group). The (formerly) amnesic women were much more likely than the nonamnesics to have been abused by a natural parent (88% vs. 38%), or by a parent figure, including stepfathers and foster fathers (92% vs. 52%). They were also more likely to have been abused by their natural father (75% vs. 24%), by their mother (33% vs. 14%), and by more than one parental figure (25% vs. 5%). On all of these dimensions, the partially amnesic group fell close to the nonamnesics. Clearly, amnesia to abuse was strongly related not only to early abuse but also to parental abuse. This is a counterintuitive finding because normal forgetting would not be higher for activities with one's parents.

FAMILIAL ABUSE

Not only were the respondents' primary abusers likely to be parents, but abuse by father figures has long been considered to be more traumatic than abuse by other people, related or not (e.g., Briere & Runtz, 1985; Freyd, 1996). In fact, the impact of abuse by fathers may be even more drastic than abuse by stepfathers. Several women expressed profound grief that their father had initiated incest, and they felt tainted. "I hate it that his blood flows in *my* veins." Similarly, although molestation by females is generally considered less traumatic than molestation by males (Finkelhor, 1984), abuse by one's mother may be a significant exception. In this study, most of the women who reported molestation by mothers had been amnesic to it (see Table 4.1), and it was usually the most painful of their memories.

Abuse by Both Parents

More than half of the survivors who viewed their mother as a sexual abuser (10 out of 16) had also experienced abuse by their father or stepfather. In several situations, the parents acted independently, but their actions were not necessarily unrelated. For example, **Adel**'s mother "comforted" her daughter sexually after her father had penetrated her. Other parents acted together. **Nedda** and **ILENE** described co-parental abuse in their homes. Although their stepfathers performed the sexual acts, these survivors viewed their mothers as sexual abusers[2] also. They sometimes brought their daughter to the abuser and watched the abuse as titillation before their own marital coupling. The little girl (in unwilling voyeurism) was then obliged to watch the adults.

Several of the respondents, in their preteen years, had shared their parents' bedroom, where intercourse occurred regularly in the daughter's presence—obscuring sexual boundaries and making the girls more vulnerable in other situations. **Norene**'s parents used their children less blatantly to enhance their own sexual arousal. She was aware that one expectation of the children's Saturday morning romp in their parents' bed was that it would stimulate the adults. The children were soon sent abruptly out of the room while the parents completed their liaison.

Other Family Members

Nearly a quarter of the women reported one or more brothers as abusers. In the literature, sibling sex is usually not defined as abuse unless there is at least a 5-year age gap. However, the survivors in this study made it clear that an age gap was not needed for a boy to intimidate, threaten, or force his sister. For example, **Anita**'s teenage brothers were a year older and a year younger than she was. Most molesting brothers were about 13 years old when they started abusing their sister. Sexual talk, spying, and handling were common violations, which sometimes escalated to coerced or violent intercourse, oral or vaginal. Several siblings were sadistic. **Patrice**'s brother was 3 years older than his sister, and he would tie her hands to the bedposts and smother her into submission. **Prudence** had two abusing brothers. She had always remembered the actions of the one who was nonviolent, but not of the other one, who had tied up and raped her regularly for 7 years. Totally amnesic between attacks, she reported, "I could not have lived knowing he would do that to me." Four survivors had brothers who, on at least one occasion, invited several friends to rape their sister. Whether this was the brothers' way of currying favor with other boys, an act of male bonding, or a rite of passage, it took place with utter disregard for their sisters. All four girls became amnesic or partially amnesic to these episodes. At least one brother also lost all memory of what he had done until some months after his sister, as an adult, confronted him.

A quarter of the women were molested by uncles and (as with brothers) in some cases by more than one. A general atmosphere of male entitlement pervaded certain families, and uncles had a relatively free hand with unprotected children. **NANCY** reported that, occasionally, there was uproar in the family when one of the uncles "fondled" a niece, but soon "the boys" would be off for a fishing trip, laughing and joking. Uncles were common abusers for members of the imprisoned group. After being used for years by a rapacious set of uncles, **Isabel** found escape as a teenager—getting sent to jail frequently for minor thefts. She was in prison for forgery when I met her.

There were a dozen grandfathers and several other elderly men among the abusers. These findings demonstrate that strong sexual obsession with children, unless publicly confronted and treated, does not vanish with age. Even impotence did not stop the respondents' abusers, but sometimes it only prolonged abuse as the perpetrator tried various ways to reach orgasm. In at least five cases, grandfathers had molested children in two or more generations. **Portia**'s grandfather had made a clean sweep of every female in at least three generations—all his daughters and nieces, his granddaughters, grandnieces, and his only great-granddaughter. Some of these victims always remembered. Others, now middle-aged, still have no memory of sodomy even though Portia got her grandfather to name all his victims before he died. Recently, Portia's sister suddenly recalled, in a blaze of pain, her own violent initiation. She had been 4 years old when Grampa took her to see the shiny cab of his new truck.

MULTIPLE ABUSERS

About three quarters (72%) of the women had been abused by more than one person. Respondents divided into three roughly equal groups—those with one abuser, two abusers, and more than two. Usually, the primary (major and typically first) abusers were close relatives. Additional abusers were divided about equally between other relatives and unrelated people. The multiple abuse happened sequentially for some women but concurrently for others. When the court removed **India** from her home because her stepfather had molested her for 7 years, her foster father continued the abuse for another 5. Her prison wardmate, **Isabel** (mentioned earlier), endured several uncles' abuse during one period of her life.

Acquaintances

Molestation by casual acquaintances, such as neighbors or the father of a friend, was experienced by at least one third of the women. It usually occurred *after* someone in the family had made the child susceptible. Repeated abuse, imposed at home or by a respected uncle or grandfather, left the child unprotected, devalued, and lonely, and it seemed that molesters could read her vulnerability. Acquaintance molestation typically involved one or more incidents of the offender handling the child's body or making her handle his. **Audrey** remarked sadly, "At 7, I thought that this was what men did to little girls." Her father's affection had been displayed only through sexual contact during toddlerhood. It ended, and he became distant when she went to preschool. She sought warmth from casual acquaintances who, one after another, molested her instead. After a terrifying attempted rape, she withdrew socially. **Norma**, at 7 years of age, was tricked and raped by neighbor boys, who were about 10 years older. Her mother took her to their minister, the father of one of the boys, and the child felt blamed for her own attack. She felt betrayed by her mother and her minister as well as by the teenagers, whom she had known and trusted.

Strangers

Ten participants (14%) had been victimized by one or more strangers, and most of them experienced life-threatening violence. **Iris**, one of the imprisoned group, had been so savagely raped by a street gang (at 8 years of age) that she nearly bled to death. A year later, her aunt was discovered fondling her "to teach her loving sexuality." A stranger brutalized **Polly** at 6 years of age on a camping trip with her parents. As a child, she remembered only that "something terrible happened" when she was very young. As an adult, she began to recall the attack, the threats if she told, and the fact that the attacker in her flashbacks "had no face." Sometimes, she thinks it happened more than once, and sometimes, she wonders if the perpetrator might have been her father. Because of her uncertainty, I have classified her in this study as "perpetrator unknown."

April was 8 years old when she came upon two strangers in her grandfather's barn. They raped her orally and vaginally, watching each other. Then they vivisected a cat to show her how they planned to kill her and described what they would do with her body. April was "out of body" (dissociated) during most of this terrifying experience. After the men finally left, she did what many traumatized children do. She tried to undo what had happened by going on with life as usual. She got dressed, left the barn, and went into her grandmother's house. Her grandmother was startled to find her sitting on the toilet, blood flowing, and declared, "You're too young for that." She gave the child a sanitary napkin and told her to tell her mother that she "had her period." But April said nothing to anyone. Her long amnesia had begun. Other abuses followed and were just as quickly lost to consciousness. Over the years, she suffered from trembling hands, migraines, wild mood swings, self-abuse, and hysterical outbursts, which spoke eloquently of her trauma. But no one heard the message. She had become, to her parents, "a very difficult child."

THE FORMS OF THEIR ABUSE

The National Center on Child Abuse and Neglect (1978) defined sexual abuse as "contacts or interactions between a child and an adult when the child is being used for the sexual stimulation of the perpetrator or another person, when the perpetrator is in a position of power or control over the victim" (p. 42). This definition is broad enough to include involvement of "another person" who watches for titillation and also to encompass sexual interactions not involving physical contact (for example, exhibitionism). It is noteworthy that my respondents, who used their own definitions of who was and was not an abuser, also included these categories.

Noncontact Sexual Abuse

Each form of abuse carries its own particular kind of distress. All are invasions of boundaries and distortions of acceptable sexuality. Most survivors were exposed to several forms, compounding the negative impact. Voyeurism and sexual talk are the two main noncontact sexual mistreatments that may be directed against a child.

Voyeurism is visual rape. Eyes can caress, feast on, or gaze at the face of a lover, but they can also follow, fix on, leer, undress, pry, and probe an unwilling target. Such invasions were reported by 46% of the respondents—for example, "I could feel eyes on me; my brother had drilled a hole in the wall between our bedrooms." A voyeur, with the help of a camera, can zoom in from a distance, snatching privacy away. **Peggy** described her father's obsession: "When I was tanning by our pool, he'd be hanging out his bedroom window taking pictures." An upsetting aspect of voyeurism is the realization that it can occur at the very moment when one is feeling relaxed and safe.

Probably even more disturbing than being subjected to voyeurism is being *forced to be a voyeur*. (I have already mentioned women who had been unwilling witnesses to parental sex.) **Ivy**'s father never touched her but, for 5 years, he regularly made her watch him masturbate. She felt dirtied, fearful, and powerless. When I attended the imprisoned women's therapy group, she pointed out, "It isn't only handling that hurts. The mental and emotional abuse and sexual threat are very damaging."

Sexual talk directed at a child is also highly distressing. Two thirds of the women (67%) experienced its demeaning and threatening impact from one or more abusers. **Paige** explained, "After church each Sunday was 'my time' with my father. We went for a long walk on the shoreline, and he told me all the obscene jokes that he dared not tell Mother. I felt so dirtied." Sometimes, sexual comments tested the possibility of a more serious violation. During repairs at **Ashley**'s home, a plumber and a carpenter (friends of the family) kept making crude remarks about her body. They upset her deeply, but her mother, who was about to leave for the store, brushed off her protests. Although Ashley begged to be taken along, she was left behind, to be raped by both men. Apparently, they felt perfectly safe, and indeed, they were.

Contact Abuse

Kissing, touching, and stroking are important messages of love to babies and young children, making them feel good about their bodies and about themselves. However, molestation should never be confused with caressing. It is not a loving misstep that slips beyond an enveloping hug, or smoothing a sad little face, or rocking a tired child. Incest is not a "relationship" or an "affair," as it may be euphemistically described. These terms imply equality and mutual, informed assent, neither of which is possible for a child. In child sexual abuse, the positive aspects of sexuality are absent or, at best, distorted. As Roland Summit (1985) put it, "the sexual experiences themselves [are not] the stuff of romantic or seductive dreams. The words 'fondle' or 'caress' are . . . better characterized as grab, rub, probe, lick, and suck" (p. 51). Adults who impose their sexual behavior on children use a gentle vocabulary to describe criminal acts.

Contact Without Penetration

External sexual handling can be more ambiguous than penetration, and it is more easily distorted by the molester. Almost all of the survivors (90%) were handled in sexual ways, whatever else happened to them. **Natalie's** description of what she endured drains any illusion of romance from the experience: "My uncle would lick my face and rub his flaccid penis over my body. To this day, I can't spell 'tongue' or 'penis,' and I can still taste alcohol and stale tobacco in my mouth."

There has been controversy over whether the form of sexual abuse determines its long-term impact. Based on this study, my belief is that the first clearly sexual contact (of any nature) by a caretaker ruptures trust unless the offender clarifies that it was his fault and that it will never happen again. Each additional episode, by the same person or others, causes further deterioration in a child's sense of her own worth and of her ability to be safe in the world. However, penetration is probably the worst offense because the child feels unsafe within her own body.

Penetration

Russell (1986, p. 143) studied a large representative sample of women who had been incest victims and demonstrated a strong relationship between severity of abuse and the degree of later trauma. She classified oral, vaginal, and anal intercourse as "very severe sexual abuse" and found they had occurred for 24% of her entire incest sample (p. 99). She also reported that, when incest had occurred with fathers or stepfathers, 26% or 47% (respectively) of the daughters had been penetrated by them. Although my study was broader in including other types of sexual abuse in addition to incest, among my respondents, the incidence of any form of penetration was much higher (81% for the total sample and 83% and 89%, respectively, for incestuous fathers and stepfathers). Probably, a major reason for the difference is that Russell's incest survivors were not from a clinical sample, whereas mine were—all of my respondents were in ther-

Table 4.2 Forms of Survivors' Sexual Abuse, by Group (%)

Characteristic	Amnesic	Partial Amnesic	Nonamnesic	Imprisoned	Total
No childhood supporter	48	27	14	17	28
Abused often or regularly	65	71	67	83	70
Force experienced during abuse					
Gentleness	83	79	80	64	78
Roughness	52	79	45	73	59
Violence	43	50	15	9	31
Torture	30	21	15	0	19
Penetration experienced	96	86	62	83	81
Oral (fellatio)	68	64	43	33	54
Vaginal	56	50	52	75	57
Anal	12	14	5	25	12
All three forms	8	7	5	25	10

apy for serious abuse, the traumatic effects of which had lasted for up to 54 years. Consistent with this interpretation, my amnesic participants had a much higher proportion of penetration (96%) than the nonamnesic group (62%). Table 4.2 shows the forms of penetration and the degrees of force imposed on the women in my study.

In a number of states, only vaginal penetration is legally considered incest (Roseman, 1992). There is public ignorance about the prevalence, and denial of the importance, of oral and anal penetration of small children. From the child's viewpoint, any form of penetration makes her feel invaded, and "used like a toilet." In the imagery of my interviewees, they endured sticky privates and their messy explosion, choked over "pee" in their throat, or bent in the "doggy" position to receive a deposit from behind.

Oral penetration, or fellatio, was imposed on 54% of my respondents. Because of the child's small size, this is the most common form inflicted on infants and toddlers. In keeping with their younger age at first abuse, more of the amnesic and partial amnesic groups endured it than the nonamnesics (68% and 64% vs. 43%). Fellatio can feel degrading to any toilet-trained child. **Angie,** burning with shame, had reasoned, "He peed in my mouth, so he must not love me." In addition, oral penetration may often feel life-threatening. During regressive flashbacks to oral sex, some respondents experienced smothering sensations and felt the choking terror of a small child. Several had almost suffocated when their throats were used to stimulate an orgasm. As adults, a number of the women attributed health problems, such as asthma, to childhood oral abuse (see Chapter 7).

Vaginal penetration was experienced by 57% of my respondents. It was especially disturbing to the older children who experienced it because it was more clearly wrong than earlier activities such as mutual masturbation and oral sex. And it was plain to many survivors that "losing their virginity" lowered their worth in society. **Pat** listened resentfully, at age 12, to her mother's advice on "saving yourself for marriage." Glaring at her father, whose eyes were fastened on his newspaper, she wanted to shout, "Wake up, Mom! You're already too late!"

Vaginal penetration was distressing physically as well. Survivors, during flashbacks, were alarmed by pain in vaginas that were too tight or too short. Many also reexperienced the heavy weight of the abuser, which created breathing problems and a powerful sense of being trapped. "I was only 97 pounds, and I'd just disappear into the mattress," said **Amy**. Flashbacks to vaginal abuse brought **Alana** to the recognition of how small she had been. She could feel the right side of her face pressed in against her father's rib cage, an outer loop of her lip trying to snatch a breath of air. Many an offender—in the throes of illicit sexual excitement—was indifferent to his daughter's plight, and the child knew it: "He doesn't even know I'm here."

Survivors who had experienced anal penetration (12%) found it "dirty," painful, and humiliating. It also left them feeling especially defenseless. Curling into the fetal position was comforting to some child victims of sexual abuse because it gave them the illusion that they could protect their mouths, breasts, and vagina, but for the victim of sodomy it only exposed the site of their invasion. There were 10% of the women, including **NANCY** and **ILENE**, who had experienced all three forms of penetration, and they felt exceptionally vulnerable—invaded from every direction, with no orifice safe.

Emotional survival seemed to require that even those women who "never forgot" needed to dissociate themselves from such experiences. As an illustration, **NANCY** told me about washing herself at the sink in her bedroom right after her father had finished with her. She was 12 years old. Suddenly, she turned toward the bed, crying out, "Daddy! Who is the girl in my mirror?" Her father muttered, "My god, what have I done?"

However, he set aside his temporary penitence for another 8 years of continuing incestuous encounters with all three of his daughters.

FREQUENCY OF ABUSE, DURATION, AND THE USE OF FORCE

Frequency and Duration

Russell (1986, p. 146) reported that a higher percentage of women considered their abuse traumatic if it had lasted more than 5 years and if it occurred frequently. For participants in this study, 5.7 years was the average duration of primary abuse (Table 4.1), and for 70% of the women, it had occurred often or regularly (Table 4.2). Because most women had been exploited by more than one offender, their victimization had extended over a still longer period of time, or it had been intensified during certain years of their lives. By their late teens and early 20s, many also experienced date rape. For the two main study groups, the survivors' level of amnesia was positively related to the duration of their childhood abuse—that is, the primary abuse of amnesic women lasted longer than that of nonamnesic women (5.7 years vs. 4.4 years). However, it was surprising that the partially amnesic group had an even longer period of primary abuse (7.4 years).

Force

The use of force certainly increases the traumatic effect of sexual abuse or assault. Many adult victims experience rape as literally life-threatening. Apparently, it was similar for my respondents as children. They were threatened verbally and behaviorally, their rapists were seen as out of control, and lust was interpreted as murderous hatred. Several believed that they would die by smothering, strangling, or drowning. Under such threats, some experienced what **Phyllis** called "the death of self."

Another highly traumatic aspect of force is group rape of children. I have already given examples of rapes by multiple strangers, rapes arranged by brothers, and rape by neighbors. A few of my survivors reported ritualized abuse, which occurred in the presence of observers. In one case, **Arna**'s parents finally admitted that they had abused her in this manner, and they are now trying to help her to heal.

My respondents typically experienced more than one level of sexual coercion during their months or years of abuse:

Gentleness	78%
Roughness	59%
Violence	31%
Torture	19%

The figures for the subgroups are shown in Table 4.2. It is noteworthy that about 80% of both the amnesic and nonamnesic group experienced gentleness in some of their abusive contacts. However, the proportion of amnesics who endured violence (43%) was much higher than that of the nonamnesics (15%), and a similar but smaller difference held for those who reported undergoing torture.

Although violence is obviously coercive, the compelling nature of gentleness has not been emphasized in the literature. According to my respondents, gentle treatment during sexual abuse was profoundly deceptive and confusing. Intimacy and abuse were paired—a conditioning that, imposed so young, is hard to break, even in adulthood. Gentleness can also set up a hunger within a child, making her extremely vulnerable to other abusers. **Alicia** experienced a fall from "princess to prostitute," as her father focused increasingly on self-gratification and his seductive behavior gave way to pressure.

Roughness during sexual abuse seemed to carry a message of indifference and callousness. Its incidence was particularly high among the partial amnesics (79%) and the imprisoned group (73%). The sense of being "used" was more clear in these cases, which were often devoid of any pretense of gentleness.

Violence was experienced by many more amnesics and partial amnesics than by the other two groups of women. Moreover, the children often knew their violent abusers—a father, uncle, brother, or neighbor. Sexual abuse by a parent who fluctuated between gentleness and violence was particularly upsetting. As **Pam** explained, every situation was unpredictable: "Dad could be extremely charming and sensual, but sometimes he was in a rage and violent." Even the sadistic mothers had been kind and attentive at times. **Abbey** looked frightened as she tried to explain: "Watch out—the look on her face would change—incredible flips that terrified me." Like soldiers in combat, these girls had to erect psychic defenses against danger and brutality (Cameron, 1994a). But unlike soldiers, most had to do so in their own home—the same place where they might also experience gentle, tender treatment.

Torture was experienced by 19% of the women. Although *torture* is not a word one normally associates with mothers, my findings require them to be linked. The enemas given by **Priscilla**'s mother left anal scarring, and **Annette**'s mother mutilated her child's genitals ("My 'potty' still hurts"). At least two other mothers displayed sadism rivaling that of Sybil's mother, who tortured her daughter in Schreiber's (1973) true story.

SEXUAL ABUSE VERSUS PHYSICAL ABUSE

In the area of physical abuse, an unexpected finding occurred. One third or more of both the amnesic and partially amnesic respondents had clear memories of physical abuse, which existed alongside their amnesia to sexual abuse. A number of circumstances may have contributed to this finding. Sexual abuse incorporates many other forms of abuse. It is, by its nature, abuse of the child's physical body as well as being psychological maltreatment. Garbarino, Guttmann, and Seeley (1987, pp. 17-18) have documented the violation of a child's emotions that occurs in sexual abuse. Sexual abuse is also neglect of the child's intimate needs through imposition of an adult's will. And sexual abuse is assaultive to the senses—sight, hearing, touch, smell, and taste—as the flashbacks of the women attested. Perhaps most important, childhood sexual abuse occurs unseen and unheard by outsiders, so there is no external validation of the child's reality.

I asked several women who had experienced both physical and sexual abuse why amnesia had been more likely for the latter. They indicated that the sexual abuse was "worse," giving several reasons: Physical mistreatment seemed more understandable, as an extension of a parent's right to discipline. **Pia** explained, "I saw it as within their right as adults, but 'unfair.' I could complain about it. The sexual abuse was degrading, shameful, and secret." **Nell** believed that physical abuse was more predictable and partly controllable:

> The physical abuse was bad. At 15, I had black eyes and a broken arm. However, there was some cause and effect: "I did X, therefore Mom did Y." I could set myself up or avoid it to some extent. But with my step-dad, the sex, the threat was there all the time. There was no way out once it started.

No rules to the game and no logic. Once it was because I didn't clean my room, and another time because I got a good report card.

Nina saw physical abuse as more external: "He would beat my butt, shake me, throw me, but at least that was on the outside. With sexual abuse, even the inside of you is polluted. You are not even safe within your own body." (Notice in this quotation that Nina distanced herself from the sexual memories by switching from *me* to the less personal *you*.)

According to **Phoebe**, the effects of physical abuse were also less permanent: "Scars, bruises, and breaks go away with time, but damage to one's sexual outlook doesn't. For the short time that the abuser gets his way, he distorts her view of intimacy for a lifetime." Finally, **Penny** saw one underlying motivation in all she had endured at the hands of her mother and her aunt:

I experienced many forms of abuse—physical and sexual abuse, neglect, abandonment, and threats to kill. All had the same theme—they were trying to take my soul, the core of who I was. That was the real evil, the real damage.

OTHER TRAUMATIC ASPECTS OF SEXUAL ABUSE

The traumatizing nature of sexual abuse was increased by other aspects of the situation. Among these were threats, duplicity and misrepresentation, game playing, humiliation, breathing problems, and even induced feelings of pleasure. Many of these undermined the child's evolving assumptions about herself and the world.

Threats in the abuse situation were both implicit and explicit. The furtive and silencing manner of the abuser suggested danger. His careful pretense the next day that "nothing happened" implied that knowledge by others was a greater threat than the abuse itself. Usually, explicit threats were added and evoked the child's fears for herself and her family. **Pam**'s father was a violent man and obsessed with his collection of guns. He threatened to kill her and her sister and mother as well if she spoke of the incest. **Andrea** was told that she would end up in a mental institution. The threat for **Nicole** was to her younger brothers. If she refused her stepfather, his direct response was to beat the little boys. For most respondents, however, the most powerful threat was internal. They felt trapped by secrecy, and the only way out—telling what had occurred —could destroy their family.

Duplicity in the abuser was profoundly disturbing, even "crazy-making," and increased the need to forget. A splitting between the public and private persona of the abuser—the "day father" and the "night father," or the "good" and the "bad" daddy—troubled several amnesic women. Experiencing flashbacks in the supportive presence of her therapist allowed **Angela** to express the confusion she could not voice as a child, "It can't be true. He *can't* be two people." Her father had come only in the dark, and he never spoke at all. By day, he acted as if nothing had happened. Once, seated on the same bed where he had treated her like a lover the night before, he gave her a spanking.

Misrepresentation was another form of duplicity. Abusive fathers often presented sexual advances as part of their parental role as educators and protectors. **Nora** explained, "The sex was supposed to be for me. My father said he was giving me 'an education in pleasure' when he presented me with a encyclopedia of sex with pictures to learn from." **Patrice**'s father entered his daughter's bedroom when her little school friend was visiting. He said that he wanted to protect them by showing them how men's bodies worked. Displaying his erect penis, he made them masturbate him to ejaculation. In a parallel lesson, this same man threw his small daughter in the deep end of the swimming pool to "teach her how to swim." **Nan**'s father, who had a similar penchant for terrorizing, took obvious pleasure in lancing a series of painful boils on her torso. He also weighed his daughter weekly, laying the tape measure over her private parts, and then shaming her with his evaluation. Were these men, who presented themselves as "good parents," social misfits? Ironically, the answer is no. They were respected in their communities and held positions of status—business proprietor, social worker, and junior high school teacher, respectively.

The playfulness that can characterize mature, loving sexuality was distorted for children whose offenders treated sexual abuse as a game because the child ran from them. Incestuous behavior often began with playful seductivity, hooking a child who was hungry for love. Then, the abuser's attention generally shifted to more blatant sexual behavior beyond the child's understanding, and his "tenderness" changed to self-gratification. The laughter of such offenders was especially upsetting. **Ava**'s stepfather, for example, started scaring her when her mother was about to go shopping, by pointing at the clock. His smile meant "My time is coming." Because her mother would not take her along, the small girl desperately tried to find a tiny secure hiding place, only to be hauled out to the sound of her stepfather's raucous laughter. For her, sex was a futile game of hide-and-seek with only one winner. Sometimes he would trick her, pretending to go out, but hiding in a closet and jumping out at her. As she fled, terrified, Ava always heard the laughter of the chase. She soon learned that she could only postpone the inevitable.

For some abusers, the blend of laughter and cruelty extended beyond sexuality. On Halloween night, **Nadine**'s father, in a hideous costume, would knock at her bedroom window, laughing uproariously when she woke, terrified. The abusers' game playing sometimes became deliberate tormenting. Several girls endured excruciating tickling, and **Penny** regularly experienced her stepfather's view of fun:

> My stepfather would torment me by holding me down or lying on top of me until I had trouble breathing. I'm very allergic to cigarette smoke, and at these times, he would blow smoke in my face, choking me. Or he would kiss me on my neck or in my mouth, reeking and slobbering. His alcoholism disgusted me. His odor, his lack of control, his appearance, his denial—they all disgusted me.

Humiliation caused by demeaning aspects of the abuse was also upsetting, especially as the respondents grew older and recognized the significance of what had happened. **Alison** recovered the humiliating memory of her brother's friends passing him money across her body. Seven-year-old **Anita** was told by a teenage molester (giving himself time to escape) to wait for him to bring her a bag of pennies. Commonly, girls who were molested by a father figure received special favors, gifts, or money from him. Looking back, they felt that they had prostituted themselves. They transposed the idea "He gave me gifts after sexual abuse" into "I gave sex to get gifts." For other survivors, additional humiliation, such as a stream of degrading sexual epithets, followed the sexual acts. Perhaps the most ironic insult of all came from young **Nona**'s father: "He threatened to spank me for not doing the sex better."

Breathing problems troubled many respondents over the years. **Alana** cannot wear any garment that must be pulled over her face. **Perri** finds herself "unable to breathe well after sundown." Respiratory problems were common for many of the women (see Chapter 7). Flashbacks (see Chapter 9) helped these women to connect such symptoms to their childhood trauma, which had usually occurred at night. Their abusers, in addition to using appeals, warnings, and threats to keep them quiet after sexual contact, generally had to silence them during the act. They did so in a multitude of ways, most of which obstructed breathing. The little girls were silenced with a hand or a pillow; their face was thrust into an armpit, a shoulder, or a mattress; something was stuffed into their mouth; the abuser sat on their face; they were choked into silence; or they were threatened with death. And many were subjected to fellatio. Gripped by the excitement of forbidden pleasure, abusers simply did not notice or care what was happening to the object of their satisfaction. Decades later, flashbacks brought back the body sensations and emotions evoked by such treatment, especially for members of the amnesic group. **Adel** re-experienced a hand covering her mouth as a 4-year-old, closing off her still-soft nose. **Andrea** recalled herself as a 10-year-old, her face crushed against her father's ribs during coitus.

Induced feelings of pleasure during abuse were another distressing issue. In incestuous families, early stroking had shaped some respondents toward more blatantly sexual acts, and they felt compromised. Later in the abuse, experiencing orgasms made them feel that their emotions as well as their physical being had been violated. Their own body had betrayed them, producing physical pleasure in the midst of despair. Some tried to hide their bodily reactions, which were seen by their abuser as proof that they "wanted it." They hated hearing smug chuckles when they had an orgasm. **Naomi** mourned, "I wish there had been no enjoyment. Then I could get angry." Not only was orgasm distressing to **Amy** as a child but, like other survivors, she eventually learned to numb parts of her body until she felt no pleasure—a talent that seriously undermined her love life as an adult. Other children were sexualized well beyond their years, making them easy targets for other abusers.

SOCIAL SUPPORT DURING CHILDHOOD

A childhood social support system can soften the impact of child abuse. Moses (1991, p. 30) reported that support of abused children by even one person enhanced victims' recovery and also the likelihood that later, as parents, they could stop the cycle of abuse from continuing into the next generation. This finding should comfort foster parents and relatives who have done whatever was possible to be helpful to child victims but who feared it was not enough.

I asked research participants whether, when they were children, there had been "at least one caring, supportive person" whom they could count on for appreciation, attention, and affection (see Table 4.2). Nearly 30% of the total sample reported that they had had no one at all to turn to as children, 56% reported having only one supporter, and 14% had two or more. The absence of support was strongly related to amnesia. Almost half of the amnesic group (48%)—compared to 27% of the partially amnesic group and 14% of the nonamnesics—lacked any truly supportive person in their lives. Even the imprisoned survivors (only 17% of whom had no supporter) felt more support than the amnesic women.

Nonsupport

Several respondents, as children, had parents who did not protect them from molesters or who even made abuse easier. **Ashley** was frequently victimized:

> Family friends made comments about my plump bottom and pawed me without reproof from my parents. Once father walked into my bedroom when one of his friends was molesting me on the bed. Father simply turned around and walked out again.

Thus, Ashley grew up in an atmosphere pervaded by a sense of male entitlement. By the age of 13, this girl had been molested by six people, including her mother when she was drunk.

In some of the women's families, not only were adults unsupportive, but they were jealous of their child's affection for other adults. Several women said that their parents had deliberately separated them from loving caretakers. **NANCY** and her mother shared her grandfather's home during World War II, and she adored her grandfather. But when her soldier father reclaimed his family after the war, he exiled the older man from their lives, and the incest began. **Pearl** "went directly from heaven to hell" at age 5. She had been raised by a loving foster mother until her mother remarried and took the child to live with her. All contact with the woman who had parented Pearl was immediately and permanently severed (along with the long golden curls that her foster mother had brushed to a shine). Despite the loss of their supporters, these children's knowledge that once they had been deeply loved helped them to grow up as survivors.

Support

Among those women who were not cut off from caring others, half had supporters who were relatives outside the immediate family. Grandmothers were the category most commonly mentioned. **ILENE** recalled, "When my mother would tell me I was rotten—no good—Grandmother was there to say, 'You know it's not so.' " The other caring people in the respondents' childhoods were quite evenly distributed among mothers, fathers, siblings, and unrelated adults. Although these support persons almost never knew about (much less stopped) the abuse, they did lay a foundation for the child's self-esteem.

Male supporters. Several women found appreciation and support from a male who did not act out sexually—a grandfather, brother, or cousin. **Natalie** confided in her 13-year-old cousin about her brother's brutality and, because she refused to talk to an adult, he became her comforter. Although a child himself, he did what he could to repair the emotional damage by explaining his own positive view of sexuality. **Audrey**, age 10, found comfort in spending time with a teenage cousin who shared his love of wild birds with her. They spent many summer hours roaming the woods together. Amnesic to her abuse, Audrey had been withdrawn and sad, but her cousin's attention and respect helped her to open up. As an adult, she was surprised to learn that he was quite retarded, for he had provided her the support she needed.

Animal friends. If support did not come in human form, some children found it in animals. **Caitlin** wrote me,

> There was no one in my entire life whom I could confide in. I had no faith in the system either—church, school, hospital, neighbors. Everyone was very effective at looking the other way. But I *could* talk and cry with my best friend—who was my dog.

She had to pretend indifference, however, whenever her father tormented the animal, because she feared for its life. **Alexis**, who was raped by her brother when she was only 6 years old, saw an owl looking in the bedroom window at her and hooting as if to comfort her and to draw her back to life. Support—wherever it came from—continued to be important in the lives of respondents as adults.

Reporting the Abuse

A particularly revealing aspect of the women's reports is the great difficulty they had in telling anyone about being sexually abused during their childhood. The majority (56%) told no one until they were well into adulthood, and four others (6%) told a girlfriend, cousin, or sister but refused to tell any adult. Some of their questionnaires explained their silence with disheartening specifics:

- No one would believe me.
- I was afraid.
- They couldn't have handled it.
- I felt alone and that no one would help—because I had done something terribly wrong.
- My whole family was part of the illness.

Was their reluctance to tell justified? Sad to say, only one of the respondents succeeded in telling an adult during childhood and receiving consolation and subsequent protection against the abuser: When **Paloma** (at age 12) told her father about her grandfather's abuse, he rocked her in his arms, comforted her, and relieved her of all guilt. However, the usual reaction was very different: 24 others told an adult, but only 5 of these were believed, and none of them were really supported. The large majority who weren't believed described the following categories of parental reactions:

- Ignoring the report—"My grandmother walked away so fast I thought she was mad at me" (**ANNE**). "I never could get my mother to believe me" (**Penny**). "My telling and feelings were ignored" (**Pat** told her mother and a school counselor).
- Silencing the child—"Grandmother told me not to ever talk like that." "Mother said it was imagination, and never to talk about it again."

- Threats—"Mother made it out to not be so bad and said that if I told anyone, they wouldn't believe me, and I would be put away."
- Punishment—"Mother punished me. I think she knew all along. She already hated me, and hated me more after I told." "I got rejection from my family and became an outsider" (after telling her stepfather about abuse by a neighbor). "My mom didn't believe me. She beat me and isolated me."

Even the five children who were believed did not receive adult support as a result. Their accounts added two other categories of adult reactions:

- Minimization—"Mother just told me not to go to that boy's house again." "Mother took me to a dentist, and he said that our neighbor was a nice grandfather and didn't *really* do anything bad to me."
- Humiliation—"Daddy was sorry for me, but Mama made a huge affair and embarrassed me deeply—threw me down on the couch, spread my legs, and said 'See what a mess you've made of this.' " ILENE reported, "Mother told me that [my stepfather] was more important to her than I was, and she would do whatever she needed to keep her husband."

Finally, there were three children whose abuser was caught in the act by a mother or both parents. The abusers were an aunt, a stepfather, and two teenage neighbors. You might think that at least these children would be vindicated and protected, but even in these clear-cut cases, the child didn't necessarily receive support. Ida's parents didn't know whether to believe her at first, but they were supportive after they hid and watched until they witnessed the abuse. Seven-year-old Arlene's mother wasn't punitive when she found her masturbating her stepfather in the shower, but Arlene did not feel able to tell her mother again when the abuse kept happening. When 6-year-old Noelle was raped by two 17-year-old neighbors, "My mother found me and told me I should never do this again. Then she took me to my pastor [the father of one of the boys], where I felt like *I* was to blame."

With adult reactions like these, is it any wonder that most of the abused children didn't even think of reporting their abuse to someone else?

THE END OF THE ABUSE

Although some of the literature on child sexual abuse has tended to view incestuous fathers as impulsive and lacking in self-discipline, many sexual offenders have been found to be planful in their abuse (Finkelhor et al., 1986). Consistent with that view, several respondents in this study emphasized their abuser's planfulness in arranging for sexual opportunities and in biding his time to avoid discovery. For example, 30 years ago, **April** and her small daughter spent a summer vacation at April's childhood home, where her father offered persuasive reasons why the 3-year-old should have her own bedroom. Decades later, this mother and daughter compared memories (recovered by April and never lost by her daughter) of both being sexually abused by him, a generation apart.

Abuse within the nuclear family, where availability and power differences provide the opportunity and means for its occurrence, is most likely to be frequent and long-lasting. Eventually, however, it does come to an end, although few of my respondents were able to stop the abuse themselves. Several women were convinced that their fathers were planful in terminating as well as initiating incestuous behavior. Terminations typically occurred at one of two stages—when the child was beginning school or entering puberty—that is, stages in the daughter's life when outside support was more likely to be available. However, a few abusers stopped their depredations still earlier, when a child was acquiring language skills. One respondent recalled being thoroughly sexualized "only up until I began putting sentences together."

For 30% of survivors who experienced abuse by fathers, the incest ceased about the time they entered elementary school. However, the most common age for fathers to stop their abuse (39%) was when their daughter was about to enter puberty, at about 12 years of age. Adolescence allowed girls more independence and a potentially supportive peer group. An additional threat to the perpetrator at this time was the possibility of exposure through the daughter becoming pregnant. At that point in time, a younger sibling was sometimes chosen as a safer object for incest. However, 26% of the fathers continued to molest the respondents beyond the age of puberty. Several of the women contracted teenage marriages that were motivated as escapes from home, and at least three fathers pursued their daughters after marriage. **ILENE** described her experience: "After my husband left for work, my stepdad would come by. I wouldn't answer the door, so he would prowl around our yard for an hour or so before giving up. God! I was grateful to have a locked door at last."

THE BOND OF SECRECY

> *I felt special. His soothing voice, saying it was our secret, made me dependent on him for comfort and for love.*
>
> **—Addie**

Secrecy is *the* essential ingredient in most sexual abuse, and especially in incest, so it was central to the survivors' childhood experiences. Sociologist Georg Simmel, analyzing the topic of secrecy, declared that a secret is a contract, and an especially powerful one, because it not only binds together those who "know" but separates them from those who do not (Wolff, 1950).[3] This double function is what makes a secret such a force for damage as well as benefit.

There is an enormous difference between healthy secrets, contracted between childhood friends, and harmful ones imposed by an adult abuser on a child. In choosing a friend with whom to share a secret, a little girl learns discernment. She also develops her capacity for close and trusting relationships. Regardless of its content, their secret sets friends apart from others and gives them a sense of power. They learn to protect their secret from those who might guess it and from their own temptation to tell. Trust, confidence, closeness, loyalty, and affection are all possible by-products of childhood secrets when equals contract together.

By contrast, the experience of my respondents is convincing evidence that a sexual secret between an adult and a child perverts the benefits described above. It destroys, rather than builds, the capacity for trust and intimacy. It distorts love and loyalty. A sexual secret between an adult and a child is not light-hearted but an obsession. The content of the secret is supremely important, and the child knows that revealing it would not only surprise and shock but could destroy someone she loves, her family, or herself. In effect, she has been given a bomb and warned not to explode it.

A small child has a tremendous need for love, attention, and affection, so she easily bonds with an abuser who makes himself her major resource. And, even though secrecy is imposed on her rather than agreed to, she feels an accomplice to what has been happening. The closer she bonds with the abuser, the more she is alienated from others and, in an ever-tightening circle of betrayal, the more dependent she becomes on him. Ironically, because secret sexuality makes potential rescuers unaware of the child's plight, she thinks her security depends on protecting the abuser. **Alma,** sadistically abused by her mother, illustrated this seeming contradiction when she said, "Mom used to hurt me a lot, but she warned me that if I told anyone I'd be put in a mental hospital where I'd fare even worse. I cried whenever I was separated from her because I thought I couldn't survive without her." The child found herself in a hostage situation, with no one negotiating her ransom. This distorted kind of closeness can continue even into adulthood. **Angie** said of her sister (who, until recently, vigorously denied having been victimized), "All the pictures in her apartment are of Dad and her together. When he was dying, she clung to him, fighting the nurses for his life. And since his death, she says that he visits her, sitting on her bed."

Secrecy Serves the Abuser
While It Sabotages the Child

The secret that binds the child to her abuser awards him all the benefits. Its value is increased by the importance of what it conceals and reinforced by the parent's "owning" attitude toward the child herself. The girl, along with "their" secret, is denied to everyone else. As an illustrative example, **Norma** told me of a survivors' meeting she had attended where three formerly incestuous fathers made themselves open to questions. Before being reported to the authorities, these men had felt no guilt about their behavior, so she asked them what they would have done if they had walked into their living room and seen their child's uncle or grandfather behaving similarly with her. In one voice, they responded, "I'd have killed him!" These possessive fathers had operated at two levels: They were clear about right and wrong for others but had savored, without guilt, their secret access to a daughter or son. The child was "theirs," and secrecy enhanced the rush of adrenaline that made this forbidden sexuality extremely addictive.

The child, in sharp contrast, is a prisoner of the secret, and she feels isolated—whether she loves, hates, or is ambivalent toward her abuser. **Nadine** had always hated her unpredictable, violent, and violating father. But, when asked whether she had ever sought help, she replied, "The idea never occurred to me." She and her father had been locked in such private combat that other people, as potential helpers, did not even exist for her.

When a child deeply loves and trusts an abusive parent, a second powerful word (in addition to *secret*) helps to seal the bond. That word is *special.* To be special to someone implies a unique relationship. But, because tenderness and caressing are only received in a sexual context, the child develops a distorted sense of love. The pairing of love with molestation in the mind of a small child is one of the cruelest outcomes of sexual abuse. As **Ingrid** said, "I thought as a child that the uncle who *never* molested me did not love me. It is only recently that I have been able to sort love out from abuse."

To be special also implies commitment, and therefore, the child feels deeply deceived when the accuser—who typically starts out seductively by focusing his attention on her—becomes increasingly narcissistic, seeking only control and sexual gratification. She feels intensely betrayed for trusting him—abandoned and made a fool of. Yet, her own sense of guilt makes her feel an accessory to the crime against herself and worthy only of abuse in future relationships. **Ariel**'s dream illustrates this feeling:

> I was dancing naked on a snowy hill when a man tried to rape me. I ran down the hill to the courthouse, where a jury pronounced him innocent because I was nude. I fled to the town for protection and the townspeople judged me guilty. Abandoning hope, I returned up the hill to the rapist.

Not only does secrecy yield all its benefits to the abuser, but it also isolates the pair in such a way that he experiences no interference and the child receives no support. Consciously or unconsciously, abusers use the principle of divide and conquer. The survivors described numerous distancing tactics employed to separate them from potential supporters —adults, siblings, and peers. Because mothers were the most likely candidates to be supporters, incestuous fathers made them primary targets of distrust. The respondents were warned that their mothers (in some cases, already seen as emotionally unavailable) would reject them if they were told about the incest. Such warnings served to widen the gap between mother and child.

Sometimes, the abuser played a more active divide-and-conquer role by making mother "the bad one." As the third party, he then sat back and exploited the growing division. "Father got custody of us girls after the divorce, and his lies about Mother made me hate and fear her. When he made us take turns sharing his bed, who could I turn to?" Another divisive technique was to paint mother as incompetent:

> Dad subtly put Mother down, making himself more important in our lives. He encouraged us when we teased her or joked about her opinions. He came off as good-natured and she as inept. We not only lost respect for her, but we also lost her presence as a support person. I feel sad now to think of what we missed giving to her and getting from her.

Abusers also made sure that the child got no help within the home from other children, either siblings or friends. **Ivonne**'s foster father isolated her from all possible supporters: "He reported every minor rule infraction to his wife and played the other children against me, causing constant fights. When I stood up for myself, he labeled me a 'bad girl' and a 'liar.' " Separation from friends was even easier to accomplish by discouraging out-of-home contacts. In some cases, the mechanisms were obvious. Several of the women had to come straight home from school, neither visiting friends nor having them over. Their dating was delayed, restricted, or subjected to voyeuristic scrutiny. Family matters were not to be discussed outside the home, and perhaps not even within it. In other cases, the means of separation were subtle. One wealthy family lived in a high-rise apartment during most of the year and on a prestigious estate in the summertime. These homes were elegant fortresses with minimal outside contact.

As offenders isolated children for themselves, they ensured the child's dependency. Moreover, the children also had good reason to be loners. They felt stigmatized—different from other people. Their secret was an obstacle to interaction with others for two reasons. Outsiders might stumble on the truth, or they themselves might give in to the constant temptation to tell. Either way, the truth could unleash its destructive power. To avoid the first danger, most respondents wore a public mask of contentment and social adjustment (their façades are discussed in Chapter 7). This appearance of normalcy helped ensure that no one would suspect their shame. At the same time, they monitored themselves when with others so that their fear, anger, and longing would not break through. Their terrible need to tell—so that they might understand the distortions of their world and learn what was normal and fair—was curbed and suppressed.

Courtois (1988) summed up the dilemma of the child-victim: "The secrecy, silence, and taboo keep her from asking for help and prevent her from getting acknowledgment and validation of her experience." Social withdrawal is one way to preserve the secret. For many abused children, amnesia is another. What better way to keep a secret than by losing it entirely? It is then unknown even to the secret bearer herself. Even among women who always remembered what had happened to them, half avoided full awareness by not labeling it as abuse, and most overlooked its impact on their lives.

The secret also kept the women out of touch with themselves and with the truth. Without social reference points, the child's only authority in the situation was the offender. Unable to accurately assign responsibility for what was happening, the survivors had typically blamed themselves. Of the formerly amnesic women, 85% believed that feelings of guilt and shame had contributed to their amnesia.

The secret incest dyad gives an offender remarkable power over a child—a power that feeds on its own dynamics. He labels sexual abuse as "special treatment" and imposes on her, without her consent, a contract of loyalty. Like a hostage, she is isolated from help and increasingly dependent on him. The longer she keeps the secret, the more implicated she feels and the more likely it is that she will be blamed if she tells.

However, the same secrecy that screens incest from view condemns it. All semblance of worthy motivation collapses before the fact of secrecy. There is a special irony when a father entices his child into a contract of silence. Confident of her trust and loyalty, he violates both. Confident of her integrity, he abandons his own. Confident that she will protect him, he endangers her. His goal, in keeping this unequal situation secret, is to satisfy his needs at the expense of his child's. The cost to her is immense, for the secret changes her relationship to the world.

SUMMARIZING GROUP DIFFERENCES

In this chapter, I have examined aspects of child sexual abuse as respondents in the three memory groups—amnesic, partially amnesic, and nonamnesic women—experienced them. Now, I summarize what I have learned about similarities and differences among the three memory groups, as well as the imprisoned group, as I examine the role of amnesia in their lives (referring back to Tables 4.1 and 4.2).

Amnesic women lived for decades without awareness of their trauma and were younger (3.7 years old) at first sexual abuse than nonamnesic women (7.0 years old). They were also more likely to have experienced sexual violence and to have been abused by their fathers. All but one of them reported one or more forms of penetration, and almost half lacked even one consistent support person during childhood. All of these differences, compared to the nonamnesic group, were large. Herman and Schatzow (1987) showed comparable results for the variables of age and violence. Three quarters of their respondents named a father figure as an abuser. (The authors did not relate this to the respondent's level of amnesia.) Illustrating the findings for this group, **ANNE**, the representative of the amnesic women, was sexually violated and tormented by her father, a respected physician. He apparently started abusing her before she was 3. The incest usually occurred on day trips and was bizarre in nature. Her only escape would have been through a field that he told her was full of rattlesnakes. The abuse took place with some regularity for about 13 years. The fact that **ANNE** had caring grandparents helped to sustain her when she began to remember in her 30s.

The *partially amnesic* women include two memory subgroups. Some minimized their memories of abuse (remembering a minor part of what they later recalled), whereas the rest separated some events that they recalled from others that they dissociated. Perhaps because of this diversity within the group, their response percentages were sometimes close to the amnesics and sometimes more like the nonamnesics. In this study, it was only when the percentage difference between the amnesic and nonamnesic women was large that those who were partially amnesic fulfilled expectations by falling in between. The following comparison of two partially amnesic women may help to illumine why they dissociated certain *abuses* versus certain *abusers.*

Pamela had always known that her father touched her inappropriately, but she was unaware of the extent of her abuse until her late 20s. The abuse had been unpredictable and inescapable. He had been randomly charming, or violent and threatening her life. Throughout her childhood, her father deliberately and consistently undermined her judgment, interpreting sexual violations as benefiting *her*—"This will help you with your husband later." At the family pool, he proclaimed, "I'm throwing you in the deep end to teach you to swim." Her abuse was too pervasive to delete from memory but too frightening to allow her to survive with full recall.

PAULA had dissociated memory of one of her abusers. She was aware from childhood that her male relatives were allowed to hit or handle females, including girl children. Complaints were useless: "Oh that's just the way he is." When her father entered a bedroom where she was being molested by a family friend, he simply walked out, as if he had interfered with the man's privacy. PAULA felt that she had grown up being silenced by gender (her brother was listened to but she was not), by racism (as a Latina in Caucasian schools), and by domination (by males and by church authorities from whom she sought help). When she finally told on her father's brother, *he* was protected, and *she* was called a liar. PAULA dissociated memory of that double betrayal.

The *nonamnesic* women never forgot the abuse, although most had not labeled it accurately nor connected it directly to their life problems. Their representative, **NANCY**, also had a father abuser, who was a blue-collar worker. Although she represents the nonamnesic women, her experience was unusually serious, involving all three forms of penetration and a 10-year span of abuse (from 11 to 20 years of age). Although she was "groomed" toward penetration much earlier, NANCY dated it from the time when her father first imposed coitus. His abuse continued throughout her teens up to the last night she slept under his roof, and he was also physically abusive. NANCY also shared important similarities with other nonamnesics—her older age at the onset and termination of overt abuse and the lower level of sexual violence she experienced. Moreover, remembering served a practical purpose for her because it sometimes enabled her to avoid the pervasive exploitation of her father. Finally, NANCY recognized that her father was abusive, and perhaps her lack of idealization was her most effective guard against amnesia. Among potential boyfriends, she deliberately looked for ones similar to the loving grandfather of her early childhood, who had given her some self-esteem and a positive male model. And she avoided boys who did not treat their mothers and sisters with respect.

The first general prediction for the memory groups in this research —that amnesia would be related to the severity of the original trauma —was borne out by findings in this chapter. It is clear that, for the research participants, long-lasting amnesia was related to characteristics of their child sexual abuse that had compounded the severity of the original trauma. This difference in the expected direction between amnesic and nonamnesic women was further supported by the fact that the partially amnesic women's scores fell between the two.

Finally, I examine the abuse experience of the women in the *imprisoned* group, whose level of amnesia was not assessed. They had typically been in early elementary school at the onset of abuse, and their abuse was more likely to involve mothers, stepfathers, and uncles rather than fathers. Compared to the three memory groups, their misuse had been more frequent and had lasted relatively long. This group also experienced more vaginal and anal penetration than any other group, and their abuse was also likely to have been rough (rather than either gentle or violent). The general impression imparted by the imprisoned women's stories is that, as children, they were used sexually with callousness and emotional indifference. Information in later chapters will increasingly fill out the picture of how their experiences were similar to and different from their counterparts outside prison.

By good fortune, I was able to interview **ILENE**, who represents the imprisoned survivors in this book. A nurturing grandmother had raised her for 3 years, but then her mother took her back after marrying a man who "admired" the child. The grandmother's continuing affirmation helped stabilize ILENE during her dreadful growing-up years. Sexual abuse by her stepfather lasted from age 3 or 4 until she married at 16. The abuse was frequent and rough, eventually including all forms of entry. ILENE reports that her mother sometimes watched. Impregnated by her stepfather, ILENE gave birth at ages 13 and 15, bearing two infants that her parents put out for adoption. Until she was imprisoned, she told no one except her first husband about these events, and he did not believe her. Although she had never forgotten the abuse, more details came to mind as she faced her past in the prison therapy group. Her memories were not vague or fragmented. For example, she could recall an entire evening as a unit and was able to explore that memory fully as she tried to make sense of her childhood. Although ILENE never dissociated abusive events from her conscious memory, she apparently managed to dissociate herself from pain. She was surprised that her memories of sexual abuse as a toddler and of her birthing of babies as a young teenager included no recall of pain. Much later, in 1998, ILENE began to reexperience that pain in flashbacks.

The negative effects of sexual abuse on each woman participating in this study were cumulative. Most of these survivors had been sexually abused at an early age, and they were still feeling the impact in adulthood. Their abuse was not erased by its termination. Its importance in the life of the child set off a domino effect, with an inexorable unfolding of results. The women's memories of the trauma were affected, they suffered cumulative damage in their psychosocial development, and they showed many symptoms of chronic and delayed posttraumatic stress disorder

(PTSD). I explore these topics in the next two chapters. First, however, I will broaden the focus of this discussion of abuse.

THE RELEVANCE OF FAMILY
ABUSE TO SOCIETAL ABUSE

I want to emphasize that the issue of child sexual abuse (and especially incest) is intrinsically related to the larger field of trauma research. The dynamics of personal trauma mirror those of any trauma perpetrated by human design. To clarify this point, I compare the personal traumatization of a child by incest with the mass traumatization of a nation under an oppressive dictatorship. There are startling similarities between the manipulation of power in an incestuous family and in a nation ruled by terrorism.

Anyhome, U.S.A., and Santiago, Chile

In the 1980s, according to Sveaass (1998), Chile was the "land of the disappeared." An "organized destruction of meaning" allowed Chile's totalitarian government to secure its hold on the nation. The Chilean government was intimidating its own citizens with the paralyzing message, "Our power is everywhere." Civilians (especially men) were vanishing without notice from their homes, the streets, and places of work. Their families were secondary victims of this terrorist tactic, which was intended to foster distrust among relatives and neighbors and hence dependency on the government. Reality was defined by those in power, and confusion was generated—nothing was what it seemed to be. No one knew why a particular citizen was singled out, what he had "done," where he was taken, or when or whether he would return. Victims were blamed for unspecified wrongdoing. Who would be next? Neighbors and relatives were isolated by distrust from each other and deprived of the comfort of communal mourning. Only a few mothers of the missing demanded answers, bravely marching in the central plaza. They were ridiculed and labeled "crazy."

The survivors of child sexual abuse in my study had been similarly controlled. The dictatorship in Chile and the incestuous parents both hid abuses behind façades of normalcy—whether of economic progress or community status. In confusing circumstances, they defined reality for those under their control, attributed guilt, and interpreted their own actions as benefiting the victim. In both situations, the lack of explanation for wrongdoing promoted distress and confusion. With no understanding of why they were targeted, victims grieved alone and trusted no one with their secret. They were paralyzed into inaction by the mechanisms of their abuse.

Whether trauma is generated in a home or in a nation, these mechanisms are similar, and further parallels will be found in other chapters of this book. All trauma, when it is of human origin, generates the sense of being helpless, hopeless, and alone in an inescapable situation.

NOTES

1. *Primary abuser* means the major, and typically first, abuser of the child. This was usually a parent, whose abuse then left the child vulnerable to others.

2. Researchers tend to define sexual abuse in terms of various degrees of handling. It is important to recognize that, in the minds of victims, a sexual abuser does not have to touch the child.

3. The framework for this discussion of secrecy is Simmel's (Wolf, 1950), but its application to the incest situation is my own.

CHAPTER 5

Cumulative Developmental Damage

As a toddler, preschooler, and for most of elementary school, I was abused by my grandfather (and several neighbors as well). My earliest memories are of Grampa molesting me. By the time I was 5, it was sodomy every time he got me alone. At age 11, I told my mother that "he hurt me," and we didn't visit him any more. But she never asked me about it because our doctor said, "it's best if children forget these things." So I had no chance to work out my shame. I finally had to deal with everything in my 30s after realizing that I had married a pedophile who abused boys.

—**Paige** in 1989

Authorities on child growth and development generally hold that the development of children toward adulthood and adult sexuality is gradual, and that parents should not rush or interrupt the natural sequence of these processes. A child's sexuality is qualitatively different from an adult's, and so a child is developmentally unprepared for the kind of stimulation and arousal introduced by an adult (cf. Freud, 1981). In particular, incest is an especially great threat to normal development. Anna Freud (1981) contradicted her father's view that incest was usually a product of childhood imagination, declaring,

> Far from existing only as a phantasy, incest is thus also a fact. Where the chances of harming a child's normal developmental growth are concerned,

it ranks higher than abandonment, neglect, physical maltreatment, or any other form of abuse. It would be a fatal mistake to underrate either the importance or the frequency of its actual occurrence. (p. 34)

Other therapists and psychologists have evaluated the lasting impact of various kinds of childhood trauma. Lenore Terr's (1990) clinical and research work, covering a wide variety of childhood traumas, includes a longitudinal study of the school children of Chowchilla, California, who were rescued after their school bus was hijacked and they were buried alive in it. She has affirmed that a whole life can be shaped by early trauma, whether or not it is remembered (Terr, 1994). Eth and Pynoos (1985), studying children traumatized by various disasters, described the differential impact of trauma at various ages. They concluded that developmental progress can be accelerated, retarded, or fixated by past traumas that influence current experiences and learning (p. 50). Other researchers (e.g., Finkelhor et al., 1986) and clinicians (e.g., Meiselman, 1990) have documented long-term damage in the lives of adults, long after the occurrence of child sexual abuse.

The present study of women who were seeking help decades after their early sexual abuse has convinced me that the damage was, for them, not only serious but often cumulative over the years before help was available. As described in Chapter 4, the participants in my research had been victimized when they were very young—close to half (43%) had first been molested before they were 5 years of age, and almost all (92%) before age 10. Their primary abuse lasted, on average, over 5 years. Moreover, because most of the respondents (72%) were abused by more than one perpetrator, their abuse had been prolonged for additional years. As a result, several developmental periods in their lives were disrupted, affecting their maturation in stage-specific ways, as will be seen in the following pages.

Several personality theorists, in addition to Sigmund and Anna Freud, have proposed that there are sequential stages in personality development, each presenting a special task to accomplish or a particular conflict to resolve. The exact definition of the stages and of the challenge that each presents varies, depending on which theorist's views are considered. For example, the first psychological task facing an infant has been defined as developing trust (Erikson), minimizing basic anxiety (Horney), overcoming an innate sense of inferiority (Adler), or feeling safe in the world

(Maslow). Despite such variations (all of which add valuable insights), the *concept of developmental stages* is widely accepted by developmental and personality theorists.

ERIKSON'S THEORY OF DEVELOPMENTAL STAGES

The purpose of this chapter is to provide a conceptual framework for discussing the cumulative developmental damage to personality experienced by the women in this study. This framework serves both to organize the material of the chapter and to help explain the results in the women's lives. I selected Erikson's (1963, 1968) developmental schema as particularly appropriate for the following reasons:

1. Erikson maintained that the personality of an individual does not develop in a social vacuum. Instead, the growing "self" matures in interaction with a particular family, culture, and time in history. Therefore, he referred to his eight phases of personal development using a term that linked personality to society—*psychosocial stages*. His view seems especially relevant when one considers that the cultural and family values of our society have permitted intimate violations (date rape, marital rape, and incest) to occur virtually unnoticed until late in the 20th century. In support of his dual concept of psychosocial stages, Erikson also emphasized the importance and relationship of personal identity and social belonging. Neither was complete without the other and, as will be seen, the survivors in this study had developed a poor sense of both.

2. Erikson's stages of personality development feature successive tasks. Each task requires a counterbalance of values (such as trust vs. distrust). A successful outcome would be positive but realistic. (For example, trust under all circumstances would be foolhardy.) The inability of a person to resolve a particular developmental task could undermine prior progress and also make later tasks even more difficult. As this chapter continues, you will realize why the survivors participating in this study faced problems at each stage and unfinished business decades later.

Table 5.1 Erikson's Developmental Stages, With the Basic Challenge and Valued Ego Strength of Each

Stage	Challenge or Task	Ego Strength
1	basic trust versus distrust	hope
2	autonomy versus shame and doubt	willpower
3	initiative versus guilt	purpose
4	industry versus inferiority	competence
5	identity versus role confusion	fidelity
6	intimacy versus isolation	love
7	generativity versus stagnation	caring
8	ego integrity versus despair	wisdom

SOURCE: Erikson (1963, p. 274).

3. According to Erikson, valuable ego strengths—hallmarks of a mature and healthy personality—emerge through successful completion of developmental tasks. With each successful stage come greater personal integration, sounder perception of oneself and the world, and more active mastery of one's environment (Erikson, 1968, p. 92). The key ego strengths, to be achieved sequentially, are hope, willpower, purpose, competence, fidelity, love, caring, and finally wisdom, which involves the integration of all these qualities (see Table 5.1).

4. Moreover, Erikson's theory is optimistic. It holds that, even if the maturation process has gone awry, the damage is not necessarily irreversible. It is possible, with determination and caring support, to build a strong sense of self in relationship with others. The process, like Erikson's stages, would need to begin with learning to trust and culminate in achieving integrity—a mature sense of wholeness and acceptance of one's life. These ideas are augmented and applied to child abuse survivors below.

THE PSYCHOSOCIAL DEVELOPMENT OF SURVIVORS

Erikson holds that, over successive stages, healthy individuals keep moving in a more positive than negative direction as they mature. Each developmental stage presents a new challenge for emerging personalities—to develop another ego strength. However, healthy people are realistic in pursuing these valued characteristics. For example, they recognize that in some situations it is better to distrust (rather than trust) or to stand alone (rather than "belong"). In contrast, exploited children—lacking the judgment, confidence, and support to discriminate—tend to develop in a negative direction. And their inadequate resolution of early stages makes later ones even harder.

Identity—personal and social—is Erikson's central concept, and it is certainly a key issue for women molested as children. According to Erikson, the self emerges through recognizing one's sameness and continuity over time. Ordinarily, one need not search for oneself, nor ask "Who am I?" as so many sexual abuse survivors do. For most individuals, identity simply matures, as tasks posed by successive life stages are mastered. However, early sexual trauma blurs that emerging sense of self and further obscures it over time.

As one traces the passage of sexually abused children through developmental stages into adulthood, one finds little that resembles the description of a healthy self. Instead, at almost every stage, further dysfunction may accumulate and, with it, a highly negative view of the self, of the world, and of one's power within it.

Fortunately, however, personality is continually dynamic. This means that there is hope for motivated people at any time of life. Elements of later stages are present in earlier ones, and vice versa. For example, a small child, tucking her teddy bear in for the night, can anticipate parenting; by the same token, an angry middle-aged woman may exercise the frustrated will of a toddler. Even more important, defeat at one stage does not preclude finding a resolution later (Elkind, 1970, p. 28). Ego strengths are not gained or lost once and for all during the time when they come into ascendance. They will be further tested and developed through successive stages of life. And injured personalities can heal. The women described in this book could not have survived emotionally during the years of their forgetting without some hope of achieving a meaningful future.

In this chapter, I discuss issues of personal development that were central to the experiences of the women whom I have described in earlier chapters. Using Erikson's comprehensive framework, I trace them over time, considering each of the psychosocial stages in turn. The old adage, "as the twig is bent, so grows the tree," is well illustrated in the developmental history of the women.

CHILDHOOD

Stage 1 (Infancy)—Basic Trust Versus Distrust

A child whose trust has been ruptured knows, from that moment, that she is alone in a dangerous world. Distrust follows her through the years and through every relationship.

—**Adel**, 1990

Erikson (1968) called the early achievement of *basic trust* "the cornerstone of a vital personality" (p. 97). Trust enriches the emerging self with the quality of hope—an enduring expectation that one's important needs can and will be met as they arise, in a world that is safe and peopled with caring individuals. In addition to receiving care, babies learn to become givers, through their smiles, sounds, and body language. In doing so, they learn the "dance of mutuality" between parent and child—getting for oneself through giving to another. In infancy, trust is embryonic and vulnerable. During the formative years of childhood, it is constantly being both validated and threatened. Even in adulthood, a breach of trust can have serious consequences.

If a child suffers sexual abuse, the younger that she is at that time, the less likely that she would have learned to trust (and distrust) appropriately. In my study, flashbacks to preschool abuse were especially common among (formerly) amnesic women. Their right to early dependency had been violated. **Adel's** strong statement (above) was supported by the women's responses to sentence-completion items on the 1986 questionnaire. Looking back on their teenage years, 61% of the amnesic women spontaneously wrote a single word after the phrase, "I didn't trust . . . " That word was *anyone*. Many partially amnesic women (54%) gave the same answer, but few of the nonamnesics (20%) did so. The imprisoned women had been especially untrusting (70%). After another item, "The future looked . . . ," one third of the amnesics wrote in the word *bleak*, underscoring their lack of hope.

Unlike the amnesic women, **Pat** had always remembered her father's frequent gropings. But she was shocked, in her 30s, to realize that he had done more than "handle" his daughters over the years. She tried to describe a revealing flashback to me: "I was 3, and he was at my baby sister's crib, making her do ... do ...." She shuddered and looked down, the sentence incomplete. Then she continued, "I tried to get away—to climb into a picture of happy children that hung over my bed." (Making an actual scene unreal and a painted one real is a poignant example of derealization.) Pat had used this escape before and would continue to do so. In her view, her sister chose a more permanent escape—dying of cancer at age 13: "I honestly believe she was 'dying to get away' from Dad." The grieving father consoled himself with a pious comment, "At least she died a virgin." His words were, at the same time, a slap at Pat, for her father had recently learned that she was sleeping with her boyfriend. Furious with her, he had screamed an ironic epithet —"Adulteress!"

Stage 2 (Ages 1 to 3)—Autonomy Versus Shame and Doubt

Wants that go unmet from childhood feel like life-and-death needs later. Even today, "not getting my way" can make me feel desperate.
                                                                      —**Phyllis**, 1992

Just as satisfaction of basic needs is essential to Stage 1, respect for individuality is paramount at Stage 2. Erikson saw this as the key period for toddlers to test their autonomy—the will to be themselves—trusting that their parents would support them, literally and symbolically, as they began to stand on their own feet. At this stage, children learn to get in touch with what is important to them, to express what they want, and to have their preferences taken into account. Parents are also supposed to protect their children from the shame and self-doubt that inexperience can bring on them. This stage should strengthen children's budding sense of selfhood by providing them with the courage to increasingly direct their own lives (Erikson, 1968, p. 114). Yet, half of the amnesic women believed that they had first been molested before they were 3, and usually by a parent.

Children at age 2 and 3 are, among other accomplishments, learning about modesty and toileting. They feel confused and shamed when behavior that is unacceptable to other people is expected of them at home (Kempe & Kempe, 1984, pp. 53-54). **Alana** remembered sobbing with shame on the back lawn, sharp blades of grass against her cheeks, after her grandfather performed cunnilingus on her. And **Noelle** was broken-hearted when her stepfather "peed in my mouth." She was convinced that he must not love her. What could be more threatening to a small child's emerging sense of self than parent-figures who see her as an extension of themselves, without even a body to call her own?

As the respondents grew older, their shame and self-doubt, the opposites of autonomy, continued. In many cases, they led to suicidal thoughts. When asked to look back on their teen years and to complete the phrase, "My goal for the future was . . . ," amnesic women, especially, wrote words like *to die.* But their suicidal ideation was typically passive. Most often, the women conveyed these feelings through phrases of shame—"I wanted to disappear" or "I just wanted to die"—rather than active words such as "I wanted to kill myself." Examples of their teenage goals were "that there would be no future," "that God would vaporize me," or "to die as soon as possible." In flashbacks 35 years after her abuse, **Ashley** reexperienced the enormous aloneness and despair she had felt at age 10 after her father had left her bedroom: "Nobody ever comes. I just want to die . . . to die . . . to die . . . to die . . . to die." In later years, these women's behavior frequently displayed the passive "little deaths" of illness and addiction.

The possessiveness of parents and the erosion of parent-child boundaries (discussed in Chapters 3 and 4) increased self-doubt among respondents like **Angie**: "Dad enjoyed giving the impression that he had magically followed me on my dates—that he knew everything we'd done." **Anita's** mother, a sadistic sex abuser, even denied her daughter's right to independent thoughts:

> There was no place to hide from my mother—I was transparent, inside out. She'd tell me, "I know everything you're seeing, doing, thinking." "Look at me," she'd say, and read my eyes. I'd try desperately to make my mind go blank, and panicked when I couldn't stop my thoughts. Even as an adult in therapy, I was sure that she knew that I was telling family secrets.

Shame and self-doubt had continued to burden the women as they matured. During the decades before they confronted the past, almost every respondent (92%) had felt "unworthy, never good enough," according to their questionnaire responses.

Hopelessness and helplessness had been the typical outcome of Stage 1 instead of trust. Now, in Stage 2, the abuse survivors were developing into human chameleons—colored by the needs, desires, and commands of others—rather than operating out of a clear sense of who they were and what they wanted for themselves. An excessive need to please became the way to survive in the world for 88% of them.

Stage 3 (Ages 3 to 5)—Initiative Versus Guilt

> *I would set myself impossible standards and unattainable goals. I was afraid of starting things, afraid of completing them, and afraid of failing—"I never do it right." I even feared success: "Yes, but I'll never make it again." The underlying message was "Why bother trying. Whatever happens, I can't win."*
>
> —**Amy**, 1987

Stage 3 revolves around initiative. This is a time period for expanding thought and action to provide a basis for realistic life goals (Erikson, 1968, p. 115). Through spontaneity, exploration, and imagination, a child can begin to achieve a sense of purpose instead of guilt as she goes after what she wants in the world. At this stage, parents hear, "Can I go . . . ?," "I want to . . . ," "I need . . . ," "Let me try . . . ," and "I'm pretending . . . " In this process, children can eagerly try new ventures, and even failures can stimulate a willingness to start over with a better sense of direction. However, a child discredited in her efforts can develop pessimism about plans, fear of failure, half-hearted efforts, and guilt over her sexual feelings.

When a healthy sense of adventure and morality results, young children are drawn toward responsible fulfillment of their own potential as well as toward awareness of what is permissible in society. However, for the research participants as children, sexual abuse generated tremendous guilt, because most of them believed that they were somehow responsible for what was happening to them. Because adults were not protecting them, safety became a primary concern, and adventurousness was replaced by caution and fear. Taking considered risks can open up new life experiences. But, early in life, inhibition increasingly deprived them of the capacity for playfulness and spontaneity. Over time, fearing the risks involved in both success and failure, they sabotaged themselves through perfectionism, indecisiveness, and procrastination.

In contrast, a few respondents became extreme risk takers—using drugs, alcohol, and/or sex as futile escapes. Rather than avoid risk, they sought it. This pattern dominated **Iris's** behavior: "By junior high, I was 'tough,' outdoing the boys in daring, shoplifting to show off, and playing with knives to prove to myself that I could handle anything."

However, most of the women (75%) felt constrained by fearfulness to be good or "better than good." They developed a cautious, restrictive way of living, which blocked full expression of their creative capacities. In adulthood, it also kept them from enjoying mature sexuality, which involves spontaneity, initiation, and freedom from a disapproving conscience. Erikson (1968) held that adults who continue to have conflicts over initiative and guilt tend to overcompensate in "a great show of tireless initiative" to feel worthwhile. He continued, "The strain ... [of being] always 'on the go,' with the engine racing even at moments of rest, is a powerful contribution to the much-discussed psychosomatic diseases of our time" (p. 120). For the respondents, "keeping busy" (75%) and "trying harder" (74%) were frequently used ways of coping during the long years before their breakthrough to awareness of past sexual abuse, and most of them paid a high price in somatic problems.

Stage 4 (Ages 6 Through 11)—
Industry Versus Inferiority

Stage 4 is Erikson's last childhood stage before adolescence. It focuses on industry. For the research participants, the first three stages had been destructive of any emerging sense of self. They reached school age without real hope that others would meet their needs; they had been controlled in such intimate ways that they had lost the will to be themselves. Their main purpose was survival—salvaging some sense of safety in their lives. An example of how a child could accomplish that, despite parental abuse, was given by **Pam:**

> At 10, I realized how serious a situation I was in, and that I was the only person who would protect me. I started looking out for my own safety. That was when I put on weight till I wasn't attractive; and I saw to it that I was never alone with my stepfather again. That was when I decided to go to college and never to have children. From my first small job, I was saving to escape.

The fourth stage afforded certain respondents (as children) a chance to strengthen their insecure sense of self by building competence instead of inferiority. For those born into middle-class homes, it was natural to cultivate reading, music, art, and writing as avenues of escape. More important, these skills allowed them to achieve some competence and to receive recognition at school. **ANNE** was one of the girls who escaped by reading voraciously—especially science fiction, which took them to worlds where "good guys" and "bad guys" were easily identified and the former always won.

School helped a number of survivors by putting them in touch with a new world of information and people. **PAULA** and **NANCY**, for example, had recognized that their own families were dysfunctional. They found —among teachers, staff, and other pupils—models and values different from those they had known. School provided a new chance at life for some girls. Rewarding escapes came through reading for **ANNE**, acting in school plays for **Alison**, and developing friendships with classmates from healthy families for **ILENE**.

In addition, certain compensating qualities that they had developed at earlier stages proved advantageous now. Coping through perfectionism, pleasing adults, keeping overly busy, and trying too hard usually brought important rewards in school, such as good grades and the attention of teachers. A number of respondents (especially those with partial or full amnesia) made excellent progress in school. Home problems rarely intruded there, and the girls won approval for their scholastic or creative accomplishments. Later, they gained status through higher education, marriage, and careers.

Moreover, their secret was safe in the classroom. Students who do not create problems are generally thought to *have* none. Although these girls already felt different from others, their façade of normalcy tended to screen their anxiety from view. How successful such façades could be is seen in **Abbey**'s wistful statement, in adulthood, to her only friend, "I seem cheerful and together, even when I'm thinking about killing myself. No one but you knows how worthless I feel."

In normal development, a sense of confidence and self-worth should be the cumulative outcome of the four stages of childhood. Instead, many respondents were driven by powerful and unhealthy patterns—distrusting people on whom they had to depend, surrendering their will to others, inhibiting their creative and exploratory urges, and (whatever their objective competence) discounting their own worth. By this time, many held themselves to a merciless standard of perfectionism that blocked pride in their own achievements. They had become skilled at hiding behind a social façade of normalcy that prevented others, as well as themselves, from realizing the depths of their distress. And now, they faced the difficult years of adolescence.

YOUTH

Stage 5 (Adolescence)—Identity Versus Role Confusion

> *Preparation for a successful adolescence, and the attainment of an integrated . . . identity, must begin in the cradle.*
> —Elkind (1970, p. 27)

Adolescence provides the chance to establish a clear sense of personal identity and fidelity to self, to friends, and to important values. Erikson (1963) speaks of this as a sense of "inner sameness and continuity" that is "matched by the sameness and continuity of one's meaning for others, as evidenced in the tangible promise of a 'career' " (pp. 261-262). As in previous stages, success at this stage is built on past success. To the extent that adolescents have been able to integrate the various self-images emerging during early childhood, they can expect to establish "a strong sense of identity based on who they are, where they have been, and where they are going" (Elkind, 1970, p. 27). Again, the research participants were handicapped. Uncertainty was far more characteristic of them at this time. They were onlookers at life. Attuned mainly to the desires and emotions of others, they found it hard to know who they were—much less what they wanted out of life and with whom they wanted to share it. This dilemma was well expressed by **April:**

> As a teenager, I never felt I belonged to any group. Painfully shy, I hung around the edges. When a kindly adult suggested, that I "just be myself," I found myself wondering, "How can I 'be myself,' when I don't know who I am?"

Respondents typically did not feel worthy of caring friendships and, instead, tended to reenact their family experience of victimization in interactions with other abusive people. Loneliness was a key emotion for

71% of the women—a serious problem at a time when they most needed peer relationships with both sexes. **Natalie** told me, "I felt like I was in the wrong place at the wrong time. Everyone else seemed to fit into whatever was happening, but I was out of sync, on the outside looking in."

In addition, rapid social changes and the loosening of community norms made escape more readily available. Alcohol could drown memories, and drugs could reduce pain. This form of escape was especially common among girls who later were in trouble with the law. Casual sexual contacts gave momentary solace to girls like **Alissa** who were hungry for affection. Initiating such contacts gave some a sense of being in control without raising hope that closeness could last. Such choices helped these adolescents hide, not only from the world, but from themselves.

To a few respondents, a negative identity as part of a gang or other deviant group seemed preferable to having no identity at all, and this choice was not limited to the imprisoned group. Other respondents sacrificed themselves to others, exhausting their physical and emotional energy by trying to be super-responsible for everyone's needs, demands, and emotions except their own. These patterns became especially evident as they entered the adult stages of personality development.

ADULTHOOD

Stage 6 (Young Adulthood)—Intimacy Versus Isolation

According to Erikson, in young adulthood, healthy people enjoy intimacy and add love to their growing list of ego strengths. Individuals who have passed through earlier stages successfully should feel in touch with their goals and dreams and competent to realize them. They will have established their independence—a firm and separate identity—and have developed mutuality—the ability to share themselves with friends and loved ones. Independence and mutuality are both needed if lovers are to find intimacy—merging physically and emotionally without fear of being swallowed up, dominated, or rejected by their partner. Healthy individuals know that commitment can enrich them as individuals, so they do not fear losing themselves in the process.

Some lucky respondents (in their first partnership or in a subsequent one) found healing through love. It even enabled them to feel safe enough to face the past. For many others, however, love was an absent emotion, and they were unable to be open and trusting. They operated more out of hope for survival than from any high expectations for their future. Many who had lived out the wishes of others brought into new relationships the unexpressed anger of many years. Most (78%) had problems with sexuality. Some added pseudo-intimacy to the façade of normalcy they had adopted long before, and their adolescent loneliness became emotional isolation in this stage. Many were still searching for the love they had not known as children, which they did not believe they deserved and never expected to receive. Longing for an understanding partner, they feared that a good relationship would never be theirs.

According to Anna Freud (1981), the after-effects of incestuous experience are either insatiable sexual longing or a powerful inhibition against sexuality. This "prostitute-or-nun" dichotomy certainly applied to a number of the survivors I interviewed.

Intimacy requires a deep trust and a strong sense of security, traits that the research participants did not generally possess. They tended to choose punitive or troubled partners, perhaps because they knew how to respond in such situations. They had been conditioned to associate love with abuse, and many of them followed a destructive pattern that Sigmund Freud termed *repetition compulsion*. The amnesic women, unaware of the past, were especially puzzled as to why they chose partners who tended to be abusive to them—physically, sexually, or emotionally—or to their children. **Audrey**, for example, had a high tolerance for pain and a low recognition of dangerous situations and people. After entering therapy, she saw herself on video and was astonished: "She looks lovable! I don't know why anyone would want to hurt such a gentle woman." Then she added, thoughtfully, "But if someone did, she'd be the one to choose because she wouldn't defend herself."

Stage 7 (Adult Years)—Generativity Versus Stagnation

For Erikson, Stage 7 is the time when dependency should give way to a mature desire to meet the needs of the next generation. Generativity can be expressed through parenting, teaching, nursing, or through a commitment to creating a better world for those as yet unborn. Caring is the ego strength that this stage contributes to a person's identity. Those who do not move in this direction tend to turn in on themselves, becoming resigned to a sense of personal stagnation and interpersonal impoverishment. Parenting was the aspect of this stage that was highlighted in most participants' accounts of their lives.

On the positive side, some of the respondents, especially first-borns, had been caretakers from childhood. As young girls, they took on the vacated role of protector to little brothers and sisters. For instance, **Nadia**, born into poverty and to unfeeling parents, had been mother to 10 younger siblings, seeing to it that they were fed and clothed, and even enrolled in school. Above all, she loved them and gave them the only cuddling they had. "It seemed that I always had a baby in my arms," she said. Other survivors whom I interviewed felt tremendous satisfaction in parenting their own children. Despite all they had gone through themselves, they managed to be really good mothers. **Andrea** told me, "My life would be meaningless without my children. I had them so that we could give each other love. They are wonderful young people—my greatest achievement."

In contrast, many of the women, who had been unable to achieve mature friendships and love relationships during the preceding two stages, found parenting difficult and deeply regretted that their childhood experiences had damaged their capacity to parent. Quite a few whose children were grown looked back on anguished years of struggle and guilt. There had been such a deficit in their own nurturing that they had not learned what good parenting was. **Alison** expressed the sense of inadequacy she had felt with her children:

> Over the years, I had often wondered at my ignorance of how to parent. My mother and father had been good role models (so I thought). Why couldn't I relax, play, have fun with my own little ones? Why was I uncomfortable with their bodies, their emotions? I often felt totally overwhelmed—as if I needed parenting more than they did. Being a good mother had been my goal in life, and I believed I was a failure at it.

Several women with adult children who were alcoholic or suicidal felt tremendous guilt about their past inadequacies in parenting. Others realized that their own neediness had blinded them to patterns that they were passing on to their children. Their abuse, decades earlier, now damaged their children's lives as well as their own. A variety of other maladaptive patterns can be seen in the examples that follow.

Some of the women had selective problems in parenting that cropped up in particular situations or times. Knowing her own background, **NANCY** had been proud of her ability to parent her small child, but this satisfaction did not last: "When my daughter turned 10 years of age—

where my own emotions had stopped—I found it much harder. I overparented, overworried, overprotected, and overcontrolled." Even amnesic women, before memories returned, could become extremely anxious when a daughter reached the age of their own past molestation. Some found themselves, without knowing why, rejecting daughters who tapped into their own pain and abusing them physically or emotionally. **Angela** had distanced herself from her children and only realized why much later: "My sudden anger often resulted in my mistreating my children. I'm still afraid to get close emotionally; it is too dangerous. I've also had fantasies of sexual encounters with my son."

At least three of the women had such intense postpartum depression that their baby's lives were endangered. For **Alexis**, this strain continued, and 8 years after giving birth, she had a homicidal episode in which she chased her daughter with a knife. She managed to gain control of herself, told the terrified child to lock herself in the bathroom, and frantically called the police. In the hospital, she was diagnosed with multiple personality disorder, and treatment began. **Alicia** was good with her baby girl but beat the child when she became a saucy 2-year-old. Her sister, visiting for a few days, shocked her by shouting, "STOP! You're acting *just like Mama!*" Suddenly, this young mother knew she was out of control and must get help.

Several survivors expressed special anxiety that their daughters might be victimized by sexual abuse. On the other hand, **Penny** found it difficult to parent her small boys because their maleness was a reminder of her abusers: "I can't even look at their naked bodies. I'm worrying about how they might use them when they grow up."

In discussing parenting, we must recognize that some women chose to remain unmarried or childless—fearing that their partner (or they themselves) might take the cycle of molestation into another generation. **Portia** gave up her child to adoption out of fear. It is her greatest regret. **Patrice**, who had been molested by her father and grandfather, recognized an intergenerational pattern when she found that her divorced husband had molested both their son and daughter. She then dedicated herself to the children's healing and, distrusting her ability to make a healthy choice of a partner, refrained from even dating.

A number of the women were convinced that they were unworthy of motherhood. They had deep guilty feelings that they had brought on abuse because they were intrinsically evil, that they had been polluted by incest, or that their own adolescent behavior—masturbation or promiscuity—had stripped them of human worth. They found evidence that God would deprive them of motherhood, citing a variety of signs—venereal disease, an ovarian tumor, blocked ovarian tubes, difficulty getting pregnant, or a miscarriage. For example, **Norene** miscarried after many months of trying to get pregnant. Demoralized and self-accusing, she embarked on an empty flirtation with a man she didn't respect and ended her marriage to a steady, supportive spouse.

Stage 8 (Mature Years)—Ego Integrity Versus Despair

Erikson's final stage of development culminates in ego integrity, incorporating all the strengths built up through the seven previous stages. This stage, like the others, should not be narrowly construed. Erikson (1968) believed that "a meaningful old age . . . gives indispensable perspective to the life cycle. Strength here takes the form of that detached yet active concern with life bounded by death, which we call 'wisdom' " (p. 140). In other words, this is a time for integration of all the ego strengths accumulated through the years. This phase includes acceptance of one's life cycle, without undue regrets, and of the meaningful people who have crossed it, and recognition that one has handled life as well as one could, given the time and place and people that formed its possibilities and limitations. In this stage, all the components of identity, gained and strengthened over the years, can blend into a harmonious and gratifying whole.

Until they dealt with the past, there was little possibility of the research participants achieving this sense of wholeness. They knew, instead, a fragmentation of self. They looked back on lives that had been disrupted at every stage. Erikson's alternative to wisdom is despair—a feeling of contempt for oneself and for what one has achieved and a recognition that the years of life remaining are too short for a new start. There was a special bitterness for women who remembered their childhood trauma long after it had wreaked severe damage in their own life and in the lives of those close to them. For various women, it had brought broken marriages, children on drugs or in prison, failed dreams, unused talents, a pervading sense of futility, or even chronic mental illness. "I can never be normal or achieve the kind of life any human being has the right to expect" was **Polly**'s sad commentary. She was not self-pitying but simply mourning what might have been. Knowing of her anguished childhood and the problems that still faced her daily, I understood her deep sadness.

SUMMARY AND PROSPECT

In this chapter, I have used Erikson's model of personality development to illustrate the cumulative developmental damage experienced by research participants over the years. This model has provided a framework to organize the women's stories of long-term consequences as they expressed them to me. Abused in their childhood years, these women had difficulties in mastering the challenges of successive psychosocial stages, and each failure compounded their past problems. In childhood, many of them learned distrust rather than trust, shame rather than autonomy, inhibition rather than initiative, and inferiority rather than competence. In youth, they were vulnerable to a diffused sense of self instead of identity and terror of closeness in lieu of intimacy. Parenting was often a troubling confirmation of their inability to nurture themselves or others, and an overview of their lives gave many of them a sense of fragmentation rather than integration.

Despite these problems, which had continued more or less seriously for decades, most of my respondents (except those in prison) had presented themselves to the world as functioning quite normally. They had plateaus of relative calm and periods of gaining strength but—during the interim between abuse and healing—they passed long silent years of accumulating damage. Nevertheless, these women *did* survive, and eventually, those who had always remembered their trauma confronted it, and those with recovered memories were catapulted into therapy. In the months and years following that breakthrough, a gradual rebuilding began to take place with the support of caring therapists.

However, unless these counselors realized the cumulative developmental damage of child sexual abuse, they were ignorant of the task before them. Their client was not simply a woman who had finally decided to face her past. Her personality still contained the unintegrated elements of an infant, a child, a teenager, a young adult, and an aspiring parent—all of whom needed to be listened to and helped toward a more rewarding future. "Telling their story" to concerned people became a crucial part of the women's healing process. Fortunately, most of the survivors who shared their experiences with me had realistic prospects of building a happier life. The strength that had allowed them to survive their trauma over the years would also help them to understand, and escape, its power.

CHAPTER 6

Amnesia and Posttraumatic Stress

My dad supplied me with alcohol and drugs from the time I was 14, and I spent my teen years in a fog, wandering the streets. Trusting the wrong people, I was often raped. As a result, my reproductive organs are ruined, and cigarette burns still scar my butt.

—**Amy**, 1986

In 1984, **Amy** had suddenly recalled her father sodomizing her as a child while his friends held her down. Since then, she has documented her therapeutic progress in a series of personal journals. In 1988, she telephoned to tell me that she had made a startling discovery. She had found a much older journal, dating from 1976 (when she had undergone treatment for addiction). It showed that her amnesia had broken 8 years earlier than she had thought. She had shared the same memory of sodomy with her counselor at that time, asking whether it might explain the many rapes (by strangers and acquaintances) that she had endured during adolescence. That night, Amy had written her therapist's response in her journal:

Pat said I was right, and explained that the 5-year-old victim part of me had enjoyed being raped (whether in fantasy or fact) by my father. In my teens, I set men up to rape me by playing the little girl seductress. I was searching for my "father-lover" in these men. Pat said that I must recognize this to be cured.

Surely, you may be thinking, Amy's early therapist must have been an untrained crackpot, and a male who was callous and chauvinist as well? No, on all counts! In 1976, many therapists—including *women* therapists such as Patricia—interpreted incest memories as childhood fantasies. Several excellent counselors have told me, with deep regret, that they had explained the memories of past clients in similar ways. Steeped in Freud's Oedipal theory, Pat had undoubtedly believed that she was helping Amy to get in touch with reality. But how did Amy react? There was no emotion in her written report; her defenses were already at work. Soon, the childhood rape was again dissociated and—along with it—that therapy session and the counselor. Eight more years passed before she felt safe enough (personally and socially) to remember. This time, her memories were respected instead of usurped.

AMNESIA AS A CONSEQUENCE OF TRAUMA

A major goal of my research was to study the nature of amnesia such as Amy's, its causes and its consequences, and when and how memories return. In earlier chapters, we have mentioned amnesia without a full discussion of what it is and is not. The priority of *this* chapter is to provide a fuller understanding of this important phenomenon. We look first at common misperceptions of amnesia that have contributed to its misunderstanding. Next, the traumatic origins of amnestic disorders are compared to the origins of dissociative disorders, along with the degree of memory loss in both cases. After noting what survivors can teach us about amnesia, we will examine how amnesia relates to posttraumatic stress disorder (PTSD) in the experience of survivors.

MISPERCEPTIONS ABOUT AMNESIA

To understand amnesia, we must first examine several distracting misperceptions regarding its nature. First, amnesia has many confused meanings in the public mind. Second, amnesia tends to be perceived as an isolated phenomenon, unrelated to anything else. Third, many people think of amnesia as intrinsically connected to sexual abuse. And fourth, terms for the process by which memory loss occurs (e.g., repression and dissociation) have been used as synonyms for the *end state* of amnesia. Let's clarify these points before proceeding.

First, there is a good deal of confusion about "what amnesia is" because a multitude of sources, claiming authority, have given it varied meanings. Television defines it dramatically, weaving story lines around characters who have lost both memory and identity. Laypersons define it subjectively as a strange sort of forgetting that they expect never to experience. The dictionary defines it semantically as partial or total loss of memory. Neurologists define it physiologically, referring to loss of functioning in various areas of the brain. Psychiatrists define amnesia clinically, in accordance with consecutive editions of the *Diagnostic and Statistical Manual of Mental Disorders* (*DSM-IV*) (American Psychiatric Association [APA], 1994). Experimental psychologists try to give it an operational definition that they can measure and test objectively.

Second, in addition to being swamped by a variety of meanings for the concept of amnesia, people have also tended to see it as an isolated phenomenon—detached from anything else. We can demystify amnesia if we recognize it as only one of many psychosocial experiences called *altered states of consciousness*. By definition, altered states of consciousness are significantly different in quality and pattern from normal mental functioning. In this respect, they are alike. They share other similarities as well, but they also differ among themselves, as the following examples attest. Here is a brief description of many of these lesser but better understood relatives of amnesia.

Both intense concentration at work and "highway hypnosis" while driving are altered states of consciousness that can make one unaware of time and place. A scholar may find the first state invaluable, but the second is life threatening. Sleep is an altered state that is universal and essential to life itself, whereas fugue (a sudden shift of one's perceived identity and locale) is rare and severely disruptive. Deep trance states can be freely entered into by mystics or evoked by fasting, solitude, or psychedelic drugs. Flashbacks involve "reliving" a traumatic event. Regression means feeling emotions or displaying behavior from an earlier age. Hypnosis is a state of induced relaxation that reduces the censoring of the conscious mind, sometimes allowing intense memories or images to surface with varying degrees of accuracy. Self-hypnosis can induce relaxation, new awareness, and greater self-understanding. Anesthesia can put a patient in an altered state where awareness and pain are reduced or suspended. It is possible to reach any of these 10 altered states (even anesthetization, under some circumstances) without the use of drugs; and most people, in the course of normal living, have experienced about half of them. Severe trauma, however, can bring on an altered state called *amnesia*, which is longer lasting and has more profound consequences than any of the ones mentioned above.

Third, many people think of long-term amnesia and the recovery of memories as being intrinsically connected with adult survivors of child sexual abuse. This belief buttresses two opposing stances: Supporters of survivors can argue that sexual abuse holds a unique position among the many traumas that afflict humanity. Supporters of "falsely accused parents" have argued that because "only" survivors claim amnesia, theirs must be "false memories." The truth is that survivors of many forms of trauma can and do display amnesia. Several researchers (e.g., Arrigo & Pezdek, 1997; Pope & Brown, 1996; van der Kolk et al., 1996) have provided documentation that amnesia is common among survivors of natural disasters such as earthquakes and fires, automobile and aircraft crashes, combat experiences, attempted suicides, criminal acts such as homicides, violent death of a parent in childhood, and adult rape experiences.

The fourth source of public confusion is that terms for the process by which amnesia occurs (e.g., repression and dissociation) have been used as synonyms for the end state of amnesia. The term *repression* is often used interchangeably with amnesia, but the words are not synonymous. Repression means that certain unacceptable, conflicting thoughts or feelings drop (or are pushed) from consciousness. As the following paragraphs will indicate, it is only one of several ways by which amnesia can occur—a particular mechanism or explanation for memory loss. Repression is not only different from and narrower in its meaning than the term amnesia, it is also less useful. Because it includes the postulated reason for memory loss, it is a slippery abstraction, which cannot be directly observed, but only inferred. Amnesia, by contrast, can be behaviorally identified and reasonably well quantified as to degree and form. Among the 60 nonimprisoned women originally surveyed in my study in 1986, 39 had identified themselves as at least partly amnesic to their abuse. By 1992, about 10 of the *non*amnesic women had recalled additional significant pieces of information about their abuse.

Dissociation is also a defense mechanism rather than a synonym for amnesia. It is the breaking apart or fracturing of one's experience into elements that are kept separate—for example, ones that are in awareness versus ones that are not, such as loss of some memories from conscious awareness. The dissociative aspects of amnesia are explained in the *DSM-IV* (APA, 1994). This volume is the authoritative psychiatric reference regarding the nature of amnesia, its origins, and its diagnosis. It states that amnesia includes a varied group of conditions, all of which involve memory disturbances and/or loss. Memory loss can range from limited to comprehensive in what it obscures, from transient to chronic in its timeline, and from mild to severe in its impact on a person's life. Amnesia can conceal from awareness memories of earlier experiences (retrograde amnesia), but it can also prevent current learning and the laying down of memories in the future (anterograde amnesia).

Disorders of Memory

The *DSM-IV* describes two major groups of conditions that involve amnesia. They are called amnestic disorders and dissociative disorders. They result from two different forms of trauma—biological or psychosocial, respectively. Amnestic disorders arise from biological traumas, such as injuries (e.g., a blow to the skull), chemical addiction (alcoholism), side effects of medication, or brain degeneration and atrophy (e.g., Alzheimer's disease). Amnestic disorders typically involve some loss of past memories and may also include inability to learn new information and establish new memories. In them, the amnesia may be transient or chronic.

Dissociative disorders are more relevant to this study, however. They are caused by severe psychosocial (rather than biological) trauma—that is, from personal or interpersonal experiences. Dissociative amnesia (formerly termed psychogenic amnesia, meaning that it is psychologically caused) is "an inability to recall important personal information, usually of a traumatic or stressful nature, that is too extensive to be explained by normal forgetfulness" (APA, 1994, p. 478).

There are many examples of psychosocial trauma that can damage memory: Among them are participating in wartime combat, witnessing the murder of a loved one, and experiencing gang rape, incest, or other threats to one's bodily integrity. These traumas involve emotionally devastating events, threat to one's body or life, violence, betrayal, or severe loss. (Environmental disasters such as earthquakes or floods can also damage memory even in the absence of physical injury.) In addition to causing dissociative amnesia, psychosocial trauma can produce dissociative identity disorder (formerly called *multiple personality disorder*) or fugue states (memory loss combined with sudden, unexpected travel away from one's customary locale, and sometimes even with assumption of a new identity). Psychosocial trauma can also cause PTSD, with memory problems as a major symptom. (PTSD is discussed later in this chapter.)

The Impact of Trauma on the Memory System

Discussions of the human memory system usually divide it into three aspects—(a) semantic memory for learned information (e.g., from school coursework such as mathematics), (b) procedural memory (such as how to ride a bike or use a computer), and (c) autobiographical memories of one's meaningful life events. Both semantic and procedural memory are *ex*trinsic (intentional) forms of learning. In them, you deliberately memorize the multiplication table or learn how to pedal a bike, acquiring usable information from outside yourself. Autobiographic memory involves *in*trinsic (unintended) learning, which is experienced within oneself. For instance, discussion of personal events such as a family reunion may evoke warm feelings or depressed emotions in those who attended it. Cues from the past (e.g., the sight of a child's bike) may trigger a sense of challenge or of uneasiness.

The biological traumas that result in amnestic disorders can severely damage the entire memory system, including semantic, procedural, and autobiographical aspects. Physical trauma can also disrupt future as well as past learning. Past memories can be erased or damaged (retrograde amnesia), and future learning and recall can be blocked (anterograde amnesia). Victims of biological trauma may be hospitalized for some time, and their memory loss is obvious to them and to those around them. For example, a friend of mine survived a terrible accident involving major head injury. All three kinds of memory were seriously affected, and her ability to create new memories or relearn old ones was greatly diminished.

In contrast, the psychosocial traumas that result in dissociative amnesia typically leave semantic and procedural memory untouched while obscuring all or part of certain autobiographical experiences. Explicit memories of trauma are ones that can be recalled and recounted. Although implicit memories, by definition, cannot be recalled, they can profoundly influence behavior. Consciousness of terrifying events (explicit memory) can be lost (dissociated) even while behavior is shaped (through implicit memory) by those same experiences. For example, a child's fearfulness of dogs can remind her parents that she was bitten as a baby. But *if no one knows* that a trauma has occurred to a child, amnesia can exist unrecognized for years, profoundly affecting the child's attitude, mood, and behavior (Terr, 1990, 1994). Not surprisingly, science understands much more about the relationship between biological trauma and explicit memory than it does about psychosocial trauma and implicit memory.

Child sexual abuse is a major form of psychosocial trauma, including (as it often does) all the elements listed above—threat, violence, emotional upset, betrayal, and loss. The abuse may be a single violent event (e.g., childhood rape) or repeated, long-term episodes (e.g., incest). It is often experienced as intolerable and inescapable and—because secrecy, silence, and separation from others characterize it—the child has no way to validate her own experience. Victims of psychosocial trauma may retain memories of it that are (a) explicit, (b) implicit, or (c) both. In this study, the nonamnesic women had survived with explicit memories intact—they could be recalled and recounted at will. The (former) amnesics had only implicit memories which, although they could not be recalled, profoundly influenced their lives. The partial amnesics had retained elements of both memory forms.

What Are the Forms of Dissociative Amnesia?

According to the *DSM-IV* (APA, 1994, p. 478), dissociative amnesia has two common and three uncommon forms, listed here in order of the extent to which personal memory is obscured. The common forms of dissociative amnesia are *localized* and *selective*. Localized amnesia is a failure to recall events from a circumscribed period of time—for example, after a car crash in which a loved one was killed, an uninjured survivor of the accident may not recall the accident or events of the next day or two. Selective amnesia blocks out some events during a particular period of time, such as events during frontline combat in Vietnam. The uncommon forms of amnesia are *systematized*, *continuous*, and *generalized*. Systematized amnesia is loss of memory for a particular kind of information, such as all memories of a certain person (e.g., an uncle) or of some kind of experience (e.g., any hospitalization). Continuous amnesia blocks out memory of all personal events from some past point in time up to the present. Generalized amnesia is a rare type, although often portrayed in movies, in which all memory of one's past identity is lost. These five subtypes of dissociative amnesia are depicted graphically in Figure 6.1, in which the black blocks represent periods of memory that are lost. Examples from the experience of respondents are given below to illustrate these amnesia subtypes but not to diagnose the women in my study.

The top line of Figure 6.1 depicts the normal state of a person's relatively uninterrupted memory for past events, which was characteristic of the nonamnesic respondents. The blocked-out periods of memory in the next two lines (localized and selective amnesia) are applicable to many of the partially amnesic women as well as the fully amnesic ones.

Localized amnesia is illustrated by the experience of survivors who lost all memories (both good and bad) for the period of time during which their trauma had occurred. The resulting memory gap was typically unnoticed or ignored for decades. **Audrey** reported, "I had no memories of family life from ages 8 to 11, the years we had a stepfather." **PAULA** lost the memory of one (but not all) of her abusers.

Among my respondents, selective amnesia typically obscured the traumatic aspects of particular time periods or events, while maintaining their neutral or pleasant elements. **Peggy** remembered her father stroking her breasts, but not the fact that he was sexually violent. **Alison** remembered the "nice young man" in her back alley, but not that he raped her. **Arlene** remembered camping weekends in childhood as pleasurable, but being molested by her father in her sleeping bag was "selected out" for forgetting. Selective amnesia can be particularly deceptive when a troubled client seeks counseling for a current problem. Arlene presented a picture of childhood that seemed innocuous or even happy, but when she planned to attend a family reunion she became exceedingly anxious. Neither she nor the therapist she consulted had suspected that her picture of happy childhood relationships was incomplete.

The uncommon amnesias can wipe out much of childhood and, sometimes, also adult years. Systematized amnesia is a serious loss of memory for only certain categories of information. For instance, **Anita** had thoroughly dissociated every element of abuse (by two perpetrators, over a 6-year period) from her childhood memories. Continuous amnesia,

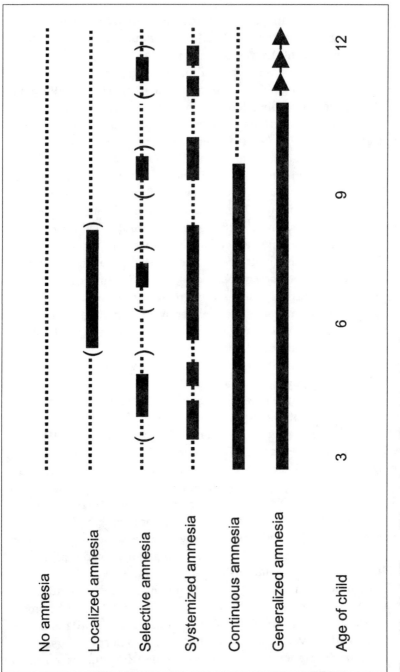

Figure 6.1. Varied Types of Memory Loss in Dissociative Amnesia

which obscures all personal memory from a certain time point onward, is similar to the "memory gap" of localized amnesia, but the gap is much more pervasive. For six women whom I interviewed, although a starting point of amnesia was obscured in very early childhood, personal memories for a major period of their life (such as the first 9 or even 14 years) were lost. **Ashley** reported, "My earliest memory came from age 14. My cousin reminded me of our attending a traveling circus the summer before, and I thought he was lying." **Angie** had similar but not entirely blank memories (perhaps also classifiable as systematized): "I had no memories of my home and parents before I was 10, but I did recall one or two school events."

None of my respondents displayed generalized amnesia with its complete loss of identity. However, one survivor continued to lose her recent past well into adulthood. **Ava** reported that she "had no past" until age 32. She gradually remembered portions of a ghastly childhood, and later referred to the past as "when I was dead." As adults, all of the women with lengthy periods of amnesia were fully aware that they lacked early memories, but they had assumed that this was normal or at least unimportant. However, such large gaps in their memories of childhood made it difficult for them to establish a continuous sense of their own identity. They were lacking knowledge of the events that had shaped who they had become as adults.

Any of these types of amnesia can contribute to a child's psychic survival by allowing her to shut out intolerable memories from her daily life. The kind of amnesia that each survivor developed probably depended on several factors: the child herself (e.g., her personality, her age at the time of abuse, her normal ways of coping), the nature of her abuse (e.g., its origins, duration, ending, pervasiveness, force, etc.), and her family situation. These factors need to be explored in future research. My impression is that each woman "forgot" whatever it took for her to survive.

It is important to clarify here that, in 1986, I did not ask for or receive any diagnoses from the therapists whom the research participants saw, nor did I ask the women themselves. I was listening to them as individuals, as recommended by Shay (1994) in the quotation that began this book. (However, I *did* ask respondents the extent of their recall of abuse, without using the word *amnesia*.) Therefore, my purpose in the above passages was merely to illustrate the varieties of dissociative amnesia, as evidenced in the experiences of these women. Indeed, some of them may well have experienced more than one type of amnesia. Alternatively, for others, amnesia may have been a manifestation of a more far-reaching condition, termed multiple personality disorder in the *DSM-III* (APA, 1980) and dissociative identity disorder (DID) in the *DSM-IV* (APA, 1994). In discussing PTSD below, I will again be referring to characteristics of that disorder and not making a clinical diagnosis of my respondents. Of course, a major symptom of PTSD is problems with memory.

WHAT SURVIVORS CAN
TEACH US ABOUT AMNESIA

Their Experience of Amnesia

The above sections show that clinical knowledge about dissociative amnesia is useful in understanding the traumatic dissociation experienced by study participants. However, in other ways, the experiences of these women were not prototypical. Until recently, authoritative views held that dissociative amnesia usually ends as abruptly as it began, recovery of memory is complete, recurrences are rare, and impairment is usually minimal and temporary (*DSM-III-R*, APA, 1987). Respondents in this study described their experiences as being different in each of these four ways. Their accounts provide a crucial perspective to add to the clinical literature.

Most of the amnesic women believed that their amnesia had not set in abruptly and involuntarily. They thought that they had been active in defending themselves against traumatic memories. (This process is described in the next few pages.)

A second difference from the usual pattern of dissociative amnesia for the women in my study was that it lasted far longer than usual—longer even than for most Vietnam veterans with symptoms of PTSD. (This topic is also discussed in the next section.) The women's trauma was extremely complex and deep-rooted. The easiest course for them was to avoid remembering until the burden became intolerable, or until society was willing to help them to carry it. For the amnesics in this study, their forgetting lasted for periods ranging from 12 to 55 years, with an average period of 36 years from the start of the abuse.

A third difference was in the amount of damage (compared to the minimal amount of impairment described in the *DSM-III-R*). The women's long years of ignorance had obscured the origin of many distressing personal and interpersonal problems. Most participants' lives had been seriously impaired because amnesia had lasted through all or most of three key developmental periods—childhood, adolescence, and young adulthood. (The cumulative nature of the damage was described in Chapter 5.)

Finally, the women's recovery of memory was neither sudden nor complete. Except in a few cases, it generally returned as fragments, slowly fitting together, and seldom providing a complete picture. For these four reasons, the experience of these women who were sexually traumatized as children seems more complex than the *DSM* description suggests. A successful therapeutic experience for them could only result from the counselor's and client's joint dedication to breaking new ground. When people who had recently remembered sexual abuse began to turn up in counselors' offices in the mid-1980s, their recovery was generally a longer and more painful process than was first anticipated, based on previous clinical experience with various types of dissociative amnesia.

Why and How Amnesia Occurred

Why did amnesia occur? Because their subjective view is a focus of this book, I asked the amnesic and partially amnesic women what purpose forgetting their abuse may have served in their lives, and how they thought it had come about. The checklist gave them a choice of responding *yes, somewhat,* or *no* and amplifying with explanations. Below and in Table 6.1, I have tallied only their unqualified "yes" answers. (Including *somewhat* would have raised most of the percentages below to the 80%-96% range.) The women's responses showed their belief that amnesia had been a useful defense, especially during childhood, and that it had been brought on by:

1. *Overwhelming distress*—memories too painful to live with (82%) and feelings of shame and guilt (79%)
2. *Security needs*—feeling that no one would believe or help them (74%) and a need to feel that their world was safe (37%)
3. *Important relationships*—desire to protect the family (58%) and love for and/or dependence on the abuser (53%)

Several amnesics spontaneously added that fear of telling may have motivated their forgetting. Such a fear was well founded, for those who did tell were disbelieved, punished, or both, as described in Chapter 4.

Table 6.1 Beliefs of Amnesic and Partially Amnesic Survivors as to Why They Did Not Remember Abuse

	Percentage Reporting
Why was amnesia needed?	
Memories too painful	82
Sense of guilt or shame	79
No one to believe or help	74
Protectiveness of abuser and/or family	58
Dependency on or love for the abuser	53
Need to believe in a "safe" world	37
How did amnesia develop?	
Repression (shoving down the memory)	82
Dissociation (separating self from abuse)	76
Controlling (keeping very busy)	63
Enduring, not feeling (shutting eyes)	47
Intellectualizing (deciding it was imagined or dreamed)	45
Idealizing (idealizing one's life or the abuser)	29

NOTE: Includes unqualified "yes" responses only.

How did amnesia occur? Amnesia—an extreme form of denial—requires enormous energy to achieve and to maintain. A battery of defenses supported it. Dissociation was probably the most powerful mental defense available to respondents as children and, as explained above, psychosocial amnesia is now called *dissociative amnesia.* Dissociation breaks up the structure of a traumatic experience, separating some or all of the elements—events, emotions, thoughts, sensations, location, time, and meaning—from each other. Dissociation served to distance respondents from overwhelming events (which, as children, they had no schema for understanding), clouding their conscious awareness even as the abuse took place.

The women who had experienced at least partial amnesia were asked how their amnesia had occurred using a checklist that omitted the term dissociation but included phrases describing some of its forms. Again, only the unqualified yes answers are reported here. The survivors responded that during their abuse they had "gone out of body" (61%), "pretended they were somewhere else" (58%), or believed that the abuse "was happening to someone else" (21%). More than three fourths (76%) of the amnesic and partially amnesic women checked at least one of these forms of dissociation. They usually based their choices on their own reexperience of abuse during flashbacks. Examples follow.

Anabel, during torturous abuse by her mother, had "gone out the window, becoming really tiny, and playing with insects on the leaves of the trees." **Portia** had "thought herself" into a picture of happy children above her bed. **Alex** looked down from above and saw the "empty, cookie-cutter shape" of a child on the ground. Each form of dissociation was a way of "not being there" that made the experience easier to forget. Dissociation seems to have occurred automatically at first for these children, and later, it was an entrenched response to further abuse. Briere and Runtz (1987) have described the way this defense mechanism can take on a life of its own and suffuse a person's later life.

The amnesic and partially amnesic women believed that they had also worked at forgetting, particularly through repression. Most of them (82%) believed that they "repeatedly shoved down the memories" until they could no longer be brought to mind. For 63%, "keeping very busy" had helped this repression process. Later, busyness became an effective, lifelong coping mechanism for keeping unwanted memories from resurfacing. (It is interesting that 67% of *non*amnesic women also used busyness as a way of avoiding what they could not forget.)

Idealization of their abuser was a defense mechanism used by many amnesics (42%), but not by partial amnesics (7%). It involved not only erasing their traumatic memories but also painting over the blank spots with pretty mental pictures that idealized their dysfunctional family, their unhappy childhood, and above all, their abuser. This process helped them to deny the possibility of abusive acts by parents, thus resolving the cognitive dissonance created by knowing that someone they trusted was betraying them. Usually, this revision of history was practiced throughout their childhood, with a lot of help from the rest of the family, and even from the community at large.

Through these three defense mechanisms—dissociation, repression, and idealization—the amnesics managed to go on with their lives until they felt safe enough to remember traumatic childhood experiences. Sometimes, other ego defenses were also enlisted in the effort. One kind of defense against remembering was the use of drugs or alcohol to fog their minds (38% for the amnesics and partial amnesics). Another was intellectualization—believing that the abuse had been imagined or dreamed (45%). These (and other) defense mechanisms were employed not only during abuse but also in subsequent years—making it possible for the women to deny that the abuse had ever occurred.

Another set of characteristics that was displayed by many research participants was symptoms of PTSD, a condition that is described and explained in the rest of this chapter.

POSTTRAUMATIC STRESS DISORDER[1]

In the 1970s, as Vietnam War veterans returned from Southeast Asia, mental health professionals became increasingly aware that the war was not over for many of them. It was relived in nightmares and flashbacks. Its effects were evident in emotions still numbed by the horrors of combat and in arousal symptoms such as hypervigilance and angry outbursts. A similar disorder pattern had been recognized beginning with World War I. In succeeding periods, it was sequentially labeled *shell shock, traumatic war neurosis,* and *gross stress reaction.* After the Vietnam War, it became known as *posttraumatic stress disorder* (PTSD).

However, the problem did not originate in the this century. Shay (1994) has documented, with passages from Homer's *Iliad,* that the full range of PTSD symptoms occurred in Greek soldiers fighting in the Trojan War 27 centuries ago. It seems that, with each recent war, the problem was rediscovered as if it were something new. And, typically, it was first viewed as blameworthy. In World War I, for example, psychosocially shattered soldiers were "cured" in hospitals (by forced recall of their horror) and quickly returned to the front. British soldiers, suffering such extreme PTSD that they were incapable of taking part, were sometimes court-martialed for cowardice or desertion and shot at dawn (Majendie, 1998).

The term PTSD was first presented and fully described in the *DSM-III* (APA, 1980). The condition consists of three clusters of symptoms that can develop following personal exposure to an exceptionally traumatic event—usually an event that was experienced with helplessness and intense fear, or horror and disorganization. The symptoms involve persistent

1. *Reexperience* of the trauma (e.g., flashbacks to its events and intrusive thoughts about it)
2. *Avoidance* of reminders of the trauma (e.g., suppression of memories) and *numbness* of response (e.g., emotional detachment)
3. *Arousal* (e.g., sleep problems, vigilance, startle responses)

All of these symptoms must last for more than 1 month to warrant the diagnosis of PTSD. The condition is labeled *acute* if it lasts less than 3 months, *chronic* if it continues longer, and *delayed* if it initially occurs more than 6 months after the traumatic event. The description of PTSD makes it clear that its symptoms can develop not only from war but from other exceptionally distressing situations such as an airplane crash, a major earthquake, a hostage takeover, the murder of a loved one, torture, or the more common trauma of rape (*DSM-IV*, APA, 1994, pp. 424-425).

Findings on PTSD Among Veterans

The findings from early studies of PTSD were limited by inadequate comparison groups of traumatized and nontraumatized veterans. However, in 1990, findings were reported from a major survey study (Goldberg, True, Eisen, & Henderson, 1990). It used well-developed instruments and a matched comparison group—identical twin brothers. All the men among 2,092 sets of twins were veterans of service in the Southeast Asia war or in other duty stations.

Results showed that 16.8% of the twins who *did* serve in Southeast Asia currently had PTSD compared to only 5% of those who *did not* serve there. The Southeast Asia war group, depending on their level of combat experience (low to high), were from 3 to 9 times as likely to have PTSD as their noncombat identical twins.

This study clearly established that PTSD was a normal response to abnormal stress rather than evidence of underlying pathology, that its probability rose with the severity of conflict experienced, and that its impact could be long-lasting. Some veterans were still seriously affected decades after their service. Moreover, their most distinctive symptoms all fell in the first cluster mentioned above—reexperiencing the trauma. Compared to their noncombat twins, veterans who had experienced a *high* level of combat were far more likely to suffer from painful memories (13 times), nightmares (12 times), and flashbacks (8 times).

Other studies of PTSD have investigated biological and psychopharmacological aspects. According to a review by Goleman (1992, p. 65), these studies have shown that wartime trauma generated a series of neurobiological changes that left affected veterans with an altered brain metabolism. There were effects in three key areas of the brain. First, the brain's noradrenaline system seemed to have been reset, making these veterans prone to adrenaline surges, even decades later (p. 65). Anything reminiscent of the original trauma could trigger a fight-or-flight alarm, and the result might be an anxiety attack that seemed totally unwarranted by the current circumstances. Second, the brain circuit linking the hypothalamus and the pituitary gland responded to crisis by triggering CRF, a stress hormone. This, in turn, stimulated secretion of a chemical (ACTH) that activated a stress reaction, compounding the effects of adrenaline surges. The response of veterans with too much ACTH was exaggeration of perceived danger; they experienced the body reactions (sweat and pounding heart) and emotions (fear or anger) of their past trauma. The third brain area that showed changes in veterans with PTSD was the opioid system, which blunts pain from injuries. It produces chemicals, such as endorphins, that act like opium to dull pain and evoke a "pleasant, detached dreaminess" (p. 66). This change may explain the second set of symptoms of PTSD—emotional numbness, apathy, lack of zest—which may alternate (or occur side by side) with contrasting symptoms such as jumpiness, nightmares, and irritability.

Thus, trauma survivors with PTSD are alert to anything that may threaten their physical and emotional safety, they overreact to any perceived danger, and they numb themselves against the possibility of pain. These three changes in the brains of trauma victims reinforce each other, producing the major symptom clusters of PTSD—reexperiencing, arousal, and numbing.

PTSD Symptoms Among Sexual Abuse Survivors

Over a century ago, Janet (1889) described PTSD-like symptoms among women victims of incest. Breuer and Freud (1895/1955), in their study of *hysteric neuroses* in women, noted two seemingly contradictory symptom clusters—intrusive-repetitive and denial-numbing. The former allowed their clients to reprocess disturbing childhood sexual events in an effort to assimilate them, and the latter provided respite when that processing grew too intense.

Gelinas (1983), one of the first of recent writers to connect sexual abuse to PTSD, held that the trauma of incest can become a time bomb of delayed negative symptoms that erupt after years of seeming normalcy. (Such a latency period may help to explain why some incest victims appear "unharmed" when they are, instead, numb—p. 318.) A victim's problems can simmer for decades, especially if there is amnesia. Gelinas proposed that the longer they go unaddressed and unresolved, the more likely the problems will have a "disguised presentation," as troubled survivors become repetitive treatment seekers.

Donaldson and Gardner (1985) further clarified the nature of sexual trauma, using the operational definition of PTSD in the *DSM-III-R* to diagnose 25 women who had experienced incest as children. Another study by Wilson, Smith, and Johnson (1985) compared a variety of survivor groups (people who had experienced different types of calamities) and found that war veterans were decidedly the most severely traumatized, except for an equal rating on PTSD for a small sample of nine victims of rape, battering, and child abuse.

Other writers have modified or clarified aspects of the PTSD diagnosis for application to survivors of child sexual abuse. For instance, Briere and Runtz (1987) proposed *post-sexual-abuse trauma* as a specific form of PTSD, featuring four primary psychosocial effects—posttraumatic stress, and cognitive, emotional, and interpersonal effects. Finkelhor and Browne (1986) elaborated on the nature of sexual abuse trauma itself by specifying four processes that contribute to trauma—traumatic sexualization, betrayal, powerlessness, and stigmatization. Courtois (1992) discussed the denial-numbing and intrusive-repetitive phases of PTSD as involving memory loss and memory retrieval, respectively. During the first phase, survivors defend against remembering, recognizing, or defining their abuse. During the second, the truth bombards them. Fredrickson (1992) summed up the advantages of the PTSD diagnosis as applied to survivors of sexual abuse, emphasizing that the label does not imply pathology; instead, the clear description of the syndrome provides a framework for survivors' experiences and alerts therapists to symptoms that they might overlook.

Both Herman (1992) and Terr (1990) have clarified the differential impacts of a short-term traumatic episode and long-term, repeated ones. Terr (1990) identified four long-lasting characteristics that originate in childhood trauma (either sexual or nonsexual). Three of these are repetitive—sensory perceptions, behavioral and body responses, and trauma-specific fears. The fourth involves "changed attitudes about people, life, and the future" (p. 19). Terr also distinguished between Type 1 trauma—a single event involving sudden shock (such as rape)—and Type 2 trauma—repeated and long-lasting situations (such as extended incest). Terr concluded that Type 1 trauma creates more vivid and complete memories than does Type 2 trauma, in which memories are typically fuzzy and spotty because dissociation becomes, over time, a way of coping. For a further, comprehensive review of the literature on PTSD and child sexual abuse, see Rowan and Foy (1993).

COMPARISON OF SEXUAL ABUSE
SURVIVORS WITH VIETNAM VETERANS
Similarities

In comparing my research participants to Vietnam veterans, let me first note the extent to which the 72 women in this study met the *DSM-IV* (APA, 1994) criteria for PTSD when they were first contacted in 1986. Had they endured events that were outside the range of expected human experience, that would be markedly upsetting to almost anyone and usually accompanied by intense fear, terror, and helplessness? Like the Vietnam veterans, many of the women had believed that their lives were in danger or that their bodies had been permanently damaged. Several told of abusers trying to suffocate or strangle them, and many had endured the physical trauma of oral, anal, or vaginal rape. In addition, a number had seen people close to them hurt. Eight reported that they were made to watch the torture of small siblings or animals, usually in ritual abuse ceremonies. Rape, incest, and ritual abuse are all possible precipitating events for PTSD, and one or more of these was experienced by at least 85% of the respondents, whereas 31% had experienced sexual violence.

Most of the research participants had also experienced the three symptom clusters that characterize PTSD. The first symptom cluster, reexperiencing, was commonplace to the women in its many forms. By the time they were surveyed, 80% of the respondents had had flashbacks, reexperiencing elements of what had happened to them, and 58% suffered from the disruption of intrusive thoughts about past traumatic events. Dreams, which tended to replay themes of helplessness, hopelessness, and terror, were reported by 61%. Even without any obvious stimulus, most of the women might be overwhelmed with emotions from the past (74%) and feel "like a kid" again (60%).

The second symptom cluster of PTSD, avoidance of reminders of their trauma and psychic numbing, had been especially prevalent before the breakthrough of memories. To avoid dealing with the past, the women had used many defense mechanisms, with dissociation and repression heading the list. Amnesia to any knowledge of abuse was the ultimate denial or avoidance, and in 1986, it was harder to find research participants who had always remembered than ones who had been at least partially amnesic to it. All the women, to varying degrees, had found additional ways of avoiding the truth over the years since their abuse. Escape through alcohol or drugs kept memories foggy for 36%, but keeping over-busy was effective for many more (75%). Some used obesity, a tense posture, or a tight jaw or crotch to discourage sexual approaches. As for psychic numbing, 65% had felt out of touch with their emotions, and the inability to enjoy life was a common complaint.

The third symptom cluster of PTSD is arousal. Among the women, 78% were anxious, 67% suffered from agitation or exhaustion, and 54% had troubled sleep or nightmares. Most had been abused at night, so bedtime (or certain hours of the night) tended to bring on bodily jerking, flashbacks, nightmares, or sensations of smothering. The respondents also were inclined to be hypervigilant and to startle easily. Several mentioned that, in social gatherings, they sat with their back to the wall where they could safely survey whatever was happening. The explosive anger typical of many Vietnam veterans seemed to be internalized by these women, and they could be unmercifully hard on themselves. Nearly all of them felt unworthy (92%) or that something was wrong with them (82%). Half (49%) had been self-abusive, 60% had suffered from depression, and 47% had experienced suicidal ideation. (Chapter 7 presents fuller details on these symptoms.)

In the varied ways described above, the symptoms of this sample of 72 survivors of sexual abuse closely paralleled those of veterans with PTSD. At the time when they were first interviewed, these women were survivors of secret battles, daily joining in combat with familiar childhood enemies—feelings of helplessness, hopelessness, and terror—that had harassed them throughout their lifetime.

The study participants were also similar to the Vietnam veterans in that they had to wait for appropriate help until laypersons and professionals became more understanding (Scott, 1990). Meanwhile, the symptoms of individuals in both groups were frequently misdiagnosed as pathological rather than as being normal responses to extreme stress. In the lives of veterans, powerful pressures were exerted to discount the ravages of PTSD, Agent Orange, and, more recently, Gulf War Syndrome. Similarly, the medical establishment ever since Freud's time had disregarded emerging evidence of the prevalence and impact of incest, thus influencing lay and clinical opinion throughout the 20th century. In the 1990s (after a scant decade of concerned attention), survivors of sexual abuse have found that new social groups, such as the False Memory Syndrome Foundation, are arising to challenge the validity of recovered memories.

Differences

There were however, at least nine key characteristics that differentiated victims of sexual abuse from Vietnam veterans, even though both suffered from PTSD. First, most veterans were men. In the mid-1980s, adults seeking therapy due to childhood sexual trauma were almost entirely women (although a substantial percentage of boys as well as girls have been sexually abused). In contrast, most studies of PTSD in the military have been of men. A recent national study of PTSD in women veterans (Van Der Wall, 1996) yielded the disturbing finding that rape while in service contributes more to their PTSD than any other factor—including, for nurses, exposure to danger and to horrendous casualties (Fillmore, 1998).

Second, many Vietnam veterans adjusted well after the war, some even feeling that military experience had been beneficial in their lives (Blank, 1985). However, only a minority of survivors of sexual abuse believe it had little or no long-term effects (e.g., Russell, 1986). Most research has verified consequences ranging from mild to serious and lasting into adulthood (e.g., Finkelhor et al., 1986; Wyatt & Powell, 1988). The women in this study all viewed their molestation as a pivotal life problem.

Third, the time lapse between trauma and seeking help in therapy was far longer for the women than for the veterans. The veterans typically first experienced the symptoms that drew them into self-help groups from 9 to 30 months after their return from Vietnam (Shatan, 1973), although for some, problems arose years after their apparently successful adjustment to civilian life (Kaylor, King, & King, 1987). In contrast, the triggers that impelled the sexual abuse survivors into therapy occurred from 10 to 55 years after the abuse began. (The mean was 30 years for all the women, and 36 years for the amnesics.) This long delay allowed the consequences of trauma to fester in their personal and interpersonal lives for many decades before being addressed.

Fourth, defensive behavior patterns were more deeply ingrained for the women. According to Kaylor et al. (1987), Vietnam soldiers had to erect psychic and behavioral defenses against stress to survive combat. After leaving the battle zone, they relaxed these defenses, and sooner or later, they experienced the effects of wartime stress in a delayed form. Exposure to danger and brutality was found to be the best predictor of serious problems later, as reported by Goldberg et al. (1990) and Fontana and Rosenheck (1993). The abused children in the current sample also had to erect defenses for survival. Sexual violence had been common, as detailed in Chapter 4. However, instead of needing to protect themselves for 1 or 2 years, most of the women had to protect themselves from early childhood onward for many years—for some, even after they left their parental home. Their defenses, early learned and long practiced, had aided their emotional (and even physical) survival in childhood but proved dysfunctional for healthy adult living.

Fifth, the veterans were usually in their late teens or early 20s during the Vietnam War, their trauma coming during the stage of life when issues of identity, direction, and intimacy are typically being resolved (Wilson, 1977). The women, at first abuse, ranged from infancy to 12 years old, averaging 5.4 years of age. Typically, they had been traumatized through several of the early stages of personality development, and with cumulative impact, as discussed in Chapter 5.

Sixth, the source of stress for the veterans lay largely in the chance events of war, sometimes made more difficult by deliberate human cruelty. By contrast, the children were traumatized by human intention—a process known to increase the length and severity of PTSD (APA, 1994, p. 424). Frequently, it was a parent, who should have ensured their safety, who jeopardized it. (For example, 41% of my respondents had been sexually abused by their natural father—75% of the amnesics.) In consequence, their ability to trust the world, their caretakers, or even themselves was seriously damaged. Among soldiers, Shay (1994) has emphasized the powerful negative impact of betrayal.

Seventh, unlike the veterans, the women had been isolated and individually traumatized during their secret battle rather than experiencing the threats in the company of others. There was no one to validate their reality, share their pain, or help them process the events that had happened.

Moreover, they had rarely told their experiences (or could not, because of amnesia). In adulthood, their early sense of isolation was reactivated for many when they began to face memories of childhood incest and found that their original family rejected them. Unlike most of the veterans, these women could not "go home again."

Eighth, partly because they had been alone during their trauma, the women were far more likely than the veterans to have dissociated it. Looking back on their childhood, many had, until recently, been unaware that it had been an emotional battleground. Amnesia had enabled them to survive, but it had grossly distorted their understanding of past reality—their family, their childhood, and their sense of identity.

Finally, these conditions intensified the impact of trauma for many of the women and created such all-pervasive consequences that the short-term therapy prescribed for many veterans was totally inadequate for them.

Relation of PTSD Symptoms to Experiencing Violence

As a final comparison, was the level of exposure to violence associated with the extent of PTSD symptoms for sexual abuse survivors, as it was for veterans? This question was studied for the 51 women who responded to the questionnaire both in 1986 and in 1992 (see Cameron, 1994a). At least 22 of these 51 participants had experienced some violence in connection with sexual abuse (most of them were amnesics or partial amnesics). Although the degree of this violence could not be exactly measured, it could easily be ranked. Accordingly, the women were categorized into three groups: those who had reported multiperpetrator organized sadistic abuse (sometimes called ritual abuse), those who had reported violence to a lesser degree, and ones who had not reported experiencing violent abuse. Mean scores for these three groups were compared on four key PTSD symptoms that were included on both the 1986 and 1992 questionnaires (flashbacks, intrusive thoughts, feeling out of touch with one's emotions, and nightmares or troubled sleep). Strong endorsement of a symptom was weighted 1.0, and moderate endorsement was weighted .5; thus the resulting scale score could range from 0.0 to 4.0.

The average score for PTSD symptoms reported by the three violence groups was 3.29, 3.23, and 2.43, respectively, in 1986, and 2.43, 1.10, and .95 in 1992. Thus, the group means varied in a pattern that was positively related to the level of violence at both times, and the group differences reached statistical significance in 1992. The passage of time also brought a significant reduction of symptoms for all three groups, although the symptoms were more tenacious in the group that suffered organized sadistic abuse. (These changes over time are discussed at length in Chapter 13.) The pattern of fewer symptoms being associated with less violence, and with greater reduction of symptoms over time, also held for scores on the three individual clusters of repetitive, numbing, and arousal symptoms (Cameron, 1994a). These findings for women survivors of sexual abuse are consistent with the report on veterans by Goldberg et al. (1990), as well as with Goleman's (1992) report on the tenacity of PTSD symptoms.

CONCLUSION *

The concept of PTSD is appropriately applied to survivors of childhood sexual trauma as well as to war combat veterans. Data from this study of women seeking therapy as adults have documented the presence of the same three clusters of symptoms that characterize PTSD for veterans —reexperiencing, avoidance of reminders or psychic numbing, and arousal. Veterans and survivors are similar in having experienced severe trauma, helplessness, despair, and disillusionment. They are also similar in having had to wait many years for the understanding and support of the American public. And, finally, they are similar in finding the symptoms of PTSD persistent in their lives.

In other ways, however, their experience differs. The women were in their childhood developmental years, far younger than the veterans at the time of their trauma, they were alone rather than in a group, and they were often betrayed by parents. Their traumatic experiences typically lasted much longer, and the memories of them were more likely to have been lost. Finally, therapy began much later in life for the sexual abuse survivors, and they generally required more time for recovery.

NOTE

1. With permission, this section uses material from my article titled "Veterans of a Secret War: Survivors of Childhood Sexual Abuse Compared to Vietnam War Veterans With PTSD" (Cameron, 1994a).

PART III

Interim Years Between Abuse and Recall

In 1986, **Arlene** had recently begun to remember her father imposing incest on her:

> I dreamed that I was in the audience at the circus. A young woman, dressed all in black and with flowing black hair, was announced as a substitute for the circus performer who should have been on stage. She was leaning against a panel ready to be catapulted into a somersault act. However, someone had put glue on the panel and, as she was flung into space, her hair and the skin of her back were torn from her. *Nevertheless, as if nothing was wrong, she completed her act.*

This dream helped Arlene to realize the dilemma she had faced as a child in a surrogate adult role. Despite her own anguish, she felt compelled to preserve a façade of normalcy before the world.

CHAPTER 7

Long Silent Years

I was the too-good child. No one could tell that I was damaged. Deny-
ing my feelings was the only way I survived, but it made me a
stranger to myself.

—Nicole

In this chapter, I describe the results of the children's sexual abuse in their later lives, up to the time when the women began to remember the abuse or to work on it for the first time in therapy. These consequences include the façades that they developed to hide their suffering, the emotions that they felt behind the façades, their personal and interpersonal problems, the coping mechanisms that they developed to survive, and the types of somatic and emotional symptoms they exhibited during the years before they received help.

FAÇADES

The validity of emotions is recognized in every culture, although each culture has guidelines as to how and when feelings may be expressed. However, the feelings of a sexually abused child are not validated. They are ignored, discounted, and mislabeled by her abuser. When such a child cries out in grief, pain, anger, or terror, even the sound of her emotion may be stifled by a hand on her mouth or throat. Her emotions are often overlooked, rejected, or punished by others as well, and she may have reason to fear the reactions of other family members. As **Adeline** reported, "Any upset on my part undermined my mother."

Something happens to an abused child whose betrayal is allowed neither recognition nor expression. She begins to deny herself the right to feel. When her emotions become too upsetting to her, too threatening to parents, or too revealing to outsiders, she masks them. Gradually, she loses touch with her own inner feelings and adopts a façade to cover them. In so doing, she may become an emotional and behavioral chameleon, trying to protect herself by reflecting the feelings and actions of those around her.

A major developmental task for the research participants, when they were children, was trying to discover guidelines outside of their home so that they could build a façade of normalcy around their feelings and actions. Most of them became observers rather than participants in life. More aware of the feelings and needs of others than of their own, they learned to present an untroubled face to the world. Although some adopted a rebellious stance, most were constrained in behavior and acted out scripts written by someone else. Beneath their carefully cultivated appearance of normalcy lay the frightening conviction that there was something terribly wrong with themselves. This self-perception was reported unequivocally by 82% of the women, and another 14% said that it was "somewhat" true of them. Examples of their written self-descriptions included the following:

- I seemed confident and self-assured, but it was a deep lie. I was in pain, denying everything.
- It amazed me that adults saw me as a joyful person. I sure didn't feel that way.
- Even when I felt as if I had a tornado inside me, others expressed pleasure that I was "such a calm person to be around."

Emotional Numbness

Most respondents (84%) felt that they were out of touch with their own emotions, (65% answered *yes* and 19% *somewhat*). Negative feelings, especially, had been submerged for self-protection. **Alison** explained:

Whenever I was put down or criticized by someone, I felt as if I had been "attacked" at the core of my being—as if my life was in danger. There was a sense of betrayal and unreality—"this can't be happening." I was also frightened by my own powerful reactions, and I tried to subdue an enormous sense of injustice. I knew that I was upset but couldn't identify anger, hate, or hurt. I was terrified of unleashing what I couldn't understand, but holding feelings in led to days of depression.

Positive feelings tended to be muted as well in the women's general flattening of affect. A few survivors had so deadened their feelings that they told me, "I was not aware of having emotions," "Love? I'm not sure that I've ever felt it," or "The only feeling I do know is fear."

Much of their behavior was driven by the primary need to be safe. In childhood, it felt essential for the respondents to know as much as possible about those around them—to figure out *their* feelings and intentions—to feel secure. They did so by listening to and watching others closely. Behind her façade, **April** taught herself to recognize the emotions of others so that she could respond safely. Later, she began to imitate their tone of voice—angry, loving, sad. Practicing these tones, she increasingly evoked the feelings in herself. This routine helped her to get in touch with her own emotions while also protecting her in a scary environment.

However, other survivors were too deeply troubled to make this connection to their own feelings. Differentness was an extremely common burden for the women (72%, plus 11% somewhat). For example, **Penny** had realized at a young age that she stood out if she did not laugh or frown when others did. She learned to fake emotions by imitating the expressions she saw on the faces of others, instantly reflecting the same joy, excitement, amusement, or irritation. "Turned outside in," as she expressed it, she felt none of these feelings herself, even as an adult. Once, watching a movie, she heard a strange noise and realized that it had come from herself—she had laughed. Another time she was surprised to find that someone had "put tears on my cheek." **Penny**'s daily experience was depersonalization—separation from herself.

Disguising Behavior

Human interaction rests on a foundation of roles, rules, and norms of behavior. These guidelines smooth relationships with others at home, at work, and in the community. The façade that disguised the emotions of a sexually abused child also shaped her behavior. Imitation—one of the ways all small children internalize the norms of society—was a high-priority activity for survivors, as in the example of **Penny**. Many became experts, not only at modeling emotions, but also at copying behavior. As **Anita** explained,

> I knew something was wrong with me, but I was also aware that my family was strange. How could I find out what "normal" was? I decided to copy people who were what I wanted to be. By observing them, I noticed what was wrong with my manners, clothes, and attitudes—and corrected them. I picked up the tiniest innuendoes and cues. That's how I learned.

This skill served Anita well over the years. She could fit in smoothly with people from any walk of life. However, their positive responses encouraged her in adulthood, as when she was a child, to live through others rather than out of her own feelings. Distressed by any hints that might suggest a flaw in her performance, she paid a high price for fitting in.

About 83% of the women saw themselves as at least somewhat "different from others," and they spent a great deal of energy disguising this perceived flaw. In the process, they learned far more about impressing others than about expressing themselves. **Paige** summarized, "I blend in and disappear, going along with whatever is happening so nobody will notice me; I've done this for as long as I can remember." **Pat** said, "I shut down a lot of feelings and acted as everyone expected in the strict life of our church." **Andrea** also led a double life: "I became whatever my caretakers wanted me to be. At grandmother's house, I was pristine, ladylike. At my father's, I was a whore."

A different sort of façade is common among child abusers. People who present a positive image of conformity, leadership, and service win respect and are viewed as models for others to admire and imitate. It is possible to hide antisocial behavior behind such a social façade. If events strip away this pretense, admirers are shocked and disbelieving, and acquaintances find it hard to accept the discrepancy between image and reality. In recent years, numerous public figures—including civic leaders, television evangelists, priests, and administrators of child care programs—have been exposed as leading double lives, using their public image to protect or even advance their own sexual deviancy.

More often, however, such people go undiscovered. Many respondents (especially among the amnesic women) grew up with parent figures who publicly subscribed to social guidelines while privately violating them. Among the occupations held by abusing parents in my study were those of doctor, social worker, nurse, minister, teacher, counselor, and mayor. These parents trained their children to protect their flawless public image. "My brother and I were good—double good," said **Ashley**, whose abusive mother, a drug user, nevertheless administered a highly respected drug abuse treatment program for many years. Like numerous other survivors, Ashley had found it mandatory to act "as if I lived in a wonderful family." Brought up in such homes, respondents were well aware that it was essential to appear normal.

Impression Management

A large majority of the women in my sample developed "as if" personalities at a young age. By my classification, 71% used impression management as a major coping mechanism during the decades between their abuse as children and their search for therapeutic help as adults. Social gatherings, family reunions, and church or school settings became stages for acting as if they were normal, healthy, and spontaneous and for displaying whatever behavior they judged would fit their role on a given occasion. Sometimes, as in **Ava**'s case, the façade could not be maintained:

> As a depressed teenager, I painted watercolors of happy people out of my imagination, and even sold some of them from a nearby store under the pseudonym "Jenay." One day, an enthusiastic woman who had purchased two paintings stopped by my home unannounced. She wanted to "meet the young painter." Finding me dejected and tongue-tied, she left shortly—obviously perplexed and disappointed.

On the questionnaire, 75% of the women reported presenting themselves as "very good." These apparently trouble-free conformers were easy for others to get along with because they simply fell in with the wishes of others. Society supported their deception. In contrast, a few respondents, especially some of the imprisoned ones, had acted rebellious rather than conforming. **Ingrid** wrote, "I always tried to be cocky and tough outside, but inside I was scared and hurt." Others, like **Ilsa**, tried to escape: "I ran away a lot. I just wanted to be alone, to think about it."

Other researchers have noted the phenomenon of impression management in sexually abused children but interpreted it in differing ways. In 1937, Bender and Blau (reflecting Freud's views of childhood sexuality) reported that the preteen victims whom they treated were often exceptionally attractive and charming, and they suggested that these children probably invited the sexual approach of adults. Unfortunately, their interpretation—cited for decades in professional literature—provided long-lasting support for the myth of the seductive child. However, other researchers have seen behind the façade of such children. For Rush (1980, p. 9), the "glossy, pleasing surface" presented by some victims was a matter for concern rather than suspicion. Forward and Buck (1987, p. 108), who described the "as if" personality, pointed out that abused children tended to present themselves before others as they thought they should be. Because over 90% of my respondents felt an excessive need to please (88% yes plus 7% somewhat), it is not surprising that so many of them chose a disarming facade. It enabled them to hide their vulnerability and helped them to move from being victims to becoming survivors. Like Eleanor Rigby in the Beatles' song, each woman "kept her face in a jar by the door."

Major impression management, such as that described, had various underlying motives—fear, lack of trust, the desire to disappear, to fit in, to excel, or to win friends—or even just the need to get by for another hour or another day. The social image the survivor projected varied with the motive that produced it. **Alana** suffered from fear so severe that she "used to pray every morning for the courage to go to school." Uncertainty about her own sense of self was **Alex**'s problem: "I would give strangers a fake name." **Nadine**, entering her teens, wanted to control her life: "I acted tough so that nothing and nobody could hurt me." **Peggy**, convinced that she "invited" molesters, tried "to be normal, not seeming seductive and sexual." Approval was **Amy**'s motive: "I tried to be very, very nice because I had nothing else to offer people." In each case, their common goal was that "no one should know the real me." Both **NANCY** and **ILENE** had to keep ongoing incest a secret well into their teens. Neither could escape while under the parental roof. ILENE even had to disguise two pregnancies by her stepfather.

Of course, not all survivors felt successful in convincing others that all was well in their world. Several believed that even the "outer me" was unacceptable, so they felt a special dread lest anyone should learn that worse lay within:

- I felt unworthy of anyone ever loving me just for myself, and for no other reason. So I didn't trust enough to let anyone see the real me and how I felt inside.

- In my teens and twenties, there was a tremendous gap between how I manifested on the outside and who I was on the inside. The outer me was a totally unlovable misfit, but the person on the inside could not even be suspected by others. I felt trapped, fighting myself, trying desperately to be someone other.

Whatever they felt inside, most respondents became quite skilled at putting on a convincing performance and presenting an untroubled face to the world. Some of them, indeed, felt that it was not enough to be "as good as" others. To feel merely acceptable, they had to be "perfect," and consequently, they displayed a high degree of achievement. Our society values confidence and success so much that even the appearance of possessing these qualities was highly advantageous to them. Pretending to feel confident, they used their intellect and talents to control their social environment. For some, acting in plays became an outlet, and two of the women told me they had won awards through taking roles in school plays: "I could inject myself into another personality and be and do whatever was needed." Their acting offered escape from self, a shield against others' seeing who they were, and it also won them praise.

Even if they succeeded in convincing their audiences—relatives, teachers, and later on, friends and coworkers—they lived with tremendous anxiety. On stage, they were constantly fearful of giving themselves away. Backstage, the mask slipped off, and the debilitating insecurities behind it often took over. "I pretended when I was with others. Alone, I allowed myself to be sad." In summary, these women paid a heavy price as they tried to live up to their own perfectionistic requirements. Observers rather than participants in life, they accommodated to the feelings and needs of others but not to their own. And the more they hid themselves from others, the more they became strangers to themselves.

THE EMOTIONS BEHIND THE MASK

What was life like for these women during the years before they sought help? On the first questionnaire, they were asked to identify predominant emotional experiences, using a checklist of paired items. (For example, were they inclined to be "cheerful" or "sad"? If both terms applied to them, they could check both items of a pair.) The results for the total group of respondents are shown in Table 7.1. On these paired items, there was a high level of endorsement of the negative qualities and a low to

Table 7.1 Negative or Positive Self-Descriptions of Respondents (%)

Percentage	Negative	Positive	Percentage	Difference	Sum
80	Nervous	Easy-going	35	45	115
78	Anxious	Calm	20	58	98
77	Depressed	Light-hearted	30	47	107
72	Untrusting	Trusting	32	40	104
71	Lonely	Sociable	48	23	119
63	Sad	Cheerful	35	28	98
59	Angry	Patient	42	17	101
31	Very bad	Very good	75	−44	106

NOTE: Pairs of items total more or less than 100% because some respondents checked both items of a pair, and some checked neither.

moderate endorsement of positive ones. The only exception was the last item, which asked whether they had tended to be "very good" or "very bad." Here the positive pole was chosen much more often, although some "very good" children felt evil inside and checked both.

A rough measure of the women's feelings can be gained from the last two columns of Table 7.1. The higher the difference in percentages between the negative and positive endorsements, the more unambiguously negative the women had felt. It was especially evident that they saw themselves as more nervous than easy-going (80% − 35% = 45%), more anxious than calm (78% − 20% = 58%), and more depressed than light-hearted (77% − 30% = 47%). The next-largest difference in this negative pattern indicated that they were more untrusting than trusting, but this finding may be rather misleading, for some women, in their vulnerability, had trusted too easily and in the wrong places.

If the sum of percentages of the negative and positive endorsements exceeded 100%, it indicated that some survivors had disguised their feelings over the years or experienced mood swings. These disguises or fluctuations were greatest for the characteristics of loneliness (71% + 48% = 119%), nervousness (80% + 35% = 115%), and depression (77% + 30% = 107%).

Within the subgroups, there were similar patterns of reported feelings, with some noteworthy exceptions. Apparently, negative traits were most often disguised by the children who grew up amnesic. Their high scores indicated that they tried hard to please powerful adults, like teachers, by acting very good (88%), yet their scores were also higher than the other groups on loneliness (80%) and sadness (68%). The nonamnesics were higher on sociability (57% vs. 40% for amnesics), despite a tendency to more anger (67% vs. 56% for amnesics) and depression (86% vs. 76% for amnesics). The partial amnesics, like the amnesics, were also notably high on acting very good (80%).[1] In contrast, half of the women in the imprisoned group saw themselves as having been "very bad." The imprisoned women were also the most untrusting (80%), were tied with the amnesics in their high level of loneliness (80%), and described themselves —every single woman—as nervous. Of course, it is possible that these retrospective responses on the questionnaire may have been colored by their current incarceration. They were the highest group on feelings of anger (60%) but, surprisingly, described themselves as lower than the other groups on feelings of sadness (50%).

I focus my attention now on three of the primary emotions that shaped the lives of the respondents over the years as a result of their sexual abuse and its results in their personal relationships. These emotions were sadness, anxiety, and anger.

Sadness and Bereavement

A profound sadness colored my growing-up years. I remember feeling a special affinity for stories of child heroes who sacrificed themselves for their country, their religion, or (especially) for their family.
—**Alana**

Bowlby's (1980) research treatise on children's loss of parents emphasized that a parent can be lost through desertion or separation as well as death. My research has convinced me that parental sexual abuse produces a special kind of bereavement—the emotional loss of a parent who should have met the child's needs for love, respect, protection, and guidance to help her to fit into society. In cases of father-daughter incest, the child may feel a double bereavement—loss of the father because his sexual misuse increasingly takes priority over parenting and loss of the mother because of her apparent complicity, or because secrecy separates the child from even the hope of her protection. Respondents have told me that they were as young as 4 years old when they decided that they were alone in the world and, with compulsive self-sufficiency, began trying to take care of themselves. Describing their typical emotions, 77% of the women characterized themselves as depressed, and 63% said they were sad.

Profound early losses of key parental relationships can create lifelong vulnerability to emotional problems, according to Bowlby (1980). As a result, psychological problems such as suicidal ideation, anxious forms of attachment to others, and serious depression may develop in later life (p. 301). These outcomes are more likely if grieving is not allowed expression at the appropriate time (p. 350). The consequences are likely to be more extreme if the child experiences multiple losses, or mystery surrounding the loss, or if her questions go unanswered (p. 351). These kinds of contingencies made the amnesics in my sample especially vulnerable in later life.

Children of incest—their self-esteem usually having been shattered by the perceived double desertion of both parents—typically hold themselves to blame. As one result, they may be drawn toward sad stories and people who are sad. In some cases, they are propelled to care for and alleviate the misfortunes of others—a process that allows them to displace their sadness outside of themselves (Bowlby, 1980, pp. 366-368). This analysis helps to explain why victims often take on the role of rescuer of others. Alternatively, however, their grief may be so buried that the victim is indifferent to the misfortunes of others. Abused children who have not grieved for themselves are more likely to abuse others, or to be self-abusive, with the same uncaring attitude.

Coping With Loss and Bereavement

Children have not developed mature ways of coping with stress, so they handle loss and bereavement differently than adults do. In general, they have four main outlets, according to Osterweis, Solomon, and Green (1984, p. 100) and, depending on the situation, they may use any or all of them. First, they may talk it out freely. After a family death, for example, some children report it to anyone they meet. It is their way of seeking support and gauging what they should feel. Second, they may reenact the trauma, struggling to master it by playing games like "funeral." Third, an explosion of anger can vent their upset feelings. Last, they may hold their emotions in, continuing "life as usual" on the surface. Unfortunately, for the sexually abused children whom I interviewed as adults, the first three of these outlets were not available.

Talking it out was certainly not an option. "Don't tell" was a mandate with incest and often also when the abuse was by nonrelatives. How could respondents, as children, have found support for such a special and secret sorrow? Most of them, like **Audrey**, felt isolated. "I knew there was no one to help me. I was all alone." Nor was it likely, in the months and years that followed the abuse, that they could ease their pain in supportive, communicative relationships with peers or adults. Their ability to experience trust and intimacy had been severely damaged and, in addition, potential peer-group friendships had often been discouraged. Until she remembered as an adult, Audrey did not understand the implications of her parents' behavior when she was a child:

> Mom wanted me to come straight home from school and not have anyone come over. If I did make friends with a girl, Dad would make fun of her voice, her hair style, or her posture.

Boy-girl relationships in adolescence were also undermined by incestuous fathers. Many of the girls were not allowed to wear makeup, feminine haircuts, or the "provocative" clothing of their peers. The attitude of a number of fathers was marked by intrusive curiosity, jealousy, or even outright vetoes on dating. **Norma** reported, "My dad said not to mess around with boys; he'd protect me from getting pregnant."

Reenactment, or "acting out" the trauma, is a second common outlet for childhood grief. It is perceived by many adults as play. Children may try to comprehend death and bereavement by "playing funeral" or by burying a dead bird. This outlet, also, was blocked for most respondents. Some of them tried to grasp their experience by "playing sex" with smaller siblings in childhood or by promiscuity in adolescence. If these behaviors were discovered, they met with severe adult disapproval from outside (as well as inside) their home, deepening their sense of shame. Rigid controls on any acting out were common in homes that harbored pervasive sexuality. **ILENE** recalled, "I was never allowed to go out on dates, and my stepdad kicked his son, Bill, out of the house permanently for making a pass at me. Bill said he only wanted what Dad got from me all the time."

Exploding in anger, a third common outlet for grief, may be tolerated when a child has lost a loved one to death. However, my respondents were not permitted to vent their feelings of deprivation and loss in a blowup that could rupture secrecy. Any expression of their negative feelings was ignored, redefined, or punished, first by others and later by themselves. Rage at their abandonment, because it was disallowed expression, was often turned inward in self-hatred. Also, their own anger was at least as frightening to them as to others. Most of them were terrified lest it break through. Besides, they wrestled with other concerns, which might be affected if they did not contain their feelings—their mother's emotional and financial security, their father's job and freedom from prison, and the safety of younger siblings. These women were trained from early years to leave themselves and their feelings out of consideration. They tested the emotional vibrations around them to fit in, to be safe—unable to express the rage that Horney (1950) held was the natural result of abandonment.

The fourth coping mechanism of grieving children, according to Osterweis et al. (1984), is to hold in their emotions and try to continue life as usual. This seemed to have been an almost automatic reaction for many respondents. **Annelise** (6 years old and deep in shock) sat on the curb and chatted with her smaller sister about the man who had showed her his "thing." She was already amnesic to his raping her a half-hour earlier. **Addie**, 11 years old, would hop on her bike to visit a friend as soon as her stepfather finished with her. It was easier for her to believe it was all a bad dream if she acted "as if it hadn't happened." And **NANCY** (from age 11 to 20), after enduring oral, anal, or vaginal incest during the night, would come downstairs in the morning, clean and neatly dressed, to help her mother with the family breakfast. All of these life-as-usual reactions were efforts to undo the trauma.

Because young children cannot sustain deep grief long enough to resolve it (Osterweis et al., 1984, p. 104), serious personal losses may cause delayed repercussions in their later lives. Among these consequences are increased vulnerability to physical, emotional, and mental problems. For the research participants, each succeeding loss—in childhood or the later years—added to the store of unresolved grief and reactivated their other losses. Like children who never allowed themselves to grieve for the death of a parent, women who could not face the enormous losses that came with sexual abuse, and especially with incest, lived vulnerable lives until they faced their grief as adults.

Anxiety and Fear

Anxiety and fear were other typical characteristics of the research participants. Anxiety was reported by 78% of the women, as shown in Table 7.1. As children, they had felt alone, without help or hope, and this had led to a pervasive anxiety. They also had more specific sources of fear. Most had feared their abuser and the abuse, but they also dreaded the possible exposure of the illicit sexual activities they were pressured into. Many were afraid that they themselves might break secrecy through some spontaneous act or emotion.

As the years passed, the women's anxiety generalized to many other situations in everyday life. They experienced fear in a variety of ways. For some, it was linked to particular types of social situations. Sitting in a closed car or attending a social gathering would make them want to escape, even though they didn't understand why. For others, observing the hyperactive antics of adolescent boys, or watching contact sports, or seeing violence in movies or television would set off anxiety attacks. **Alexis** found herself, on several occasions, sobbing so uncontrollably in a theater that she had to leave. The depiction of cruelty or injustice had set her off. For 2 years thereafter, she "healed herself" by watching innocuous preschool programs on public television with her youngest child. Occasionally, a respondent had rendered her fears manageable even earlier. **Nell** explained,

> I took pride as a teenager in my ability to overcome my fears. I used a kind of "behavior mod" technique, progressively testing my fear of the dark till I could leave my lights off, and gradually challenging my fear of heights.

Other women, who were victims of extreme viciousness, had carried feelings of buried or overt terror through all of their lives. **Alison** told me in 1990, "My primary feeling is fear. From the third grade on, my hands shook all the time." **Adel** expressed her constant terror in a letter to me: "Fear sits on my shoulder. I must be so careful. I have only to turn and look at him, and I am lost." At the time she wrote me, she was recovering from her latest suicide attempt.

The depths of fear that such respondents felt can be better understood by considering the history of **Ariel**. She believed that, from infancy, she had never bonded with anyone. When she was a young child, her father took her and her brother weekly to a place where they were sexually shared with his friends. As she grew older, fear overwhelmed all other emotions. Only alcohol, provided by her father, dulled her pain. By age 14, she was drinking every day and wandering the streets. She felt she was looking for affection, but instead, she found repeated rape and torture. In 1986, she told me why and how she had learned to protect herself: "I am so afraid to be on the earth. I must guard my boundaries. I do not show you who I am." Women like Ariel, who were so badly traumatized, continued to live in fear until they placed themselves in a healing environment where they could learn appropriate trust—in some cases, for the first time.

Anger and the Urge to Kill

In 1987, in a famous court case, Cheryl Pierson was convicted of manslaughter and given 6 months in jail for hiring a classmate to kill her father. He had abused her sexually and physically from the age of 11 until his death when she was 16. She had plotted his murder after seeing signs that he was also starting an incestuous relationship with her 8-year-old sister. My research participants were full of sympathy for Cheryl. Their typical comments were, "I'd have let her off" and "She deserved a medal." One woman was convinced that the judge couldn't afford to release Cheryl because doing so might trigger killings by molested children all across the country.

Many of the women in the nonprison groups had lived with stifled anger, and some with murderous rage. Several had come close to killing an abuser—their own, the battering husband who succeeded him, or their child's molester. Others turned their hate inward, becoming self-abusive or suicidal. A number of these women loathed the "unhappy child" within them and wanted to destroy her. Still others experienced hatred for a daughter who was a reminder of themselves in childhood. The examples below illustrate these various attitudes.

Six respondents reported that, as preteens or teenagers, they had seriously thought of killing an incestuous parent to end an intolerable situation. At 13, **Polly** was afraid that her father would try to kill her and that her mother would be unable to stop him. Several times, she talked with her younger brother about how they might kill him instead: "Maybe Joey was just going along with me, but I was serious." **Alex**, at 11, had settled on a method—stabbing her father with a large knife while he watched television. However, Perry Mason movies convinced her that a jury would call that premeditation. And how could she, a child, convince them that it was self-protection? Imagining a trial, she could think of only three words in her own defense: "He was mean."

Amy, at 15 years of age, actually came within seconds of killing her stepfather:

> One afternoon, Frank was in the hallway, beating up on Mom again, and I'd had it. I went up to their bedroom and got his gun. I just pointed it at him from halfway down the stairway, not saying a word. Mom and he stared at me in alarm. She kept asking me to give her the gun. Instead, I cocked it. The click sounded loud and reassuring. I felt power for the first time, looking at Frank's face, pasty and scared. I could pull the trigger any time and that's what I wanted to do. But I knew I would be "put away." I thought about it for several minutes while I kept the gun aimed at Frank. There was no hurry. Finally, I decided that he wasn't worth going to prison for. I handed the gun to my mother.

Portia ended her stepfather's advances by brandishing a butcher knife and telling him she'd kill him if he ever touched her again. **Norene** told me that she cannot count the number of times and ways she had fantasized killing her brutal father. In 1995 (anticipating seeing him at a family wedding), she dreamed repeatedly of ripping him to shreds, gnashing, gnawing, tearing at his flesh like an animal.

The women were more often aware of fury on behalf of others than of themselves. They typically felt powerful empathy for all assaulted children. **Andrea**, on learning during a visit to the police department that there were 23 registered sex offenders in her small community, experienced a powerful fantasy of stealing their addresses and making her rounds with a shotgun. Several women (some before their amnesia lifted) experienced out-of-control rage at the sexual abuser of their child. **Pia**, whose 6-year-old was beaten up by a teenage molester when he found he could not take off her snowsuit, set off to find him with intent to kill. **Phyllis** saw flashing images of herself plunging a knife—over and over—into the body of her former husband. He had just admitted having their 6-month-old baby perform fellatio on him, remarking, "I didn't think it was important." Neither of these women had a weapon on hand, but a third one, **Ivonne,** did and used it against her daughter's abuser. She is in prison.

A victim's anger at a childhood molester can be transferred and compounded years later against an abusive spouse. It is hard for survivors of childhood molestation to choose healthy partners—the respondents often reported that they could not recognize or "did not deserve" one. Some of the women found them only in second marriages or in lesbian relationships. Commonly, the respondents had been in at least one relationship as an adult that was physically, sexually, or emotionally abusive, and sometimes thoughts of murder tempted them. **Nedda** fled her house in horror when she found herself about to kill her husband while he slept. **ILENE** went to prison for killing her husband with the gun he had threatened to use on her. The difference between imprisoned survivors and ones who were free was not so much in the nature of their angry impulses as it was in whether they acted on them.

Self-Hatred

Self-hatred can be another manifestation of anger at the original abuser. Children often find hatred and rage against an abusing parent too dangerous, so they turn it inward. In a flashback to childhood, **Allie** found herself saying in the same breath, "I hate you, Daddy. I wish I was dead." Over half of the amnesics went a further step, idolizing their abuser in addition to denying their anger and loathing of him. The hatred deflected from him was typically directed inward from childhood on, creating alienation from themselves. Horney (1950) has called such self-hate "a cruel and merciless force" (p. 115). It allowed my respondents no compassion for their own suffering and fueled suicidal ideation in 65% of them (47% *yes* plus 18% *somewhat*).

A number of the women considered suicide while they were still schoolchildren and acted on their thoughts in varying ways. Some were actively suicidal. **Ashley,** age 11, got out the family gun and searched 2 hours for the bullets. **Penny,** age 15, swallowed every pill in the medicine cabinet, including her dog's medicine. Others tempted fate—walking on railroad bridges, or across the top of a high waterfall, or swimming in Lake Erie during a lightning storm—letting chance determine whether they lived or died. Some lived carelessly, suffering the "little deaths" of multiple injuries. **Patrice** reported, "I was a mass of scars and broken bones. Mother said I was very clumsy." Still others were passively suicidal, longing to be rescued from life by illness, accident, or the hand of God. Two of these, at bedtime, used to ask God to let them die during the night. For others, as adolescents, death had been their "hope for the future," and two of them had wanted it "as soon as possible."

Passivity had been typical of most of these children's suicidal ideation. They had so little feeling of control in their lives that they tended to wish for death rather than to take matters into their own hands. When they became adults, obsession with suicide continued to be more common than attempts, but these women were also prone to psychosomatic illness, self-abuse, and accidents, as described in later sections of this chapter. (Considering the course of their lives, one wonders how many sexually abused children have actually committed suicide. In most cases, their stories can never be told.)

The Disposable Child

When the women directed murderous hatred inward, it was often focused on their "inner child"—the child they had been. Most survivors knew, intellectually, that they were not responsible for their childhood trauma, but more than a dozen of them were chagrined at how harshly they rejected—and separated themselves from—their childhood self. They resented returning to that little girl in flashbacks. Women who were ordinarily compassionate could be merciless toward the little girl inside them: "She got me into all this. Why didn't she fight?"

Angela recovered memories of being savagely raped as a child by two men in her grandfather's barn. She told me,

> I am appalled at the anger I have at the little 8-year-old who was raped and tortured. She is what separates me from people. She didn't beg for life; she wanted to be killed. She didn't fight back, didn't struggle. She only moaned and whimpered, and to me she is ugly and despicable. My head knows it was not her fault, but part of me absolutely loathes her—intense hatred that turns my stomach—despising her pain, her helplessness, and wanting to destroy her.

NANCY has never forgotten her abuse. In her 30s and 40s, before she got help, she was aware that she carried within herself, and hated, the little girl she had been. Blocked through the years in all attempts to get help, she could not conceive of healing that inner child; she just wanted to get rid of her. It seemed that this "disposable child" encapsulated all her pain and filled the core of her being. She found herself obsessing about how she might "cut her out" and leave the rest of herself alive. However, the child and the woman were inseparable, and her body registered her desperation. She went through a complete hysterectomy, hemorrhoidectomy, and two throat operations. She recognized later that she had used surgery to attack the sites of sexual invasion, the parts that carried her intolerable secret.

Such self-hatred also damages a mother's relationship with any child who reminds her of herself. **Carla** wrote me that she had seemed a confident and outgoing woman until her daughter was born under terrifying circumstances:

> I was left alone in a dark labor room until, frightened by increasing pain, I realized my call-bell didn't work. My screams eventually brought help but, by then, my daughter had torn her way out into the blackness and was lying wet and wailing between my legs. In the weeks that followed, postpartum depression and loathing for my child overwhelmed me. I could not bear to touch or care for her. I abused her, and for 12 years, I was under psychiatric care. I now understand that the circumstances of her birth had brought back the self-loathing I had felt during childhood rapes in a dark bedroom. My little girl was *me*, and I hated her. I almost destroyed us both.

Whether or not a survivor remembered her own molestation, she was likely to become anxious as her child reached the age of her own sexual abuse—a phenomenon that has been termed *anniversary reaction* (Hilgard, 1989). Several women became extraordinarily fearful for their daughter's safety. Others, like **Audrey**, found themselves rejecting a daughter who mirrored their own child-self:

> I hated it when she cried or whined, when her misery rasped across my nerves. She was not supposed to be unhappy. I had silenced the child within me, and now my daughter had resurrected her, and together they voiced a duet of pain. At the time, I didn't remember my own abuse, so I was unaware that my Dad had gotten to her also.

In sum, one or more of the emotions that we have been discussing —sadness and grief, anxiety and fear, anger, and even self-hatred—were pervasive feelings under the women's usual façade of normalcy during the long years before they began to deal with their childhood abuse.

CONSEQUENCES OF ABUSE
OVER THE YEARS

Now that I have examined the protective façade adopted by the survivors during their long silent years, and the emotions hidden behind it, I turn my attention to the personal and interpersonal problems they experienced, the coping mechanisms they used, and the body symptoms that expressed some of their underlying pain. On their first questionnaire and during the interview that followed it, they described personal consequences of their abuse, which can be summarized under three headings: (a) negative self-perceptions, (b) maladaptive coping styles, and (c) long-term somatic problems. A fourth set of consequences, symptoms of post-traumatic stress syndrome (PTSD), was touched on in the preceding chapter and is amplified here.

Some influential research on child sexual abuse has downplayed its long-term consequences (e.g., Henderson, 1983) as well as its immediate impact on children (Kinsey et al., 1953). However, other studies have increasingly confirmed the force and endurance of its impact. Finkelhor et al. (1986), in their review of empirical studies, summarized evidence that sexual abuse is a "serious mental health problem, consistently associated with very disturbing subsequent problems in a significant portion of its victims" (p. 163). They concluded that the best-documented long-term consequences were anxiety, depression, poor self-esteem, feelings of stigma, isolation and distrust, self-destructive behavior, and tendencies toward drug abuse and revictimization (p. 162). By the mid-1980s, negative self-perceptions were being used by all key researchers as one measure of the impact of sexual abuse (e.g., Russell, 1986; Wyatt & Powell, 1988), and this pattern has continued (Briere & Elliott, 1994).

Negative Self-Perceptions

Among my respondents, there was an extremely high endorsement of unfavorable items that indicated low self-esteem and a negative self-concept. Table 7.2 presents, for the entire sample, the percentage who gave an unqualified "yes" to a self-descriptive term. As the table shows, these women saw themselves retrospectively as having been "never good enough" (92%). They had felt something was wrong with them (82%), they blamed their unhappiness on their own deficiencies (76%), and they had long felt "different from others" (72%).

Table 7.2 Self-Perception of Survivors During the Interim Period, by Group (%)

Self-Perception	**Amnesic**	Partial Amnesic	**Nonamnesic**	Imprisoned	Total
Unworthy, never good enough	**92**	93	**90**	92	92
Excessive need to please	**76**	100	**86**	100	88
Something wrong with me	**88**	86	**81**	67	82
To blame for my problems	**76**	79	**90**	50	76
Problems with relationships	**72**	93	**81**	100	83
Different from others	**84**	64	**67**	67	72
Didn't fit in	**80**	64	**57**	75	69
Uneasy with peers	**68**	57	**62**	83	67

NOTE: Unqualified "yes" responses only.

These negative self-concepts led the survivors to a variety of problems in interpersonal relationships. Most of them became "people pleasers" (88% yes) and tried to hide their inadequacies from others, as discussed above. On other self-descriptive items, the women reported experiencing a high degree of social fear, feeling out of touch with their emotions (65% yes—see Table 7.5), uneasy with peers (67%), unable to fit in (69%), lonely (71%), and untrusting of other people (72%—see Table 7.1 for the latter two items). The consequences in their lives included strained and distant social relationships (83% yes), problems in intimate and sexual interactions (78%), depression (60% yes), and, for many, the suicidal feelings described in a previous section (47%). (See Table 7.5 for a detailed breakdown of this last group of symptoms.)

The survivors' attempted solutions to these problems were quite variable, and some were more successful than others. As a result of their loneliness, many of the women tended to search for parenting figures in their friends or partners. A few gradually found supportive and healthy friendships. One woman's choice of friends changed over the years before she remembered her abuse, as she unconsciously sought various types of parenting figures in friends or partners. Her first friend was a nurturing mother, and her second husband was a "good father," but she had never felt equal to them. Gradually, she built a network of caring people about her. After she remembered her abuse, she felt the presence of her friends' loving support, and she gained increasing self-esteem. As an alternative pattern, instead of seeking parenting figures for themselves, other respondents became parenting figures to others. Some tried to buy friendship by always doing things for others, whereas others became rescuers to avoid facing their own problems.

Sexually, abuse survivors may become promiscuous or may avoid sex entirely. Some choose to be lesbians, whereas others experience the usual problems of women in our culture in exaggerated form. As a teenager, **Ariel** was a goody-goody, who publicly stated that she was offended by games like "post office." In contrast, **Penny** solicited boys in high school. **Nona**, who became nonorgasmic, explained, "When I get horny, I start being afraid. At some point in the past, I refused to give [my abuser] the satisfaction of reacting, and it's hard to turn myself on again so many years later." Similarly, **Angie** said, "I was so inhibited sexually, I tried not to have a lower part."

The respondents who became sexually promiscuous in adolescence often did so as a way of dealing with issues of control: "I have some control if I say when, where, and how." **Anita** gave a dramatic example:

> It was easy to control boys by giving them sexual pleasure. I decided to win their love that way, remaining indifferent myself. Then I could reject them and take pleasure in hurting them. But it didn't work. They ended up using me and then leaving. Many years later, I realized that my plan had grown out of my need to regain power. I had tried in the only way I knew.

Unfortunately, revictimization was common for many of the women. As children, almost three quarters (72%) had been molested by more than one person. A number of them reported having suffered date rape or stranger rape as additional traumatic events in adolescence and young womanhood. Revictimization also often resulted from their choice of an abusive partner in marital relationships, although nearly a quarter (23%) had never married. Many of the respondents' first marriages were to abusive people. In these cases, their memories generally returned during happier second marriages when, at last, they felt safe enough to remember. **Phoebe** had taken longer than most to find a good relationship. As a young woman, she turned down a proposal from a fine young man whom she "loved too much" to marry. She couldn't bear for him to find out "what she was really like." Each of her early marriages further convinced her that she was "not worthy" of love and tenderness. Her first three husbands were, in turn, womanizing, nonsexual (except during rape), and domineering. With her fourth husband, she was finally able to face the past as well as to build a satisfying relationship.

LONG-TERM COPING STYLES

Coping behaviors adopted by child victims may reduce psychic pain, both during the abuse period and during the interim years before help is sought. However, these behaviors tend to generalize and elaborate, becoming increasingly maladaptive over time (Briere & Elliott, 1994). Glasser (1976) described several dysfunctional ways in which individuals try to escape pain in stressful situations, and these illuminate the coping mechanisms of many survivors prior to their entering therapy. One is giving up hope after futile attempts to improve one's life (a process that Seligman, 1975, has termed *learned helplessness*). The person's priority becomes hurting less rather than getting more, and these individuals settle for minimal living. They live with resignation, numbed emotions, and blunted spirits. A second choice is to divert the pain elsewhere. One can act out, settle into depression, paranoia, or psychosis, or express one's difficulties through psychosomatic ills. A third choice is escaping pain through addiction to drugs, sex, or other negative ways of achieving a rush of pleasure and relief from pain.

The negative coping styles of suicidal efforts and self-abuse, which some respondents displayed, are described at greater length elsewhere in this chapter. Drug or alcohol addictions were major escape mechanisms for 36% of the women. Sleep was another form of escape for over half of the respondents (58%): "I sleep to forget, because I don't want to face the day. I just want it to be over." Other means of escaping the pain that were reported by the women were overeating, sexual activity, and distractions such as television or movies.

A variety of more positive coping styles were reported by participants in this study, as displayed in Table 7.3. During the years before they dealt with their abuse, the highest proportion of these women coped by methods involving effort and maintaining control—by seeking to win approval from others (79%), trying harder (perfectionism) (74%), and keeping busy (75%). These mechanisms can be understood as aspects of the other-orientation of survivors who felt unworthy and who strained to earn acceptance in their daily lives.

These coping styles enabled many of the women, whatever their burdens, to be responsible and productive people who contributed to society in various significant ways. Some of them were remarkable overachiev-

Table 7.3 Coping Styles of Survivors During the Interim Period, by Group (%)

Coping Style	**Amnesic**	Partial Amnesic	**Nonamnesic**	Imprisoned	Total
Effort					
Seeking approval	84	71	81	75	79
Keeping busy	80	86	67	67	75
Trying harder	84	71	76	50	74
Escape					
Sleeping	48	43	76	67	58
Alcohol/drugs	40	36	24	50	36
Support					
Religion	48	29	57	25	43
Talking about feelings	36	21	29	17	28
Therapy (nonsexual)	32	21	14	17	22

ers, such as teenage **Perri,** who typically practiced the violin for 8 hours each weekend. Similarly, **Ava** summarized her method of coping: "I became a workaholic—always on the go and leaving no time to think." On top of many other activities, she was raising foster children abused in infancy. "This was the most difficult part of my life, but I couldn't give them up. At first I saw them as some kind of punishment. However, dealing with these damaged children was the key to unraveling my own life."

Other more positive forms of coping included various ways of seeking comfort and support. The women found support, to varying extents, in religion (43%), artistic or dramatic expression (42%), talking about feelings (28%), and therapy (22%), as well as with friends and relatives, pets, or nature.

The differences between the amnesics and nonamnesics on these coping styles were fairly small and nonsignificant. Both groups coped primarily by trying harder (84% and 76%, respectively), seeking to win approval from others (84%, 81%), and keeping busy (80%, 67%). The amnesics had a tendency to use more dangerous escapes (i.e., drugs or alcohol) than nonamnesics (40%, 24%), whereas the nonamnesics were higher in escape through sleeping (48%, 76%). Also, during the interim years between childhood abuse and its confrontation in adulthood, amnesics had been somewhat more likely to seek support from counselors for depression, relationship problems, or addictions (32%, 14%), although not for sexual abuse.

LONG-TERM SOMATIC PROBLEMS

Researchers have found survivors of sexual abuse to have many somatic symptoms, and these symptoms are often closely connected to the individual's habitual coping styles. Gelinas (1983) considered such symptoms disguised representations of sexual abuse, which might serve to hide the past from both counselor and counselee. Physicians frequently find problems in infants, preschoolers, and early adolescents that seem to be real medical complaints but that are, in reality, masked sexual abuse (Kempe & Kempe, 1984, pp. 66-68). Some of these symptoms in minors are abdominal pains, air swallowing, hyperventilation, depression, sleep disturbances, changes in school performance, truancy, running away, suicide attempts, drug overdoses, pregnancy in the early teen years, genital injuries, and venereal disease.

In 1986, I asked the research participants, in an open question, to specify any health problems that they had experienced during the interim years. In 1992, on the basis of those responses, I constructed a checklist of long-term health problems and gave it to the women who answered the third survey. I also asked them to specify both the past and the current status of these ailments (from *worse* to *no longer a problem*). The major types of items listed were eating, respiratory, gynecological, and head and jaw problems. In addition, the questionnaire asked about additional body-related symptoms—accidents, self-abuse, an oversoft voice, and general unwellness—that had been mentioned in earlier interviews. The information presented below came from responses to the health problem checklist and from follow-up telephone interviews.

During the decades before they sought help, 91% of my research respondents had at least one of the somatic complaints listed in Table 7.4, and 76% had more than one, for an average of 3.4 problems per person. Their symptoms seemed to be of four general types. First, there were clearly medical problems, such as the need for a hysterectomy. Second, there were physical problems that seemed to be psychosomatic in origin—bulimia, for example. Third, there were psychological symptoms, such as severe pain that had no apparent physical cause. Fourth, there were seemingly impossible symptoms, such as being able to hear everything that occurred while under full anesthesia during surgery. The data did not permit a clear distinction among these four categories, so in Table 7.4 the past somatic ailments reported by survivors are classified according to the body area affected.

Table 7.4 Somatic Symptoms During the Interim Period, by Group (%)

Somatic Symptom	Amnesic	Partial Amnesic	Nonamnesic	Imprisoned	Total
Any eating or weight problem	83	92	81	60	82
Compulsive eating	67	50	62	20	57
Anorexia nervosa	11	8	19	0	12
Bulimia	6	8	6	20	8
Any gynecological problem	78	83	75	40	75
Premenstrual syndrome	61	25	44	60	47
Other menstrual problem	17	50	44	40	35
Unexplained pelvic pain	22	33	6	20	20
Head and jaw problems					
Headaches of any kind	67	67	69	60	67
Migraine headaches	44	58	50	20	47
Tight jaw	56	58	50	40	53
Teeth grinding	44	50	31	40	41
Respiratory problems					
Allergies	22	75	56	40	47
Oversoft voice	33	25	25	40	29
Asthma	22	8	19	0	16
Miscellaneous problems					
Self-abuse	56	58	44	20	49
Generally unwell	44	50	38	40	43
Accidents	33	42	25	0	29

NOTE: Unqualified "yes" responses only (occasional missing data). These somatic symptoms were measured retrospectively *after* the crisis of recall (*N* = 51 on third questionnaire).

Table 7.5

Problems Involving Weight and Eating

Disturbances related to eating and weight were the most common past somatic problems, reported by 82% of the respondents. Feelings of being overweight had troubled most of these women, creating a poor body image and low self-esteem, particularly because our society values slimness so much. Anorexia nervosa or bulimia were reported as past problems by 6 and 4 of the women, respectively, out of the 51 respondents in 1992. Considering that the National Institute of Child Health and Human Development has estimated that one teenage girl in 200 ($\frac{1}{2}$ of 1%) develops anorexia nervosa, this problem was about 12 times as frequent among my respondents. Compulsive eating was another common problem for the women (57%), which suggested the addictive nature of food—it was the "substance of choice" for many of them. **April** remarked that she hadn't thought of eating as a coping mechanism until she attended a gathering where sexual abuse perpetrators were present. There, she found herself where sexual abuse perpetrators were present. There, she found herself saying "I've got to eat . . . I've got to eat" as she searched frantically for a candy machine.

Several women had experienced sudden weight gains at key points in childhood when their abuse was initiated or escalated. **Abby**'s weight zoomed between the ages of 6 and 7, and **April** went from normal weight to 160 pounds between the 7th and 8th grades. For both these girls, their sudden weight gains accompanied a period of sexual abuse. **Petra** gained 130 pounds after becoming sexually active in her marriage. **Alicia** had painstakingly lost 40 pounds but, seeing her father again after 20 years, she quickly put half of the weight back on.

Food carried a multitude of meanings to the women. It meant nurturance and love to some, evoking nostalgia for parenting figures who had cooked "special" foods for them—their grandmother baking cookies or mother fixing hot cream-of-wheat on a rainy morning. Food was an anesthetic to others, who had learned to use it to soothe their pain. "Instead of listening to my feelings, my mother used to say, 'Eat this.' " Food was like a drug to some of the women, and as their tolerance for it grew, they needed more to escape their unhappy feelings. Food could also be a way of maintaining some control when other individuals tried to dictate their lives. No one can make an anorectic eat, nor a bulimic stop eating. Sadly, however, neither can the woman herself.

Some women consciously chose obesity to discourage male advances. **Angela**—pretty, blond, and willowy—had been raped by several acquaintances. Blaming her good looks, she ate herself into a stout, protective matronly figure. **Priscilla**, newly divorced, was frightened by the attentions of a coworker, so she went home and ate three pints of ice cream. The women who chose to gain weight had a common goal. Feeling vulnerable and helpless in their normal bodies, they tried to make themselves undesirable. But they paid a high price because many of them loathed the fat that protected them. Their excess weight held a variety of meanings for the respondents. It tended to deaden their own sexual feelings as well as reduce the interest of others. It was a protective layer, cushioning them against men. In serious obesity, bulging thighs and abdominal layers almost obscured the genital area. Accordingly, losing weight could feel dangerous. **Pamela** told me, "When I lost weight through dieting, I found myself wearing an overcoat in summer weather."

In the years after they remembered their abuse, body symptoms held less power over some of the women. **Arna** gradually lost over 100 pounds without dieting. Better ways of coping began to emerge or were deliberately chosen. For example, **Nadia** found journaling helpful and reported, "When my feelings come out on paper, the food doesn't go in."

Migraine Headaches

Migraines are brutal headaches, with symptoms that can include hours or days of pain, nausea, and vomiting, as well as disturbances of vision, mood, and thought processes. Population estimates indicate that about 10% of American women have migraine headaches, yet 47% of my research participants had suffered from them. Australians call migraines "trap headaches," believing that they arise when a person feels emotionally blocked in some important way. In view of the fact that migraines are related to serotonin levels in the brain (Brody, 1988), it seems possible that the women's migraines may have developed because the trauma of serious sexual abuse affected their serotonin levels.

Migraines may bring such distress that a victim can be incapacitated for several days. Many of the survivors had been tormented by them. **Alison** had reached a dose of almost 150 mg of Valium per day in a vain effort to win relief. For many respondents, these headaches occurred most often around the time of menstruation, when the chemical and hormonal balance of the body was shifting. In therapy, **Anita** concluded that her menstrual cramps were reminiscent of her forgotten sexual abuse and that her migraines may have blocked emerging memories.

Jaw, Throat, and Respiratory Problems

Nearly all of the participants had experienced jaw, throat, or respiratory symptoms (88%). I group these together because the women, by the time I interviewed them, tended to associate these symptoms with childhood experiences of fellatio. Nine of the women reported that they had had temporomandibular joint disorder. Like a larger number of other respondents, they had long been puzzled by the tight set of their jaws, their clenched teeth, and their inability to open their mouth wide. They had repeatedly been asked by dentists and school music teachers to "open wider." **Andrea** concluded that her clenched jaw had been a stubborn defense against oral abuse. A similar problem, mentioned by several women, was bruxism (tooth grinding), especially during the night. This can wreak havoc with the mouth and jaw, as **ANNE** knew all too well: "I've had problems with my teeth forever. Within a few months, I had five root canals, numerous fillings, and bridges as well."

Several women had experienced sore throats that were chronic or situational (e.g., during pregnancy). They tended to associate them with fellatio or with the way they were silenced as children. The inside of **Carole**'s throat still bears the scars of a never-forgotten early oral attack, which kept her near death for months. **Norene** gets excruciatingly sore throats when she needs to cry. Flashbacks have allowed her to remember an elbow jammed against her voice box. **Addie** was molested from infancy, as verified by her mother, who heard her baby cry and walked in on an abuse scene. Over the years, Addie has had severe upper respiratory problems—even before she was a year old, she had whooping cough and two bouts of pneumonia. Similarly, **Paige** had pneumonia six or seven times as a young child. **Alicia** had a problem with coughing for several years prior to recall: "I was always wanting to clear my throat of phlegm. Recently, I've been coughing in the night. Last night, the cough became retching and the phlegm turned to 'semen'."

Other respondents complained of allergies. **Natalie** reported, "I had allergies all the time and everywhere—in the heat of summer deserts and in frozen winters when nothing bloomed. I don't need a Philadelphia lawyer to know it wasn't the environment—it was me. I couldn't cry, so my nose was always running."

Gynecological Problems

Three quarters of the research participants (75%) reported some kind of gynecological problem: premenstrual syndrome (PMS), reproductive problems in miscarriages or childbirth, or gynecological surgery. From age 11, **Alex**'s menstrual cramps were so excruciatingly painful that she would black out from the pain. **Audrey** recalled, "The PMS was especially bad last year. Each month I had less and less time free from it. A friend stayed with me during the worst times because, otherwise, I would beat up on the kids. My behavior was weird—out of control."

Several women, who had problems getting pregnant or had suffered miscarriages, told me that they believed God must really be angry with them—they felt they didn't deserve a baby. Others were deliberately childless because they feared they could never be good mothers. For three other women, childbirth—with all its happy expectations—was a nightmare experience. Consequently, they found themselves unable to care for their own baby. When **Amy** gave birth to her first child, the event triggered terrible memories that hit her "like a ton of bricks." Both her abusers (father and stepfather) came to visit her in the hospital, and she forced her new memories aside. "Nothing was wrong, and I gave them each a big hug." However, when her newborn son was brought to her, she was afraid of him and went into a hysterical anxiety attack. Soon, her body was swollen with hives, and she was deep into postpartum depression.

For some respondents, gynecological surgery aroused intense physical sensations or emotions such as shame, fear, and guilt. **Arna** felt tremendous guilt for many months afterward. Three other women barely escaped exploratory surgery for severe and mysterious pain in their reproductive organs. In their cases, abuse memories began to emerge prior to the operation, and the physical pain left.

EMOTIONAL PROBLEMS

Self-Abuse

Gritting their teeth, shutting their eyes, and enduring pain had been ways of dealing with abuse for many of the survivors when they were children. For many, creating their own pain was just one step farther. In the total sample, 49% reported having been self-abusive, and some of the remainder may not have identified the way they treated themselves as destructive. Self-abuse was more common among amnesics (56%) and partial amnesics (58%) than among nonamnesics (44%). It was characterized by a strong compulsion—far stronger than addiction to drugs, according to **Peggy**. Whether a respondent was digging her fingernails into her skin, yanking out her hair, pushing sharp objects into her rectum, or cutting her vagina, each one seemed to feel that she "couldn't stop herself." An even more serious self-destructive incident was reported by **Alana**, who told me the following story:

I poured oil into the frying pan, and turned up the heat. I watched it simmer, then boil, then smoke. Finally, when the oil was on fire, I carried the pan to the sink and carefully poured it over my hand. Then I drove myself to the hospital.

Apparently, the emergency room doctors didn't perceive this as a cry for help.

I asked self-abusive respondents why they had felt "out of control" when they hurt themselves. Ironically, their motivation (looking back) had apparently been to regain control in one of several ways. Some were punishing themselves—for their "bad" sexual behavior, or for feelings of anger that were disallowed in their families, or to confirm their low self-esteem. Others found that inflicting external damage distracted them from the pain they experienced inwardly. Still others lived in dread that "something bad" was inevitable, and as their anxiety grew, self-abuse ended the waiting. Several had used self-abuse to anesthetize themselves to pain. **Phoebe** explained,

My arms are scarred. During class, I'd rake them with my fingernails—up and down, over and over—until the blood came. And all the time, I'd be thinking, "I'm getting better and better at not feeling."

The ability to "not feel" pain came up fairly often in conversations with the women. Several connected it directly to their molestation: "I was not going to feel anything from the waist down." This ability to anesthetize pain in local areas tended to generalize to other parts of the body. **Annette**'s friends forced her go to a doctor after she tore loose the inner ligament of her knee. When the doctor moved the damaged knee at a 30-degree angle, Amy admitted that it "sort of hurt." Most survivors seemed to assume that pain must be endured, and several volunteered that they could handle a lot of it. "When it came to pain, I took it in stride—even childbirth."

These survivors had learned their patterns of self-abuse in childhood. **Nona**, fearful of what would occur when she went to sleep, used head banging to keep herself awake. **Pam**, extremely anxious and full of self-hatred, hit and bit herself, banged her head, and chewed her nails until they bled. Others, unable to talk about incest, had shown their visible (and self-inflicted) wounds to caretakers in bids for nurturance.

Suicidal Ideation

Of course, the ultimate self-abuse is suicide, and 47% of the women unequivocally reported having had suicidal feelings during the interim years before they sought help. For some, these feelings were sudden and overwhelming: "God take me. I don't want to be on earth another moment." For others, they were chronic. Trauma at an early age "destroys a child's sense of the future," according to Lenore Terr (1990, p. 163). When asked, on an open-response question, how the future had looked to them as teenagers, 30% of the amnesics independently wrote down the word *bleak,* whereas 9% said there was no future. Findings such as these reveal that many abuse survivors already felt dead inside. For them, suicide was not a leap but only a short step. Sometimes, suicidal ideation was an obsession. **April** said,

> I saw a knife and I wanted to stab myself; I saw an embankment and was drawn to drive off it; I saw a fire and wanted to put my hair in it. My wrists itched, like they were begging to be cut.

As mentioned earlier, some participants tempted fate by reckless or dangerous acts. For others, suicidal ideation was very passive. Asked to complete the sentence, "My goal for the future as a teenager was...," 21% of the amnesics wanted to die. Yet death, as well as life, seemed out of their control. Someone or something else would save them from living longer. Minor health problems convinced **Alicia** that she was dying ("Soon it will all be over"), whereas **Angie** hoped that a plane crash would ensure that she "wouldn't have to try anymore." For **Annie**, the wish was not conscious: Driving on a busy freeway with her dominating husband, she felt suddenly desperate to "escape" his demanding voice. Her hand was pulling on the door handle before she realized where she was.

We have no way of knowing how many children, adolescents, and adult men and women kill themselves because of sexual abuse. The brothers of two survivors in my study killed themselves in their teens. One did so after being sexually abused by their stepfather on a camping trip. The other killed himself in remorse after his parents encouraged him to gain sexual experience with his sister.

Accidents

Accidents constituted another form of self-abuse for 29% of the respondents. Dissociation undoubtedly made these women more vulnerable—they were less aware of their surroundings whether they were driving a car, confronting a hazard, or simply working around a hot stove. Carelessness contributed also. Many of the women had been indifferent to burns, cuts, or bruises, often not knowing when, where, or how they had happened. Self-punishment was another factor, because "accidents" were more likely to occur when the women felt down on themselves. Some of the accidents were life-threatening: "Speeding along the freeway, I had no concern for safety. I totaled two cars." The women's pattern of accidents had sometimes started early in life. For example, **Pat** ran into the side of moving cars three times before she was 6 years old.

Sickliness

Over the years, 43% of the survivors had been sickly, and their general malaise had usually started at a young age. **Patrice** missed 156 days of school in 1 year. **Peggy** was constantly sick, although the doctors could find nothing wrong. Many of the survivors' stories included statements like "I was just not well," "I didn't feel good," and "I was exhausted all the time." These women had lacked both energy and bodily stamina. In some cases, as children, they had exaggerated or faked illness to receive attention, but usually, their unwellness was very real. It was also scary. Hypochondriasis—abnormal anxiety about health—troubled several women: "Even today, with *anything* physically wrong, I'm almost nonfunctional with fear of dying."

SYMPTOMS OF PTSD

Today, many researchers consider trauma symptoms to be a major and complex consequence of repeated incest (e.g., Briere & Runtz, 1987; Freyd, 1994; Herman, 1992; van der Kolk, 1987). Children who have been sexually abused, especially by family members, constantly ask themselves "Why me?", and 47% of my respondents reported having felt suicidal. Orbach (1988) concluded that children become suicidal when they feel trapped and incapacitated in an unresolvable situation. Research by Pennebaker (1990) has demonstrated the negative health effects of being

Table 7.5 Posttraumatic Stress Disorder (PTSD) Symptoms During the Interim Period, by Group (%)

PTSD Symptom	Amnesic	Partial Amnesic	Nonamnesic	Imprisoned	Total
Avoiding/denial/numbing					
Numbed emotions	72	71	57	58	65
Depression (withdrawal)	64	57	57	58	60
Suicidal feelings	52	57	38	42	47
Sexual problems	80	93	67	75	78
Reexperiencing/arousal					
Flashbacks[a]	92	79	65	82	80
Intrusive thoughts[a]	64	43	67	45	58
Troubled sleep/nightmares	52	50	57	58	54

NOTE: Unqualified "yes" responses only (occasional missing data).
a. These two PTSD symptoms occurred *after* the crisis of recall instead of during the interim period ($N = 51$).

unable to confide one's distress to other people, and he declared that "the mind torments itself by thinking about unresolvable issues" (p. 104). Certainly, an unresolvable issue faces most child abuse and incest victims, who are unable to tell about their abuse for fear of creating immense problems for themselves and/or their family. This conflict is a key source of their obsessive, intrusive thinking and other traumatic symptoms.

As described in Chapter 6, high percentages of the participants in this study reported suffering from the three clusters of PTSD symptoms—repetition of experiences, avoidance or psychic numbing, and arousal reactions. In particular, they displayed the PTSD symptoms of flashbacks, intrusive thoughts, feeling out of touch with their emotions, and nightmares or troubled sleep. Table 7.5 shows a breakdown of these symptoms for the several groups of respondents. On most of these characteristics, the amnesic group was somewhat higher than the nonamnesics, and the difference was especially great on the presence of flashbacks (92% vs. 65%).

CONCLUSIONS

In summary, whether respondents had been amnesic or nonamnesic to their sexual abuse over the interim years, very high proportions of them had felt pervasive negative emotions of sadness, fearfulness, and anger. They had also developed unfavorable self-perceptions and pessimistic views about life in general, and nearly half had had periods of suicidal feelings. Among the consequences in their lives were long-term health difficulties including weight and eating issues; jaw, throat, and respiratory problems; gynecological problems; self-abuse; accidents; general sickliness; and symptoms of PTSD.

However, many of the women had also responded to their abuse by developing coping mechanisms that helped them to survive it. Some of these coping styles were maladaptive in the long run, such as escape through substance abuse, oversleeping, or compulsive eating. However, others were socially valued, such as keeping busy, seeking the approval of others, and trying hard to maintain control over their life. As a result of these coping styles, many of the women were able to hide their problems from others by maintaining a façade of apparent balance, conformity, and achievement that obscured their internal fears and low self-esteem. In the next chapters, I explore what happened when memories of their childhood abuse broke through or became impossible to ignore any longer.

In closing this chapter, it is important to note that, since this long-term study began, there has been an impressive expansion of research into the link between childhood trauma and long-term consequences. The study of survivors of sexual abuse has helped to bring awareness to this critical human concern. Brief notes on two major studies will illustrate some of these recent findings.

In 1996, Neuman, Houskamp, Pollock, and Briere reported a meta-analytic summary of 38 rigorous research studies on the long-term impact on women—psychological, somatic, and behavioral—of being sexually abused as children. Among the symptoms studied were many that this book describes: PTSD, anxiety, anger, depression, dissociation, low self-esteem, substance abuse, somatization, self-abuse, suicidal tendencies, and interpersonal problems. All of these symptoms were significantly related to the occurrence of child sexual abuse, and the relationships were especially strong for women who were in populations of clinical patients.

In 1998, the National Center for Chronic Disease Prevention reported results of a major ongoing study of the link between adverse childhood experiences—including various forms of child abuse—and adult health problems (Felitti et al., 1998). The population studied was 9,508 representative adult members of the Kaiser Permanente medical care service. Based on members' self-reports, the findings showed a strong relationship between the number of adverse childhood experiences and health risk behaviors in adulthood (e.g., alcoholism, smoking, sexual promiscuity, depression, and suicide attempts). Moreover, as the number of adversities went up, the number of adult risk behaviors increased. Similarly, the likelihood of poor physical health and serious diseases such as heart, cancer, diabetes, and skeletal fractures increased with the number of adverse childhood experiences. The investigators viewed the adult risky behaviors as coping devices, which often arose from childhood trauma, and they recommended early childhood interventions after adverse experiences to promote later lifelong psychological and physical health.

Intervention is an important goal, but the task is daunting. For example, 22% of the Felitti sample had experienced child sexual abuse. Can society afford to have so many hurting children speak out? Will we listen to them? Will we take action?

NOTE

1. These self-description measures were not intended for detailed analysis, but some of the patterns presented are quite consistent with other information comparing the emotional experience of subgroups in Part II of the book.

CHAPTER 8

Triggering
of Memories

My husband and I were doing our "Tarzan and Jane" thing. Tom was hooting like an ape while he chased me through our house. But suddenly, as he pinned me to our bed, the laughing face above me became my stepfather's, and I was small and terrified.

—**Amy,** in 1986

This chapter examines the psychic events that finally catapulted the women into confrontation with the past—providing knowledge of past events, recognition and labeling of the abuse, and awareness of its impact. This process eventually ended the tyranny of the past. The first part of the chapter examines the clues that built up over time, disrupting the women's lives. Among these clues were changes in their symptoms, their feelings, and their dreams. The second part of the chapter describes the process of breakthrough into the remembering stage of recovery.

During the long years that had intervened between the women's trauma and their breakthrough, the survivors had largely "forgotten" their abuse—amnesics through amnesia and nonamnesics by ignoring painful memories. All the respondents had developed powerful defenses against the truth, defenses that had protected them through adolescence and well into adulthood. These defenses had been essential to their survival in a world that, until recently, was unprepared to believe and help them. Objectively, the women had functioned quite well, gradually strengthening themselves, but over time, the strain of avoiding past reality was catching up with them. Each woman, in her own way, had been moving toward confrontation with the past.

In Part I of this book, I identified three key factors that distinguished amnesics from nonamnesics. They were (a) knowledge of their abuse, (b) recognition of its sexual nature, and (c) awareness of its impact on their lives. The nonamnesics had always known what had happened to them, and half of them had recognized it as sexual abuse. However, most were unaware of how it connected to the many serious problems they experienced, as adults, in daily living. A few nonamnesics had wrestled from time to time with their memories, trying to make sense of the past. But most told themselves that they had "gotten over" the abuse and, refusing to deal further with those painful memories, they shoved them out of their daily lives. These women typically coped passably until problems built up overwhelmingly and the banished memories had to be faced at last.

The amnesics had more seriously dissociated themselves from the truth. They had no conscious knowledge of abuse—much less its sexual nature—and so they had no explanation for their problems. They had to break through all three levels to get at the truth. Over time, their energy had been drained by an inner struggle between the continuing forces that maintained amnesia and memories that sought release. They could not understand why daily living seemed exhausting and unrewarding. In despair, some had numbed themselves into mute resignation and depression. Others had anesthetized their pain through substance abuse. Still others had fought to gain more control of life—to make it simpler and safer. Typically, memories did not come back for the amnesic women until they had reached some level of security.

As the years went by, it became harder for the respondents to maintain these compromises with truth. For the amnesic women, hints of the past had been accumulating to the point that they could no longer be ignored or explained away. For the nonamnesics, "getting by in life" had become a precarious balance that was difficult to maintain. Internal and external pressures were beginning to overwhelm them. There was also a buildup of symptoms that had been there, less intensely, all along. These survivors were increasingly aware of operating under stress and could no longer pretend that they were functioning well. Their already strong feelings of inadequacy deepened. Some felt that they were barely holding their lives together.

In the pages that follow, I examine in more detail the accumulation of events that led the women to confront the past and the process of memory breakthrough.

EARLY CHALLENGES TO DENIAL

Usually, a trail of clues, unnoticed at first, led to ultimate understanding. Looking back later, amnesics were especially astonished: "It was right there all along—I just didn't recognize it." Their unconscious had for years been speaking to them in a variety of languages—bodily symptoms, emotions, sexual problems, compulsive self-abuse, and strange dreams and fantasies. These earlier, unrecognized hints prepared them for the powerful breakthrough of memories that came later. This process is clarified below, as I examine the buildup of clues, especially for amnesics, prior to the triggering of memories.

Body language. One of the strongest clues over the years was body language. Some women's body stance gave off a message to others that was unintended. **Ariel**, for example, was unusually pretty and wondered why boys, and later men, were wary of her. She gradually connected this to the "stay away" rigidity of her posture. It was a long time before she took the next step and wondered why her body had assumed such a defensive stance. Other respondents had given off "come hither" body messages, which placed them in danger when decoded by victimizers. **Andrea**'s sensuality, instilled by early abuse, led men in the street to think she was inviting their sexual attention, and **April**'s vulnerable air instantly alerted abusive people, who tried to revictimize her.

In addition to these obvious body signals, there were more subtle, implicit signs that a respondent may have noticed in herself and perhaps puzzled over. Most of these were aspects of defenses that the women had developed against dangerous contacts with males. For instance, an especially soft voice defused anger; sweaty palms made her avoid shaking hands; skin that "crawled away" when a man touched her arm kept her aloof. Other examples of body symptoms included a sharp startle reaction at any unexpected voice, sound, or presence; teeth that clenched and ground in the night; an unusual tightness in the crotch; and a sleep posture that protected her crotch. These women had, unwittingly, trained their bodies to "protect" them from further experiences with now-forgotten abuse (cf. Terr, 1994).

The women's bodies signaled them of earlier, forgotten trauma in a variety of other ways. Some of these included feelings of being smothered ("I found it hard to breathe after sundown"), silenced ("I choked when I tried to speak out"), handled ("It became intolerable to have my breasts touched"), undergoing an oral attack ("I had incessant, unexplainable sore throats"), and being raped ("I was puzzled, after a friend proved totally disloyal, that my vagina felt raw for 2 weeks").

Emotions. Clues had also been presented by the women's emotions, which tended to be numbed, explosive, or erratic—or, for some, all three by turn. Anger was so dangerous to **Penny** that she convinced others (and herself) that she had none. When **Adele** experienced negative emotions, she could not tell whether she felt rejected, hurt, angry, fearful, or sad. Her tender feelings were numbed as well. For other women, however, feelings exploded into expression—extreme and inappropriate to the situation that elicited them but germane to their past experiences. Unpredictable mood swings caused the women who suffered from them (24% of all respondents and 29% of the amnesics) to feel out of control.

Sexuality. Patterns of sexual behavior and feelings also increasingly hinted at the women's past abuse. Over time, they had experienced a variety of attractions, compulsions, and inhibitions. A common problem, with serious consequences, was their sexual attraction to men who would not make good partners and lack of interest in those who would. Their childhood conditioning had paired sexuality with abusive persons—men who were narcissistic, dominating, or cruel—and this conditioning often resulted in unhappy relationships and marriages. Some respondents, overly sexualized as children, had compulsively sought numerous sexual partners during their teen years. They were looking for attention, affection, loving words, and touching but sex was the only way they knew to win closeness. Usually, they were bitterly disappointed at how consistently tenderness ceased following their partner's gratification. **Pamela** felt compelled to make boys lust for her so that she could then break their hearts, but their interest typically waned before she could carry out her vengeance.

Strong sexual compulsions troubled some women in adulthood. These compulsions frequently brought shame even if they were not acted on. **Anita**, as a puritanical teenager, was tormented by a constant desire to stare at men's crotches, and she also experienced a strong temptation to display herself. **Angie** felt driven to have affairs with married men, continuing her childhood role as the "other woman." **Natalie** sought multiple casual encounters, one-night stands that didn't evoke her longing for a caring relationship. She thus controlled partners by initiating sex on her own terms, reversing her earlier patterns of helplessness. After disappointing experiences with males, **Abigail** temporarily found comfort and understanding in a lesbian relationship.

Some of the women were, at times, both promiscuous and inhibited. However, inhibition was more common among the respondents, and it took both particular and general forms. Avoidance behaviors covered a wide range of sexual expression. Typically, certain activities, such as oral sex, tongue kissing, or caressing of breasts were avoided or merely endured: "The joy of loving each other freely was taken from my husband and me years before we met." Sometimes, old resentments were triggered. A gentle request from a partner might feel like a selfish demand: "If I knew he wanted a particular caress, that was what I *didn't* want to give. I was ashamed of being so withholding."

As memories surged toward awareness, some amnesic women experienced a widening distaste for certain, or all, sexual contacts. Others grew increasingly out of touch with their sexuality: "I came to feel that I had 'nothing down there'—no desire, no feelings, NOTHING." Prescription drugs for depression sometimes contributed to this lack of sexual interest. About 80% of respondents reported that they had experienced sexual problems over time, 30% had never married, and some of these had never experienced sexual contact outside of abuse.

Self-abuse. Another clue to past events was a growing pattern of self-abuse. Sometimes, it focused compulsively on body orifices. Several interviewees had forced objects into their vagina or anus, sometimes even sharp instruments: "The compulsion was *powerful*—far stronger than my earlier drug addiction. I couldn't resist it until I remembered one of my mother's boyfriends doing the same thing to me." A less obvious preoccupation with orifices was reported by **Alison**, who "picked on herself" in a multitude of ways:

> I had always hated anything like scabs in my nose, wax in my ears, or mucus in my throat. Now, I couldn't stand them, and felt compelled to get rid of them. I strained my throat by constantly coughing up the slightest phlegm.

> I was startled when my doctor asked me why I "abused my body" by
> scratching inside my ears and nose. I had no idea that anyone could know. I
> was glad that he didn't examine my scalp: I usually had 15-20 bloody scabs
> under my carefully groomed hair.

How did Alison explain this to herself at the time? She decided that she
must be the "nervous type."

Dreams were another common source of hints about the women's past
abuse. Prior to remembering, many women had a period when dreams
carried a mysterious message that was later easily deciphered through
hindsight. For example, **Pat** had learned a lot during 3 years in a group
working on their dreams, but, on rereading her dreams *after* remembering, she was startled to find how full they were of violent symbolism. As
the women moved toward breakthrough, their dreams of danger became
more bloody. **Alex** dreamed of dying:

> I was sitting on the floor of a hospital room while the nurse put sheets on the
> examination table. I had been feeling ill, but now blood started flowing
> from between my legs. The nurse spoke urgently, "You MUST get on the ta-
> ble." I was too weak, and the blood became a stream, carrying with it all the
> tears of my life. It seemed that I was giving birth to death. Consciousness
> faded as I heard the nurse screaming for the doctor.

The victims in **Paige**'s dreams were often small children: "Someone
was stabbing babies. There were naked bodies, cut up and bloody, all
around. Terrified for my 2-year-old, I bundled her up and hid her." Some
women could not remember their dreams, but their sleep was so troubled
that they woke exhausted in the morning as if they had been struggling
all night long. Indeed, they had been.

When they were children, many of the women had dreams that contained symbols such as snakes, which sometimes entered their bodies.
Some, like **Pia**, had repetitive escape dreams: "I would be flying, flapping
my wings with all my might, trying to get away from a monster." Others
had repetitive pursuit dreams that involved a rapist or a terrifying "man
with a knife," who followed respondents through the years in their sleep.
For some, he frequented their fantasies as well. Several women had
"seen" him hover in the shadows of their bedroom or had sensed his presence just outside their door.

As the women got closer to a memory breakthrough, the symbolism
and themes of dreams often emerged more clearly. **Phyllis**, for example,
had begun to explore her childhood in therapy when, dropping off to

sleep one night, she had a startling minidream: Digging with her hands for something buried, she found only a sticky substance. She held her hands up against the sunlit sky, and was revolted to find that they were covered with feces. Other women began to believe that something was quite wrong—typically, they thought, with themselves.

Combinations of clues. For most women, anomalies of thought, emotion, or behavior had combined to give hints of the past. An example is the trail of **Addie**'s experiences over the years: She had hysterics at age 7 over a tiny worm in her breakfast berries, a plan for suicide at 10, deep depression when she was 14 after viewing a comedy about infidelity, a teasing request at 19 that her boyfriend tie her wrists, a sudden compulsion at 21 to place her firstborn in her father's unwilling arms. Each of these experiences had carried its own personal logic at the time. Consequently, respondents tended to respond to the trail of clues with slightly increasing puzzlement rather than with suspicion that these might be important messages.

However, as the clues accumulated and surprising feelings and symptoms became more focused and intense, suspicions became harder and harder to deny. For **Alana**, the upsetting thoughts focused on her father:

> I increasingly avoided visiting my widowed father in the next state. He was charming but terribly self-centered, and I felt nauseated whenever he expected a hug or kiss. It was almost unbearable when he called me by my mother's name, expected me to wait on him as she had, and had me sleep in "her room." It seemed to me that her bed still smelled of her. I felt guilty that I could not be a more dutiful and loving daughter to my dad. Summing up my frustration to my husband, I complained, "He treats me like Mother and makes me sleep in her bed." Two years later, I realized the significance of my words.

Other amnesics, after remembering, also found ample evidence that there had been some level of knowing underneath their amnesia.

PRELIMINARY THERAPY

The amnesic women were more likely than nonamnesics to have had some therapeutic experience at some time during the years before they began to deal with their past (32% vs. 14%). Not yet knowing about their abuse history, they had usually addressed symptoms such as strained relationships, depression, or dependency on alcohol (40% vs. 24%) or on food (67% vs. 62%). For a number of the survivors, their substance of choice had been a powerful agent in keeping memories contained. Using it brought speedy relief; their painful feelings were numbed, and their memories were muted. However, use of these substances carried penalties as well. Eventually, many of the addicted women sought help from organizations such as Alcoholics Anonymous or Weight Watchers. These programs emphasize positive coping mechanisms, being responsible for oneself, and getting in touch with one's feelings. Those who enrolled began to feel more self-directed and hopeful as their emotional numbness, undergirded by substance abuse, lessened. With the power of their addiction reduced, these women were able to examine their lives more honestly than ever before.

As the survivors moved closer to awareness, more of them sought therapy or entered self-help groups. Because most of them first sought help in the 1960s or 1970s, prior to widening social and professional knowledge of the impact of childhood sexual trauma, their therapists generally did not understand the turmoil that lay below the presenting symptoms of the amnesic women. Also, if nonamnesics awkwardly mentioned having had childhood sexual contact with adults, some therapists dismissed that topic as "not the real problem." Generally, the women had other obvious problems needing attention, and therapy that built a trusting and supportive relationship proved especially effective. Many of the women gained in strength and self-knowledge through this early counseling and came away (as others did from self-help groups) with a greater repertoire of effective coping mechanisms as well. Moreover, the survivors who engaged in therapy were addressing a major deficit in their childhood by finding caring listeners who validated their perceptions and believed in them as people. Seeing themselves in a more positive light, gaining stronger egos, and finding supportive people gave them strengths that would be sorely tested later.

When their breakthrough came, women who had learned the benefits of counseling earlier were more likely to seek therapy again. Others sought it when they felt overwhelmed by personal or interpersonal problems. **Annie** had been desolate after her husband had an affair, which tapped into her vague childhood feelings of being sacrificed to others. His contrition brought them back together, but her agitation grew. She started raking her fingernails across her abdomen after lovemaking.

Soon, she became obsessed with plunging a knife into her belly. It made sense to her—she could let the pain out. Eventually, she was committed for evaluation at the county mental hospital. There a callous psychiatrist placed her in a holding cell with two psychotic men, one of whom proceeded to explore her body. For 2 nightmarish hours, a good friend stood with her hand against the window glass, until she could get Annie released. That friend helped her find a therapist and join a church self-help group for troubled women. Annie was in that supportive context when her memories broke through.

A similar crisis developed for **Alicia**. Feeling deeply troubled, she told her husband that she thought she needed counseling. His response was that she "wasn't that disturbed." A week later, he came home from work to find their toddler wandering around the house alone and his wife curled up in terror behind their bedroom bureau. When she saw her husband, she cried out, "Daddy, don't let him get me." Months later, she was able to joke about that day: "Tom decided that counseling wasn't such a bad idea after all." Gradually, women like these—who came to therapy with serious presenting problems—were able to pursue their memories of the past in the presence of a counselor they could trust.

Nonamnesics, more often than amnesics, entered therapy because they felt overwhelmed by life (33% vs. 12%; see Table 8.1). Psychic damage accumulated in their lives until it reached crisis proportions. Over the years, many of them had made a shaky truce with the past and didn't want to risk reexamining issues that had been set aside. Eventually, however, the balance shifted, and it became too dangerous to ignore the past. **Nellie**, who was already overweight and chronically fatigued, experienced several major losses in close succession. Her mother died, she lost the job that had given her a feeling of worth, and she underwent a hysterectomy. At this point, her depression and obsessive thoughts about past abuse necessitated therapy. **Norma** became extremely agitated as her niece approached the age at which her brother (the child's father) had molested her. Molestation memories—too intense to push aside any longer—demanded her attention.

Another nonamnesic, **Nelda**, who also had always tried to ignore her past, finally felt so overwhelmed that she quit her job. "For many months," she said, "I had put myself in gear each morning and zombied through the day, feeling nothing. At night, I took myself out of gear. When

Table 8.1 Triggers for Returning Memories and Help-Seeking, by Group (%)

Trigger	**Amnesic**	Partial Amnesic	**Nonamnesic**	Imprisoned	Total
General context					
Feeling safe	44	36	24	75	42
Feeling overwhelmed	12	0	33	17	17
Specific triggers					
Hearing about someone else's abuse	44	50	43	42	44
Body contact (surgery/massage/sex)	32	57	24	33	35
Contact with similar person/setting	28	36	24	25	28
Dreams/nightmares	20	29	19	42	25

NOTE: Unqualified "yes" responses only (occasional missing data).

I finally had no more energy to keep this up, I knew I must deal with the abuse." **NANCY**'s story of her life-crisis was particularly poignant:

> Paul came home from work early that day because he was really worried about me. He found me standing dazed in our bedroom and insisted on knowing what I had in my hand. I showed him the pills that would have ended my life. Paul was desperate. "*What* is so *terrible* that you can never tell me?" I was planning to kill myself anyway, so I told him about the horrible years with my father. Dad had warned me that if I ever told my husband, he would leave me and take our children away from me. Instead, Paul took me in his arms and said, "Now that I know, you and I can work this through together."

FACTORS THAT AIDED REMEMBERING

In the 1980s, more than in any past era of history, society was ready to recognize childhood sexual abuse and to extend a helping hand to its survivors, whether they had always remembered their abuse or were only recently beginning to do so. Increasingly, women who could no longer maintain the delicate balance in their lives moved toward therapy. The counseling setting provided them with security and support. This was especially important because these women had felt unsafe ever since early childhood. Amnesics who were coming out of amnesia, and nonamnesics who could no longer ignore the impact of past events, were learning that it was not only safe but essential for them to deal with the past.

Personal security was another important factor prior to the breakthrough of denial. Many survivors had reached a fairly safe time in their own personal life and were ready to confront what had happened so long ago. As shown in Table 8.1, the women's unqualified "yes" answers indicated that this was a more important factor for amnesics and partially amnesic women than for nonamnesics (44% vs. 36% vs. 24%, respectively).[1] When their "somewhat" responses were included, the importance of personal safety to the amnesic women was emphasized dramatically (68% vs. 36% vs. 24%). Indeed, half of the amnesic women believed that the "need to feel safe in the world" had been one explanation for their forgetting in the first place. Their later security had been hard-won. They had tried over time to create a stable and safe environment in which to live, but they had no understanding of the motivation underlying this driving need.

For most survivors, the process leading up to facing their past was quite gradual because they were generally fearful of risk. By the time they began to deal directly with their past, many were in a relatively secure position, with more self-understanding, more occupational and financial stability, and more emotional support than at any previous time in their lives. About 20% of the women had already experienced at least one supportive therapeutic setting, which they had entered for the various reasons discussed earlier. Many had proved themselves vocationally as diligent, dependable workers and, despite their low self-esteem, had won respect for their competence. Some felt loved and secure for the first time in their lives. About one third of the respondents had made a reasonably healthy choice of an intimate partner, often after leaving earlier abusive relationships. Others, following early struggles with loneliness, had become more adept at making and keeping good friends. For still others, the feeling that they were valued and loved had come through religious conversion or spiritual experiences. Despite all of these positives, however, the survivors still struggled with daily living.

Separation, either from threat or for introspection, was another factor that created a safer setting for dealing with the past. Geographical and emotional distance had separated some women from the families that had raised them. They then had a chance to test their own values and their ways of looking at life. For several women, the death of an abuser contributed to the sense of safety. **Penny** and **Alison** recovered their memories at such a time. **Nyla** felt suddenly released when her uncle died and, for the first time, told her husband of the burden she had carried from childhood. Two other women, who had finally decided to deal with their memories, followed their therapist's recommendation to enter a mental health facility, which gave them a brief and much-needed retreat from everyday pressures.

Of special interest, 75% of the imprisoned group felt that their incarceration had provided a "safe time" to examine the anger, grief, and fears left over from their child sexual abuse. Shut away from other responsibilities, and highly fortunate to have been included in a therapy group, they could let out all their feelings. **ILENE** was one of those who benefited. Earlier, while out on bail during the period before her trial, she had met the man who married her just before her sentencing. After her incarceration, he encouraged her to join the group, and she felt that it could help not only herself but their relationship. Other imprisoned women who expected to be released were also motivated to examine their lives before returning to the outside world.

The passage of personal time since their childhood was on the side of all survivors. Examining the past as mature adults, and recognizing that sexual abuse is never a child's fault, they could relinquish the self-blame that had weighed on them as children. The contrast between then and now was especially dramatic for the amnesic women. The last time they had consciously focused on their abuse, their tools had been the thoughts and emotions and behaviors of a child. As adults, they were better equipped to face the memories, could use more effective means of coping with stress, and could expect more support from others. Counseling became an important resource for all these women. Some faced their past trauma only after they had come to trust a counselor who had worked with them first on other presenting problems. Most, however, sought therapy because the ordeal of returning memories mandated it.

Pressure from another was occasionally involved. A concerned friend or partner pushed some survivors into getting help. **Portia**'s husband knew that she was bothered by "something" that she would not talk about, and he confronted her during a marriage counseling session. Another woman received caring advice at a workshop: "Stop worrying about others and pay attention to yourself." It was a totally new idea to her, but she took the advice and stopped her busyness long enough to listen to what was going on inside her.

AN EXAMPLE—APPROACHING BREAKTHROUGH

ANNE's story illustrates many of the principles presented above. She had repressed all memory of her trauma and had been making the world safer for herself for some time before her memories began. At age 28, she had established herself, independent of her family, 1,200 miles from home. She was studying to be a social worker and, in the process, was getting to know herself at deeper levels than previously, improving her level of competence and her capacity for friendship. She was also looking more objectively at herself and the family that had raised her, and she found it puzzling that she remembered so little of her childhood.

ANNE had been raised in an "ideal family," or so it had seemed to people in the community where she grew up—and to her as well. She had thought herself privileged. Her father had a successful medical practice, her mother kept busy with community work, and the family was active in the church. The image was impeccable, even to the brightly colored petunias that danced in the window boxes of their large and gracious home. Why, as a child, had she dreamed repeatedly of hiding something hideous under those blossoms? Why, at 9 years of age, had she ransacked the house, looking for bullets for the family gun so that she might kill herself? Why, as an adult, did she struggle with the feeling that she must be "crazy"?

Working with sexually abused children in the course of her counseling internship, ANNE began to remember more about her childhood. This opening up was accompanied by terrifying nightmares of earthquakes, fire, and atomic bombs. But she also dreamed of receiving a gift. She was about to open Pandora's box:

> It was a beautiful white gift box, tied with pink satin ribbon (my favorite color as a child). A bow was carefully looped on top. But I could not lift the lid because wide brown mailing tape—many layers thick—joined it to the box. Suddenly, the brown tape disappeared, leaving only the ribbon in place. An ominous vapor was escaping, curling out from under the edges of the lid.

ANNE's world, as she had perceived it, was about to explode, and the experience would be life-changing. A high degree of security had been essential before she could recognize that she had been out of touch with her own reality since babyhood.

BREAKING THROUGH DENIAL

> *You really have to want to know.*
> **—Alicia**

Feelings of personal security alone were not enough to break through the survivors' amnesia. The situation might be ready to explode, but the fuse must still be lit. What was it then that ruptured denial for women who had, for decades, lived by ignoring clues to the truth?

The first questionnaire sent to the participants in this study asked them what had triggered recall of their abuse (or triggered the decision to deal with never-forgotten abuse). They usually checked multiple answers (see Table 8.1), suggesting that several factors—together or in sequence—had brought their memories to the fore.

I will now examine the main findings in Table 8.1 and then discuss various triggers to memory in more detail. Information about someone else's abuse was a factor in triggering recognition of their own abuse for close to half of the respondents (44%). For over one quarter (28%), a precipitating factor was a situation reminiscent of their trauma or the presence of someone who reminded them of their abuser. For about one third, memories were first stimulated through physical contact—this included surgery or giving birth, body massage, and sexual contact. About one quarter were helped to recover memories through dreams. (Hypnosis, flashbacks, and artwork also tapped into unconscious memories for some of the survivors.) Clearly, there was more than one trigger for many of the women. Any of a wide variety of experiences in the present could help to initiate recovery of memories of abuse. This diversity is evident in the situations described below.

There were only minor differences in the specific triggers reported by the two main groups of survivors. Amnesics checked somewhat more items than did nonamnesics. (The remembering process was more laborious and traumatic for them than for women who had always known what had happened.) However, these two groups were very similar in their reports of all five specific triggers shown in Table 8.1. Women in the partially amnesic group were a bit more likely to mention a similar person or setting as a trigger to recall, and they were considerably higher in mentioning body contact as a factor. The imprisoned group members were higher than the other groups in mentioning dreams or nightmares as triggers. In addition, the prison setting and its occupants were frequently reminders of their past abuse.

Among the overlapping answers to the question about triggers, some were shared by most of the women, and others were highly individual. For most survivors, the first explosion of life-changing recollection was usually set off by some stimulus similar enough to the original trauma situation to elicit unhappy memories. Laboratory studies of learning and recall have demonstrated that recall is greatly improved if the original context is evoked (e.g., Bower, 1981). Although repressed traumatic experiences differ from deliberately learned material, reports from my respondents suggest that their first fragmentary recall of abuse was likely to occur in a context that included elements similar to those of their childhood trauma. In other words, there was an important match between the original abuse situation and the situation in which memories (whether repressed, denied, or distorted) broke through or were at last redefined. In fully 89% of their reports, something in the present reminded the women of the original abuse situation.

Factors that had been hints prior to breakthrough now became compelling pieces of evidence, when triggers—one, or several in sequence—awakened old traumas. For example, a television dramatization of abuse, a dream, and a sexual experience might combine to break down a woman's denial. The stimuli came from varied sources—the women's personal or work situation; media reports on abuse; persons, settings, or contacts that reminded them of their own childhood abuse; and emotional or bodily experiences. I examine each major trigger in turn.

Hearing About the Abuse of Others

In the 1980s, there was a great increase in mass media reports about molestation, about sexual abuse in educational and recreational settings, and about incest. The media were especially instrumental in publicizing information concerning child sexual abuse because they latch onto any human interest topic that captures public imagination. They feature it in the news, on special programs, and on talk shows. In addition, educators lecture about new topics of interest, and researchers study and report on the phenomenon. Public knowledge and concern escalate together. This is what happened with the topic of child sexual abuse. Information, crime statistics, personal stories, class discussions, expert testimony, and courtroom dramas about child sexual abuse catapulted the topic into public scrutiny.

A number of my interviewees reported that hearing descriptions of abuse or of its symptoms and ramifications, on television or in a classroom, began to bring their own trauma into awareness. A television documentary, for example, created a multiple impact—cognitive, emotional, visual, and auditory—that helped some women make a personal connection to the material presented. Several described their stunned reaction with the words "It seemed they were telling my story." For amnesics, sexual trauma was no longer merely hinted at. Many of them had a sense of horrified recognition. For nonamnesics, their intellectual views and emotions on this topic meshed for perhaps the first time, and the connection between what had happened to them and their problems with daily living became compelling.

Several women found themselves sobbing uncontrollably at a real or dramatized description of sexual abuse. The movies *Sybil* and *Nuts* haunted other survivors just prior to their recall and were almost unbearably painful. Sometimes, it was a newspaper story about child sexual abuse, or descriptions in a book, that unlocked the past. A publisher's representative at a convention told me of a woman delegate who, leafing through exhibit books about abuse, had suddenly turned pale and gasped, "I remember." Sometimes—in the more open discussion of the topic among friends, sisters, and other relatives—the knowledge of someone else's abuse evoked a respondent's own trauma. **Adele**'s reaction was almost fatal: "My sister told me about her abuse before I was ready to deal with the remembering. I started going downhill so fast that I was barely alive. Already tiny, I became anorexic."

Sometimes, siblings worked together to assemble the past. **Ashley**'s therapist had encouraged her to draw scenes of her childhood. When pictures of huge parents and strange happenings began to emerge, Ashley "knew" without remembering that she had experienced parental incest. She recalled that her brother used to sleep with a knife under his pillow, and she telephoned him. At first, he discounted her intuition, but her call quickly triggered a breakthrough for him also. Together they pieced together the story of a tormented childhood, in which both parents had been abusive, as had an uncle.

However, learning about a survivor's abuse did not usually trigger the memories of her siblings, no matter how strong the emotional impact. Another person's memory—even a sibling's—is not the same as one's own. In addition, there was usually little motivation to share such a troubled legacy. (Chapter 11 describes in more detail the typical denial by siblings not only of their own abuse but of the respondent's as well.) One of my students informed me, "Mother told me that Dad had sex regularly with my sister when she was a child, and I felt as if the breath was knocked out of me." This student has strong suspicions about her own early sexual experiences but has chosen to avoid the anguish of exploring them. Similarly, **April**'s siblings say they have no memory of their own sexual abuse, which her father admitted to her.

A Similar Person, Situation, or Contact

Victims helping victims. Many of my respondents were employed in helping professions, such as counseling, teaching, or nursing. Several had been drawn to working with victims of various kinds of abuse even before remembering their own trauma. These cases were examples of children who had never been rescued but grew up trying to save others. In the process, they had moved closer to dealing with their own issues. For some of them, listening to the story of incest from the lips of a particular patient or pupil evoked highly personal emotions. **Ava**, a social worker, reported that she became intensely anxious, wanting to get away from her client's voice and her words. **Annette**, helping a pupil take her uncle to trial, was appalled when the lawyer working *for* her pupil remarked, "But I really believe that, within the family, the child is equally culpable." **Peggy** reported that, in the process of cofacilitating a group of sex offenders, she redefined her own remembered experience as abuse. **Abbie** and her husband were having problems with a foster child who had been removed from a sexually abusive home. While they were attending a seminar on abuse, Abbie found herself startled by the speaker's description of the doll-play of abused children. It fit herself as a child perfectly, and she brought this fact up with the therapist she was seeing for depression. In another case, **Nan** and two friends—sharing personal accounts of remembered abuse—were all precipitated into therapy "as if by a chain reaction."

Learning of a similar event. Several amnesics broke through their amnesia shortly after learning about the sexual trauma of someone close to them. **April** told me, "Last summer my niece was raped at gunpoint, and I was overwhelmed by my emotions. I didn't know what I was feeling or why. In trying to get help, I found an incest group." For **Arna**, the abduction, rape, and murder of a child near the hometown where she herself had been almost killed years earlier had a similar impact. **Angela**'s memory was triggered when she found out about her own daughter's abuse. As she simultaneously faced what her husband had done to her daughter and what her grandfather had done to her, she was overwhelmed with confusion, betrayal, and pain. Several amnesics, having blocked awareness of their own sexual abuse, were unaware that the same aggressor (or another one) was repeating the pattern in the next generation. Typically, their child's abuse came to their attention only after they had remembered their own, and they were able to offer strong support to the child. **Nadine**, taking her abused daughter to therapy, finally admitted that she needed help with her own never-forgotten abuse. Listening to her child, she experienced shock, disbelief, deep sadness, and a great deal of pain—as if it were happening all over again.

Occasionally, the mere possibility of a similar event occurring for a daughter caused such extreme agitation and overprotectiveness that a survivor was propelled into therapy. **Nina**, for example, became especially anxious when her child reached the age of her own abuse. "My daughter was *me* at that age." Both amnesics and nonamnesics were vulnerable to this kind of overidentification with their daughters. This blurring of boundaries had precipitated child battering for two amnesics, whose self-hate was projected onto their small children. **Alexis** was beating her 2-year old when her sister shouted, "Stop! You're just like Mama!" **Audrey** came terrifyingly close to killing her child, but she gained enough control to order her daughter to lock herself in the bathroom while she called the police. Subsequently hospitalized, Audrey learned that dissociated personalities within her had originated in her hideous childhood. For both of these mothers, their own violence against a child impelled them to remember their own childhood abuse.

Experiencing a similar event. Examples of victimizing events that stirred recollections of the original abuse included date-rape, burglary of the survivor's home, the poisoning of a family pet, and the actions of an abusive "friend" or coworker. These events evoked powerful feelings of violation, disillusionment, anger, or despair in several respondents. Two survivors experienced severe throat or vaginal pain because these situations tapped into a deep well of unresolved emotion. The result was feelings that seemed even more extreme than the situation warranted and were a surprise to both the woman and those who know her. However, it is important to realize that these emotions *were* appropriate to the original trauma, which sometimes began to be remembered at such times.

A similar time, setting, or activity. Therapists are well aware that holidays can be low points for their clients—evoking nostalgia for happier times or reminders of unmet needs. Betrayal that is associated with "happy" events seems especially devastating. Two formerly amnesic women whom I have talked with had memories of parents molesting them during holiday periods. As an adult, **Alison** had been avoiding her mother but expected to see her again at a Christmas gathering:

> Anxious and irritable, I was idly blow-drying my hair when I saw—as if on videotape—my own molestation. I suddenly tuned in toward the end of it: "Wait a minute. Back up. I'd better rerun that!"

Body Interventions

Incest, rape, and other forms of sexual abuse write themselves so physically on the human body that often it is the body that portrays the unconscious during the years of forgetting. (In Chapter 7, I described the multiple physical ills that can express childhood sexual trauma during the years of repression.) Frequently, too, it is the body that helps to bring forth memories later. Bodily interventions such as therapeutic massage, giving birth, and surgery of the reproductive organs are potent triggers to memory. Such interventions share the characteristics of many sexual abuse situations. Beds, sheets, blankets, vulnerability, the prone position, the dissociation involved in anesthesia, someone touching one's body or moving its parts—all these are similar elements that can evoke memories of abuse. **PAULA** began to have uncontrollable flashbacks after she was disabled by a hysterectomy. "I felt almost out of my body, seeing what and who my uncle was. He visited me when I was fresh into memories, and really scared me—extreme, 'under the bed' panic."

Therapeutic massage involves so much touching, and such varied degrees of pressure, that it is almost inevitable that it will evoke memory or recognition of some past bodily experiences. Examples include physical injuries, events involving some part of one's body, and abuse experiences. These recollections may range from minimal to overwhelming. Deeper memories and emotions are much more likely in cases where there has been a lengthy and trusting relationship between the client and the body worker.

The experience of body workers indicates that bodily trauma is often written into specific areas of the body where it occurred—"held, locked in, or stuffed" there, in the common jargon of the therapeutic massage field. Examples include a return of pain at the site of an old injury; tension in the throat, jaw, or crotch; or pain in the throat from holding back emotions. Sensitive therapists may also note a client's difficulty in breathing deeply or her inability to cry, which may indicate past occasions of smothering or even strangulation. For victims of child abuse, silence was almost always enforced during the abuse, and the tears, sobs, and screams that were denied then seem to have remained within the body. Massage can allow these powerful emotions to emerge at last. When they come out in body work decades later, the cries of a desolate or terrified child can burst eerily from the body of a full-grown woman.

Here are two examples of abuse experiences that were apparently locked into the body of my respondents. **Abigail** reported that pressure on a certain spot behind her left knee had made her jackknife on the massage table as if from a blow to the solar plexus. For 15 minutes, she thrashed about violently, as if she were fighting for her life. Her graphic movements seemed to suggest the presence of an invisible rapist. The "attack" ended with Abigail retching over the edge of the table and sobbing like a small child. Similarly, therapeutic massage evoked a particular aspect of **Anita**'s trauma. When the therapist ran his hands firmly down her arms to the wrist, she reexperienced being similarly restrained during a gang rape by her brother and his friends when she was 9: "Everything just exploded in my head—pictures, the pain, shouting for my father, the taste of blood in my mouth." It is important to note that both of these women had been in body work with a trusted massage therapist for many months before their startling breakthroughs.

Sexuality, whose later patterns can be profoundly affected by child sexual abuse, is another avenue for remembering. The sexual context provides both a similar setting and a similar activity to trigger memories. A body contact that had previously evoked no disturbance was the catalyst that suddenly broke through **Addie**'s amnesia: "My husband had often wrapped himself around me at night, but this time, I remembered the weight of my father. I jumped out of bed, screaming." For **Amy**, some slight variation in the playful "Tarzan chase" quoted at the beginning of this chapter was the trigger that released her memories of sexual abuse by her stepfather.

Surgical and birth procedures also provide settings reminiscent of abuse, and anesthetic drugs produce altered states of consciousness. In addition, surgery mandates rest, which prevents the use of busyness to ward off memories. Childbirth—the emergence of a new life—reminded some survivors about their own infancy and childhood events or raised fears about their adequacy as parents. The birth of **Andrea**'s baby set off a series of graphic nightmares. A hysterectomy was the stimulus for memories that put **Allie** in the psychiatric wing of the hospital for a while. **Phyllis** barely avoided exploratory surgery to determine the cause of a mysterious pain in her groin. The night before the operation was to be performed, she remembered incest.

Altered states, such as dreams, hypnosis, and regression (in addition to anesthesia) are reminders of dissociation experiences during molestation. **Priscilla** experienced three successive short dreams: First, she saw simply a headboard on a bed. Second, a man was sitting against the headboard. Third, he was beckoning a small and frightened child, with his smile disclosing a silvery front tooth. The dreams made her uneasy. Weeks later, a relative gave Priscilla "an old snap of you with your father," showing that at that time her father had had just such a silvery tooth. Dismayed, she recognized the man and child of her dreams, and her denial was broken.

For my respondents, hypnosis, if used at all in the recovery of memories, typically did not bring the first recall. It was sometimes needed, like forceps, to ease the difficult birthing of traumatic memories, or later in therapy when serious blocking was interfering with a woman's progress. Sometimes, it elicited nothing new, but in **Polly**'s case, it brought back a startling memory. Apparently, her stepfather had her hypnotized, at 5 years of age, to give her a posthypnotic suggestion to forget the fact that he had raped her. Hypnosis, in adulthood, proved an ironically apt therapeutic tool in this case.

Perhaps the most convincing breakthrough of denial comes in spontaneous regression. It is a stunning experience to hear the words or sobbing of a preschooler coming from one's own lips, or to find that one's handwriting has become that of a second grader, as in the case of **Carla**. She was a counselor who appreciated the importance of "listening to one's self":

> I had been working late. As I turned the key to my car door, I felt a strong compulsion to go back to my office and write "something" —I didn't know what. I returned to my desk and picked up a notebook. Slowly, haltingly, childish printing took shape, forming my uncle's name over and over. Then, as time slowly passed, I found myself filling the book with horror.

Regression provides the ultimate "similar context," allowing powerful elements and emotions from a past trauma to be replayed in the present. It is also an important component in the flashbacks that are described in Chapter 9.

Therapy as a trigger? About one third of the amnesics had—in the years prior to remembering their abuse—tried therapy as one way of coping with the many symptoms that troubled them. Therapy at that time had triggered no memories. In the 6 months *after* the breakthrough of memories, counseling helped 54% of them to remember and face forgotten abuse in a safe setting, and additional survivors profited from counseling subsequently. Most (72% of the amnesic women) had apparently started to remember their abuse through other triggers and then went into counseling. A few had been in therapy for months or years before uncovering sexual abuse. Only one woman checked counseling as her only trigger to remembering. Her memories started, and multiple personalities were revealed, in a hospital therapy group in which she was placed after she had almost killed her daughter. None of the participants in my research reported the kind of "implanting" of memories that has been alleged by recent criticisms of the validity of recovered memories. In fact, even a therapist's mild labeling of memories more often tended to create denial rather than belief.

Among the nonamnesic women, who had never forgotten their abuse, a few (14%) had tried therapy at one time or another. Usually, in their sessions they had not revealed their remembered abuse or, if they did so, the therapist had minimized it. Their breakthroughs came later, when 65% of them sought help in the first 6 months of trying to deal with their past abuse. The predominant factor in their starting to deal with their past seemed to be not that it was safe for them to remember, but that the memories and other results of their abuse were creating too many problems in their lives.

NEXT STAGES

Once reality had broken through for the respondents, similar triggers—evoking the past through emotions, thoughts, and sensory experiences—further opened up the awareness of amnesics and nonamnesics alike. Clues that were previously unnoticed came gradually into central awareness. The breakthrough of their denial and their subsequent review of the past were unsettling experiences for survivors who had always remembered their abuse but who had denied its power in their lives. Breakthrough was still more cataclysmic for women who had been entirely amnesic during their past lives, and the truth returned only slowly over months or even years. Flashbacks, which were experienced more or less frequently by practically all of the amnesics and most of the other women, brought to the respondents a deepening awareness of the travesty of their childhood. The next chapter examines flashbacks as a major avenue to remembering in the women's continued processing of their trauma.

NOTE

1. A similar table in Cameron (1996) inadvertently used *yes* plus *somewhat* responses for some of the comparisons.

PART IV

Remembering
and Healing

My dream is sepia-colored, like old photographs. Daylight fades slowly as an ancient sailing ship that will take me to a new country is readied for voyage. Family and friends huddle round me on the dock, voices subdued, reluctant to let me go. They cannot come with me to the land that stretches faintly on the farthest horizon. Other persons, whom I do not yet know, must guide the ship through dangerous waters to our destination. Now, as the ship moves away from the dock, I stand at the stern, watching familiar faces grow smaller and smaller. Will we ever be together again? Finally, I turn away, and move toward the prow of the vessel. The wind blows my hair back from my face as I peer into the deepening darkness. I do not know what lies before me. I only know that it is right for me to go.

—Alison, 1986

A s survivors began their journeys back into the dark regions of childhood memory, they sensed that their lives would never be the same again. They themselves would be changed in the process and so would all their relationships. It would be a challenging trip and a strange one. To move forward in their lives, they must first go back.

CHAPTER 9

Flashbacks and the Crisis of Recall

With flashbacks, I have the feeling of actually being back there in body, mind, and soul. It seems like the abuse is happening all over again.

—**Anne**, 1989

The chapters in Part II and Part III focused on the experience of childhood sexual abuse and the personal impact of recognizing its occurrence in one's own life. Now, I examine flashbacks, a major means by which survivors learned about and better understood their past.

The material in this chapter is closely related to the section of Chapter 6 on posttraumatic stress disorder (PTSD). PTSD is a cyclical condition. Its alternative symptoms of numbing versus reexperiencing and arousal are like a coin that can expose two different sides. This chapter examines the opposite side of PTSD from that described in Chapter 7. During the long, silent years between childhood abuse and its confrontation in adulthood, the numbing/avoiding/denial phase of PTSD was ascendant. But when the memories were confronted, voluntarily or involuntarily, the reexperiencing/arousal phase of PTSD was dominant. Previously, the PTSD symptoms were protecting the survivors from remembering their abuse, but with the advent of flashbacks, they were helping them to remember.

THE NATURE OF FLASHBACKS

Naming the Symptom

The word *flashback* was first used in connection with Vietnam veterans who, as a psychological aftermath of battle, suffered from PTSD. Flashbacks are experiences of reliving a past traumatic event as if it is occurring now—usually with vivid imagery and extreme emotions. Flashbacks can be stimulated by a current smell (e.g., gas), sight (an accident victim), sound (a gunshot), taste (canned meat), or touch (a hand on one's shoulder). For Vietnam veterans, this reexperiencing often occurred long after the war (see Chapter 6).

At first, it was popularly thought that flashbacks were nightmares, or sudden thoughts of war, and limited to soldiers—just as, more recently, many people thought that severe amnesia was limited to the sexually abused. However, further study showed that flashbacks constitute a sudden reexperiencing of *any* past trauma. Gradually, the word became common in newspaper and journal articles describing similar reactions (either immediate or delayed) to personal or group trauma as well as battle—being raped, witnessing a murder, or living through a community disaster such as an earthquake or tornado.

The abused women participating in my study were also veterans who had been caught up as children in a trauma beyond their understanding, and they were still affected by it decades later (Cameron, 1994a). Because the experience of Vietnam veterans had taught our nation about delayed reactions to trauma, these women were beneficiaries of a more sympathetic public attitude.

Flashbacks were common to my respondents in the weeks and months following the breakthrough of amnesia. In the case of these survivors, the term flashback means the reexperiencing in adulthood of a traumatic sexual event from childhood. The original event may have been singular (a rape, for example) or frequently repeated (e.g., incest) in the early life of the person having the flashback. It may be experienced visually, bodily, or—to a lesser degree—with sounds, smells, or tastes and it generally is accompanied by strong emotional reactions.

Flashbacks have sometimes been called hallucinations because they can be viewed as "sensory perceptions not associated with real external stimuli" (Kaplan & Sadock, 1988, p. 173). This usage leads to confusion because the sensory flashbacks of trauma survivors *are* associated with real external stimuli—not in the present, but in the *past*. The term *halluci-nation* is further problematic because, although hallucinations are not indicative of psychotic disturbance unless reasoning is also impaired, the public views hallucinations as highly negative, abnormal events. For survivors of trauma, flashbacks do not imply pathology but, rather, a normal response to extreme stress. Because the term *hallucinations* is misleading, the neutral term *flashback* is generally applied to survivors of any kind of trauma.

For the adult survivor of trauma, flashbacks are a dissociative, or altered state of consciousness—one that involves separating from the present and regressing to sensory, emotional, or cognitive experiences of the past. As such, flashbacks provide a context for recalling previously denied memories laid down during similar dissociative states years before. This process can be viewed as an example of state-dependent learning and recall (see Bower, 1981, for research findings about state-dependent learning).

The flashbacks of the women in my study were recurring phenomena, especially common after amnesia was breached. Typically, the flashbacks were involuntary. They could not be willed to come or go. A particular flashback might repeat day after day, starting out rather mildly and growing in severity over its occurrences until the survivor recognized the reality of some particular episode of abuse. As an example, this might mean repeatedly suffering from the force of a perpetrator's blows or penetration and experiencing increasingly severe variations of the attack until the abuser's actions and the survivor's feelings were more fully recalled. This quotation describes **Adelle**'s experience:

> Flashbacks didn't give me all the bad news at first—how strong the cramps were, how sharp the intrusions. Each time a body experience repeated, the scenario worsened. I'd try to stave it off by concentrating on the sights and sounds of television. But I couldn't stand sports, war pictures, the news, or nature programs where animals attacked each other. Instead, I rented films for children. I'd stay up till I was utterly exhausted, hoping to fall asleep before the flashbacks came on. But that seldom worked.

Some survivors had been aware of sensory flashbacks—especially visual ones—years before they knew what they were or what they meant. These experiences were frightening intrusions and increased their concern that something was wrong with them or that they were "crazy." Frightened, they usually had not shared these experiences with others, not even with a therapist. Their caution was fortunate because, until recently, such perceptual disturbances were usually thought to be evidence of psychosis. Indeed, several of the women had been labeled psychotic prior to breaking through their amnesia. As Ellenson (1985) has pointed out, in discussing survivors of sexual abuse, "The fear of being crazy was unwarranted. The fear of (false) confirmation of the fear *was* warranted" (p. 155). Even today, uninformed mental health professionals may not recognize the significant differences between symptoms displayed by trauma survivors and schizophrenics. For example, schizophrenics are more likely to have auditory than visual hallucinations, and tactile and olfactory experiences are unusual for them (Kaplan & Sadock, 1988, p. 260).

The Variability of Flashbacks

The flashbacks that survivors experienced were quite variable. They could be brief or lengthy, superficial or deep, sudden or slow to arrive, simple or complex in their content, involving only one of the senses or several. They could be brought on by emotions, physical pain, or situations reminiscent of childhood ones. Different survivors reported different typical patterns, but most women experienced various kinds of flashbacks over the course of their remembering.

First, flashbacks differed among themselves in the time involved. There were mini-flashbacks, which lasted for seconds—a tiny blip on the screen of memory—and lengthy ones that went on for an hour or more. A few women experienced a dissociated state for several days, feeling barely connected to the here and now. The presentation of time *within* flashbacks varied also. A memory might return in "real time," or much speeded up and condensed, or in slow motion.

The complexity of flashbacks varied also (and not always in correspondence with the time elapsed). Some flashbacks were superficial experiences, barely tapping into the past—much like a dream. But, often, the women experienced two worlds during flashbacks—reliving past feelings and events while being aware of the present time and place. Occasionally, a flashback was so compelling and totally involving that a participant briefly lost touch with present reality. **Alexis** reported, "I felt I was being held by some terrible force." After a particularly horrifying memory, and fearful of losing herself in the past, she managed to phone a friend. **April** went further out of touch. Deeply dissociated, she briefly lost awareness that she was safe in the presence of her trusted therapist and "fled from her stepfather" out the office door.

Not surprisingly, in view of such reactions, therapists encouraged certain clients to experience serious flashbacks in a supportive context whenever possible. For a few women, a hospital stay provided a sanctuary where a terrifying event could be more safely revisited. Therapists of these survivors may have facilitated the reliving process, but they did not "bring on" their clients' flashbacks. (Only **Pat**'s therapist used sodium ambutal, for instance.) The presence of a counselor provided a safer-than-usual context for allowing memories to surface. An upcoming therapy appointment might be enough to keep a frightening memory from surfacing earlier.

Flashbacks differed in intensity, too, and this aspect generally changed with time. At first, they typically provided some recognition that abuse had occurred but included little or nothing of the child's reaction to the abuse. Later, flashbacks tended to become increasingly multifaceted, providing a fuller picture of the child's sensory, emotional, and intellectual response to what had happened at different ages during extended abuse. Some flashbacks also grew in intensity, increasingly revealing more severe forms of abuse. **Pearl,** for example, reported, "They get worse and worse, but I'm better at handling it."

Flashbacks varied in the content that was (sooner or later) revealed. Of course, the content depended, first and foremost, on the form of abuse remembered—handling, oral contact, or forcible rape, for example. Moreover, a single incident generally was presented with more specific details than were repeated incestuous contacts. Recurrent incidents of parental abuse tended to run together as a kind of generic memory. However, particular watersheds in incest—such as the first entry, first use of force, or the child's sudden recognition that she was trapped in an exploitive situation—usually produced more specific sensory and emotional details illuminating these "moments of truth." The contents of such a memory might escalate over several weeks in repetitions of a particular flashback until, after a final denouement of its most upsetting aspect, that particular flashback ceased. For example, one of **Ashley's** flashback series dealt with recurring motions of flinging her head from side to side as if avoiding oral contact, and this series led up to an especially repulsive event—ejaculation by her abuser that sprayed her face and hair.

Despite the distressing nature of their flashbacks, most of the respondents felt determined to pursue information about their past abuse as a matter of psychic survival. The nature and variability of their flashbacks will become increasingly evident as this chapter progresses and the differences among the women are explored.

Characteristics of Flashbacks

Infants experience the world through emotional and sensory impressions long before their cognitive abilities have fully developed, and as they grow older, they continue to process experience through their senses and emotions. Because the women were mostly quite young when first abused, it is understandable that their flashbacks reflected this strongly. Sexual abuse assaults all of the senses, and the upset and fear experienced by the victims in childhood came through in their flashbacks. The child saw body parts that frightened her: "His penis seemed to move with a will of its own." She heard words that offended even if they were little understood: "After church each Sunday was 'my time' with my father. We went for a long walk in the woods, and he told me all the obscene jokes he dared not tell mother." She smelled or tasted sweat or semen. She could feel that her throat and her breath were jeopardized. "I could feel his fingers tightening on my voice box." Her emotions were discredited and her thoughts censored: "You like this, don't you?" Even her place in space was not respected when a child was picked up and deposited at the will of another. **Carrie** reexperienced her cousin lifting her upside down by one leg while his rough finger explored her vagina. **Amy,** in tactile flashbacks, felt her naked body being dragged up and down over her father's genitals when she was only a toddler.

The research participants generally experienced flashbacks, whether or not they had been amnesic to their earlier abuse. Comparisons between the amnesic and nonamnesic groups of women are presented later, but first I consider their commonalities (see Table 9.1). The proportions stated here should be viewed as descriptive, rather than directly generalizable to other samples.

Memories generally came in surges (for 53% of the respondents) and over a total period of many months (54%) rather than in one brief period (11%). They were more likely to come in bits and pieces (57%)—rather than as whole memories (19%)—and for close to half of the women they came with gathering intensity of emotions and seriousness (43%). During

Table 9.1 Flashbacks: Preliminary Sensations and Timing, by Group (%)

Characteristic	**Amnesic**	Partial Amnesic	**Nonamnesic**	Imprisoned	Total
Preliminary sensations					
Uneasy/ominous feeling	**64**	71	**70**	55	66
Moving/drifting away	**56**	71	**45**	64	57
Air seems close/stuffy	**32**	36	**35**	18	31
Timing of memories					
Over many months	**68**	57	**55**	18	54
In one brief period	**4**	21	**15**	9	11
In intermittent surges	**48**	50	**55**	64	53
With gathering intensity	**52**	57	**15**	55	43**
As bits and pieces	**72**	71	**45**	27	57*
As whole memories	**8**	7	**30**	36	19

NOTE: Unqualified "yes" responses only (occasional missing data).

*p < .05. **p < .01. Difference between amnesics and nonamnesics, one-tailed.

their flashbacks, a majority of the women (60%) had experienced themselves crying and grimacing like a child.

Table 9.2 summarizes the varied sensory aspects and other components of the respondents' flashbacks. A large majority of the survivors (76%) had visual images of their abuse. Sometimes, they observed the scene as if through the child's eyes (61% of the women), and sometimes in a dissociated way, as if from outside the child (54%). In some of their flashbacks, 47% of the women experienced the sense of sound, and 50% experienced the sense of smell. They heard seductive words, threats, and degrading names. Their reports mentioned the smell of sweat, blood, or semen, and a few women also mentioned tastes. All of this sensory input was powerful, but often, the most compelling form was tactile (experienced by 50%). Tactile, visceral sensations in flashbacks included feelings of being handled, probed, hit, flattened, or invaded as a child, as well as the victim's bodily reactions to these impositions. Survivors of sexual abuse tend to call such visceral sensory fragments *body memories*, but the term does not imply that the skin and muscles possess brain cells and can think.

The women usually experienced various kinds of flashbacks over months and sometimes years, and their variety accounts for the high percentage of women that checked each of the items. All flashback experiences were regressive by definition, usually taking the survivors back to childhood years and gradually portraying a sketchy personal history of

Table 9.2 Varied Components of Flashbacks, by Group (%)

Component	Amnesic	Partial Amnesic	Nonamnesic	Imprisoned	Total
Sensory components					
One or more senses mentioned	96	100	90	91	94
Visual	84	86	65	64	76
Normal viewing	80	57	40	64	61
Dissociated viewing	60	71	50	27	54
Kinesthetic/visceral/touch	64	50	30	55	50**
Olfactory	60	36	30	82	50*
Auditory	52	36	45	55	47
Regressive components					
Feel crying/grimaces of a child	68	64	40	73	60
Emotional component	76	64	70	91	74
Thinking component	56	71	55	36	56
Dream symbolism	64	43	75	55	61
Impatience to remember	24	21	40	55	33

NOTE: Unqualified "yes" responses only (occasional missing data).
*$p < .05$. **$p < .01$. Difference between amnesics and nonamnesics, one-tailed.

those years. Individual differences in the flashbacks were influenced by the time and nature of the abuse being recalled (e.g., early childhood vs. late childhood, single vs. repeated, or forcible vs. gentler abuse); by the identity of the perpetrator (parent, acquaintance, or stranger-rapist); and by the time of recall (e.g., soon after the breakthrough of amnesia vs. late in the recovery process). For example, **Audrey**'s first breakthrough flashback to incest in early childhood involved mild emotion (apprehension) and a sensory sexual stimulus (touch). Months later, her flashbacks to escalating abuse, at older ages, included multisensory responses (touching, seeing, hearing, smelling), powerful emotions (fear and sadness), and cognitive reactions ("He's weird. I don't want anyone to know.").

Emotions, which were experienced by 74% of the women during flashbacks, ranged from restrained to overpowering. These emotions usually intensified as escalating abuses were revealed over time. However, the women generally reported feeling increasingly capable of managing the process of recovery, thanks to therapy and their increasing self-confidence.

Differences Between Amnesics and Nonamnesics

In addition to the patterns for the entire sample of respondents, there were also some noteworthy differences between the flashback experiences of amnesics and nonamnesics. The women who had been amnesic had a multitude of questions about the past to answer because they had been ignorant at three levels: the fact of the traumatic event, its meaning, and its impact on their lives. They had to start understanding from scratch and to learn about these aspects while also fighting an urge to deny what they were learning—an urge that had certainly contributed to their earlier amnesia. The nonamnesics, although they had always remembered the traumatic events, had often been ignorant of their real meaning and almost certainly of their full impact on their lives. They had to reinterpret what they had always known so that they might grasp it more realistically.

It is understandable, therefore, that the flashbacks of the two groups differed in form and content and in the way in which they occurred (see Tables 9.1 and 9.2). Amnesics were more likely than nonamnesics to find their flashbacks extending over many months (68% vs. 55%) and less likely to have them during one brief period (4% vs. 15%). Amnesics were much more likely than nonamnesics to recover memories in bits and pieces (72% vs. 45%) and with gathering intensity (52% vs. 15%). The amnesics were less likely to have surges of flashbacks with gaps in between (48% vs. 55%), and much less likely to regain whole memories at once (8% vs. 30%). Fewer amnesics were impatient to remember and put everything into perspective (24% vs. 40%), probably because the amnesics were torn between their need to know the reality of their childhood and fear of what they would find out.

Even 6 months after learning that they had been abused as children, amnesics were highly likely (76%) to have serious trouble believing what they were remembering. Understandably, this denial created great stress. They were torn between feeling crazy and believing a horrifying truth. Even some nonamnesics (24%)—in the face of family denial—had trouble believing abusive events that they had never forgotten. The likelihood of this was increased if they had mislabeled these events or minimized their impact on their lives. Now, they had to recognize them as sexual abuse and reexamine their families of origin and their childhood. For example, **Nell** had half-believed her uncle, who had called his attentions "a special way of loving," and now she had to reinterpret them as "a callous way of taking."

Amnesic respondents were also more likely than nonamnesics to report experiencing each of the sensory aspects and most of the other components of flashbacks (see Table 9.2), and some of these differences were quite large and significant. In addition to being more likely to have flashbacks in general, the amnesics experienced them more often through their various senses and through regressive emotions. More amnesics than nonamnesics had visual flashbacks (84% vs. 65%) and auditory ones (52% vs. 45%). The differences between these groups were even larger and significant for tactile or kinesthetic memories (64% vs. 30%) and for memories involving smell (60% vs. 30%). These differences may reflect the fact that, at the time of their earliest abuse, amnesics were younger than nonamnesics, and consequently body sensations, smells, and emotions were more important interpreters of their world than than later in childhood. Moreover, the amnesic women, with more betrayal by parents in their background, were more likely to have dissociated during their abuse.

The only flashback component on which nonamnesics were higher than amnesics was in recognizing past events through dream symbolism. **ILENE** had never forgotten most of her abuse, and she was more inclined to intrusive thoughts than to flashbacks. Sometimes, she would recall a particular event and the details would replay so that she could grasp, in clearer context, what had happened. For **NANCY**, also, intrusive thoughts were extremely distressing.

Dissociation

The dissociation seen in the women's flashbacks is understandable. Dissociation can be an effective way to escape from powerlessness in an inescapable situation. During their abuse as children, the women had frequently dissociated from the experience. Indeed, many of the amnesic respondents believed that a major reason for their amnesia lay in the fact that they had found ways to "not be present" during molestation.

There can be a wide range of types and degrees of dissociation. As seen in their flashbacks, various women had used any of the following forms, which are listed here in increasing order of extremity:

Dissociation to other thoughts. "I shut my eyes, gritted my teeth, and thought about other things until it was over."
Dissociation from pain. "I just tried to endure, and avoid the awareness and pain." "Anesthetizing fits in here. I anesthetized the feelings in the lower part of my body."

Dissociation from one's body. Many of the women had, as children, gone "out of body," observing the abuse objectively and indifferently— usually from above, near the ceiling. Their dissociation was from both their body and their feelings. They could "know" what was happening without experiencing it. One woman fantasized putting her rag doll in her place—"He doesn't know the difference."

Dissociation to other places. In these instances, the child "went else-where" during the abuse. Her choice might be to go into a picture hanging on her wall, into the wall itself, into the closet, or out the window. Some went to a remembered or fantasized place—a beach or a flower garden. Shutting down their senses and their emotions, they dissociated from every aspect of the abuse experience. "I really left my body. I wasn't there. Only after I hopped back in my body did I realize that I had been absent."

Dissociation from one's self. Here, there was separation from the child's body *and* identity. This dissociation extended to depersonalization—the self was changed to non-self (i.e., the child's body that she saw being molested was not her own).

As reported in Chapter 6, 61% of the amnesic and partially amnesic survivors had gone out-of-body, staring indifferently from the ceiling or a corner of the room at what was happening to their bodies; 58% had pretended they were elsewhere; and 21% had pretended that the molestation was happening to someone else. Because many of the respondents reported having had more than one of these experiences, it is evident that a given woman could have varying degrees of separation in different flashbacks, or even within the same recurring one over time. The separation from self in visual flashbacks seemed to be a way for the women to distance themselves from the painful experience. As a survivor begins to leave the substantial protection of amnesia, she may need a lesser defense to tide her over—a reduced amount of dissociation that allows her enough distance and time for memories to surface and for her to recognize that they concern herself.

The Woman as Witness for the Child

Flashbacks were doubly useful to the remembering process when they involved two levels of awareness—the child's and adult's perspectives on the abuse. The past and the present eventually needed to be integrated, and this was more likely to occur if the women were able to experience past feelings and events while still remaining aware of their present time and place (an ability that their therapist could help them to achieve). Here is an example, based on an interview with **Alana**:

> As the flashback began, I was about 10 years old. I was lying helplessly, feeling deeply discouraged and totally under my father's control. I could make no sense of his activities—"I don't know why he does this"—and I saw him as a "wild man." I was crying silently, my throat aching from the strain, because Mom would die if she came in and found "this" Daddy.

As the flashback faded, the remembering woman became increasingly aware of her father's callous exploitation and of how demeaning the sexual abuse had become. Bringing an adult perspective to this scene, Alana could realize and label her father's pathology. Also, although she was afraid to identify too closely with so much pain, she was beginning to feel compassion and admiration for herself as a child. Until she was able to combine the adult and child perspectives—that is, while her abusing father remained "not-Daddy" and the child "not-me"—she could not become a whole person.

Remembering Takes Time

I need to remember, but I don't want to know.
— **Phyllis**

One third of the women (33%) were impatient to remember, but they felt ambivalence as well. They were understandably afraid of what they might recall, and half of them (49%) wrestled for many months with recurring denial of what they were uncovering. Continuing episodes of denial were especially common for the amnesics (76%) and to a lesser extent for the partially amnesic women (57%)—significantly more than for the nonamnesics (24%).

For some survivors, the first stunning revelation came like a flash of lightning, but the rest usually took a long, long time—months and sometimes years. This was especially true for the formerly amnesic women. **Andrea** later complained to her therapist, "Why two years of flashbacks with just bits and pieces of the past? Why couldn't I have remembered all this at one time? I could have handled it!" But her therapist explained,

"You forget where you were emotionally when you first started remembering. To find out everything, when you remembered nothing, would have hospitalized you. You needed to gradually get used to the idea and the extent of your abuse."

Traumatic memories should not be rushed, and responsible therapists encouraged the survivors not to overload. It took time for each woman to bring memories into awareness, to deal with them, and to integrate them into her picture of the world. None of the women received all the missing puzzle parts at once. As shown in Table 9.1, memories usually came in surges followed by breaks that lasted for days, weeks, or even months. They came in bits and pieces and not always in sequence. There was usually a gathering intensity in the emotions experienced and in the severity of what was remembered. Eventually a picture of the abuse emerged and made sense. In accepting past reality, each woman had to redefine her entire childhood, her family of origin, and her own self.

FLASHBACKS AS MULTIFACETED EXPERIENCES

Premonition of Flashbacks

> *The atmosphere is so apparent I can feel it. The then and now come together and swallow me up in fear.*
>
> **—Angie**

At first, flashbacks came to the survivors with little identifiable forewarning, but later, most of them learned to identify typical precursors. According to their checklist responses, these took the form of uneasy, ominous feelings (for 66% of the women), a sense of moving to another time or place (57%), or sensations of closeness and stuffy air (31%; see Table 9.1). These preliminary sensations could last for minutes or hours. Occasionally, respondents experienced uncomfortable feelings for several days before a particular flashback. The preliminary atmosphere might vary for any given woman as well as between women, but there were no statistically significant differences between the memory groups.

Each type of premonition mentioned above as being associated with the beginnings of a flashback can be related (at least in part) to the original abuse situation. The uneasy, ominous feelings paralleled the anxiety that survivors had felt as children when they had been aware of certain omens that portended the occurrence of intermittent or regular abuse. The barking of the dog when the abuser came home, "that look" in his eyes after supper, the squeak of flooring at night, the click of a cigarette lighter, or the turn of a doorknob had signaled his presence and the likelihood of sexual abuse. The respondents' sense of shifting out of the present time and place is understandable also, because 76% of the amnesic and partially amnesic women believed that a major reason for their long amnesia was dissociation during molestation—pretending they were elsewhere, going out-of-body, or viewing the molestation as if it was happening to someone else. Similarly, they related the sense of stuffy air and difficulties in breathing to being silenced as children in the multitude of ways described in Chapter 4.

In addition to their checklist responses on the first questionnaire, the women volunteered other descriptions of their premonitions. Before flashbacks, some felt increasingly dizzy, nauseated, or headachy; others felt floaty, woozy, or disoriented. A "cloud" drifted across their thoughts; they "faded back" into their bed as the flashback came on; or their limbs became "tingly" or "so numb and heavy that I could hardly move them." Some respondents were warned by emotions that were inappropriate to the present or by bodily jerks or strange distortions of facial muscles. For **Portia**, nostalgia for her grandfather and the "good old bad days" came first: "A lover who was bad to you was, nevertheless, a lover."

A few women told me that they had no advance cues. They simply found themselves back in a childhood abuse situation—"being there, and little." Others spoke of flashbacks that came instantaneously, like a lightning bolt, and went away just as suddenly. They were unprepared for a moving-picture scene of a brother overpowering them or for the sudden bodily feeling of anal rape. Their long experience in acting "as if" everything was normal proved useful because these flashbacks sometimes occurred in a public setting during the long months of recall.

THE SENSORY DIMENSIONS OF FLASHBACKS

Now, I will delve more deeply into the nature of the women's flashbacks and the sensory modalities in which they occurred. As Table 9.2 indicates, in their flashbacks, the survivors reexperienced past sexual traumas through sensory memories (94%), far more than through recall of their cognitive processes (56%). Their flashbacks were most often visual (76% of the women). Also common were ones felt tactilely in the body (50%) or auditory (50%) and olfactory (47%) experiences. Only a few women mentioned memories involving taste.

Visual Flashbacks

When vision was the primary sensory experience, the flashbacks of the women exhibited one of three degrees of separation of self from the abuse, as described under Dissociation. There could be

- no separation (e.g., she was "in" her body during the molestation). I will refer to these as *subjectively viewed* flashbacks because they were viewed through the eyes of the child.
- separation from her body (e.g., she was out-of-body during the molestation, as in seeing her abuse from the ceiling). Patients in surgery sometimes have such an experience. I will refer to this and the next category as *objectively viewed* flashbacks because, in them, the viewer was detached from the scene.
- separation from her body *and* identity (e.g., the child's body that she saw being molested was not hers).

Subjectively viewed flashbacks were seen through the eyes of the respondent's child-self. As examples, she saw "hate" in the rapist's eyes, the smile on her stepfather's face, or the change in her mother's expression. Or she saw a "big person" approaching her. Sometimes, the flashback seemed to be censored: "I see my father's naked body down to the groin; I can't look further." In a visual-emotional flashback, **ANNE** was apparently a tiny child, sitting or crawling on the floor, and monitoring her sense of safety in the presence of her father: "I see only from his shoes to his knees. I'm fearful or relaxed depending on whether his shoes are pointing toward me or away." A snapshot of ANNE as a toddler, standing beside her father, shows a distinctly frightened little face.

A few respondents reported extensive and vivid details in flashbacks to molestation as seen through the child's eyes. Two examples follow, one of which took place in a poor home and the other in a wealthy one.

I can see my uncle sitting on the old reddish metal kitchen chair—the kind you see in *I Love Lucy* shows, with a marbled plastic seat and back. He's heavy, so he sits with his legs apart. At his feet, the vinyl flooring is dirty and eaten away by rats and roaches. As usual, my uncle makes me come over and sit on his lap. He touches me all over whenever my parents aren't looking right at us. They never seem to notice. No one cares.

In this flashback, **PAULA** was about 10, and there was a sense of weary repetition in her description. You can imagine her staring at the shabby flooring to avoid her uncle's eyes whenever he came to visit.

One of **Phyllis**'s flashbacks was to a single unexpected childhood experience, when she sharply focused on a strange occurrence. Her remarkably detailed description of the chair was verified by her mother after the flashback, but the child never saw the chair again after she was 5.

I'm about 3, happily sitting in my favorite Grampa's lap in the big room. Grandma's in the kitchen. But then he starts moving me back and forth across his legs. What's happening? Something is different. My good feelings are gone. I look at Grampa. He's in his church suit. I see the back of the chair behind his head. It is covered with tiny stitches in different colors [tapestry]. I can see them one by one. I see carved wooden leaves on the chair arms, and smooth green carpet below. I feel waves and waves of warm feelings. I don't know why Grampa is doing this moving. I must pay attention. I'm trying to understand.

As an adult, **Phyllis** has recalled other times when "Grampa did strange things."

Objectively viewed flashbacks were seen like an image that was projected on a movie or television screen. **Perri** reported,

I see silent moving pictures of myself with Dad and feel only disgust. I want them to stop. I want to escape. There are quick scenes of my Dad and me in action. I put my hands over my eyes to dispel the images. I'm never alone when this happens; it's always in a room full of people, like during a church service.

Similarly, **Alicia** described a recurring image that always caught her unawares: "Everything is going along normally when suddenly a scene of mutilated kittens comes up again." In recounting this, she raised her outspread hand in front of her eyes as if shielding herself from the sight. She has experienced this upsetting vision from childhood, sometimes fainting when it happened in her school classroom. The image still remains unconnected to anything in her past, and its origin may never be clear.

Tactile Flashbacks

Tactile or kinesthetic flashbacks are ones that involve touch or visceral feelings. They were experienced by 50% of the survivors. In some cases, they were triggered by bodily sensations similar to those experienced during the abuse incident—for instance, when certain body spots were touched during sexual contact or during deep body massage. Often, however, they were simply fragmentary sensations that repeated until more clues made sense of them. These examples were reported by various survivors:

The weight of his body pressing on mine.

His scratchy beard against my skin.

My brother's hand over my mouth.

Sticky fluid on me, making me feel disgusted.

The sharp jab of his fist in my solar plexus, doubling me up.

My teeth chattering uncontrollably, my head pulling to one side.

My face being flattened, and my shoulders shaking.

The pain of his penis inside me, feelings of anguish and shame.

Patrice described a series of body feelings: "I feel the sharp penetration, then the banging, banging against the end of a too-short vagina. I'm out of my body, looking at us from just above." As an adult, Patrice slept with her hands one on top of the other, protectively between her legs.

Auditory Flashbacks

Auditory flashbacks were often of brief but critical moments:

His voice calling me dirty names after the sex.

Threats of what he'd do to me if I ever told anyone.

The click of a cigarette lighter, warning me that he is near.

The wailing sound of a preschooler, with no one to comfort her.

This last example is a reminder of the fact that many of the women found themselves crying like a very young child during some of their flashbacks. For **Abbie** this was common:

During flashbacks, my crying sometimes sounded like a child of 7 years of age, or 6. Occasionally, it had the forlorn, wailing quality of a preschool child. Once, I had such a flashback in my therapist's office. When the crying of a unusually young child was subsiding, she asked me what I wanted to say. I answered, puzzled, "I have no words."

Flashbacks Involving Odors

Smells (50%) were not as common as visual images in flashbacks. However, their impact was powerful. Olfactory flashbacks might be stimulated by an odor present in some daily experience, or they might arise without the stimulus of any present odor. They were also frequently part of a more complex visual or tactile flashback. Instances of all three types can be seen in these examples:

- I found my husband making his favorite sardine sandwich and was nauseated, associating the pungent smell with semen.
- Tobacco smoke in my face or the smell of sweat takes me back to the memory of the man who attacked me.
- During flashbacks to my grandfather's bedroom, there is once more the odor of his pipe tobacco, and the smell of food cooking in the kitchen below.
- As a tiny child, I hid under low-slung furniture in a futile effort to escape my stepfather. Flashbacks bring back the smell of old furniture and carpet dust—and the feeling of mounting terror.
- I sometimes smell my mother's personal musky body odor.
- I reexperience the odor of my brother's stale sweat and breath.
- He sat on my face. All I could smell was his anus.

A more complex memory involving smells was reported by **PAULA.**

My uncle and aunt lived in a huge house when I was a child. Years later, I visited my widowed aunt, and we sat again in their guest parlor as she talked of how "wonderful" my uncle had been. An old musty odor still clung to that room and, sitting across from her, I began to feel severely claustrophobic. Suddenly, I realized that she was sitting in the chair he had used, and his picture hung on the wall just above her head. I felt nauseated, experiencing again the duality that was my uncle—hearing the nicey-nice words that changed to meanness when he was with me unobserved.

Flashbacks Involving Taste

Flashbacks involving taste were relatively uncommon, but occasionally, they involved the taste of cigarettes, or semen, or blood. **Anita** recalled her rape by three boys: "I kept shouting for Daddy, so the boys who were raping me stuffed a sock in my mouth. It split the corners of my mouth and I couldn't breathe. In the flashback, I could taste the blood."

Flashbacks Involving Multiple Senses

Some flashbacks were multisensory. When I interviewed **Arna,** she told me that 2 years earlier, she had remembered, without emotion, that her 18-year-old brother had raped her when she was 6 years old. Several days after our interview, she telephoned to tell me that, for the first time, she had experienced the attack. The flashback she described had involved sight, sound, and touch, as well as feelings of betrayal, helplessness, fear, and pain. There was also a clear narrative.

> My sister, looking real cheerful and mysterious, coaxed me to go upstairs. My biggest brother, Mama's favorite, was in his room and he made me take off my panties. Then he raped me. It hurt so much, and I was bleeding. Right after, he made me get up, dress, and go downstairs. Mama was standing at the foot of the stairs—smiling. I only saw Mama smile four times, and this was one of them. As I looked at her, I knew that she knew what had occurred and that she had wanted it to happen.

Arna continued, "I went through hell yesterday when I finally lived it again. I could feel that damn, slippery, slimy stuff when he dropped his load in me, and I didn't want to be alive any more. But now, I'm free. I'll never be used by other people again." She added, as an afterthought, "Yesterday, I actually *bled* from my vagina—and I'm 66 years old."

Sound was the most upsetting aspect of flashbacks for **Pamela**, who had been partly amnesic to her experiences with predatory relatives. Her family was poor and had numerous children, for whom she (as the oldest) was the primary caretaker. She had to sleep on a cot in her parent's room while the smallest child shared their bed. She was regularly an unwilling listener to sexual intercourse and described a frequent flashback to the recurrent, always-remembered scene:

I'm back there again—about 12 years old, trapped, with no choice but to be there, and no way to tell my anger. Thinking and thinking: "I hate my mother." She's always telling me sex is dirty but making noises at night as if she likes it. All those unwanted lives, and she's pregnant and sick again. So she gives me all the washing and ironing and cleaning. I'm staring at the dingy green wall and the plaster scaling off the ceiling, but I can see the shape of their bodies and their movement under the old gray army blanket and hear every sound. I reach inside myself and find only unmet longings for someone to care about me. God, why did you make me, just to feel empty? Why am I here? Tell me that I'm not a mistake, that I didn't just happen from two people doing sex without love. I stare at the ceiling, crying inside myself till I can fall asleep again.

No Face on the Abuser

There were also flashbacks where key elements were conspicuously missing. Several women spoke of there being no face on their abuser during flashbacks. After such an occasion, **Paige** would shout, "Why won't you show your face?" But, at the same time, she knew she didn't want further evidence that it was her father who had molested her: "As long as I don't see his face, I can maintain some doubt."

Similarly, **Pia** can't see the face of the stranger who raped her and threatened her life when she was 5 years of age. Sometimes, she thinks that there were other attacks. Sometimes, she wonders whether it might have been someone she knew. Her father, for example, can be violent and cruel. Two or three times when she was small, he brutally killed her cat's litter. She is disturbed that she is drawn to men with similar personalities. Now, as an adult, she occasionally feels stalked. She has found mutilated animals or birds on her porch and sometimes she has received weird phone calls. Perhaps, she thinks, she will remember more about her abuse later. Meanwhile, she is working through a lot of feelings in therapy and also in her own reading. She is growing emotionally and mentally and is developing a strong sense of direction for her life.

Emotions Then and Now

Three quarters of the women (74%) experienced a return of childhood emotions in some of their flashbacks—desolation, aloneness, despair, fear, sadness, and (less frequently) anger. "There's no one to help. No one ever comes. I'm all alone. I just want to die." In confronting their past, more and more, the women were choosing to examine their abuse without running from the feelings that it evoked. The emotions they felt during this remembering period were more intense than those they had experienced before they dealt with the past. Then, feelings of sadness, anger, and aloneness had been more numbed, diffuse, and harder to identify—weakened by being spread out over time. Occasionally, the feelings had erupted inappropriately, puzzling and embarrassing the survivor. But generally, the past had intruded into the present by draining her of energy and aliveness. During the remembering stage, however, these emotions were far more acute because the women were allowing feelings to surface during a condensed period of time.

The turbulent and conflicting emotions aroused by childhood incest, and equally by its memory in adulthood, came through poignantly in an entry from **ANNE**'s journal: "Today, I felt again the old despair, sadness, disillusionment, anger, and helplessness. I was crying out against his unfairness, his blindness—yelling my hatred and feeling my love."

The following excerpt from **Angela**'s journal describes a flashback that typifies the hopeless, lonely, and sad emotions of a girl enmeshed by incest. Anger, briefly surfacing, is turned against herself:

> My face contorted as soon as I tried to rest. I found myself crying with unspeakable sadness. I was 10 years old. He'd left, and I was all alone: There's no feeling between my legs. When I knew he was coming, I had pulled up the "nothing" feeling like a little blanket between my legs. Then, I wouldn't feel it happen. Now, suddenly, I feel real mad. My fists double up. I hit out but there's nobody there. I begin to punch on my legs and tummy, and then harder and harder between my legs until I hurt. I keep on hitting myself until I'm exhausted and the tears flow freely. I feel so sad—so very sad.

As a child, she had anesthetized the pain through denial and other coping mechanisms. Now, she was allowing herself to experience that pain so that she would not need to carry it through the months and years ahead.

LEARNING TO LIVE WITH FLASHBACKS

I have used the analogy of a jigsaw puzzle for the process of putting new pieces of memory together. **Ava** used a similar one. She thought of remembering as rather like assembling scattered frames from an old movie reel. More and larger segments gradually appeared, and eventually, perhaps, most of a scene. The picture was fragmented or blurry, especially at first. On later occasions, color might be added, or even sound. There was no way of knowing how much clearer or more complete the picture would eventually become, nor how much effort must be expended in trying to make sense of it. However, after a major flashback had pulled some abusive episode together, the past and its impact on the present usually became more understandable, and the woman's energy (which had been drained in birthing the memory) was recharged.

The Timing of Flashbacks

The timing of flashbacks varied for different women. For many, they were most likely to erupt when she tried to relax or get some rest. Relaxing involved letting go of preoccupations and defenses that had been active during the day. Also, resting typically meant lying down, with all the associations that position carried with it. Most women experienced their flashbacks away from their place of work, in a situation where they were better able to handle whatever developed. However, some found them intruding at their busy workplace, where other distractions prevented dealing with them in detail. Still others experienced them in the safety of their therapist's office, after learning how to discourage them when they were alone.

Flashbacks are basically a knee-jerk reaction to internal or external stimuli, and they can rarely be controlled by willing them to come or go. If they could be hastened, the women who were impatient for truth would not have endured the slow unfolding of their memories. And others, exhausted by a daily barrage of flashbacks, would have found reprieve by commanding them to stop. However, because lack of control had characterized their childhood abuse, it was important that they achieve increasing control over the reliving of that abuse in the present. Given the involuntary nature of flashbacks, how could this be accomplished? The answer seemed to be twofold: (a) by gaining awareness of internal and external stimuli that released or inhibited flashbacks and (b) by adopting a positive attitude toward flashbacks.

Awareness of Internal and External Pressures

A situation of chronic stress followed the women's crisis of first memories. They typically found their internal (experiencing) life on overload.

Yet their external (doing) environment continued to produce home and work duties. Respite in one area or the other was essential for many of them. At times of intense internal turmoil during the remembering, the survivors were forced to simplify their external environment. They were generally encouraged by therapists to cut back on obligations as a positive step and to elicit support and understanding wherever it could be found. **Amy** shared her dilemma with her good-hearted employer, and he offered her reduced hours. They agreed instead that she should feel free to leave work whenever she felt overwhelmed. She seldom did so but treasured that generous option. **Nora** took a year's leave from work. **Peggy**, a perfectionist, was astonished in looking back at her first post-breakthrough year: "I neglected so many 'essential' household chores, but somehow our family survived quite well."

When a survivor's external environment was exceptionally demanding, that was not the time to deal with heavy memories. **Norene,** an exhausted high school teacher, could predict the pattern of her flashbacks: "Probably there'll be a status quo till school lets out and then I'll have a really rotten June." **Ariel** had to learn the hard way: She took a 3-week tour of Asia at the peak of her flashbacks and found herself externally overwhelmed as well. In unfamiliar cities, all five of her senses were assaulted by unusual sights, sounds, smells, tastes, and tactile experiences. The combination of inner and outer stimuli made her afraid she was "going crazy," and there was no one available to help her ground herself.

Learning to Control Flashbacks

Some survivors, prior to breakthrough of their memories, had been aware that certain situations troubled them. For example, watching contact sports, sitting with others in a closed car, or standing at a crowded cocktail party made them almost desperate to escape, long before they could understand why this was so. After breakthrough, as flashbacks became more a part of their daily life, they gradually realized that certain people, settings, events, or feelings stimulated or deterred flashbacks. For instance, sitting in a certain chair or thinking about their childhood tended to bring on flashbacks, whereas a brisk walk or an entertaining television program tended to discourage them. These women could achieve some indirect control of flashbacks as they evoked, avoided, or left the kind of emotional or physical setting that encouraged flashbacks.

By attending to their own needs in this way, they acknowledged their own importance. They deserved attention in and of themselves. This was an important lesson in self-trust.

Releasing flashbacks. Efforts to encourage or release flashbacks seemed to require a lowering of the defenses of body and mind. Just as relaxing at the appropriate time can facilitate the birth of a child more than pushing and shoving can, deep relaxation and breathing exercises tended to release some flashbacks that were hovering, annoyingly, just below the surface of memory. **Addie** released emotions, reduced excess tension, and (sometimes) evoked a flashback by lying down alone on her bed and allowing herself to descend into upwelling emotions of sadness or fear. Telephoning a friend before or after made her feel less isolated. **Penny** learned to use deep relaxation or self-hypnosis techniques when an important memory needed help in coming through. In doing so, she was turning altered states of consciousness, which had accompanied the abuse, to her benefit.

Deferring flashbacks. Other study participants needed a reprieve from flashbacks. During their working day, busyness (a major coping mechanism for many) had helped, but by bedtime, they were drained. However, bed stimulated flashbacks, and when sleep came, it was fitful or beset by troubling dreams. Another problem, which especially plagued **Audrey** at bedtime, was "jerking," which seemed to release daytime tension. Asked to explain what she meant, she answered, "You know those sudden little jerks you give when you start to fall asleep? Well, multiply them by 5 or 10, and that's what happens repeatedly for half an hour as soon as my body relaxes. I sometimes give poor Jack an awful kick!"

    Phoebe was taught by her therapist how to defer a flashback that was erupting at a bad time. Because flashbacks are altered states of mind that transport one into the past, the goal was to ground herself firmly and clearly in the present. She was told to make all possible contacts, mental and sensory, between herself and the here and now. She told herself exactly where she was, touched parts of her body and felt the texture of the carpet beneath her feet, listened for the sounds of everyday life—the refrigerator's hum, the sound of a lawnmower outdoors—noted the objects that surrounded her in the room and their varied colors, and so on. Then Phoebe decided how she wanted to "put away the flashback" (and its contribution to self-understanding) for a better or safer time. She chose to visualize a neat set of mason jars with calico labels, one for each problem she encountered. She would put one in a jar, fasten the lid, set it on the shelf, and promise, "I won't leave you there. You deserve attention, so I'll be back to let you out." This example illustrates the healthy use of suppression (wise deferment of problems for later attention) instead of the re-repression of memories (refusal to deal with them).

Impatience and the Need to Know

Abraham Maslow (1970) said that human beings who seek fulfillment have a strong need to know and to understand. The need for understanding is particularly keen when one has suffered from a traumatic event. And, if the trauma is caused by human actions—especially if one has been betrayed by a close friend or relative—the need to understand why this occurred is likely to reach obsessive levels. Over half of the study respondents (57%), when confronting the crisis of recall, were haunted by the question "Why me?" (cf. Table 10.1). Although this question is sometimes viewed as self-pitying, its basic nature is a desperate search for meaning, especially in situations that can never be resolved (Emerson, 1986).

Many of the respondents felt that their recall of the past was tortuously slow when major questions about their childhood remained unanswered. A typical reaction was "I feel great anger about not knowing sooner about my problems." However, at the same time, denial continued to plague the survivors because it had taken them so many years to become fully aware of their past abuse. Even nonamnesics, who had always remembered childhood rape or incest, sometimes doubted that it had really happened. Some were again tempted to deny that it was "that bad" or "that callous," whereas others wavered toward thinking they had "misunderstood" the intentions of the perpetrator—themes that had been powerful in past years.

It was even harder for amnesics to believe memories that had been absent from previous awareness. The slow recall and partial memories in the early stages of remembering were discouraging. However, their quest for truth was relentless because most were determined never to fool themselves again. Occasionally, a sibling or relative helped (deliberately or inadvertently) by verifying some aspect of what they were remembering—the wallpaper of a bedroom, an old workshop, a medical treatment, or an uncle's sexual perversions. Gradually over time, evidence accumulated, and tiny and large pieces of the puzzle fell into place. Eventually the picture emerged clearly enough to be compelling. Doubts diminished to an occasional flicker in their mind, and external affirmation seemed relatively unimportant (although some validation was received by most of the amnesics). For instance, **Allie** believed that her flashbacks fell off as her confidence grew, and she stated, "I have validated my own reality."

When the survivors knew "enough" about their abuse, learning further facts or experiencing additional incidents of abuse was not only superfluous but self-punishing. As **Priscilla** said, "I don't need to see every cow, horse, and rooster to recognize a barnyard." Then, it was time to move on to other parts of the healing process. For **Ashley**, putting together the picture was rather methodical:

> I felt at times like a detective, collecting evidence against my own father. Only when it became overwhelming could I convict him in my own mind. What I've remembered and reexperienced about my life is so different from what I had made myself believe. The family I grew up in, I don't even recognize. It's blown sky high. In flashbacks, it didn't even occur to me to call Mother. She was nowhere around. Nobody to help me, nobody to come. As for my father, I thought at first that the abuse was infrequent and, in his distorted view, "loving." But what I've experienced at times was close to brutality. There's no way he couldn't know that I was hurting physically and emotionally. *No way*. It's fantastic. If I'd read it in a book, I'd think, "the God-damn fucking bastard," and I've had to realize that my own father did all that to me. I could not put the two men together—this man and the father I knew by day. I've put them together now by dividing him in half. However you might diagnose him, he's two different persons to me.

The Process of Confirmation

As they gradually progressed in their recovery, the survivors whom I studied tended to move from (a) focusing predominantly on past memories to (b) integrating them into the present and, finally, to (c) living *in* the present and *for* the future (see Figure 9.1). Eventually, through this process, each woman reached some sense of completion regarding her abuse. Confirmation of her new insights came in many possible forms.

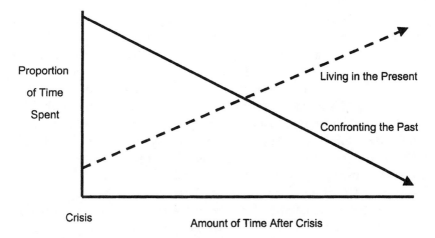

Figure 9.1 The Shift in Temporal Focus Over Time During Recovery

External corroboration of abuse. In many cases, incomplete memories were supported or validated by external evidence—an old diary entry or medical report, another victim, a witness to abuse, or confirmation (usually partial) by the abuser. Two thirds of the amnesic survivors eventually gained this kind of validation.

Narrative memories (which were never lost) provided a context for understanding involuntary regressions or flashbacks. For example, **Alicia** doubted flashbacks to incest at night in her parents' bedroom. But then she recalled her parents sleeping in a tent during the summer, and she remembered that her father, a veteran with PTSD sleep patterns, frequently came inside.

New recognition of inappropriate and intrusive family patterns often developed after survivors began to talk openly and objectively about their family life in individual or group therapy. In this process, behaviors and attitudes that had not previously been recognized as boundary violations became obvious. Half the nonamnesics had not defined what happened to them as either sexual or abusive. And many amnesics had not recognized certain remembered family patterns as intrusive or inappropriate. The women's new perceptions of family life made incest seem less incredible.

New information sometimes made puzzling sensations understandable. **Andrea** often awoke with the feeling that her wrists were tied. An older cousin's offhand remark supplied a relevant context: "Your brother was a mean kid—he used to tie you up."

As another example, ever since **Cynthia**'s childhood, she had felt sharp pain and fear whenever she saw an old-style car gearshift (the kind with a round knob on top of a long rod). She thought she might have been injured by one as a child. At age 55, she suddenly recalled her grandfather taking her to see his new truck when she was 4 years old. This happy cognition (and her image of his shiny truck cab) "disappeared in a blaze of rectal pain." That 30-second memory informed her that she had been sodomized. (Previously, she had always believed that her grandfather, who had abused all females in her extended family, had "only" handled her.)

Memories merged into a pattern that made sense. When survivors had recalled and put together "enough" puzzle pieces of memory to form a compelling (if still incomplete) picture of abuse, they often could accept some ambiguity. They felt they did not have to know "everything."

Survivors increasingly respected themselves and their perceptions, recognizing the strength and integrity of the child they had been and of the woman they were becoming.

The crisis of recall was a watershed in the lives of respondents, clearly separating the time before and after they faced their childhood trauma. During that crisis, most survivors experienced florid symptoms of PTSD. **Arlene** called it "the hurricane within." The women were overwhelmed by emotions, physiological arousal, nightmares, hope, and despair. Living through this stress was their top priority at that time, and all their life energy had to be harnessed toward survival. As the crisis passed, there was a period when remembering took top priority, as many fragments and occasional whole memories forced themselves to the forefront of attention in flashbacks. The women's past demanded attention if their present was ever to make sense, and if their future was to be freed from the grip of trauma.

A Positive Attitude—Flashbacks as Friends

As was discussed in previous chapters, PTSD is not a pathological diagnosis but a normal response to intolerable stress. Similarly, the symptoms experienced by my respondents over the decades *before* break-through can be seen as their way of dealing with past trauma until it was possible to face it squarely. And flashbacks *after* breakthrough are not pathological but are efforts of the body and mind to bring about healing. A positive attitude toward them allowed many survivors to feel more in control of their lives.

An important part of taking control of one's own remembering lies in accepting the process while also finding ways to make it less draining. By flowing with (rather than fighting) flashbacks and intrusive thoughts, these survivors learned the secrets of the abuser's power so that they could be free from it. Flashbacks could be seen as friends—although sometimes they visit too often and are perhaps awkward in their timing. It was these flashbacks that helped rememberers to get down into the past, to explore it, and to destroy its impact. **Petra** described how she learned to deal with them: "I pay close attention to flashbacks when they are insistent. Others tend to repeat old information, and I tell them to come back when they can be more helpful."

In ways like these, survivors took charge of their own healing. They re-called past victimization, not to wallow in it endlessly, but so that they could put it behind them and move on. **Patrice** said, "I defeat my abuser by *allowing* him to return." When viewed as part of the healing process, symptoms such as intrusive thoughts, changeable emotions, and flash-backs became less intimidating. As the women resurrected the past—with its memories of being helpless, hopeless, and alone—they freed themselves from its power in their lives. And through the struggle, they took charge of their own future, recognizing their own personhood and improving their relationships to those around them. These developments are described later in Chapters 13 and 14, but first, the following two chapters summarize the survivors' own personal responses to their re-turning memories of abuse and the reactions of their relatives and friends.

CHAPTER 10

The Personal Response to Remembering

I never anticipated the profound disruption of remembering the past,
nor the rewards of knowing and understanding it.

—Annette

Imagine that you have been working for years on a giant picture puzzle of your life. You cannot seem to get it to make sense. Suddenly, a tornado descends, flinging the pieces to the ceiling. They land helter-skelter, and you must start all over again. But this time, you have certain key elements you did not even know were missing. As soon as you put them together, many other pieces click into place. Slowly, a picture begins to emerge, but it is not the one you expected to see, nor is it one you want to look at. The pieces of memory that you had before—how do they fit in? Which of them are real, and which are distortions? Furthermore, additional new pieces—large and small—gradually appear. You must sort them out and snap them into place around the core section. It isn't an easy task nor a speedy one. All the foundations of life—your values, perceptions of the world, understanding of parents and family—must be fitted together in a new way. This chapter introduces you to that process.

A LONG PROCESS

Tedeschi and Calhoun (1995) have pointed out that an experience of trauma is a watershed marking off "before" from "after." For survivors of early sexual abuse, however, their trauma is multilayered. It was integrated into their identity even as that identity was being formed in childhood, skewing their perceptions, emotions, thinking, and behavior. Especially if they dissociated their trauma experience, their "life story" tended to resemble a fairy tale rather than history. Moreover, in the crisis of recall, remembering survivors become retraumatized by their own personal reactions and by those of others around them. To heal, they must incorporate both of these phases of trauma into the narrative of their life and deal with the consequences of both.

After the first breakthrough of memories, further remembering was a long drawn-out process for my respondents, and it produced many changes in the attitudes and behavior of the women as they worked their way out of amnesia. These shifts, and the fluctuations that accompanied them, demanded many adjustments from each woman and from those to whom she related. The interpersonal and social responses to the breakthrough are the subject of Chapter 11. This chapter focuses on the personal effects of remembering—first, the survivors' complex responses to the initial breach in amnesia (or in denial in the case of nonamnesic women) and, second, their later reactions during the slow process of remembering what had happened to them.

Reexamining Past Idealization

Past years had to be reexamined in the light of new knowledge. A child who had forgotten incest, for example, might have substituted cheerful pieces in the jigsaw puzzle of her life for those that were frightening. Many of my respondents, imagining themselves as growing up in a safe and kindly environment, idealized their abuser and created in their minds the best of worlds:

> I thought of our family as close and supportive. Mom and Dad were "perfect" parents and highly respected in the community. Dad was head layman at our church and the foundation of our lives. We were *so* proud of him, and Mother was his chief supporter.

It was not surprising that **Adelle,** growing up in such an idealized home, felt guilty for being depressed and sad—"What is wrong with *me*?" Such self-blame typically continued into adulthood. When memories of abuse finally broke through, she struggled to sort truth from fiction in her

childhood and to determine whether, when, and how these new memories fitted in. She also began to assert her own identify instead of seeing
herself as "her father's daughter." In the process of challenging their
former foundations, women like Adelle found unanticipated strength
within themselves.

Facing the truth was a somewhat different experience for nonamnesic
women than for amnesic women. Some of them had not labeled their experience sexual abuse, and most had denied its impact on their lives. Realization was a shock, as **Nicole** reported:

> They've always been there—vivid memories of all kinds that I never told
> anyone. But I thought something like that couldn't have had such an effect.
> I had all kinds of phobias. I couldn't drive or go to the store. I pushed it all
> aside till it burst in my face one day. Otherwise, I would have sat around
> and vegetated till I just decayed. I had been in therapy for some time, but
> nothing worked until I started dealing with the abuse.

For the amnesic women, there was sudden recognition that one's
childhood, one's parents—yes, even one's life to this moment in time—
were not what one had believed them to be. The more that childhood and
parents had been idealized, the greater was the psychic shock. The impact was cataclysmic, and the conflict it generated was overwhelming.
Over half were tempted to commit suicide. These survivors were torn between their new insight—the click of recognition—and a desperate need
to deny it. Everything from the past was thrown into question. What *was*
reality in the face of massive contradictions between old memories and
new? **Alexis** wrote,

> Suddenly, I did not know my origins, and those who parented me were
> strangers. I was born into a world I do not now recognize. Even the pres-
> ent—my own identity—was uncertain. Who was I if the values that shaped
> my way of living were grounded in falsehood? I had to face the fact that a
> major part of my life was so intolerable that I had wiped it out of existence,
> that the world was more evil than I ever imagined. My only escape was to
> believe that I was going insane.

Most of the amnesic women I interviewed had lived quite successfully
by society's standards and had appeared much like others, even though
they secretly felt that they were barely holding themselves together.
These women had wrestled with life and had developed the ability to endure. Formally or informally, they had worked hard at improving them-

selves, their home and work situations—trying to find satisfaction in life. Some had gone through extensive counseling—individual or group therapy—and others had done soul-searching through Al-Anon or Weight Watchers. Over time, they had tackled a variety of problems but had not triggered memories of sexual abuse. These efforts had developed in them a strength that enabled them to deal with their traumatic memories later.

These amnesic women often became more insightful as they drew closer to their core issue. A middle-aged woman remarked wryly, "I feel a lot of kinship with the onion. I had to peel off so many layers to get to the center." Finally, the women knew what they were up against. They had named the problem at last and were ready for the hardest battle—salvaging the past and integrating it into the present.

PERSONAL REACTIONS TO THE INITIAL BREACH OF AMNESIA

The first fragmentary memories were usually only a sample of what was to come in the long process of remembering. (One woman, however, said she got a brief "table of contents" of what had happened, how it fitted into her life, and what its impact had been.) What was important was the click of recognition in the breakthrough because it convinced the women that they had indeed forgotten life-damaging events.

Initial memories tended to be more factual than emotional: "I was raped as a child." "My uncle pulled down my panties and rubbed me." "My father got into my bed and I was scared." An amnesic woman might even know intellectually that she had felt shamed, fearful, or helpless as a child, but it was usually some time before she experienced these dissociated emotions as connected to the memories. The factual knowledge was enough for her to handle for the time being, and it set off powerful repercussions. Even though it usually took a while for a woman to connect her childhood emotions to particular memories, she often found a storm of feelings unleashed around the fact that she had been sexually abused. Her world would never be the same.

In the days that followed, there were strong reactions. For many amnesic survivors, the intervening years seemed to disappear: It seemed as if the rape had happened yesterday or the molestation had occurred last night. Agitation and exhaustion competed, as the women felt too electric to rest but too exhausted to perform their usual tasks. "I felt extremely anxious and agitated, as if electric currents ran through all the parts of my body, and they were miswired." "I couldn't stand any noise or chaos for weeks." The women's normal coping mechanisms were acutely upset. They needed time and space to absorb the force of reality breaking through. Some, like **Angela**, fought against it:

> Being "dead" was familiar—the only thing I knew. I was OK with that. Not this remembering. When it happens, I feel, "God take me. I don't want to be here."

In some ways the pain was not different from that experienced over the years. However, previously, the feelings of sadness, anger, and aloneness were diffuse and harder to name, and the respondents had been scarcely aware of the toll taken on their energy and feelings of aliveness. Their unhappy feelings had been spread out over time, although sometimes erupting in an explosion of inappropriate emotion that left them and those around them puzzled and embarrassed. Now, instead, they experienced everything more acutely because they were more aware of its meaning and were dealing with many early events together, in a concentrated period of time. They were reliving them without the dulling of anesthesia, addiction, and denial that had formerly obscured what they felt. They were allowing themselves to fully experience past pain so that they need not bear it as a dead weight through the years ahead—so that they would clearly know who they were, what they thought and felt, what they wanted from life, and who they wanted to share it with.

Regression

During the first few days and weeks after the breakthrough of memories, the women at times found themselves feeling and acting like small children. They suddenly realized that their chin was quivering, or that they were, toddler-like, rubbing tears away with the back of their fists. They needed to be comforted and protected and to tell their story over and over, as they had been unable to do many years ago. The counselors (who were called into this crisis situation or who had already seen the client for other problems) could reassure them that their reactions were normal. During the crisis of initial recall, the women needed to flow with what was happening and to give priority to their own needs.

Relief and Understanding

Many respondents experienced relief that their lives made sense at last. They were not "crazy" as they had secretly feared. At last, they could answer the nagging question "What's wrong with me?" and, for the first time, know that it wasn't their fault. It was as if someone had hit them with a truck, but no one had tended to their wounds. After **Ashley**'s breakthrough in the counseling office, her therapist made sure that she was driven back to her home. There, she lay on a sofa while a friend sat beside her, holding her hand. For over an hour, fragmented sentences tumbled out, connecting decades of fear to the childhood rape that she had just uncovered:

> Oh, now I know why I've been so afraid and on guard . . . not able to look men in the eye. . . . Oh, now I know why trust feels so dangerous! . . . That strange fear of being hit. . . . Oh!! The doctor moving my legs when I had a caudal. . . . Feeling nauseated by violent scenes on TV . . . the dizzy spells . . . weird compulsions. . . .

All of a sudden, so many things in her life made sense. However devastating the new knowledge, there were certain immediate rewards. Over half of both amnesics and nonamnesics reported that they felt a sense of relief (63% and 57%, respectively) and a flood of new understandings (54% and 57%).

New discernment about their previously stressed existence gave most of the women determination to do whatever it took to find their way through to the truth. Knowledge that trauma had occurred, recognition that it had been severe abuse, and awareness of its impact provided a passport to freedom for women like Ashley. They finally had an answer to many disturbing questions. They were not crazy, evil, or worthless, as so many had believed. Instead, they could take pride in having survived as well as they had. However, knowledge that one had been abused was not enough. **Pat**, whose dreams of molestation had made her feel crazy, reported, "Life was great for about a year—just knowing that I hadn't made it up. But then I had to *deal with* what had happened."

Troubling Emotions

Even women who felt relieved to know that there was a basis for their problems did not escape disillusionment, grief, and horror. There were still painful emotions and agonizing questions. The amnesic and nonamnesic women were similar in their experience of guilt (63% and 57%, respectively) and in asking "Why me?" (54% and 62%). These concerns are related because both carry the feeling of being at fault. The question "Why me?" implies "Why was I singled out? What did I do to deserve it?" It led to other questions as the women tried to make sense of their abuse. The search for meaning obsessed many women in the months ahead— "Why did he use me?"; "Why did God let this happen?" (cf. Emerson, 1986); "Why did no one help?" As their awareness of our abusive society broadened, many asked, "How can I live in a world where this happens to so many little children?"

At the other extreme from women who experienced relief as well as dismay, there were ones for whom sudden remembering was starkly negative. One stayed drunk for days and tried to overdose on drugs. Several cried nonstop. The most salient characteristic of all these reactions was that emotions were raw, powerful, and changeable. This was a sign of new life and growth, but it was terrifying to women who had numbed their feelings from childhood or who had been relatively out of touch with them. It was important for them to realize that these feelings were not really new. The feelings were the same ones they had known as children, the same ones they had carried through the silent years of denial. Then, they were held within, unacknowledged, while the numbing cycle of posttraumatic stress disorder (PTSD) held ascendance. Now, they were owned and more safely externalized. Their very intensity told how much energy had been sapped from living to keep them contained.

Choosing Not to Remember

Occasionally, a therapist has discussed with me the fact that some clients are close to awareness of sexual abuse before they are strong enough to work on it. One client's current problem (e.g., addiction) may require attention first; the fragile self-esteem of another needs strengthening; or a network of social support is important before a third client is ready to face the past. Also, therapists have pointed out that some clients can handle an onslaught of memories, whereas others need to move slowly, integrating each new memory over a period of time. In cases such as these, the client and therapist are not avoiding recall but monitoring memories only as the client is ready to deal with them.

I have also talked with several people who say that they are unwilling to deal with the past. Intellectually, they realize that they were sexually abused as children—that knowledge was only muted. They may even infer what occurred and suspect who their abuser was. For example, **Andrew** told me that his mother or the maid molested him, and he has guessed the nature of the abuse. He has deliberately chosen to believe it was the maid and to block any further information about the past. At least, people like Andrew have the comfort of recognizing that there is a reason—beyond themselves—for certain problems that they continue to experience. However, few amnesics have such freedom of choice. For most, if a first memory comes, more will follow—whether they feel ready or not.

Denial

Throughout the survivors' anguished remembering, there typically persisted the contrary theme of denial: "It can't be true." How slow this theme is to die. The formerly amnesic women suffered many recurring doubts about their new memories. Amnesia and other forms of denial had allowed them to survive childhood, and these defenses would not be easily abandoned.

It is important to recognize that the emphasis in denial is on "It can't be true" rather than "It isn't true"—on "He couldn't have done such things" rather than "He didn't do them." The rememberer constantly questions how something so terrible could have been done to her, how it could have been done by that particular person, and how it could possibly be blotted out of consciousness. The enormity of it just does not fit with her prior view of the world. Trauma has shattered that view (Janoff-Bulman, 1990).

Differences Between the Groups

The first questionnaire included a checklist on which the research participants indicated their immediate responses in dealing with their abuse. Some of the ways in which the several groups of respondents were similar have been described above, and all of their responses are presented in Table 10.1. In addition to their similarities, there were also a number of notable differences between the amnesic and nonamnesic groups.

Table 10.1 Immediate Reactions to Breakthrough, by Group (%)

Reaction	Amnesic	Partial Amnesic	Nonamnesic	Imprisoned	Total
Denial	83	43	24	25	48***
Horror	67	50	24	33	46***
Disillusionment	57	36	29	58	44*
Suicidal feelings	54	50	29	17	40*
Agitation/exhaustion	67	71	52	83	67
Change in sexual feelings	54	21	24	17	33*
Normal coping fails	63	64	43	33	52
Escape to alcohol/drugs	21	21	5	25	17
Grief	67	50	57	50	58
Anger	58	64	81	67	68
Guilt	63	50	57	42	55
Why me?	54	43	62	67	57
Relief	63	36	57	50	54
New understanding	54	29	57	50	50
Need to talk about it	50	43	71	25	51

NOTE: Unqualified "yes" responses only (occasional missing data).
*$p < .05$. **$p < .01$. ***$p < .001$. Difference between amnesics and nonamnesics, one-tailed.

Even though all research participants found the breakthrough had profound immediate effects, the different levels of prior knowledge, recognition, and awareness that distinguished nonamnesic women from amnesics influenced their immediate reactions. Amnesic women were much more likely than nonamnesics to experience denial (83% vs. 24%), horror (67% vs. 24%), and disillusionment (57% vs. 29%). They were also much more likely to feel suicidal (54% vs. 29%) and to try to escape through alcohol or drugs (21% vs. 5%).

Such differences underscore how important it is that defenses not be broken down prematurely in therapy. Indeed, several women were hospitalized just before or right after remembering. For some women, suicidal feelings were triggered by shame or by facing the intolerable truth about a parent or relative. However, for others, self-destructive and suicidal symptoms decreased sharply. Stubbornness led **Audrey** to vow, "I'll be damned if I'll let him kill me, too!"

More amnesic women than nonamnesics experienced a disruption of normal coping (63% vs. 43%). The nonamnesics had a long history of coping with the partial truth of their past. Moreover, amnesic women were much more likely to have immediate changes in sexual feelings (54% vs.

24%). **Anita** reported, "It felt as if all my sexual feelings were miswired and were exploding chaotically." Generally, the initial sexual response was distress or a fluctuation between approach and avoidance. Only two women experienced liberated rather than inhibited sexuality.

As to their feelings, both groups experienced grief for their stolen childhood (67% vs. 57%), but fewer amnesic than nonamnesic women were angry at those who had taken it away (58% vs. 81%). **Adelle,** for example, tried for some weeks to view her father's abuse as loving and gentle. The need to talk about their feelings with others was initially less powerful for amnesic women than for nonamnesics (50% vs. 71%). Having never discussed any part of their trauma before, the amnesics' shock and denial on first remembering were restraining factors. Nonamnesic women, by contrast, were more likely already to have a partner or friend who had been aware of some of their past and been supportive about it.

PERSONAL REACTIONS IN LATER STAGES

The first breakthrough of memories was followed by a gradual unraveling of the past, highlighted from time to time by smaller crises of especially painful recollections. For many women, recall came rapidly at first and then more gradually over the next few months (although for some the pace was reversed). The experiences of all their past years were repeatedly examined in the light of the new information, much of which came from the flashbacks described in Chapter 9. This was a difficult time, but it was marked by signs of real progress in salvaging the past, destroying its negative power, and making use of new strengths. The impact of this process was felt in many personal ways that are examined below. The data in Table 10.2 came from the women's responses to a portion of the first questionnaire, where they described the reactions they had in the first 6 months after breaking out from denial or amnesia.

About half of both amnesic and nonamnesic women were having new memories by this time (48% and 57%, respectively). For the amnesics, these memories were likely to be additional details that fleshed out their embryonic memories. Many of the nonamnesics were recovering suppressed incidents that helped them put their past in perspective. Large majorities of both groups were also understanding the impact of their abuse more clearly (64% and 81%). Their current feelings were similar to but more acutely painful than those that had troubled them over the

Table 10.2 Reactions 6 Months After Breakthrough, by Group (%)

Reaction	Amnesic	Partial Amnesic	Nonamnesic	Imprisoned	Total
Denial of memories	76	57	24	27	49***
Intrusive thoughts, obsessions	64	43	67	45	58
Regressive experiences, feel like a kid	76	64	81	55	72
Raw, changeable emotions	68	57	76	64	68
Grief	84	57	62	36	65*
Anger	64	57	76	73	68
Need to scream	60	36	48	73	54
Need to hit out	40	50	48	36	44
Changes in sexual feelings	60	36	57	45	52
Changes in marriage/relationship	52	43	52	55	51
Changes in friends	48	43	48	55	48
Problems with relatives	40	43	57	18	42
Problems in coping with work	52	43	38	36	44
New memories	48	50	57	73	55
New understanding	64	57	81	82	70
Need support from:					
Therapy	92	86	67	73	80*
Friends	76	71	57	73	69
Family	52	36	33	64	45
All three of these resources	52	36	10	45	35***
Desire to confront abuser (if living)	60	17	39	20	38

NOTE: Unqualified "yes" responses only (occasional missing data).
*$p < .05.$ **$p < .01.$ ***$p < .001.$ Difference between amnesics and nonamnesics, one-tailed.

years. For example, about three quarters of each group described themselves as having raw emotions (68% and 76%), and since their breakthrough, reports of grief experiences had risen in both groups (to 84% and 62%). The women were constantly reminded of how troubled they really were and of the amount of pain they had shoved out of mind or avoided through amnesia. For many, PTSD symptoms made daily life difficult —intrusive thoughts (64% and 67%), flashbacks, bad dreams, or startled responses to noises or people tormented them. One woman had thought that remembering would suddenly explain and resolve all her problems, but, like other respondents, she had to recognize that recovery was not a simple process.

Despite their momentous breakthrough, the women typically continued to waver in believing their new perceptions of the past. Many former amnesics were haunted by the fear that they had "made up" their new memories. After all, their glimpses of the past were still fragmentary, and they "might be mistaken." Moreover, if these women tried to talk to siblings or even close friends, they almost always met protests that their father, stepfather, or brother could not possibly have done such horrible things. Consequently, the denial of amnesic women took every possible form, and 76% of them reported it as a continuing problem—a figure much higher than for the nonamnesics (24%).

To a lesser extent, the nonamnesic women, too, reverted to old defenses. Even after directly facing the wrong that had been perpetrated against them and its impact on their lives, about one quarter of them still tended to deny what had happened or its impact on them. Even **Nina**, who clearly remembered 10 years of abuse perpetrated by both of her brothers, said that she still had moments of thinking that she must be crazy—that the abuse had never really happened.

The Need for Support

Social support was essential to recovery for both amnesics and nonamnesics dealing with their childhood sexual abuse for the first time. This was not the time for tightly contained therapy, where a problem would be worked on solely by the therapist and client. The woman needed all the support she could get—from her therapist, counseling group, friends, family, and coworkers. However, it was hard for her to reach out to others because her trust had been badly damaged, and she feared further betrayal.

The most immediate need was for therapeutic support. A caring counselor, listening to accounts of terrifying flashbacks and of the disbelief of relatives, could make a client feel really heard for the first time: "I'm so sorry for what you had to go through as a child, and for what you are still going through." Support from concerned friends and loved ones could sometimes have similar effects.

Support from individuals with similar backgrounds was also important. Women in the throes of dealing with past abuse could gain understanding of the remembering process through self-help groups for adults molested as children (AMACs) or through reading personal accounts written by survivors. Both of these sources, although hard to find in the 1980s, provided them with affirmation that they were not alone or crazy.

Their past and their present could be shared with others who were having similar experiences. Another important kind of support was society's increasing recognition of the reality of childhood sexual abuse in the 1980s, and public expression in the mass media of concerned attitudes toward adult abuse survivors. In contrast, there was much less public sympathy for survivors in the 1990s.

Comparing the memory groups, the need for social support was felt most strongly by amnesic women, who had to work through more layers of forgotten material than the nonamnesics. Therapeutic support ranked as most needed (by 92% of amnesics vs. 67% of nonamnesics). Need for support from friends came second (76% vs. 57%) and then support from family members (52% vs. 33%). The greater deficiency of the amnesics can be seen in the fact that 52% of them indicated their need of all three of these resources, compared with only 10% of the nonamnesics.

Sadly, however, confirmation of memories, or even credence or support, was unlikely to come from those who might be most in a position to help—members of the family of origin. Typically, a survivor's story undermined beliefs and coping styles that had enabled a damaged family to operate through the years, and family members generally rallied to defend the family's image from attack. The survivor usually found herself on the outside as soon as she hinted that all was not well in Camelot, and she generally remained unwelcome as long as she persevered. (Chapter 11 discusses such interpersonal relationships in detail.) A survivor's closest relatives typically became the people by whom she felt most abandoned. Such experiences provided compelling evidence as to why these women could not "tell" when they were children.

The desire to confront their abuser fluctuated repeatedly for survivors during the healing process. Six months after remembering, 60% of amnesic women, compared with 39% of nonamnesics, were anxious to confront their abuser. However, very few of the amnesics were ready to do so. Most were motivated by a powerful need to have the abuser say "Yes, I did it. It was my fault, and I'm really sorry." In other words, they wanted to have their difficult-to-believe memories confirmed by the one person who knew the most about the abuse. Unfortunately, he (or she) was the person least likely to help. Instead, he was likely to protest and proclaim what she had feared—"You're crazy!"— thus compounding the denial and ostracism that she experienced from other members of the family.

Emotions

With remembering, the anxiety, guilt, and unreasoned fears that many women had experienced behind their calm exteriors over the years made sense at last, and these emotions began to lose the power they had derived from their hidden subversion. However, anger and grief took much longer to be expressed and resolved. As these feelings struggled to find outlets, the respondents typically were afraid of getting out of control and felt as if they were riding herd on wild horses. They had a special terror of unleashing anger, for it had been bottled up inside them for so long that, often, it had turned to rage. Once turned loose, could it ever be contained? A petite woman, unburdening herself in my office, said with quiet restraint, "I am so angry that I could tear out that wall of books with my bare hands." It was often many months before a survivor could express such fury that someone had been so insensitive to her pain. In doing so, she needed a place where she could feel the cleansing effects of anger without damaging herself and others.

Emotional moods tended to fluctuate widely for most of the women at this time, and these feelings could no longer be numbed. Now they were powerful and demanded outlets. The proportion of survivors who acknowledged strong anger remained about as high as at their breakthrough point (64% of amnesics and 76% of nonamnesics). Many women felt a need to scream out their anguish (60% and 48%, respectively) or to hit out (40% and 48%), which they sometimes expressed by slamming their anger into pillows that could safely absorb it. Amnesic women were more likely to express grief (84%) than anger (64%), whereas the nonamnesics expressed grief (62%) less often than anger (76%).

Illustrating these feelings, **Alana** was distraught that there was no place to freely scream her pain and grief:

> As a child, I was hushed and smothered and frightened into silence. As a woman, I may scream during therapy—*if* I smother the sound with a pillow, but that's what my stepfather did to me. Why may I never be heard?

Similarly, the issue of screams led **Pamela**'s therapist to offer her a Saturday appointment when nearby offices were vacant. However, she felt the need to scream on other days as well. In desperation, she walked a noisy truck road night after night so that she could scream as each vehicle was passing. Her therapist felt bad but knew that screams from the clinic could bring a police officer to the door. Pamela bitterly volunteered to tell her would-be rescuer, "You're 30 years too late."

Sadness and grief took many forms for these women. Sadness for the children they had been, and for the lost years, was agonizing for many of them. Grief was especially overwhelming for those who had lost forever the possibility of marriage and parenthood or who had experienced a series of abusive relationships. Others grieved for the years during which they had drowned their anxiety in alcohol or had surrounded their bodies with protective layers of fat. Still others, who had remained ignorant of their own molestation, now found to their dismay that they had been unable to protect their own child or grandchild from incest or sexual assault.

Problem Areas

Large segments of both the amnesic and nonamnesic groups reported similar areas of life that were problematic for them. These were changes in sexuality (60% and 57%, respectively), in marital relationships (52% and 52%), and in friends (48% and 48%), problems with relatives (40% and 57%), and problems in coping with work (52% and 38%). As reported above, about two thirds of each group were experiencing intrusive thoughts and flashbacks as well as raw emotions. These reactions contributed to making sexual contact difficult and intimate relationships strained—for higher proportions than at the breakthrough point 6 months earlier. For example, **Patricia** reported,

> When I get horny, I start being afraid and picking arguments with my husband or wanting to hide in the closet. Yet, I have orgasms freely in flashbacks. Apparently, all the machinery was intact when I was a child. At some point, I refused to give "him" the satisfaction of reacting, and it's hard to turn myself on again so many years later.

As mentioned above, relatives tended to close ranks against a woman who was dragging skeletons out of the family closet. Work problems were somewhat more common for amnesic women, who were more prone to flashbacks and dissociation, which interfered with their normal functioning, as well as to other PTSD symptoms.

Responses to the women's new discoveries varied greatly. Changes in friendships developed as survivors reached out for understanding and support. Some of these changes were positive. Some listeners became un-tiring supporters, filled with compassion. The survivors who experi-enced this tended to have made healthier contacts in the years prior to the breakthrough, and they were often astonished to realize that they were much loved. However, fair-weather friends vanished when survivors who had been rescuers entered their own time of desperate need. NANCY—who had been a stalwart support to mother, sisters, and trou-bled friends—found herself deserted. Even the sympathetic friends who stood by the survivors were drained by the distress of women in such acute crisis. Other people seemed indifferent or pretended not to hear their agonizing accounts of abuse. Perhaps some of these accounts tapped into unexamined areas of their own lives. **Phyllis** told me, "I lost all my friends." But then she added in a surprised tone, "But that's OK!"

Often, it was other survivors in therapy groups who filled the gap in providing support. During all this personal and interpersonal distress, a major lesson that was learned by most of the women was that they could depend on themselves.

Positive Feelings

By the time I sent the first questionnaire to the survivors, they had typi-cally been dealing with their memories of abuse for about a year, and they felt that they had already grown in a positive direction. Many women (54% of the respondents) said that they felt "adult" for the first time, even though a roller coaster of emotions could sometimes carry them back to childhood within seconds so that they might feel like a kid as well (72%). They began to "expect the unexpected," to relinquish rigid self-control, and to have increasing faith in their own personhood. Table 10.3 summa-rizes the women's reports of the positive characteristics that had emerged in their lives.

The women's emotions become self-affirming rather than dangerous. They learned that honest anger is pure and energizing and that it can be safely released. They found that tears of grief can cleanse and heal, un-blocking the flow of loving feelings toward others as well. Laughter be-gan to lighten their heaviness. **Peggy**, age 37, remarked, "I never knew what people meant when they talked of their 'love of life.' Now, for the first time, I'm beginning to feel it for myself."

Table 10.3 Positive Characteristics Experienced in the Healing Process,
by Group (%)

Positive Characteristic	Amnesic	Partial Amnesic	Nonamnesic	Imprisoned	Total
Deeper relationships	58	57	81	73	67
Rejoice in own strength and courage	67	43	76	82	67
Pride in surviving past trauma	67	57	71	64	66
Glad for new chance at life	62	57	62	82	64
Aware/in touch with own feelings	71	57	62	64	64
Feel in charge of own life	67	36	62	64	59
More centered/whole/integrated	62	36	48	73	54
Have more energy and creativity	71	29	33	64	50

NOTE: Unqualified "yes" responses only (occasional missing data).

Needs and Temptations in Therapy

As mentioned above, the survivors strongly felt the need for therapeutic support when they began dealing with their memories of childhood sexual abuse. The first questionnaire asked them about the kinds of support they wanted in therapy, and their answers are shown in Table 10.4. The greatest need that they expressed was to be believed, respected, and cared about as worthwhile individuals (83%). Their next most important needs were to have their strengths and progress affirmed (76%) and to gain information about what was happening as they moved through the recovery process (76%). Also important was the need to receive compassion when they were in pain (69%). Finally, a smaller majority stated the hope to have their experience as abuse victims and survivors validated by others who had had a similar trauma (61%). The imprisoned women were particularly high on most of these items—not surprising in view of their incarcerated situation—whereas the differences among the other subgroups did not show a systematic pattern.

The respondents also reported on the temptations that they were experiencing and needed to resist in dealing with their past abuse. They showed less agreement about these than about their needs in therapy (see Table 10.4). The majority (59%) mentioned the danger of remaining stuck in the victim role rather than progressing to new, healthier relationships. Related to that idea, 45% noted the danger of constantly obsessing about the past. The second-strongest temptation that the women expressed was their eagerness to try to rush the recovery process and "get it over with" (54%). Similarly, 49% mentioned the danger of expecting therapy to solve

Table 10.4 Needs and Temptations in the Healing Process, by Group (%)

Aspect of the Healing Process	Amnesic	Partial Amnesic	Nonamnesic	Imprisoned	Total
What are needs from therapy?					
Be believed, respected, and cared about	79	100	80	75	83
Have my strengths and progress affirmed	71	71	75	92	76
Be informed about recovery process	67	79	80	83	76
Get compassion when in pain	62	71	70	75	69
Have my experience validated	75	43	50	75	61
Temptations experienced					
Stay stuck in victim role	46	85	60	58	59
Try to rush recovery process	62	46	55	42	54
Expect to solve all my problems	50	38	55	50	49
Obsess about the past	33	69	30	67	45
Avoid working on most painful parts	29	38	40	50	38

NOTE: Unqualified "yes" responses only (occasional missing data).

all of their problems. On the other hand, 38% admitted that they were often tempted to avoid working on the most painful parts of their problems. The partially amnesic survivors were particularly likely to express the temptations to stay stuck in the victim role and to obsess about the past, whereas the formerly amnesic women were relatively low on those temptations and also on avoidance of working on the most painful parts of their past. The imprisoned women—again reasonably, in view of their situation—were high in obsessing about the past but low in trying to rush the recovery process.

Reliance on Old Coping Mechanisms

During the months of remembering, the respondents experienced extraordinary stress. It is not surprising that they fell back on old coping mechanisms that allowed them to escape for all-too-brief moments or hours. The women's coping mechanisms after their breakthrough period are shown in Table 10.5. Keeping busy and trying harder were old favorites that had enabled the respondents to accomplish objectives and have some sense of control while also blocking intrusive thoughts and feelings. In the months after they sought help, these mechanisms were still used by 60% and 54% of the women, respectively.

Some escapist coping mechanisms also remained quite popular. Eating provided comfort and helped to numb overwhelming emotional feel-

Table 10.5 Coping Styles After Breakthrough of Memories, by Group (%)

Coping Style	Amnesic	Partial Amnesic	Nonamnesic	Imprisoned	Total
Keeping busy	58	62	70	45	60
Trying harder	58	54	55	45	54
Escapes					
Oversleeping	38	38	50	45	43
Compulsive eating	42	38	65	27	46
Television	38	15	35	27	31
Suicide temptation	29	38	15	27	26
Drugs/alcohol	8	23	5	36	15
Positive methods					
Art/music/writing	38	54	55	64	50
Journaling	46	38	55	45	47
Treating self well, having fun	33	15	55	27	35
Exercise	42	8	35	45	34

NOTE: Unqualified "yes" responses only (occasional missing data).

ings for 46% of the respondents—42% of the amnesics versus 65% of the nonamnesics, who used this escape more than any other group. Sleeping was an important escape for 43% of the women because the flashback period was such an exhausting time. However, this figure was lower than the 58% reported for the interim years before the breakthrough period (see Table 7.3). One survivor told me, "AMACs are very tired women." Sleep was also a way to bring closure to an especially painful day. However, sleep for some amnesic women was likely to be disrupted by dreams, flashbacks, and convulsive jerking reflexes. These women were bone-weary but afraid of what the night would bring. Television was a popular escape for 31% of the respondents—its bright, resounding images could often distract their senses and delay the onslaught of yet another flashback.

More life-threatening escapism—a temptation toward suicide—was reported by 26% of the respondents (including 29% of amnesic women and 38% of the partially amnesic group), as the magnitude of the recovery process became more and more apparent to them. This level of suicidal feelings was substantially lower than the 47% reported for the long interim period after abuse (Table 7.5) and the 40% reported as an immediate reaction to the breakthrough of memories (Table 10.1). However, the more current reports were critical ones because these women were feeling a desire to end their life during a brief period of months—an acute symptom, not just an occasional one over the decades since their abuse. Fortunately, none of the respondents actually took her own life during the course of the study.

For many of the women, suicidal temptation had ceased. These survivors now knew that there had been an explanation for their lifelong problems, and they bent their energies to achieving an improved life. Suicidal feelings were only 15% in the nonamnesic group. Encouragingly, drug and alcohol use was only 15% for the whole sample and was down to 8% for the amnesic women.

New Coping Mechanisms

The women were also learning new ways of coping that were positive rather than escapist. By the time of the second questionnaire (2 years after the first and about 3 years after their breakthrough), about half of the respondents (47%) had been journaling—keeping a diary of the process of their healing. This was an excellent way of getting in touch with, expressing, and clarifying feelings. Some women wrote directly from turbulent emotional states rather than using intellectual processing, allowing their journals to tap into feelings they were unaware of. For them, an inner censor was bypassed, and they were occasionally startled at what they found themselves writing. Unedited, free-flowing notebooks accumulated over the months, providing the women with evidence of how they had cycled through the ups and downs of remembering. These journals also kept track of flashes of memory that had bubbled into consciousness only to submerge again. They recorded progress over time as the women moved through the healing process. The journals were both records and validation of what had happened, of the impact of events, and of the women's small and large victories in working through their problems.

To survive the onslaught of emotions, thoughts, and new memories, most women had to radically simplify their lives. All nonessential activities dropped off—and they found there were many of these. Homemaking tasks became unimportant, and spouses and children looked after themselves more than ever before. A young wife and mother said, "My standards of cleanliness and cooking really fell off for a year, but our family survived." The women's job duties were expedited, and appointments were minimized. A professional woman reported, "Each day, I managed to make it through top priority jobs and then came home and collapsed." These women, many of whom had believed that their world would fall apart if they were not perfect, learned that their greatest responsibility was toward themselves.

Self-caring and being good to themselves tended to develop for many respondents because the crisis of remembering mandated putting themselves first to ensure their own emotional survival. Being good to themselves was a new coping mechanism for many of the survivors—reported by 35% of the whole sample, including 55% of the nonamnesics. However, it was not an easy change to accomplish for the half who had been self-abusive over the years (cf. Table 7.4).

Many respondents began actively seeking ways to treat themselves well—broadening out from their typical previous rewards of food and sleep. Artistic expression (such as painting, writing, or music) was gratifying to 50% of the women. New memories and satisfaction from their accomplishments were positive outcomes of the time they spent on new activities.

One third of the respondents (34%) reported pursuing some form of exercise by now—examples were jazzercise, aerobics, walking, running, and swimming. In contrast, prior to remembering, they had reported athletic activities much less often (12%). Exercise was therapeutic as well as physically healthful, especially for women who were depressed. It stimulated endorphins that promoted a sense of well-being and forced a change in the women's heart rate and breathing. Many survivors had had such unhappy experiences of being trapped, smothered, and silenced that their breathing had been decidedly affected. Exercise required them to breathe faster, deeper, and more loudly than they would have allowed themselves to do otherwise. Also, exercise typically required a change of scene, getting outdoors or being with other women. Some of the respondents found a partner in their chosen activity, whom they talked to regularly. This provided them with an extra chance to ventilate about their problems, but it usually meant sharing views on more upbeat topics as well.

"Having fun" was another positive aspect of the women's treating themselves well, but this capacity came far more slowly. Fun involves elements of risk, spontaneity, and disinhibition. The respondents tended to suffer from an inability to enjoy themselves (anhedonia). Therefore, therapists who sought to counterbalance the painful work of remembering for clients often found them unable to specify a list of fun activities. As

Andrea remarked, "I can think of lots of events that others consider fun, but I would find myself just going through the motions." Sometimes, the first evidence of a shift came in a dream, such as her following example:

> I was all by myself in a child's amusement center. Instead of hundreds of colored balls to play in, there were live furry kittens and puppies and baby rabbits 3 feet deep. I rolled around freely in that mass of softness without hurting them at all. It was a freeing, joyous celebration of the sense of touch. It was fun. It was healing.

Andrea also found models for a happier self among children who began to populate her dreams—ones with spontaneity, eagerness for life, willingness to risk, and an open expression of all their feelings.

Increased Knowledge

> *Ignorance is not bliss. It sure didn't put a song in my heart.*
> —**Anne,** 1989

One third of the respondents (33%) were impatient with the slow process of reexperiencing past emotions and memories (cf. Table 9.2). This was more true of nonamnesic women (40%), who already had a reality base into which they could plug new information and awareness. The amnesic survivors had been far more horrified and disillusioned by their breakthrough (cf. Table 10.1), so their desire for information was lower (24%), being offset by a strong fear of what they might find out. They were having to reconstruct, memory by memory, the reality of what their childhood had been. However, there were some for whom the "need to know" what had happened to them was almost desperate. Until the pieces came together, they could not know which of their new and old memories were real and which were distortions.

Although amnesic women were troubled by their own questioning and denial of new memories, they were at least as concerned with the reality of old memories that they had carried through the years before the recall of abuse. Was there any truth to the belief that their mother and father were kindly and loving? What about the values on which they had based their lives? Were these values founded on the twisted views of their parents? They needed to remember because their problems had stemmed from *not* remembering. *Not* to know had been their defense mechanism. Now, truth was essential for them. They wanted to get control of their memories, to work them through, and to get all of the injuries out in the open.

BEST AND WORST PARTS OF REMEMBERING

In 1992, 6 years after the first questionnaire, I sent the survivors a third questionnaire, in which I asked them about the best and worst aspects of working through their memories. Their responses revealed a great deal about the process of confronting childhood sexual abuse. A few of the women checked nearly every one of the "worst parts" and very few of the "best parts," indicating that they were still having a very difficult time in dealing with the past, but most saw strong positive aspects as well. The percentage of women listing each aspect is presented in the text below.

Worst Parts

The worst aspect of remembering for most women was the overwhelming emotions, which had been stifled and disallowed in childhood and later suppressed by themselves, and which now found an outlet (checked by 62%). Grief, anger, shame, and terror gripped the women with such power that they were afraid they would lose control. At times, they were overwhelmed by sadness, immobilized by fear, burning with shame, or so filled with anger that they felt they could kill.

To come to the realization that there was nothing wrong with themselves, the women had to give up many past beliefs. The second-worst part of dealing with the past was admitting how seriously sexual abuse had influenced their lives (58%). Related to that was having to recognize who had abused them (33%)—usually a relative. They had used an arsenal of defense mechanisms over the years to keep themselves from looking at what had happened and who their abuser had been. It took great courage to give up these defenses—to face the past and to admit that it had distorted their lives. Their abuse had shaped the goals they had selected, the work they were doing, the friends they had chosen, the intimate relationships they had formed (or avoided), their ability to parent, and their health—every aspect of living.

Recurring doubts and denial (48%), especially for amnesics, were a problem for years as the women alternately fled from the truth and em-

Recurring doubts and denial (48%), especially for amnesics, were a problem for years as the women alternately fled from the truth and embraced it. It took many months for them to realize the full extent of the impact, but that became clearer as time went by. A number of the women's answers were related to discouragement (30%), which set in from time to time because of the long time that recovery was taking (56%) and the difficulty of changing old patterns (54%). It was hard for them to see their improvement (34%), and they worried whether they would ever get over the past (44%).

Another group of items highlighted the survivors' close links with the past. At times, they felt stuck in the past (50%)—even lost in it. It sometimes seemed more real than the present (20%), especially when intense flashbacks engulfed them (36%), or they relived what had happened to them (24%), or they tended to lapse into old ways of behaving (26%).

A final major difficulty for 46% of respondents was the loss of support they experienced as adults when they began to examine the past. Most felt abandoned by their relatives and families of origin—an experience that helped them understand why they could not tell as children and why so many of them had found forgetting the best way out. This abandonment was especially devastating to women who had previously fantasized their family life as having been warm and close. Suddenly, they faced a past full of horror, and they faced it alone. By contrast, abandonment was an unhappy feature, but not a priority problem, for those who reported "It was nothing new—I never *did* have family support."

Best Parts

Although facing the reality of their abuse—its extent and its impact on their lives—was one of the worst aspects of the healing process, it was also a freeing experience for the survivors. Almost immediately after confronting their memories, 54% of the women felt a sense of relief (cf. Table 10.1). And 6 months later, despite the shock of that awakening, 70% had been grateful that they now understood the impact of their childhood trauma more fully than they ever had before (cf. Table 10.2).

Looking back 6 years later, the survivors reported that the best parts of the healing process were finding that they were not crazy after all (70%), that the problems they had wrestled with for years made sense at last

(68%), and that truth was replacing distortion in their view of life (50%). These three items all dealt with the nature of reality, and almost all of the respondents (90%) checked one or more of these features as one of the best parts of dealing with the past. These benefits increased with time as more and more pieces of the puzzle of their lives fell into place.

The second major area of benefit dealt with relationships. Experiencing the concern and support of others (50%) and the deepening of certain relationships (36%) were other important rewards of the healing process. The respondents' capacity for friendship and intimacy had grown, and 62% of them expressed one or more of these two benefits. Even more important, they had gotten to know, respect, and love themselves, and they no longer depended on the approval and control of others because they had become their own persons. They described being more centered within themselves (64%), being in tune with their own emotions (50%), and having a new appreciation of themselves (52%). Fully 82% of the women endorsed one or more of these qualities that described a new sense of personal integration.

The final area of benefit was a feeling of autonomy. The respondents appreciated getting a new chance at life (52%), and they felt more in charge of their lives (52%)—what they needed and wanted. Three quarters of the women (76%) endorsed one or both of those items. Many of them (48%) also affirmed that they now had more energy and creativity to use in achieving their goals.

During recovery, the survivors had occasionally been surprised by having "peak experiences" (Maslow, 1971) in which they felt intensely alive and aware and whole. They had seen these as glimpses of what their future might hold. Some also reported the more stable and lasting experience of reaching a new plateau—a sense of growth that seemed to have been sudden but in actuality had been long under way. Plateau experiences are characterized by a profound shift in attitude toward oneself, others, and the world. Both kinds of experience bring a keener and more intense appreciation of life. But, in my perception, the high plateaus also brought to some of the women a growing sense of peace that I began to see in their faces, hear in their voices, and feel in their presence.

SUMMARY

Six months after their breakthrough, both the amnesic and nonamnesic women were experiencing new memories and more understanding of their lives but also turbulent emotions. They needed social and therapeutic support anywhere it was available. Both groups found themselves wrestling with interpersonal problems—in sexual, friendship, and work relationships—and many of them had suicidal thoughts. They experienced recurrent doubts about the reality of their memories, and they still had difficulty in letting out the anger, grief, and pain that they had bottled up for so long. However, they were beginning to experience more positive feelings and to develop new and healthy ways of coping, although they still often fell back on their older and less constructive coping patterns.

Six years later, the respondents looked back on the process of dealing with their memories and saw both good and bad aspects. They had been flooded by unwelcome emotions, and they had had to give up their defenses of denial and numbness. They also had felt frequent discouragement at the long process of recovery, sometimes felt "stuck" in the past, and wondered whether they would ever get over the effects of their abuse. However, the positive aspects outweighed the negative ones. The survivors felt great relief at finding that confronting their memories had finally made sense out of their past problems and symptoms, giving them a better grasp of reality. They felt a new sense of personal integration and also of autonomy in being in charge of their lives. In addition, many of them had found unexpected reservoirs of concern and support from other people around them and had strengthened their important social relationships.

CHAPTER 11

Reactions of Others

I dreamed that a rattlesnake had taken over a child's bedroom. Her family warned her not to touch it, but the little girl grasped it firmly by the neck. The house shook to its foundations.

—NANCY

Traumatized people who "come home" from their ordeal do so with new emotions, attitudes, and behaviors. This is true whether the returnee is a veteran of hand-to-hand combat, a "comfort woman" who endured sexual slavery, or a woman facing memories of severe child sexual abuse. Family and friends can be seriously affected by changes in these survivors, which are disruptive of relationships and difficult to understand. This chapter examines the interpersonal crisis precipitated by my respondents' memory breakthrough—impacts on their close friendships, on the women's original family, and on their partners and children.

Dealing with previously unconfronted memories was usually a long and slow process. During this time period, the survivors needed the support and caring of loved ones and friends. They also needed a responsible counselor and, usually, group therapy with others who could share and understand their experience. It was a difficult time for all concerned, but the fact that the women had the courage to deal with a painful childhood is testimony to their strength and determination.

THE RESPONSE OF FRIENDS

It is important for traumatized people to be able to share their feelings, but it is hard for others to listen to their story, especially as it unfolds over time. The second questionnaire, in 1988, asked about the emotional support that survivors had received from their friends. In response, 34% said "much," 30% said "some," 26% mentioned lower amounts or actions that blocked their progress, and 10% reported that they hadn't told their friends about their childhood abuse.

The more specific reactions of friends to the women in this study were highly variable. Some friends were infinitely supportive. Others rapidly grew weary of listening to the survivor's pain. Some were sympathetic at first but expected the recovering survivor to "get over it" by some fixed point in time. Some could hear about a stranger rape but changed the topic or excused themselves if a family abuser was mentioned. The respondents found it hard to remember that such reactions had to do with the listener's own fears. As the women talked with other people about the problems they were confronting, whether before or after memories returned, they lost or gained friends in intriguing ways, as illustrated in the following examples.

Over several decades, **Andrea** had unwittingly prepared for her breakthrough through her choice of friends. During her amnesia, she had sought therapy from time to time for a series of emotional problems. She had also struggled to achieve a clearer sense of self and to bring meaning to her life. Through all these efforts, she had grown stronger and more mature. Early in adulthood, she had selected friends who were mother and father figures, knowing that she needed them but wondering why. Later, she chose more equalitarian relationships with people who were committed to self-growth. However, she was always afraid these friends would reject her if they really knew her. When the breach in her amnesia occurred, and her façade dropped away, she found she already had a small network of supporters, and it grew as she became a more open person. She was warmed and encouraged by the caring of these friends.

Other respondents found that their supposed friends fell away, or they themselves chose to reduce contact. Before dealing with her memories, **Patricia** had been a rescuer. Ignoring her own inner turmoil by tending to the troubles of everyone else, she had become a magnet for needy, selfish, dependent people. As she confronted her own truths, she realized that these friends were really parasites who were constantly draining and never nurturing her. She found that she was no longer willing to accept such an uneven exchange, and she had no time for people who would not support her in her own time of crisis. Many women found friends leaving them instead of the other way around. However, the desertion of friends who proved uncaring was usually found to be a minor loss, especially as the women grew stronger within themselves.

A few of the women held unreasonable expectations. **April**, for instance, decided that if she had to go through such a painful remembering process the least others could do was listen to her entire tale of abuse. She was constantly frustrated by nonsupportive responses. Others, like **Anita**, simply found her friends' responses generally disappointing: "A victim needs friends who don't play 'Twenty Questions' or change the subject—friends who won't tell you someone else's story and then say, 'Yours isn't so bad.' I haven't found any such friends yet."

The survivors needed to share upsetting childhood events that no caring person had ever listened to, and it was hard to edit their stories now. Many, however, much as they longed to talk freely, recognized that others could not handle all the "gory details" that were coming through in flashbacks and nightmares. They became like Geiger counters, ultrasensitive about to whom they could talk and what each person could endure. **Arna** found that she kept a mental account of which friends could handle what kind of information and how much of it: "Between therapy sessions, I would contact friends as I needed to. But I often felt like a big balloon filled with noxious gas, which I was obliged to vent only a little at a time so that the poison would not overwhelm those around me."

Many of the women (48%), however, described making new friends and deepening relationships, even in the first 6 months after their breakthrough. Especially helpful were friendships developed in therapy groups where AMACs shared their struggles and progress with survivors like themselves. In doing so, they became more honest in their relationships and increasingly compassionate toward others.

Frustration at the Skepticism of Others

The women needed all the support and validation they could get as they went through the difficult process of remembering. Unfortunately, disappointments were common. For example, a coworker asked **Portia** why she hadn't refused her father's sexual overtures (at age 5). Anyone who can ask that question ignores the power of authority, physical size and strength, love, fear, and dependency in the life of a child.

The general public, even with the information that is now more widely available than in earlier years, cannot comprehend the complexity of what happened to these women in childhood, nor of the repercussions affecting them in the present. The survivors were pressured by many listeners to "put the past behind you." Typical questions and comments (spoken in ignorance or even from genuine concern) during the remembering and recovery process, included the following:

- Why would you want to dig all this up?
- Is it wise to keep trying to have flashbacks?
- I thought you'd be over this by now. It's been several months.
- Why bother with all this therapy? It seems to be making you upset.
- Shouldn't you get on with your life?

It was hard for a survivor's friends to realize—just as she could not have imagined in advance—how unfinished the past can be. Recovering amnesics had had no idea of how much weight from the past they had carried through the years. And that burden was with them still. Each new memory seemed like an event that had just occurred, and consequently, the women's emotions and bodies were raw. **Arlene** explained, "When flashbacks take me back to Dad having sex with me at 10, my back hurts and I get cramps like a period. Afterward, I have to soak in a hot tub to ease the pain." A similar problem occurred for **Alicia** just 3 days after recalling a childhood rape, when she had to take a prearranged airplane trip:

> I felt as if I'd been hit by a truck, and I asked a stewardess in the airport if there was a place I could rest. I told her I had been raped. It seemed irrelevant that it was four decades ago. She took me to the employee lounge and her concern was healing.

During the remembering process, the women found it painful to have family, friends, relatives, or coworkers question their grasp on reality. Yet it was the need to stand firm against the pressure of others that helped build the self-confidence that they had lost early in life through sexual abuse. When a respondent found her rationality and stability questioned—when her flashbacks were termed symbolic or fantasy, or when someone suggested that her memories came from "another lifetime" —she felt anger, but also she frequently found a new strength and conviction. She resented the usurpation of her memories—for instance, another person interpreting her flashbacks to childhood assault as merely representing current aspects of her life, such as unfair working conditions, a bad business deal, or an abusive marriage. She was sure she knew the differences between fantasy, symbolism, and reality.

Amy gave an example of a fantasy that she had experienced 7 years before her memory returned. It affirmed for her now the fear and pain she had held inside through the years:

> Our conference group was asked to fantasize a small lake in a meadow, and I imagined mine—set among wild flowers, peaceful, blue and shining on a sunny afternoon—a hummingbird darting back and forth over the surface. Then, we were asked to look at it in cross-section, and I found my lake *deep and troubled*—brown and black and blood-red—boiling against the thin surface skin that held it back. I knew that one touch of the hummingbird's piercing beak could send something horrible exploding over the countryside.

Late in her recovery, Amy had a dream that displayed important symbolism. It seemed to her to represent both the effort and the rewards of overcoming childhood sexual abuse, and it provided a dramatic contrast to her years-earlier fantasy:

> I dreamed I was walking through grassy foothills with my husband. The rough slope of the mountain suddenly looked tempting to me, and I spontaneously decided to test my strength by climbing as far as I reasonably could. I would meet my husband later. I climbed with difficulty, and the slope grew steeper and more and more challenging. But I felt invigorated and proud that my strength was holding up. I wouldn't think of stopping now. I felt sure that I could go all the way to the top. After a long while, I was nearly there and paused to catch my breath. Looking around, I saw that my husband had been with me all the way, giving me space to prove myself. With my last strength, I pulled my head and shoulders over the rocky ledge at the top. I had done it! I had reached the top! And now, stretched down and away, on the other side of the mountain— where we were headed—lay the most beautiful country I had ever seen.

Fantasy and symbolism, such as the examples above, are metaphors that can provide a variety of insights. They can be supportive indications of survivors' actual feelings and events. In contrast, memories—experienced through the senses, the emotions, and the mind—are based on past events rather than on representations. The women's memories helped them find reality, and even if the resulting picture was incomplete and somewhat flawed, it was far more honest than the idealized picture of family life that had blinded them through the decades.

THE RESPONSE OF FAMILY MEMBERS

> *It's a constant struggle to stand by your truths. That's the real battle, because it's such a lonely road. To believe against the opinion of your whole family, you have to be strong.*
>
> **—PAULA**

The great majority of my respondents who turned to their family or relatives for support quickly realized why they could not "tell" as a child. Their story was too threatening to the family members. Only 14% reported that their family and relatives gave them "much" emotional support, 10% received "some" support, 70% got reactions ranging from little support down to blocking their progress, and 6% entirely avoided telling their family members.

If an adult survivor now told her family of a rape that she had endured as a child, with no one knowing or helping, the idea was appalling to them. To accept the news would be to admit that her parents had somehow failed her, so most family members appeared not to take the account seriously. If they did give the account credence, their common reaction was to say, "That was all long ago. Put it behind you and get on with your life." This reaction was especially likely if the rememberer, fearful of upsetting the family, had described the event in an off-hand way, minimizing the experience and not revealing its impact on her over time and into the present—of course, she herself might just be learning more about the event's impact and so be unclear about it in her own mind. Fortunately, there were some caring individuals who were exceptions to the general inability of family members to be truly supportive when childhood rape was remembered.

However, when the abuse was at the hands of someone the family trusted, the situation was far worse—especially if the offender was a parent, a brother, or someone who was idolized. Only two women whom I interviewed found immediate, solid support from siblings. Generally, brothers and sisters didn't want to believe that a loved or respected uncle, a sibling, or a parent had done such things. In addition to general skepticism, another motivational factor prevented belief in such allegations—if siblings allowed themselves to believe that such abuse had happened to one family member, that opened the possibility that they themselves might also have forgotten similar abuse. If the perpetrator was a family member, in most cases the respondent's mother was still married to the offending father or stepfather, or was still protective of her predatory son(s). She was torn apart by her daughter's accusation, and for her, the quickest way back to "normal" was to have the accuser retract her charges.

The phrase "killing the messenger" who bears bad news comes from ancient Greece, but the theme lives on. Adult survivors who disclosed incest to their families—just like child victims who tell (as reported by Summit, 1983)—tended to be viewed as the problem. They were pressured to accommodate by giving up their own perceptions, their own truth, and their own integrity. However, in a similar fashion, the reciprocal form of pressuring also sometimes occurred. For example, a survivor, desperately in need of support and fearful for other potential victims, might put unbearable pressure on siblings to accept these new and horrible truths.

Disbelief or minimization was the common response of relatives. They often tended to see a recovering amnesic as disturbed or vindictive. A substantial proportion of the women were called crazy—especially by the abuser, if they confronted him. Experiencing this reaction clarified for survivors why they had been unable to tell as children. In other families, relatives who had genuine love and concern for a rememberer tried to find kinder explanations for what she was experiencing. They might view her not as crazy but as "mistaken" in her interpretation of memories, as **Alison** reported:

> My brother suggested that my memories about Dad were symbolic. Or perhaps they came from another lifetime (though he doesn't believe in "past lives"). I think that the hardest burden in all this was my siblings' disbelief, and the way they protected their grown children from even minimal information about what I was remembering. I felt so very lonely and betrayed.

I learned from interviews that when a respondent who had been molested by a brother or uncle was at least partially believed by the family, she was usually expected to handle the inevitable strain or to settle the matter quickly with an easy forgiveness. After a brief conversation, and perhaps an indifferent apology, the families expected to "put all this behind us," and they often tended to throw the abuser and the abused together at family get-togethers. To the survivors, *together* was a poignant word—mingling fear, anger, dependency, a strange obligation, and painful shreds of nostalgia. Several women told me that *they* were ostracized with their burden, whereas their molester's feelings were protected, and he had free contact with other children and grandchildren in the family. For example, **Phoebe**'s mother—after learning that her son had molested Phoebe for years—gave his small daughter a book for children about sexual abuse. She said nothing to her son or his wife. Was the 5-year-old supposed to learn and practice self-protection?

Typically, family members tried to contain and minimize the story, believing (or trying to convince themselves) that "the past was past," the offender had changed, and he was no longer a danger. In most cases, however, an abuser doesn't "grow out of" sexual molestation—even up to senescence—without having his behavior exposed and undergoing treatment (Meyer & Romero, 1980; Soothill & Gibbons, 1978). Men in their 80s have been arrested for incest. As one example, **Paloma**'s abuser had molested three generations in his family. Each discovered instance was assumed to be the only one, no police report was ever made, and no warnings were issued within the family. There were other cases in my sample where members of at least two generations had been molested by the same person.

A correspondent told me that she had written 16 letters to family members about a dead grandfather whom she was certain had molested children in two or more generations. She received one answer only, from an aunt who appreciated her message. Another woman wrote warning letters to her adult siblings, who used their father regularly as a babysitter, telling them about his abusing her when she was a preschooler. Her letters were unanswered and ignored.

The Death of Innocence

It is important for a survivor to realize—for her own understanding of what is happening—the dilemma faced by her original family, especially if they have viewed themselves as close and supportive through the years. She feels again the terrible aloneness of her childhood—by day, and even during her sleep. **Audrey,** for example, dreamed that she was on a boating trip with her parents and siblings. Each family member had a separate cabin. She was in trouble, but every door was shut to her. The only sound in the dream was her own screaming.

The rememberer who is desperately trying to stay within the family may badger her relatives to believe her. **Alana** reported that her family members felt "victimized by the victim," as her sister protested. They were experiencing their own pain and their own bad dreams. The depth of the impact could be measured by the nightmares of relatives. Alana's sister dreamed of entering her own living room and finding her beautiful daughter laid out in a coffin. About the same time, Alana's grown son dreamed of backing the family car over his toddler. The revelation of incest within a family is incredibly painful—the "death of innocence" for all concerned.

A Crisis of Relationships

Several women told me of hesitating to share their memories with a particular member of their family, such as their mother or grandmother, because that person would be so devastated on their behalf. But when **Peggy** revealed her terrible secret, she found that her mother actually seemed indifferent and minimized what Peggy's brother had done to her. Being the mother of both parties, she was terribly torn by the news. Moreover, Peggy realized later that her earlier sparing of her mother had been self-protective as well. She had feared the nonsupport that she was now experiencing.

A crisis of relationships for both the rememberer and her original family members is especially likely if the abuser was the father, and the resulting division is agonizing for everyone. The sister of one rememberer said, tears in her eyes, "This is the first time in our lives that I haven't been able to be with you in facing a problem." The two sisters found themselves displacing anger at the situation onto each other until an honest exchange helped them become more empathetic. The one who was remembering, **Ashley,** expressed frustration that her sister, Jean, refused to believe her memories about their father and was critical of her need to tell other family members. Jean answered,

But they are *your* memories of him. My memories say that this is impossible. You're pressuring me to accept what *you* believe against all my own intuitions. I'll try to keep an open mind if you stop pushing me to accept every new "truth" *you* uncover. I have to process this at my speed.

These sisters were better able to accept their differences after this discussion. However, most respondents were less successful in maintaining relationships with family members, and some were cruelly abandoned.

Standing Alone

The women desperately longed for reassurance from their original family in the crazy-making world of emerging memories. In actuality, they hardly ever received the support they needed from family members. However, they found that nonsupport had certain unexpected advantages. It graphically showed them what their situation must have been like as a child and why they could not have sought help. They knew again the loneliness and shame of their early years. They felt deserted and blamed, but they also learned that waiting to be rescued was pointless. Some respondents broke away from their family of origin, at least for a while, to find a valuable new resource—their own strength. **Charlene**'s reaction was adamant: "If you don't believe me, Mom, I don't need you in my life!" If survivors tried to reunite with their family later on, their degree of success depended on all parties' mutual capacity for growth and compassion.

A key issue for many survivors whose abuser was still living was whether to confront him or her and demand accountability for the abuse. A related topic was forgiveness—whether she could find it possible within herself to forgive the abuser and others who had ignored or covered up his actions. Both of these topics are discussed in Chapter 12.

THE RESPONSE OF PARTNERS

Most of the women with whom I talked were married or in close relationships. Their partner played a key role in the process of remembering. It was not an easy role, but there could be important rewards for him and for their relationship in the long run. Three of my respondents had lesbian partners, and in general, the women seemed similar to the male partners in their responsiveness to the survivor's recollections.

Much change would take place in the rememberers and in their relationships, and of course, the partners would have their own needs and personal problems, which usually took second place for a while. Some of the survivors had grown up passive and other-directed—avoiding any show of self-centeredness and winning acceptance by "being there" for others. Suddenly, they seemed to vacate the helping role, and their family's needs tended to go unmet. At this point, *they* were the needy ones, and they became tremendously turned in on themselves. This was hard on a marriage, but 71% of respondents who had partners felt that they tried to be understanding and to support them emotionally (59% said they gave "much" support). The situation was similar to that of a woman having a long and difficult pregnancy—giving birth to pain—and this called forth a loving partner's nurturance and his adaptation of his sexual needs to hers. There were some exceptions, however. One woman, **Nell**, never told her husband about the distress she was experiencing. He was a man who, when it came to sexual contact, simply said "You owe me."

Naturally, husbands grew restive as time went by and their wife's changing moods followed each other. Because they had no idea what might be coming next, they wished this major adjustment period didn't have to continue. **Phyllis**'s husband protested, "I didn't do anything wrong, but you're taking your past abuse out on me." **Alma**'s husband told her much later that he had found the situation so difficult that he had wanted to leave her, but loyalty and love made him stay. At least four of the respondents' marriages did break up eventually. Judging from information that I gleaned during interviews, nonmarried partners were quite likely to drop by the wayside, especially if neither party had a long investment in the relationship.

When a survivor was suicidal or required hospitalization, her husband was fearful of possibly losing her as a companion *and* as the caretaker of their children. These men paid a high price for another man's wrongdoing, and this was especially distressing if the abuser was still alive. The family budget of one respondent was drained by expensive therapy bills for her and her children, while the abuser took a holiday in the Bahamas. Partners also suffered from some by-products of their wives' unexpressed anger at the perpetrator.

When rememberers were having disturbing flashbacks, it was particularly difficult for their partners to know what to do. It is hard to witness someone in such recurrent pain and distress, so the partners' own anxiety was usually aroused. Also, they might believe that the flashbacks were too severe, too upsetting, or simply "bad" for the survivor. Consequently, they might try to intellectualize what was happening or to direct the woman how to "control" her flashbacks. Instead, it was more helpful if they shifted their focus away from thinking toward empathizing with the woman's experience (Peter Danylchuk, personal communication, January, 1987). In many cases, a partner could be most supportive by simply being present ("You're safe. I'm right here") and quietly encouraging the survivor to get in touch with her feelings, to allow the flashback to happen. The following account from **Ava** shows how helpful that can be:

> I was just wild. Nothing would stop the flashbacks. I ran out of our bedroom, into the bathroom, and was convulsing under the shower, sobbing and swearing and in utter despair. Suddenly, I realized that he had followed me and was standing there quietly, just being near me, and it felt so comforting. I wasn't alone.

After a flashback, the survivor may (or may not) want to talk about it. It is important for this to happen only when she feels ready. She may find the memory barely tolerable at first and not want to discuss it right away.

The following two examples illustrate many of the difficulties that the men had in understanding what their mates were going through. **Adelle**'s husband, Jim, described his experience as follows:

> At first, I tried to give Adelle advice and direction, but it didn't work. I was so frustrated. I'd say, "Can't you see that you ought to . . . ?" And of course she couldn't. I wasn't in her place, and she couldn't follow my schedule for understanding. She had to recover at her own pace and in her own way, whatever they were. I realize that I can't make her past different from what it was. It wasn't of my doing, nor hers. It's not something that she did *to* me. It's out of my hands; all I can do is help her pick up the pieces. I've accepted that as a fact.
>
> Of course I get upset that she's been hurt so badly, but I'm no longer overprotective or intrusive. Sure, I've gone through anger, frustration, and denial while she has been remembering. Being in the 12-step program for spouses of addicted persons has helped. Now I basically accept what has happened and her right to work it through.
>
> She's doing really well—moving through different phases more or less fast. Lately, she's been going like gangbusters, and the frenetic pace is exhausting for both of us. Sometimes, I still get very frustrated, feeling as if I'm walking on eggshells as I tune into where she's at—trying not to snap at her and add to her burden. Meanwhile, I have no outlet. While I'm taking

care of her needs, who takes care of me? This is not something that I can
bring up if I'm out with the guys for an evening. There are help groups, but
they are filled with women. The men who need them are out there, but
where are the groups for them?

In this account, it is important to note that Jim doesn't take responsibility away from his wife. He is patient, appreciative, listens to her, and tries
to respond to her emotional needs. But he has problems himself: His
needs aren't being met, and there are no groups where he can share his
problems and receive support. Husbands of rememberers often need social support, just as their wives do, but there is little available for them. In
some cases, husbands did find it helpful to see their wife's therapist on
occasion to discuss their own concerns and questions.

Alexis provided another example of improved couple understanding:

> I was so emotional. My husband took me on a weekend outing to make me
> feel better. All I wanted was to talk and cry. All he wanted was to "fix it" for
> me (he's a typical adult child of alcoholics). Finally, we decided to go
> through your questionnaire together and, through it, we each came to un-
> derstand the other. I had thought that he wanted to shut me up because he
> was ashamed of the incest, and of me. I learned that it was his love for me
> that made my pain so hard to witness. He realized that he could help by en-
> couraging my feelings to flow instead of blocking them.

It was a credit to these men that so many developed a great capacity to
balance fathering their wives with husbanding them. It was partly because of the kind of men they had married that some amnesic women had
been able to find the courage to remember the past and to deal with it.
Gentle partners were especially able to nurture the troubled child in their
spouse whenever she emerged, especially if their wife let them know
"what age she felt" at a given time.

As a recovering woman emerged, stronger and less dependent than
before, the relationship had to shift. The nurturance that she might have
craved when she married, and which increased to support her as she
dealt with upsetting returning memories, might seem smothering later
on as she emerged into strength. The husband who was a good father to
the hurt child might seem like a controlling father as his wife grew more
self-reliant. However, for couples who were able to work through these
shifts, the relationship was strengthened and became better and more
open and honest than ever before.

As time moved on, the partner generally met a stronger and more flexible woman, and one who was appreciative of all the support she had received. Although adjustments were frequently needed because both parties had grown and changed, in good relationships the lines of communication were opened up, and the needed changes could be made. However, in at least four cases, divorce left the woman with multiple additional problems. It was difficult for her to make another major adjustment in addition to dealing with her memories, even if the divorce was for the best.

Impact on Sexual Relationships

Sexual relationships are extremely sensitive to aspects of the physical, psychological, and interpersonal problems of an individual or a couple. Certainly, when a woman remembers childhood sexual abuse, it will have a profound impact on her sexual feelings. Following the breakthrough experience, 56% of the amnesic respondents reported a change in their sexual feelings, and 6 months later, about half of the whole group of respondents (52%) were experiencing similar changes in sexuality.

It is important to realize, however, that the couple's previous sexual relationship was probably already affected by the past events that she had never dealt with. Various women had been aware of reactions that they didn't understand, such as "wanting to escape" when her husband put his arm around her in bed, resenting and avoiding any sexual act that he especially asked for, or losing all sexual feelings for months at a time. **Penny** told me that she really had had "no trouble that way" but then listed "minor exceptions" that added up to serious sexual dysfunction.

These women had pretended that everything was all right or denied to themselves and their partners that sexuality was a problem. Some, who were aware of their own dissatisfactions, had found it impossible to communicate sexual concerns. Most didn't know what was the matter, so how could they explain? Their partners were even less aware. Dealing with memories of sexual abuse made it mandatory for couples to be more open.

For most of the women whom I interviewed, the sexual relationship went through a series of changes during the remembering period. The more a couple could accept whatever developed and flow with it, the sooner the ups and downs could level out. One couple lightened their experience with humor: "Feast or famine" was one of their slogans, and "This week's no-no" was another. During the remembering period, the women generally needed more personal space, less sex, and more influence on when and how love making took place. This, of course, required much patience and understanding from their partners. Frustration was inevitable at times, but often their mutual commitment was deepened.

Sexual difficulties frequently occurred for women who were remembering abuse. **Abbie** gave an example:

> My husband wants sex in the middle of the night, and I've just realized that was when my father used to wake me. The memory is too fresh, and I haven't discussed it with Bob. So I shut off my feelings and endure, and afterwards I go downstairs and cry.

In situations like this, no one should underestimate the task faced by the partners of survivors. If they were emotionally healthy people, they hadn't intended to marry a little child, and they would rather not have to relate to their partner in that way. This was particularly true of the sexual relationship. It was hard for them to know "where she's at" at any given time, so communication was crucial. My respondents found it helpful to express their needs of the moment clearly, and even to tell their partner "how old" they were feeling from time to time. One sympathetic husband said, "Tell me when you're feeling small and if you just need to be held and caressed."

Angie, like some other respondents, had thought it unfair to avoid sex with her husband even when she was regressing to childlike emotions. When her husband realized that she had sometimes allowed sexual intimacy at such a time, he was upset. He felt that her silence had *not* been considerate of him. Instead, it had put him unwittingly in the position of reenacting her childhood abuse. He said, "I have no interest in being sexual with a child." His words chastened her but also felt comforting and supportive.

After the women's recovery of memories of abuse, their sexual reactions (and hence the impact on their partners) ranged from minor to serious and from temporary to long-lasting. Some women found little change in their love life. Many experienced new sexual problems such as those just mentioned. However, on a more positive note, quite a few respondents experienced a surge of love and appreciation for their supportive husbands, together with reduced sexual inhibitions. A few women told me that they developed sexual feelings for the first time: "I never knew what it was all about before!"

Typically, however, the early reactions were more likely to be negative or unpredictable. This was often a difficult time, and a few women temporarily found sexual contact to be physically and emotionally intolerable. **Carole** could not allow herself to be touched, even by her children. Fortunately, such responses tended to moderate or fade with time. It was also a difficult time for husbands. **Pamela's** husband withdrew, haunted by guilt about his own innocent childhood sex play; meanwhile, Pamela believed that her memories had revolted him. Obviously, they needed to talk about these feelings, and fortunately, they did. A major dividend for such couples was increased communication and honesty about their sexual feelings.

The process of remembering—and especially the flashbacks that accompany it—tend to define certain sexual behaviors (at least temporarily) as too threatening. For example, to a woman who is currently flashing back to suffocation under oral attack, similar love making will feel like rape. It is crucial for a recovering woman to learn to explain her reactions and her needs to her partner. She can no longer accept behavior that feels abusive—no matter how lovingly it is intended. As another example, if she never particularly liked having her nipples stimulated, she may now find it intolerable. She herself may not know why that kind of touch made her feel ridiculed or intruded on, but the fact that it did has to be respected.

The kinds of sexual problems that arose for the survivors varied widely. For women who continued to want sexual contact, certain body areas and particular kinds of sexual behavior gave satisfaction, but others brought to the surface upsetting fears, flashbacks, or negative reactions that they had barely noticed in years past. Some of the shifting needs they shared with their partners were:

- Leave the light on so that I'll know it's you.
- I have a bad time with smells. Let's shower together first.
- Please just hold me as close as you can.
- Please take as long as possible before you enter.
- I want you, but I don't want to be stimulated.
- Don't put on deodorant before we make love.
- I can't handle anything tonight.

The women could usually accept these feelings once they recognized them, and they could experience and appreciate having them honored by a loving partner. Their partners were often surprisingly supportive, and the situation itself evoked a great deal of compassion and caring. One man expressed his unchanged feelings to his wife in these words: "You are so much more than anything that happened to you, and what you have gone through has helped to make you the person I love."

SUMMARY

Recovery of memories of child abuse among the sexual abuse survivors I met affected everyone who was close to her. Her friends had varied reactions. Some were highly supportive, although they often were skeptical or had trouble understanding her changing emotions and reactions. Others dropped away, and the new friends who replaced them were frequently other survivors who could share the woman's experiences more completely. More difficult than losing a friend was alienation from part or all of one's family in cases where incest was revealed. Unfortunately, despite the loyalty of a very few family members, the typical response of relatives was denial or minimization of what had happened to the woman in childhood. The victim was most often disbelieved and frequently ostracized as being herself the problem. Only 1 out of over 200 perpetrators ever volunteered his guilt, but respondents were often urged to "forgive and forget" despite the absence of any signs of acknowledgment, regret, or recompense from their abuser.

The survivor's partner had a particularly difficult role in dealing with her daily ups and downs, but his support and help could speed her recovery and strengthen their relationship over the long run. It was difficult for spouses to understand and react appropriately to the rememberers' shifting course of moods and symptoms, but many of them successfully provided the empathy and nurturance that their partner required. Their sexual relations were often sharply affected by the returning memories, and each partner needed to be alert and sensitive to the other's current reactions and emotions. However, with open communication and patience, these challenges could be met, and the result was often a stronger and more committed marital relationship.

CHAPTER 12

Confronting the Abuser

I've been carrying this burden too long. It's your responsibility. I'm giving it back to you.

—**Nina**, 1990

Words cannot convey the turbulent emotions of the survivors when, as adults, they first considered confronting an abuser who was a family member. Sorrow, rage, terror, and longing tumbled over each other. Typically, many months intervened between thought and action. For some, intense feelings gave way to emotional numbness (the avoiding stage of posttraumatic stress disorder [PTSD]), which had characterized the interim years. Confronting their abuser, especially in cases of parental incest, was certainly one of the most important steps the women took toward integrating the past and moving on, and it was also one of the most difficult. For many, it marked a major transition between remembering and resolution—between dealing with the past and embarking on an increasingly rewarding way of living. That is why this chapter on confrontation precedes the concluding chapters in Part V.[1]

SEEKING FAMILY SUPPORT BEFORE CONFRONTING THE ABUSER

I realized that even though all my family and relatives might turn against me, I still had to do it. The alternative was to lose myself.

—**Arlene**, 1994

Trauma victims desperately need support in dealing with their experience, whether it has just occurred or is being relived decades later. Before confronting a parent abuser, my respondents typically spoke with siblings about what they were remembering. In the great majority of cases, they met with disbelief, anger, or accusations. Throughout history, recipients of bad news have "killed the messenger," either literally or figuratively. No one wants to hear bad news. Even after earthquakes, people wear T-shirts proclaiming "Thank you for *not* telling me about your experience."

However, stories of human atrocities (a category that applies to much of child sexual abuse) are even harder to listen to than tales of natural disasters. Counselors and researchers who deal with traumatized people are not surprised by attempts to silence survivors of child sexual abuse. They have witnessed similar silencing and rejection following many other types of traumatic situations:

- After their release in 1945, Jewish holocaust survivors were advised not to talk about their experiences. Moreover, they were not welcomed in the newly established state of Israel because they were seen as "victims" who had gone meekly to the Nazi death camps (Lipstadt, 1994).

- America's "atomic veterans" were soldiers who, without their foreknowledge, were placed at different distances from nuclear bomb test explosions in the Nevada desert in 1945. (The U.S. government was secretly using them to assess the effects of exposure to nuclear radiation.) They later found themselves ostracized by groups of veterans, which regarded soldiers endangered by their own government as less worthy than those endangered by "the enemy" (Grahlfs, 1995). Vietnam veterans faced similar rejection as "losers" (Shay, 1994).

- After World War II, many "comfort women" returned to their hometowns in various parts of Asia. They were young women who had been abducted and enslaved by the Japanese military to serve in brothels for Japanese soldiers.[2] For the following 50 years, they were silenced by shame, by their families, and by their cultural norms (Lies, 1998).

Similarly, the respondents who participated in my study were torn between their need to tell family members about their new (or finally acknowledged) memories of abuse and the threat that their story posed to these relatives. As adults, they faced the same dilemma that they had faced as children. Their truth threatened the family of which they were a part, and no one wanted to know.

Typically, relatives urged survivors (*if* it really happened) to "forgive and forget." **ANNE** found that advice ironic: "I had done the forgetting part for decades. As to the forgiving, I still couldn't remember half of what I was supposed to forgive." **Angela** remarked wryly, "Mother told me to 'give it to God,' but He kept giving it back to me." Occasionally, a counselor tried to impose a personal bias. **Priscilla** left a therapist who insisted that she make an immediate and total break with her family. **Nadine** stopped meeting with her pastor, who pressed for "Christian forgiveness" without hearing her pain. These women had commonly bowed to the will of others since childhood, and now, they felt it essential to listen to their own inner voice.

CONFRONTING THE ABUSER

It's a constant struggle to stand by your truths because it's such a lonely road.

—**Audrey,** 1993

When first approaching their siblings, survivors generally anticipated dismayed, but supportive, responses. Instead, they felt abandoned. When they wanted to take the next step—to confront the relative (father, mother, brother, or grandfather) who had abused them—they met with active opposition. They were told that the perpetrator was now "old, ill, or a changed person." Or, word might get out and it would "ruin his reputation." Or, it would "devastate" his innocent wife. They were also told that it had happened "so long ago," and no children were now in danger. (In several cases, a survivor told her brothers or sisters about a potential danger to their children from the children's grandfather, who was currently being used as a sitter for the children, but the survivor's siblings were incensed by the warning.)

Denial of threatening news may be a primary root of such opposition, but family members may also misunderstand the meaning of a proposed confrontation. The term is likely to conjure up the image of a malevolent, gratuitous attack. Actually, confrontation is a direct consequence of childhood sexual abuse, and it is intended *for* the survivor rather than *against* the abuser. Its essence is bold, face-to-face communication. Moreover, confrontation is not a task for a victim but for someone who is done with being victimized. The tone of it may be matter-of-fact or highly emotional, but the message should be conveyed directly and without apology.

Confrontation can be a giant step forward, but it is not necessary, advisable, or even possible for every survivor. The experiences of my respondents (all but four of whom eventually confronted if it was possible to do so) have convinced me that key decisions on this issue must belong to survivors alone. Fortunately, very few of the women's therapists considered confrontation mandatory or tried to push it prematurely. They were, instead, supportive of their client as she wrestled with questions, options, feelings, and a responsible plan for carrying out whatever decision she made.

Whether to Confront

Few of the respondents confronted their abuser spontaneously. And few did it early in their remembering. They mulled the idea over for some time. Six months after they began to deal with past abuse, 46% of the women with a living abuser felt "a desire to confront." But among the formerly amnesic women, the figure was 63%. Their slow recall made them, at times, almost desperate for information, but they were also fearful of what they might learn. Even if they were not fully aware of it, they first wrestled with two questions: one about remembered abuse—Is it true?— and the second about taking action—Will it help?

Is it true? The first question was one of conscience. The women were extremely cautious about making accusations, even within their own minds. (For example, **Abbie**, when first flashing back to her group rape at age 9 by her brother's friends, thought that her brother had raped her also. As her memories clarified, she felt guilty. Her brother had "only" stuffed a sock in her mouth and held her down for the others.) Survivors who had been amnesic to their childhood trauma were intermittently tormented by doubts that their returning memories were real. During the years intervening between abuse and remembering, they had lived under the influence of the avoidance and numbing phase of PTSD. Once in a while, some hint from the past had intruded on them, causing puzzling reactions. Now, as traumatic memories returned, the intrusive-arousal phase of PTSD was dominant (although denial returned when their emotions felt unbearably intense). Even women who had never forgotten their sexual abuse as children had frightening episodes when they thought "Maybe I really am crazy, and it never happened." Before risking confrontation, survivors had to give full affirmation to the question "Is it true?" Otherwise, fear of making a wrongful accusation, or of the power of the abuser, could send them into suicidal depression.

Will it help? There were powerful factors that favored confrontation, and others that argued against it. The favorable motives were all related to healing. First, confrontation put the survivor in charge, perhaps for the first time. The helplessness and hopelessness that had possessed her—even as an adult, and especially in the presence of the offender—were based on past reactions. Now, it was she who initiated confrontation. The abuser's only choice was reaction, and even nonresponse was an answer, revealing a good deal about him. Second, confrontation set the record straight, designating what was done, who did it, and what the consequences had been. Euphemisms for the act, justifications for the actor, and minimization of its devastating results were stripped away. The truth lay raw and unconcealed.

Third, confrontation provided closure for unfinished business. Past feelings that were unspoken, unasked questions, and unrecognized injuries finally found a voice. Fourth, confronting the abuser clarified relationships. Sexual abuse, especially if it started at a young age, had distorted reality for the child—love was linked to sex and sex to exploitation. Family roles of the adult and child were also confused. Through confrontation, the survivor could begin to understand why her abuser had breached a relationship that was her birthright, and she could recognize her own integrity even as a child. Fifth, preparing for confrontation released emotions, which were previously unrecognized and unexpressed, in a direct and mature way.

Obviously, the points above suggest a positive answer to the question, Will confrontation help? These survivors recognized its tremendous potential for healing. However, they also experienced deterrents to confrontation. One deterrent was the possible impact on the abuser or family members. The same protectiveness of others that had silenced them as children constrained the women as adults. Their concern for the offender ranged from childlike thoughts ("I'm afraid it would hurt his feelings") to carefully weighed viewpoints ("I'm not sure if it's fair to help myself by hurting her").

There were also personal deterrents to confronting. Amnesics, slowly recapturing memories, were often unsure of facts that they needed to feel confident in a confrontation. Some feared that the abuser might have a heart attack or stroke, especially if their siblings had expressed such a warning. **Anita**, who finally sent her father a letter against the wishes of her half-sister, spent agonized days waiting for word of its impact. Her anguish was excruciating: "I thought my body would break apart, or that I would die of pain." When a report finally came back, her half-sister said, "You were lucky. He didn't die." Survivors also worried about their own capacity to handle repercussions: "I'm under enough stress without alienating my siblings further." Another poignant concern (which they recognized as irrational) was fear of rejection by the parent. The respondents' words betrayed regressive emotions, such as "I'm afraid he'll be mad at me." **Angie**, considering a meeting with her father, awoke one night from a terrifying nightmare of abandonment: "His face was livid and he shouted, 'You're *not* my daughter.' "

In addition to concerns about confrontation's impact on oneself or others, realistic expectations dissuaded several women from confronting. They had no hope for other than a negative outcome. **Polly**, raised in a "crazy family," had never been able to get her parents to face reality: "No possible good could come from trying to talk to them." It is understandable that even the strongest motives to confront may be overcome by concerns such as these.

Readiness to Confront

The amnesic women, especially, were overwhelmed by unanswered questions and wanted to confront long before they were ready to do so. Later, if they came to terms with recurrent denial and determined that the act of confronting would not be too costly, they could make plans. Clear and realistic goals were signs of readiness for two reasons: First, they reversed old patterns by giving initiative to the survivor, rather than the perpetrator. Second, success did not depend on him. **Andrea**'s experience shows both of these advantages.

At first, Andrea had longed for a confession of guilt from her father (to halt her recurring denial), an explanation (to silence the "why" of undeserved pain), and expressions of regret and apology (to show concern for her past and current distress). Before confronting, she had to recognize that these goals were out of her control. Her objectives must depend on herself and not on him. Confrontation must be an honest message from herself, not a petition to her father. Instead of expecting a confession, she told him of his guilt. Instead of asking why, she spoke of her own disillusionment. Instead of hoping for his penitence, she expressed her own pain. In other words, during confrontation, she operated out of her own integrity, which his response could neither diminish nor enhance.

Occasionally, confrontations gained more than was expected. **Pia** told me that she made a list of realistic goals for herself that did not depend on her grandfather and a wish list that she could implement only if he were responsive. She had not seen him in the 35 years since she had told her parents of his "hurting" her. They did not know how sadistic the abuse had been or that he had sodomized all of his girl descendants for years. Once, as an adult, she had written to him without receiving a response. Now, when she confronted him in person, the old man admitted his actions and expressed regret. In response, Pia convinced him to accept her help, before he died, in writing to all of his victims in the three generations that he had abused—letters in which he accepted all blame for his actions. The success of Pia's confrontation had not depended on any response from him, but having a wish list enabled her to bring some resolution to others whom he had harmed as well.

PREPARATION AND ACTION

The respondents told me about their confrontation experiences in 1988, on the second survey, and also in interviews after the third survey in 1992. Among the 45 giving relevant information, the abusers of 21 were already dead, so actual confrontation was impossible. However, about half of these women had imagined confronting their offender in absentia and had often gained a feeling of closure from that exercise. Of the 24 women whose abuser was still alive, all but 4 (83%) eventually did confront him or her in some manner and frequently more than once or in multiple ways. The methods that they had used by the time of the 1988 survey were letters (67%), face-to-face meetings (50%), and telephone calls (28%).

Most of the survivors were unpracticed in asserting themselves, and their abuser was typically the person with whom they were least secure. Thus, confrontation was an especially powerful test of their ability to take a stand. Moreover, powerful emotions can obscure carefully chosen goals, so they needed to anticipate the response of their molester, their own reactions, and elements in the situation that could make them vulnerable.

Fantasizing a meeting proved an excellent way to rehearse for it. Imagining confrontation occurred naturally—even obsessively—for women like **Alana**. However, in therapy, an added element was attention to exactly what happened in a fantasized interview:

> The idea of confronting my aging father evoked a terrifying image with far more emotion than reality: We're boxed into an 8-by-8-foot room at the top of a high building. I try to talk and, as usual, he tunes me out like a trivial television actor. As I fade from the screen, he dials in a more notable person—himself. The rage I feel comes from always losing "myself" in his presence. I can't bear to have it happen again. I can see only two alternatives—to strangle him by his scrawny neck, or to escape the sight and sound of him by leaping to my death.

This example shows how imagining can bring previously unrecognized feelings—such as fear and rage—to the surface.

Obviously, Alana was not yet ready to challenge her abuser face-to-face if even the thought of doing so evoked her childhood helplessness. Examining this fantasy with her therapist showed Alana that being "wiped out" was her Achilles' heel, but she remembered that her father often reread letters, so she decided to write him as her first approach.

Other survivors found role-playing a confrontation helpful. The symbolism of theater was especially appropriate to those who had been "handed a bad script" as children and who were determined to exchange it for a better one. To reduce stage fright, they tried a variety of scenarios, anticipating all possible responses: What part do I choose to play? How might he upstage me? What old cues could upset me? Once sure of their role and well rehearsed, these women felt ready.

Deciding How To Confront

In choosing a method, time, and location for confrontation, the respondents, usually with the help of their therapists, tried to increase their sense of safety. At a very young age, they had lost personal autonomy—control of their own bodies, thoughts, and emotions. Consequently, confrontation must be a declaration of independence from the power of the abuser. It was important to make the situation as different as possible from that of their victimization. Then, the time, the setting, and the events had been out of their hands. Now, they made sure that every possible decision was theirs because, by default, all others would be the abuser's. *They* seized the initiative, *they* determined the time, *they* chose the setting, and *they* set the agenda. These principles were important whether they made contact by a phone call, a letter, a face-to-face meeting, or some combination of these three.

About half of the women who had confronted by 1988 had done so only by letter or, less often, only by telephone. It was rare for their first effort to be in person. There were advantages and disadvantages to each method. A telephone call allowed a survivor to surprise a relative who might not have agreed to a meeting, and to do so from a safe distance. She had some privacy because she could disguise her emotions, and she could use written notes to remind herself of what she wanted to say. To escape, she had only to hang up the receiver. However, these features cut two ways because the reactions of the offender were screened as well, and he too could hang up.

The confronters usually found it easier to express themselves in writing than by phone or face-to-face. Letters were most chosen because they made it possible to say exactly what was intended and to do so safely from a distance. A letter might be a minimal two-sentence statement of strength, reporting that a survivor had remembered incest and was recovering well, or a full description of wrongs. Writing a first draft often uncovered emotions that needed to be recognized and handled before proceeding, and it helped the writer clarify exactly what she wanted to express. Also, letters could be held for several days, reread and modified before they were mailed, and a copy could be kept.

The disadvantages of letters were that they were usually less powerful than face-to-face confrontation, and they did not allow a survivor to see and hear the first reaction of the recipient. Indeed, she usually received no answer at all. However, almost all the women used a letter as at least part of their confrontation. It proved a good choice for the initial communication and also for follow-up. Another option, of course, was writing a letter that was never mailed. Doing this proved to be a turning point for **ILENE** in prison.

The most personal setting for confrontation was face-to-face. About half of the respondents chose such a meeting, which was usually preceded or followed by a letter or telephone call. There were real advantages to using several ways to communicate. Some women asserted themselves sequentially, first with caution and later with power. **Adeline** was able to send a confronting letter many months before she felt strong enough to meet her offender face-to-face. Other women dovetailed the advantages, and neutralized the disadvantages, of two methods. For example, **Pamela** wanted the impact but not the threat of talking face-to-face with her parents, so she used a letter to invite them to discuss "an important matter" in the presence of her therapist. The meeting brought up new issues, which she then pursued by phone. In her case, the flexibility of having several ways of taking a stand was even more clear after the fact than beforehand. In sequential confrontation actions, some women repeated their assertive contacts at various stages in the spiral of their recovery, whereas others used a different means to confront a second or third abuser.

Questions about in-person meetings (how? when? where?) were usually addressed even more carefully than were other ways of taking a stand. As children, most survivors had known neither safety nor support, so now they needed to be assured of both. If they felt revictimized, it could be a drastic setback. **Pat** wanted to confront her father, who was a gun collector, but she was blocked for years by a visceral fear that he would murder her. When she finally decided to meet him, she let him know that she had filed letters that would be turned over to the police in the event of her death. Even when the women were not in such evident danger, it was important for them (and their therapists) to recognize how psychically threatening the abuser had always been to them. They needed a situation for confrontation that was as safe as possible.

Support was also essential for the survivors because so few had had support people in childhood. Helpless, hopeless feelings of abandonment had been conditioned into their lives, and confrontation must help extinguish these. Increasingly, these women became their own strongest support, but most of them also developed a mutual network of caring others—partner, friends, and colleagues. Some were finding supporters and friends in groups of other survivors. When a woman was determined to talk face-to-face with the offender, she usually had several people who could support her.

I was once with a group of survivors who were discussing a good place for a confrontation meeting. There was general agreement that the location not only should maximize protection and support for the woman (and escape if it was needed) but also should minimize these for the abuser, thus reversing the experience of childhood. The question of "turf" was important. For example, people generally feel strongest at their own home or place of work. A survivor would put herself at a disadvantage if she went alone to the abuser's home, whereas meeting him in her therapist's office could provide both support and structure. (Of course, feasibility had to be considered too—the first alternative might be feasible and the second impossible.)

A public restaurant provided **Natalie** with neutral territory and a friend at a nearby table. She wanted to convey an image of strength, no matter how shaky she felt. Such a setting provided subtle curbs on the offender's potential efforts to intimidate her through anger or sarcasm, and his emotions were less likely to get out of hand. There were no interruptions from the telephone, the doorbell, or family members, as there might have been at her home. **Nora** found that raising her voice, which had been silenced in childhood, now had the power to make her abuser stay and listen against his will.

RESULTS OF THE CONFRONTATION

After all the survivors' preparation and concern, how did their offender(s) respond? In 1988, 18 women had confronted one or more abusers. They reported all reactions from the abusers, so the following percentages add to more than 100%—some women had confronted more than one abuser or reconfronted the same abuser. In these interactions, 28% of the women had received no response—their words or letter were ignored, or the offender left the room or hung up the phone. Total denial was the response to 44%, with exclamations such as "May God strike me dead if ever I did any of those things!" Four of the women (22%) were told by the abuser that she had "misunderstood" his behavior. Overlapping these groups, 44% had their sanity questioned (in slang or elegant phrases): "You're nuts," "You were always crazy," or "You have some mental aberration." Only 22% heard even a partial admission of the abuse, sometimes accompanied by anger, and often retracted later. Regret was not ex-

pressed by any of those confronted, although later there were two peni-
tent deathbed confessions, such as the one to **NANCY** mentioned below.

By 1992, several more respondents had obtained confirmation of their
abuse. Two had succeeded in court cases against abusers (**ILENE** re-
gained custody of her son, and **Adelle** put an abusive therapist out of
practice). Three others filed legal reports on close relatives who had recently abused or endangered a child. No respondents sued their childhood abusers on their own behalf. In some cases, certain relatives were
now validating the survivor's abuse or reporting instances of past abuse
to themselves or their children. A few offenders who had strongly denied
any abusive behavior gave limited admissions of their actions: "Guys
didn't think that kind of thing was wrong back then."

The denial by offenders should not be surprising. Incest and child sexual abuse are regarded as the most despicable of crimes, even by felons.
Rosenquist (1932-33), interviewing prison inmates, found that their denial of guilt varied with social condemnation of their crimes. Only 15% of
men imprisoned for nonsexual felonies denied guilt after conviction,
compared to 56% of rapists and 70% of incest perpetrators. Similarly, in a
racially volatile era, Weinberg (1955) reported that black inmates convicted of raping white women were less likely than incest offenders to
claim innocence.

Typically, respondents made more than one attempt to talk to their
abuser about the abuse, and sometimes, they had more objective success
in later attempts than at first. For example, **NANCY**, who had been mis-
treated and invaded from childhood until she left home at 20, was called
to her father's deathbed. He had walked out on earlier meetings, but
here, he finally gave a grudging admission of his incest.

How did the women feel about the results of their confrontation? Initially, their reaction was often disappointment. The decision to confront
had not been made lightly. They had risked much in taking a stand and, it
appeared at first, had gained little. Flat denial—"You need therapy for
your memory, not for incest"—revived **Pauline**'s childhood belief that
she had imagined or dreamed her abuse. **Norma** briefly doubted clear
memories that she had never forgotten. **Pat,** whose fragmented memories
had been hard-won, experienced a huge backslide into the darkness of
doubt and depression. Each woman who challenged her father had
hoped that he would take responsibility by saying "Yes, I did it." His re-

fusal to do so marked the day she gave up hope of ever having a "real" father, but it also marked a new freedom to be her own person.

For example, **Alison** felt immediate relief when she met in a restaurant with the mother who had sexually abused both her and her brother. Speaking up had been essential to her: "I was on one side of a bridge. On the other side was freedom. I *had to say the words* to get there." Her father and uncle (also abusers) were now dead, but she reported, "I felt as good as if I had confronted them as well."

Sooner or later, confrontation clarified certain issues for every survivor who attempted it. Almost all of them (83%) recognized the pathology of their abuser, and half were impressed with their own recent growth. A few discovered, to their chagrin, that the offender still had some control over them, but about half recognized that his power was finally ended and that they themselves had broken it. With time and the working through of feelings related to the encounter, these survivors experienced more and more satisfaction with what they had gained.

Survivors whose abuser had already died felt deprived of the chance to know for certain whether their abuser would deny guilt, how he would interpret the events they described, and how he would assess responsibility. It was important to these women to have an experience of meaningful closure that met their particular needs. **Phyllis** found it helpful to write a letter to her dead father. **Naomi** found release in role-playing a showdown. **Amy**, along with her therapist, urinated on her abuser's grave: "It was so appropriate. He was underneath me and couldn't get away; I used my body against him with the ultimate disrespect." There was black humor in her account.

Case Examples

In real life, there are probably no ideal confrontations, and the three examples that follow illustrate the many facets and foibles of such encounters.

1. **Penny** was preparing to confront her stepfather for the first time, and she had accelerated the schedule because her supportive therapist was moving out of state. It was scary, but at least her mother now believed her and agreed to be home. When Penny stopped by her parental home, she sat down near Herman and gave him the letter in which she had recorded

the history of his abuse. Herman looked it over as casually as if it were the daily newspaper. "So what's your problem? You were always fantasizing—dressing up in your mother's nightie, trying to seduce me, and saying it was the other way around." Penny responded by standing up to leave. She had at least taken a stand and didn't want to spoil it. But Herman kept ridiculing her until she became enraged and began hitting him with her purse. As Herman started to grab Penny, her mother intervened and took her sobbing daughter outdoors. By now, however, Penny felt out of control. Her stepfather's new red Cadillac was parked out front. Over and over, before she left, she scrawled a lipstick message on his windows: "Herman is a child molester." That night, Penny slept little. She felt that she had failed in the confrontation.

However, by the next day, she realized that she had broken her stepfather's power over her, and her emotional outburst had allowed her to vent previously inexpressible rage. Penny's therapy group laughed at the lipstick messages left on Herman's car, and one of them wrote a comical tribute to Penny that everyone sang to the tune of "Rudolph the Red-Nosed Reindeer." They finished with howls of laughter, especially when someone impishly suggested that they could take the song as a "singing telegram" to Herman's place of work. Such fantasies are freeing. Penny's encounter had become a cause for celebration and gave that group of survivors a new sense of empowerment.

2. **Arna** had imagined a confrontation in advance and realized that she was too fearful to meet with her father. Consequently, she used a letter, and later a telephone call, to inform him that she was recalling his abuse. Two years later, she was ready for a face-to-face meeting, and her sister (who had formerly been resistant) was willing to help set it up. Arna told her father about the impact of incest on her life and, for 2 hours, she challenged his every evasion. Afterward, as she tried to assimilate what had happened, she realized that she had gotten nothing but denial and digression from her father. But, within herself, Arna had received far more—knowledge that she had at last stood up to him, pride in her own courage, and recognition of her progress.

Arna had also gained information about her father that he had never intended to convey—his narcissism, defensiveness, and inability to feel any sympathy for the child whom he had harmed. Before leaving him, she had asked if he could "imagine that the incest had really happened" and express how she would have felt. "Yes, I can," he replied. "You would be resentful; you would brood over it; and you would try to hurt me." What more did she need to know about a man whose only concept of incest was how it could injure *him*?

3. **Ashley** confronted her grandfather for the third time on his 99th birthday, in an act that exemplified the determination of survivors. The old man was almost deaf, he could scarcely speak, and he was dying. He asked her if there had been a breach between them. Sitting by his bed, and (to her own surprise) holding his hand, she told him again that he had sexually abused her as a child. As before, he said he had no memory of it, but this time there was no denial. Instead, he looked at her and asked, "But it didn't bother you?" She answered, "Yes, it did. Every day of my life." A look of utter consternation flashed across his face. It was the only time he had ever validated her pain. He told her that it was right for her to tell him and that he was deeply, deeply sorry.

Did Ashley feel a rush of forgiveness for the years of abuse? No. Only a sense of peacefulness that deepened in the days that followed. A month later, her grandfather died. His nurse told Ashley that, toward the end, he pleaded over and over in a childish voice, "Leave me alone. Leave me alone." Ashley remembered that her grandfather had once told her that two people had sexually molested him as a child—a neighbor girl and his older brother. "But," he had declared, "it never hurt me."

THE RELEVANCE OF CONFRONTATION TO ISSUES OF SOCIAL JUSTICE

Early in this chapter, I pointed out that survivors of trauma are often silenced. Here, I return to that issue within the larger context of human rights violations. In an incestuous family, the social fabric is ruptured by the abusive relationship. A similar thing has occurred—on an enormous scale—in nations like Chile, where thousands of citizens "disappeared" in the 1980s, and in Bosnia and Rwanda in the 1990s, where innumerable men were slaughtered and women raped by their countrymen—even by their neighbors. These human rights atrocities in other countries have been widely publicized, but the rupturing of the social fabric that occurs in incestuous families usually goes unrecognized. The survivor who speaks out against another family member is almost invariably blamed for breaking up the family, whereas actually she only broke the *silence*. It is rarely acknowledged that the family structure was previously broken by the perpetrator.

Lest readers feel that my linking familial sexual abuse to national genocide is an out-of-scale comparison, let me explain the linkage. The 72 women who composed the original group of survivors in this study were assaulted by over 200 people, most of them members of their own families. Almost all of those 200 abusers committed legally punishable crimes against children. Yet none were ever charged, few admitted any guilt, none made recompense, and hardly ever were their actions known in the larger society beyond the family. In this study, by a conservative estimate, natural parents alone were responsible for 260 years of child sexual abuse, and that figure assumes only a single victim in the family.

In the aftermath of serious trauma, social justice is mandatory for the healing of individuals, families, and nations. As I understand social justice, it is grounded on four principles that must be applied when human rights have been violated. These are truth, accountability, recompense, and social recognition. To achieve truth, there must be a determination of facts. In accountability, the guilty party accepts (or is assigned) responsibility. With recompense, the guilty party is expected to ease the damage. With social recognition, the larger society labels the wrong and oversees the administration of justice.

How were these principles followed within the respondent's family, the society within which incest occurred? First, the survivor of incest tried to assemble the truth about what happened to her as a child. She had a head start if she had always remembered her abuse. Otherwise, she had to gather facts in bits and pieces over a long period of time with little or no help from family members. Did the abuser help the child-woman whom he had harmed in this search for the truth about her past? No, he did not. Only 1 of the women's 200-plus perpetrators ever approached a survivor (his cousin) as an adult to say how sorry he was that he had sexually abused her as a child.

Second, the survivor tried to hold the guilty party accountable, but almost invariably he neither accepted responsibility nor expressed regret. When the women confronted their abuser(s), a typical response was to claim that nothing requiring forgiveness had happened except for her audacious accusation. "A brutal assault" was one man's description of his daughter's confronting phone call.

Third, some of the survivors sought compensation of some kind for their suffering. In this regard, it is hard to imagine what could be adequate reparation for a life that had been skewed from early childhood. The idea of financial reparations was hardly ever considered, but other more meaningful forms of recompense might have been remorse from the abuser or assistance from family members in establishing facts about the survivor's history of abuse. None of my respondents sued for compensation, but I have talked with one woman who did. In the course of our conversation, I asked her what she would most like to say to her father-abuser if he were to walk through the door. She replied without hesitation, "It's not the money, Dad. I just want justice."

Among my respondents, there were only two instances where monetary compensation was proposed. **Nona** asked the brother who had abused her years before to pay for her therapy. He agreed but then reneged when he realized that to do so he would have to give up an expensive hobby. His acknowledgment of her truth as a part of their family history could have been a major form of compensation, but he has refused to admit to their parents the incest he imposed on his sister. Only one pair of parents (after 10 years of denial) accepted their guilt, offering to compensate **April** with emotional support and financial aid. Since then, they have given her both emotional and financial support as she resurrects her life. However, they also promised to furnish April with full knowledge of her abuse to speed her healing, but they have provided no further information to her, nor have they ever confessed their maltreatment of her to her siblings.

Fourth, many survivors sought social recognition. They tried to get family members—their personal society—to label the wrong and facilitate justice being done. Typically, family members deplored such a crime but insisted that it could not have occurred in their home. Families were very loath to acknowledge and accuse one of their members of sexual abuse, even to relieve the suffering of his victim. On the contrary, in many cases, evidence was hidden from a survivor by relatives who could have revealed it.

What about the role of the larger society beyond the family in labeling incest as wrong and administering justice to punish and prevent it? Unfortunately, the broader society is almost always unaware of instances of child sexual abuse—so successful is the family, including the victims and survivors, in concealing the secret. When we talked in 1998, **NANCY** reflected on the lack of justice in her case:

> He stole three girls' youth. We were isolated from each other, in separate bedrooms, scared and trying to survive. My father should have been tried by society, and sentenced to a life term in prison. Instead, his daughters paid, each in a separate prison of helplessness, distrust, and fear.

Our society is definitely concerned about child sexual abuse and has passed laws and regulations intended to prevent or punish it. But unfortunately, those laws are ineffective in situations where criminal offenses against a child are hidden, and those include the vast majority of instances of incest. As for adult survivors (the abused children who are now grown) who seek legal justice, such cases have virtually disappeared from U.S. courtrooms, largely because of orchestrated campaigns of intimidation against therapists and prominent supporters of child sexual abuse survivors. This topic is discussed further in Chapter 14.

Certainly, legal cases must never be fought with memories (of the accuser *or* the accused) as the only weapons. Concrete evidence must be submitted in cases presented to a court of law. And certainly our society is far too litigious. But it is ironic that lawsuits abound for thousands of lesser wrongs, whereas those who suffered unspeakable crimes are silenced when they can finally put voice to what they endured.

I believe that survivors who speak out within their own family system (or in court) are usually seeking the justice that eluded them through childhood and into the present. They are saying "never again" to the personal holocaust of incest, and they are saying it on behalf of future victims. The first incest survivors to speak out on television had their faces obscured for anonymity. Similarly, the first "comfort women" to tell their ordeal veiled their faces in shame. They were breaking 47 years of silence, and that took enormous courage. But soon the veils were gone, and comfort women marched unashamedly in front of Japanese embassies in the countries from which they were abducted. They demanded that Japanese history books be rewritten to include their story. They demanded apology and reparations. Five years later, the government offered partial apology and a large cash payment for each of the few remaining survivors. Most of the women, poor though they were, turned down both. The apology fell short of full accountability, and the money came from concerned Japanese citizens rather than from the government that had enslaved them (Betzner & Jensen, 1995).

Rwandan and Bosnian survivors of genocide are testifying at the trials of war criminals and choosing to do so publicly at great personal risk. They want their story to be told, their faces seen, and their voices heard. They feel driven to witness to the wrong because that is the only way they can find meaning in what they endured. One survivor of a Rwandan church massacre, where thousands were slaughtered by their neighbors, hid several days beneath corpses in order to live, in order to testify. And as a consequence of testifying, he told a reporter, "I *know* I will be killed."

Survivors of human rights violations, victims of many different forms of trauma, are seeking justice by setting the record straight. Among them, survivors of childhood sexual abuse are trying to ensure that those who follow after them will not have to experience similar betrayal. This is not an easy task to accomplish. I hope that all of their stories that were given voice in these pages will contribute toward reaching that goal.

NOTES

1. With permission, this chapter incorporates material from my article titled "Women Survivors Confronting Their Abusers: Issues, Decisions, and Outcomes" (Cameron, 1994b), which explores more thoroughly the procedures and consequences of confronting an abuser.

2. About 200,000 Asian women and girls, mostly from Korea, suffered this fate, but most of them did not survive to return home.

PART V

Moving Beyond Trauma

One of my former students, aware of my research, told me about her grandmother who, at age 93, had been living in a nursing home since she broke her hip a year earlier. Prior to that, she had been looking after herself in her own home. Her three marriages had ended in divorce (rare events at the time). She had kept herself extremely busy all her life, so her confinement now was frustrating. With her usual ways of coping taken away, the old woman began to experience fragments of a lost memory. Deeply troubled, she shared her recollections with her middle-aged daughter (my student's mother), until the story emerged of her rape at age 5. Over and over, she repeated the emotional and sensory experiences —the pain, the terror, the aloneness, the shame. "My mother," said my student, "is a compassionate, gentle person. She just listened and consoled until, at last, Grandmother made peace with that awful memory, and the need to talk about it faded away. Not long afterward, she died."

There is a common saying about negative childhood experiences: "Children forget these things." Yes, children do forget. But, more often than people realize, *adults*—young, middle-aged, or elderly—remember. And, if caring listeners are available, these survivors of early abuse can move through, and beyond, the trauma.

CHAPTER 13

Changed Lives

*I was grown-up as a child and childlike as an adult. Now, at last, I am
a woman.*

—Alison, 1992

Key questions that the research participants had been asked in 1986
were repeated on the questionnaire in 1992 so that change could be
individually measured for the women who had responded to the first and
third surveys. The 93% response rate was remarkable, comprising 51 of
the 55 women who could still be reached.

The 1992 responses of the whole group of survivors provided an overall picture of how the women felt they were doing at that time. In addition, each woman's responses on the repeated items were compared with
those she had given 6 years earlier, providing an objective measure of the
degree of her self-reported progress toward healing in those years. (The
women were very unlikely to remember their previous answers to the
questions that were repeated in 1992.) As before, the questions were usually presented in checklists, with space provided for further comments.
The topics covered provided an analysis of changes in the women's ways
of coping, ego strengths, psychological symptoms, somatic symptoms,
and symptoms of posttraumatic stress disorder (PTSD), and each of these
topics is discussed below.

The overall finding of this longitudinal study was that there had been
important progress in all of these areas. These survivors had indeed
changed their lives. This was true not only for the individual women but

also for the various memory subgroups, and comparisons of the changes shown by the various subgroups are reported below. I now examine the information provided by the third survey in each of these key areas of adjustment.

COPING STYLES

The ways of coping that the women described themselves as using in 1986 and in 1992 are shown in Table 13.1. Inspection of the percentages for these coping mechanisms in 1986 shows that, prior to facing their memories, respondents drove themselves intensely. They expended great personal effort on getting through the day, tried to please others rather than being centered within themselves, and used busyness to distract themselves from their anxieties. They also sought escape from their concerns through sleeping, compulsive eating, and—for some women—drugs or alcohol. Religion provided a respite for some, as did creative outlets such as music, art, drama, or writing. However, for most, ways of tackling their feelings directly by talking with supportive others or with a therapist were low on their list of coping mechanisms during past years.

These ways of coping that they had clung to for decades would not change overnight, no matter how unproductive they had become. However, the crisis of memory precipitated an emergency situation for most respondents. Previous means of coping failed for many of them, and nearly half had suicidal feelings. Even the nonamnesics, who had never forgotten their abuse, were suddenly in touch with new truths about their past. The enormity of what the women were uncovering—hard as it was to bear—nevertheless forced them to find new ways to handle their lives. A less disruptive impact might not have precipitated such changes.

The asterisks shown in Table 13.1 indicate the significance of the differences between 1986 and 1992 in the percentage of women who used each of the coping mechanisms, comparing each of the 51 respondents in 1992 with herself in 1986.[1] By the time those 6 years had elapsed, the respondents had radically reversed their earlier patterns of coping, and healthier patterns had become dominant. They were now more inner-directed rather than driven. These were huge changes because they constituted a movement away from being other-oriented, judging themselves, and operating on the basis of what others thought of them. Instead, they shifted

Table 13.1 Comparison of Coping Styles During Interim Period (Before Breakthrough of Memories) to 1992, by Group (%)

Coping Style	Amnesic (N = 18) Interim	1992	Partial Amnesic (N = 12) Interim	1992	Nonamnesic (N = 16) Interim	1992	Imprisoned (N = 5) Interim	1992	Total (N = 51) Interim	1992
Effort										
Trying harder	83	17***	75	17	81	19***	40	40	76	20***
Seeking approval	83	6***	75	8	75	12***	80	20	78	10***
Keeping busy	72	39*	83	50	62	44	80	40	73	43**
Escape										
Eating	67	67	50	33	62	50	20	0	57	47
Sleeping	44	6**	42	17	75	25**	80	0	57	14***
Alcohol/drugs	44	0**	33	0	31	0*	40	0	37	0***
Support										
Religion	50	44	33	50	62	69	20	40	47	53
Talking about feelings	39	72*	25	50	31	75*	0	80	29	69***
Counseling (nonsexual)	33	56	25	50	12	56**	0	40	22	53**

NOTE: Unqualified "yes" responses only (occasional missing data). Data for both time periods are for the 51 respondents who answered the third questionnaire.
*p < .05. **p < .01. ***p < .001.

to getting support and finding outlets for their own internal feelings. In focusing on centering within themselves and expressing their own feelings, they had become their own persons for the first time.

Trying harder and seeking approval (the women's most popular coping methods in 1986, with over 75% endorsement) had dropped precipitously to 20% and 10% yes responses. Keeping busy had also dropped sharply but was still acknowledged by 43% of respondents. The women were now facing life quite confidently, but they also had learned the value of accepting support—talking out their feelings, using therapy, and participating in religion had moved to the top three places with over 50% endorsement. Their old escapes through sleeping and alcohol or drugs were nearly abandoned, although almost half of the women still used eating as a way of combating anxieties.

Therapy

The respondents' commitment to working through what had happened to them helped them be far more assertive about meeting their needs than they had ever been before. Immediately after their memory breakthrough, therapy jumped from ninth place in this list of coping mechanisms to first place, and it remained in second place in 1992. Similarly, "talking out feelings" jumped from eighth place to fifth place after their breakthrough and eventually to first place in 1992. Long-term therapeutic support had been especially necessary for the survival of amnesics, over 60% of whom had felt suicidal in the face of horrifying new truths about their childhood. Through it, they learned to replace old defenses with more successful means of coping, which were now becoming firmly entrenched in their lives.

Half of the survivors were still maintaining a therapeutic contact in 1992. However, few of them had been continuously in therapy because it was costly, even at the reduced rates that many counselors offered to survivors. Most had taken breaks of several months to a year or more. These interruptions usually came during periods when they felt relatively stable and were coping more easily and successfully. Some women simply returned to their therapist occasionally for a "tune-up" to keep their lives running smoothly or to bring a caring counselor up-to-date on the positive events and feelings that were increasingly enriching their lives. For others, a new stage in the healing process might bring them back into therapy to deal with new issues.

It was intriguing to find that a number of the survivors had worked with as many as five or six counselors over the years, and almost all had seen more than one. The first few months of facing traumatic memories were likely to test the fit between the survivor and a therapist. Later, changing therapists according to their shifting needs made good sense to the women. One therapist might be especially skilled in dealing with grief, another with flashbacks, a third with family dynamics, and still another with growth. The women also left therapists who proved to be unskilled, untrustworthy, or inclined to impose their own views. As **Angie** commented, "I became hypersensitive to *any* form of abuse."

It is hard for me to picture, as critics of therapy for sexual abuse survivors have alleged, that these survivors were under the control and suggestive influence of "recovered memory therapists." My respondents, once they had committed themselves to facing a traumatic past, seemed strongly self-directed and increasingly able to be assertive about meeting their needs in therapy. Their written comments about incompetent therapists were often excoriating. They pronounced them "bombs," self-absorbed, untrustworthy, controllers, or ignorant (of women's issues, incest, and appropriate resources). For example, **Iona**, who had never forgotten her father's five years of regular masturbation in front of her, was irate at two male therapists who had invalidated her trauma. They had made comments like "That has nothing to do with your sexual problems now" and "That wasn't incest, so you can forget it." If they had taken her abuse more seriously, Iona might not be in prison today. The women quickly stopped seeing such therapists.

The recovery process was a slow one, taking place over many months and years in the lives of survivors. Some of the changes came quickly, but most occurred almost imperceptibly. It was hard for the women to realize how much improvement they were actually making. For some respondents, the whole process—remembering abuse; enduring flashbacks; rethinking the past; examining old attitudes, values, and coping patterns; resisting the desire to give in to old patterns; and wrestling with relationships—was all-consuming and extremely taxing. They had to work hard to keep their spirits up to deal with each new aspect of the old problem and to create a difference in their lives.

In their interviews, some respondents volunteered that they eventually found a well-rounded therapist who had the caring, flexibility, and integrity necessary to move with them through all the complexity of a changing, growth-producing process. As they grew and changed with his or her help, the survivors came to like and respect themselves more, and they felt deep appreciation for all those who had traveled with them on the long journey to their past and back again. A number of the women who were no longer in therapy volunteered that they had learned coping skills that allowed them to handle more of their own needs but that they felt open to accepting help when it was needed in the future.

Only one of my respondents, in 1992, wanted nothing to do with therapy. **Alicia** had peered into her personal Pandora's box just enough to know that she wanted to nail down the lid for good. She felt, however, that a year in therapy had given her added strength and some understanding of her problems. In my later follow-up in 1995, she asked for no further contact regarding the study, and I have respected her request.

Two other women, **Arlene** and **Patricia**, could no longer get the therapy that they valued and desperately wanted—one because of severe financial reverses and the other because her husband refused to support it. During our phone interviews, both of them confided that every day was a burden to them. Their voices and their 1992 questionnaire responses showed serious discouragement and a tragic need for the counseling support that was unattainable for them. Arlene, who had a diagnosis of multiple personality, had one truly successful therapeutic relationship with a counselor who was promoted to a different locale, and Arlene was still grieving her loss. However, in 1997, she wrote me that she had turned her life around by deliberately applying the understanding and coping skills that therapist had taught her. She had moved far away from her abusive family and had taken training for a better job. A year later, she wrote me enthusiastically about her new job and her joy in having become engaged to be married: "Things are getting better and better in my life. I never dreamed that I would be able to really love a man."

Many of the women had found safety and understanding in survivor groups, where they were able to get in touch with their own pain and to witness that of others. Some said that was the only place they could really open up and "let it all hang out." There, they did not have to edit or "ration" what they wanted to divulge, nor to shut down their emotions. In such groups, they learned to be open and honest and to feel compassion for each other. They also learned a deeper level of intimacy and trust. A few survivors had been fortunate enough to find other people, outside of such groups, who responded positively to them when they dropped their façades.

Other Supports

In 1992, religion was mentioned as a support by about half of the women, several of whom described it as a deepening spirituality. An earthly father had contaminated their childhood view of "God as Father," but their current religious emphasis seemed more mature and grounded.

A strong network of supportive people was an important factor in the healing of most respondents. Friends sorted themselves out quickly when facing a survivor in crisis. Respondents who had previously tried to escape their own problems by taking care of others reported that their "fair weather friends" dropped out of sight. There were other friends, and many relatives, who simply could not tolerate being close to so much pain. However, compassionate people became more evident in the respondents' lives, and many of them came to recognize how much these caring others valued them.

The women's abuse of drugs and/or alcohol dropped off sharply, from 37% in 1986 to 0% in 1992. In contrast, eating as a comfort/escape mechanism decreased only a little, and nearly half of the women reported it as a common practice in 1992. However, by then, their former self-blaming attitudes toward their eating patterns moved toward greater acceptance. Also, exercise became an important coping mechanism for 39% of the women. They reported that it brought multiple benefits—deeper breathing, better muscle tone and trimness, and a sense of well-being that was probably linked to the release of endorphins in the brain.

Television watching was another activity that continued to be reported as a supportive coping mechanism by over one third of the women. After their breakthrough of memories, watching TV had often proved helpful in forestalling imminent flashbacks or giving a respite from intrusive thoughts. TV's bright colors and varied sounds stimulated the senses, and even a childish cartoon could sometimes take their thoughts away from past trauma or present unhappiness. Watching a good comedy or drama could engage their attention fully for a time and also demonstrated that there were other issues in life beyond the seemingly all-engrossing one of sexual abuse. Thus, the powerful escape of television helped some desperate women to get through many difficult days.

There were also respondents who made moderate, selective viewing of television a positive resource in their lives for information or cultural enjoyment. Some of the women found themselves drawn to dramatic or informative programs on abuse or rape, in an effort to understand what had happened to them. However, others totally avoided such topics. Survivors who watched soap operas typically picked out a particular character to identify with. One respondent, before her memories returned, had identified with a character who learned that she had multiple personalities. Another was fascinated by a woman who was imprisoned (for several months of television time) in a well. The heroine's helpless, hopeless situation was a symbol of the survivor's own life situation and helped her to work through her own feelings.

In summary, the women changed and grew in important ways, particularly in how they chose to cope with stress. They increasingly took a proactive stance on their own behalf to protect and strengthen themselves rather than automatically reacting defensively or using the most available escape mechanisms.

EGO STRENGTHS

As discussed in Chapter 5, the respondents had experienced developmental damage in their early childhood. Because each developmental task laid the groundwork for those that followed, that damage had been cumulative. Abused at a very young age, the women had failed to master fully the challenge of each subsequent psychosocial stage. In Erikson's terms, their childhoods had been marred by their learning distrust rather than trust, shame rather than autonomy, guilt and inhibition rather than initiative, and inferiority rather than industry and competence. In youth, they had developed a diffused sense of self instead of identity and a feeling of belonging and terror of closeness instead of intimacy. In adulthood, parenting had often been a troubling confirmation of their inability to nurture themselves or others, and an overview of their lives gave them a despairing sense of fragmentation rather than integration.

The 1992 questionnaire asked the women how they *now* saw themselves, compared to before they had dealt with their abuse. The items on the questionnaire were descriptions of the qualities specified in Erikson's

Table 13.2 Mean Change From 1986 to 1992 on Erikson's Developmental Stages (Reported on Third Questionnaire, $N = 51$)

	Stage	Change	Significance
1	Trust	.90	.001
2	Autonomy	1.42	.001
3	Initiative	1.15	.001
4	Industry	1.17	.001
5	Identity	1.06	.001
6	Intimacy	.56	.001
7	Generativity	1.09	.001
8	Integrity	1.31	.001

eight stages of life, which combine to constitute a strong self. The respondents were asked "Please compare yourself to where you were before you remembered/dealt with your childhood trauma" on each of the following eight qualities:

1. Able to trust and hope
2. In charge of your life, know what you want, ask for it
3. Able to act on ideas, create, risk, play, be spontaneous
4. Able to complete tasks, achieve
5. Identity, belonging, and friendship
6. Can be intimate, love freely
7. Caring for others, specially those who are young
8. Seeing your life as a whole and accepting it

The respondents were given four choices, which were scored as follows: *Less than before* (–1), *Same amount* (0), *More* (+1), and *Much more* (+2). Mean scores for the whole group of respondents were calculated, indicating the degree of change on each of the eight qualities during the period from 1986 to 1992, and the significance level of each change is shown in Table 13.2. In addition, for each quality, the women wrote free-response answers regarding their "strongest area" and "growth needed."

In all eight areas, the women saw themselves as doing significantly better by 1992 than before their breakthrough. (A fair amount of the change shown in Table 13.2 had already been achieved by 1988, according to the second survey.) The women's greatest feeling of progress was in the areas of autonomy and integrity. They saw themselves as more in charge of their lives, centered, and whole. The average improvement scores for amnesics were generally slightly better than for nonamnesics, with the exception of the stages of intimacy and generativity (parenting).

I also asked the women which characteristics they found hardest to change. The responses added to more than 100% because several women chose more than one hardest stage—two of them even chose all stages as equally difficult. (Their choices in answering this question certainly do not imply that they found other behaviors easy to change—for example, none listed initiative, even though many had difficulty with it.)

For about one third of the survivors (38%), behaviors related to intimacy (Stage 6) were the most difficult to change—love, sexuality, and relationships. However, two thirds of the respondents felt that they had improved even here. Trust (Stage 1) was another elusive quality for 23%, and one that was required by intimacy—consequently, 11% of the women checked both. Identity (Stage 5)—belonging, making friends, and achieving a sense of oneself—was hardest to achieve for 19% of the respondents. Their loneliness in high school years tended to become isolation in early adulthood (Stage 6), reflecting the problems of that stage, as well as of trust. These stages are especially linked because intimacy must be built on a strong sense of identity and on the ability to trust others enough to commit oneself to friendship and love.

The cumulative impact of these problems over time was still evident in these women's lives. And yet it is important to realize that most of them were feeling significantly more confident and satisfied by 1992 than before they began to wrestle with their memories.

PSYCHOLOGICAL SYMPTOMS

In the first questionnaire, the women were asked how they had felt during the years before their breakthrough. As you will remember from Chapter 7, their answers were dismayingly bleak. Therefore, most of the same self-description checklist items were repeated in 1992, asking the women how they felt about themselves now. Table 13.3 displays the frequencies for the key group of self-perception items that were repeated (as before, only for the 51 women who responded in 1992). Again, the significance levels of the changes are shown for the amnesics, the nonamnesics, and the total sample of survivors. The table shows that, for the total sample and both subgroups, all five negative feelings had decreased dramati-

Table 13.3 Comparison of Self-Perceptions During Interim Period (Before Breakthrough of Memories) to 1992, by Group (%)

Self-Perception	Amnesic (N = 18)		Partial Amnesic (N = 12)		Nonamnesic (N = 16)		Imprisoned (N = 5)		Total (N = 51)	
	Interim	1992	Interim	1992	Interim	1992	Interim	1992	Interim	1992
Unworthy/never good enough	89	11***	92	25	88	0***	80	0	88	10**
Different from others	89	39***	67	58	62	12**	100	0	76	33*
Something wrong with me	94	22***	83	33	81	0***	80	0	86	16***
To blame for my problems	83	0***	83	8	88	6***	40	0	80	4***
Excessive need to please	78	11***	100	33	94	6***	100	0	90	16***

NOTE: Unqualified "yes" responses only (occasional missing data). Data for both time periods are for the 51 respondents who answered the third questionnaire.
*p < .05. **p < .01. ***p < .001.

285

cally and significantly over the 6 years. All of them had dropped from being endorsed by a huge majority of the respondents (75% or more) to a small minority (ranging from 33% down to 4%). These changes are amazing. It seems as if we are looking at two different groups of women and, in a sense, we are.

When the respondents' more qualified "somewhat" answers to these items were considered, they showed that these signs of psychological distress were not only less frequent but, in cases where they were still present, were less severe than before. The clear conclusion from these findings is that the women were feeling a great deal better about themselves. In addition, they were more discriminating. For example, several of those who still felt that they were "different from others" now saw this as a positive characteristic—affirming their courage, hard work, and capacity for growth. Others distinguished between self-blame (which had been so prevalent in their lives) and their new sense of responsibility for their lives.

SOMATIC SYMPTOMS

As shown in Chapter 7, survivors of sexual abuse are prone to long-term somatic symptoms. Consequently, the 1992 questionnaire gave the respondents a list of 23 health-related problems and asked them to check any that they had experienced over the years before they began to deal with their sexual abuse and to rate the current status of these problems. The options that they were given to rate their present condition were: *Worse, Same, Better, Much better,* and *No longer a problem.* Table 13.4 displays their responses to the same 16 health problems that were discussed in Chapter 7, combining the answers "Better," "Much better," and "No longer a problem" into one category labeled *improved.* The first column of numbers repeats the data from the final column of Table 7.4, showing the percentage of the whole group of respondents who reported each problem in the past. The next three columns present the women's responses in 1992—first, the number of women who reported experiencing that particular problem in the past, then the number who reported improvement in 1992, and finally the percentage of those experiencing the problem who now felt improved.[2]

On average, the respondents checked eight health problems that they had experienced during the course of their life since their abuse. Across the list of problems, about three quarters of the women who reported

Table 13.4 Somatic Symptoms During Interim Period (Before Breakthrough of Memories), and Improvement by 1992, for Total Sample

Somatic Symptom	Percentage Reporting for Interim Period	Number Mentioning in 1992	Number Improved [a] in 1992	Percentage Improved [a] in 1992
Eating problems				
Compulsive eating	57	28	18	64
Anorexia nervosa	12	6	5	83
Bulimia	8	3	3	100
Gynecological problems				
Premenstrual syndrome	47	22	15	68
Other menstrual problem	35	18	12	67
Unexplained pelvic pain	20	10	7	70
Head and jaw problems				
Headaches of any kind	67	24	16	67
Migraine headaches	47	21	17	81
Tight jaw	53	27	17	63
Teeth-grinding	41	20	16	80
Respiratory problems				
Allergies	47	23	13	57
Oversoft voice	29	14	12	86
Asthma	16	7	5	71
Miscellaneous problems				
Self-abuse	49	24	21	88
Generally unwell	43	23	19	83
Accidents	29	14	10	71

NOTE: These somatic symptoms were measured retrospectively *after* the crisis of recall ($N = 51$ on third questionnaire).
a. *Improved* includes "better," "much better," and "no longer a problem" responses.

having each of these previous somatic complaints said that it had improved or disappeared by 1992, and hardly any reported it as worse. It was impressive that the percentage improvement for the various somatic symptoms ranged from a low of 57% to a high of 100%. That is, on each of the somatic problems, large majorities of the respondents reported that they had improved. Some of the problems, of course, had diminished prior to the breakthrough of memories. For instance, several of the amnesic women began to remember their abuse only after conquering alcoholism or other addictions. By 1992, the respondents were looking after themselves much better. They were more attentive to their health and exercise, many had arranged to have corrective surgery for various conditions, and they were less tense, anxious, and depressed.

PTSD SYMPTOMS

As a final topic, a key group of PTSD symptoms was included on the 1992 questionnaire, and the answers of the 51 respondents were compared with their answers in 1986. Just as with the somatic complaints, highly significant positive changes were evident on all of these PTSD symptoms, as shown in Table 13.5. In 1986, unqualified "yes" answers had been given by over half of the women to all but one of the symptoms (on that one, 47% said they had been suicidal), and the percentages ranged up to 78% for flashbacks and sexual problems. In 1992, the percentage of women reporting each of these problems had dropped to 25% or less (as little as 4% for suicidal feelings), and the reduction on each of the seven symptoms was highly significant.

For most of the time between the respondents' abuse and their confrontation of it in adulthood, their predominant PTSD symptoms had been numbed emotions and various forms of denial. This blunted reaction to earlier trauma had been interrupted from time to time by emotional reactions that were inappropriate to their present reality, by disturbed sleep, and by unrecognized flashbacks. With the crisis of remembering, the arousal/reexperiencing symptoms came to ascendance—nightmares, flashbacks, intrusive images and thoughts, and emotions that threatened to get out of control. Also, during that crisis, the numbing, avoidance, and denial symptoms recurred frequently when the intensity of remembering became too hard to bear. During recovery, all of the PTSD symptoms abated markedly, some more than others, as more of the women mastered the trauma that had plagued them for so long. The PTSD symptoms for them—as for war veterans—had a marked tenacity but, over time, these became weaker, appeared less frequently, and they were more easily resolved. The most common continuing problems were difficulties in sexual relationships (25%) and troubled sleep and nightmares (24%). Most notably, recurrences of suicidal feelings and of numbed emotions were reported by only 4% and 6% of the respondents, respectively.

EXPECTATIONS FOR THE FUTURE

In the 1992 survey, the survivors evaluated their own progress and what the healing process had meant to them. Of course, this was not the end of the journey for them. As they shared their experiences with me—gener-

Table 13.5 Comparison of PTSD Symptoms During Interim Period (Before Breakthrough of Memories) to 1992, by Group (%)

PSTD Symptom	Amnesic (N = 18)		Partial Amnesic (N = 12)		Nonamnesic (N = 16)		Imprisoned (N = 5)		Total (N = 51)	
	Interim	1992	Interim	1992	Interim	1992	Interim	1992	Interim	1992
Avoiding/denial/numbing										
Numbed emotions	72	6***	75	17	56	0***	40	0	65	6***
Depression (withdrawal)	67	22**	58	8	62	0***	40	0	61	10***
Suicidal feelings	61	6**	50	8	38	0**	20	0	47	4***
Sexual problems	83	33**	92	42	69	6***	60	20	78	25**
Reexperiencing/arousal										
Flashbacks[a]	94	17***	83	33	62	0***	60	20	78	16***
Intrusive thoughts (obsessed)[a]	67	6***	50	25	62	13**	25	20	58	14***
Troubled sleep/nightmares	56	17*	42	42	62	13**	60	40	55	24*

NOTE: Unqualified "yes" responses only (occasional missing data). Data for both time periods are for the 51 respondents who answered the third questionnaire.
a. These two PTSD symptoms occurred *after* the crisis of recall instead of during the interim period.
*p < .05. **p < .01. ***p < .001.

ously and openly, as in the past—they were well aware that they would go on growing and changing. The women's answers to two questions on the 1992 survey were particularly striking, and I summarize them here in some detail.

Where Would You Be Now If You Had Not Dealt With Your Sexual Abuse?

Respondents were forthright in answering this open-ended question. The word *dead* leapt out from the responses of the largest group of women (42%). Sometimes, it was the only word given, but in other cases, the breadth and depth of the dying came through, as in this response from **Andrea**, a pretty young wife and mother:

> If I wasn't physically dead from suicide, recklessness, or addiction—I would be emotionally dead. I hated myself and everyone around me. I felt nothing. I didn't give a damn.

This type of response was closely linked to amnesia. Amnesics were significantly more likely to mention death than were nonamnesics (65% vs. 25%). Their emphasis on death may be less surprising when we recall the high rate of self-abuse (56%) and suicidal feelings (52%) among amnesics during the long, silent years.

The negativity of the death theme carried over into four other free-response categories that survivors presented—bad relationships, helplessness, addiction, and loss of self. One woman stated comprehensively, "I would be dead, divorced, or drunk." Nearly one third of the women (30%) emphasized bad relationships. They believed that, without help, they would have stayed in a "dead" marriage or "destroyed" a good one. Several responded that they would have been unable to initiate or maintain any intimate relationship—for example, "going from man to man looking for love."

For 26% of the women, the question above evoked the feelings of helplessness and hopelessness that had engulfed them in childhood. They believed that, without help, they would have remained trapped, stuck, or imprisoned in dysfunctional patterns of paranoia, fear, and depression—unable to extricate themselves. Several thought that they would have been institutionalized.

In the category of addictions, 20% of the respondents stated that they would have remained addicted to drugs, food, or sex. Finally, 16% emphasized loss of self. They would have missed the self-development, achievements, and creativity that they were now experiencing. Instead, they would have been living with self-hatred, self-abuse, accidents, and psychosomatic illnesses.

Will Survivors Who Deal With Their Sexual Abuse Eventually Get Over It?

This was the second striking question. The dream of "getting over it" had been a beacon of hope for many of the women. It had illuminated their painful journey into the past and their difficult climb toward recovery. "Trying harder" had always been one of their favorite coping mechanisms, and they brought a great deal of perseverance to their efforts to deal with their past abuse. For months, and even years, many were motivated by the conviction that, if they tried hard enough, they would get over their childhood trauma. Their chief question was how long the process of healing would take. "When will you be over it?" was also a question frequently asked, or hinted at, by those around them. (Depending on the sensitivity of the inquirer, the question might mean "How long do I have to put up with your complaints?" or "How can I bear to see you go on suffering so?")

The respondents had often asked the same agonizing question of themselves. Now, 6 years after the first survey, it stared at them from the last page of the third questionnaire—did they believe that survivors who deal with their sexual abuse will eventually get over it? The form allowed them to give multiple responses, and the women's answers showed a marked change from their earlier expectations. Only four (8%) answered "yes." Ten (20%) checked "no," typically adding a qualifier to that seemingly disappointing response. Overwhelmingly (92%), the respondents were convinced that the past abuse lost its power in their lives rather than disappearing. This conclusion, however, did not seem to dismay them. A large majority (70%) now believed that abuse issues came up less frequently and were increasingly manageable—this seems both a positive and a realistic expectation. Nearly half (48%) responded that survivors would govern their lives rather than being controlled by the abuse, and 40% said that the abuse would grow less influential in their lives. The most prominent subgroup differences were that amnesic and partially amnesic women were more likely to say that survivors never really get over their abuse (24% jointly, compared to 6% for nonamnesics). Looking at the other side of the picture, nonamnesics (88%) were more optimistic than amnesics (65%) about abuse issues becoming increasingly manageable.

In the mid-1980s, I frequently heard therapists interviewed by the media suggest that recovery from childhood sexual abuse would take "about a year." However, it soon became obvious that healing was not so simple. The experiences of war veterans with PTSD and Jewish holocaust survivors also indicated that recovery from severe trauma was a long-term process, at best. Sexual abuse survivors who felt they had "graduated" from therapy later experienced further ramifications of abuse in their lives, tapping into new layers of pain that they needed to work through. Many returned to their therapist or sought out a different counselor who could better understand these new problems. In the 1980s, it was rare for these women to find a therapist who could deal with all that must be worked through—the crisis of remembering, flashbacks, confrontations with family members, reassembling the past, relinquishing familiar but outmoded patterns of behavior, and developing more effective coping mechanisms. By the 1990s, the therapeutic needs of the research participants who had first entered counseling in the mid-1980s were apt to be quite different because the women themselves had changed in many ways.

The survivors whom I interviewed had typically begun therapy with the assumption that the process would have a clear completion—an end point when they would be "over it." They anticipated that life would be smooth, and nirvana would come. This would be their compensation for all that they had suffered as children, adolescents, and adults. It would also be restitution for the huge efforts that they were investing in the recovery process. They had expended tremendous energy over the years—first in shoving down traumatic memories and then in deliberately opening them up to examine them one by one. It is no wonder that they would expect some massive reward—somehow, justice would triumph in their world. They had not foreseen the many hurdles that they would face—cycles of progress and setback; change that was often slow, minuscule, or imperceptible; the tearing down of old patterns and comforting coping mechanisms in the process of making gains; and so much discouragement along the way.

The flaw in their expectations lay in their belief that life was going to change—to become much kinder to them—that there would be changes in their outward existence, and the world would be a better place. However, in some ways, the world, or certainly their view of it, became worse. They discovered evil in men and women that they had never conceived possible in the process of understanding their own background and the experiences of others like them. They recognized events in the lives of little children that were nearly incomprehensible. And yet they had to acknowledge that these things not only happened to other children but had happened to themselves. They learned about human depravity.

However, in addition to these agonizing lessons, the survivors learned how loving and caring and supportive other people can be. They learned to find the support they had not received (as children or as remembering adults) from their families of origin—receiving it from other survivors, from partners, from therapists, even from casual acquaintances with whom they chose to share their experience. They came to realize, as they faced the hatred, fear, anger, sadness, and distrust within themselves, that there were people they could trust and love rather than fear. In addition, they were able to see major changes in themselves. In the process of therapy and healing, they looked inward to examine formerly hidden aspects of their lives, and they found many positive resources to replace their former feelings of inadequacy.

Life could still be difficult, and problems at work or in their relationships continued to emerge but to a lesser degree. They found they were able to face situations and people and interactions that before would have seemed intolerable. This was possible because of the therapeutic work they were doing. As a result, they felt able to manage their lives more and more successfully, as 70% indicated on the 1992 questionnaire. They felt in charge of themselves, their lives, and their goals—they recovered the autonomy that had been aborted in their early childhood years. They were operating out of their own feelings and needs rather than simply reacting to other people.

These women were becoming powerful in ways that they had never dreamed possible. But were they "getting over" their sexual abuse? **Norma** summed it up:

Will we get over it? The question itself is an insult. It diminishes the wrong that was done to us, and the achievements we have made in working it through. We are forever changed, but we have turned that change into a positive.

Norma was right. It *is* an insulting question. It demeans the significance of the past abuse and disputes the fact that one can never undo and wipe out such trauma. It also minimizes the tremendous effort that the women were putting into recovery. Getting over it?—no, that ceased to be the issue. Instead, the women's emphasis was on an inner transformation that created such changes in their emotions, their coping, their ways of dealing with others, and their approach to life that they became in many ways different people. The core of their personality blossomed, and the pain of what had happened to them as children diminished.

The survivors had reviewed their entire lives and were determined to relinquish patterns that were no longer productive. Concentrating on building their strength in the present and for the future, they were living in each day rather than living in the past or in the days to come. As **Priscilla** put it:

> I went through the bottom of the barrel and I was still alive. Nothing, I know, will be beyond my capacity. There will be times that will be extremely difficult, but I know I have the strength to endure. There will be times that I will be flung back into the trauma, the emotions, the pain. Something in the present will turn that switch and I will feel again the pain, the sadness, the anger—but I will know even in the depths that it is not as bad as it has been. I will know that I will come out of it faster than I have in the past, and at a new level of growth.

The respondents found that they had grown in strength, in the range of emotions available to them, in the conviction of their values, in the honesty with which they faced others and themselves, and in their commitment to justice in the world. They had developed a compassion that was evident to people who knew them. They were able to receive love from others around them, but most of all, they loved and respected themselves.

The recovering women could feel for their inner child who had endured so much. They could care for her and nurture her with a tenderness that she had never known and that they had not realized they were capable of giving. That child would always be there within, signaling past distress, reminding them of spontaneity and joy that had been forgotten so long. But she was no longer locked away, as in the past. She was part of the woman of today, who could fluctuate from strength, determination, and competence to spontaneity, joy, and play—because that little child and she were one person at last.

NOTES

1. Because the percentages in this table are for the 51 repeat respondents, they differ slightly from those in Table 7.3, which includes all 72 initial respondents. The significance levels are computed only for the two main memory groups, where the results are more stable because these groups are larger than the other two, and for the total sample of respondents.

2. Because of the relatively small numbers of respondents who reported many of the problems, the significance of the improvement figures has not been calculated, but the percentages of improvement demonstrate momentous changes in the women's lives.

CHAPTER 14

Epilogue:
Gaining Closure

Seeing your manuscript means that our stories are out. Alone, there was no connection, no place to go with them. But now I see my life, intermingled with others', written down on these pages. Someone in authority really cared and took the time to listen. This book became a voice for me.

—**NANCY**, 1998

An underlying theme of this book has been clarification of trauma survivors' experience over time. A group of determined women has shared with us their personal experience of childhood sexual abuse and the ways in which that played itself out in their lives. They have helped us to understand how abused children feel, why early betrayal is so devastating, and how it can affect every aspect of adult life. However, these survivors have also shown us that, with commitment to recovery, they were able to move into a rewarding way of living.

In this chapter, our theme shifts from clarification to closure. This chapter not only concludes the book but also reports on closure in the experience of the survivors. After I sent the book manuscript to the publisher, while waiting for reviewers' comments and suggestions, I decided to conduct a final survey with the 51 survivors who had remained in contact over the years since 1986.[1] The result would be a 12-year longitudinal study of their trauma experience and recovery, with up-to-date information on their progress. I found that three respondents had died by the autumn of 1998, but in our last preceding interview, each of them had been taking charge of her life. For example, **Alicia**'s customary response to the salutation "Have a good day" had become "I *intend* to!" And **Audrey**, who was estranged from her family, had chosen to move close to a kind relative, who helped her, at age 75, to enjoy new interests and people. I was astonished and delighted that I was still able to reach 44 of the remaining 48 survivors (92%). I felt somewhat rueful to be approaching them yet again because the book was still "in process." However, all of them were glad to be interviewed once more, confirming their remarkable allegiance to the project; and several emphasized benefits that I had not foreseen. For example, **Pamela** told me, "The repeated contacts kept me aware of my own progress. I look at the little markers along the path and realize I fought every inch of the way."

This chapter briefly reviews the overall changes in the lives of these survivors from 1986 to 1998. First, it describes their current marital, parental, and occupational status. Next, it examines changes in key trauma symptoms that had plagued them—low self-esteem, signs of PTSD, and problems with psychosocial development—to see whether the improvement documented in Chapter 13 had stabilized or continued further in the last 6 years. The chapter also touches on the current public debate about the validity of recovered memories and how the women felt about the widespread attention paid to that issue. Then, it explores the extent to which the respondents had managed to gain closure with members of their family of origin. Finally, it reports how the women felt about participating in this study for so many years.

THE UNIVERSAL NEED OF TRAUMA
SURVIVORS FOR CLOSURE

Natural disasters and accidents. When a disaster brings trauma to people's lives, the survivors—both those who escaped and those who are bereaved—feel a tremendous need to understand the truth about what happened. Only then can they process the experience and gain some sense of meaning and closure. To outside observers, their quest for the truth may seem obsessive. For example, when TWA Flight 800 crashed into the Atlantic Ocean, millions of dollars were spent in reconstructing the tragedy and recovering the maximum possible number of bodies from the ocean floor to satisfy relatives of the dead. Everyone—both authorities and the public—wanted to learn whether the crash was an accident or caused by human design.

Similar quests were launched after the Canadian ore ship *Edmund Fitzgerald* sank without warning during a storm on Lake Superior in 1975

(Farnquist, 1996). Over the next two decades, grieving relatives of the 29 drowned seamen instigated five different expeditions to learn the exact cause of the disaster. None were successful. The last effort was funded by the Canadian Navy and a local tribe of Chippewa. This time, the seamen's relatives were satisfied. The expedition had been launched through generosity, carried out with respect, and concluded with a service that was held for the relatives, who were joined in their common grief. The ship's bell was brought to the surface to be engraved with the names of the dead and placed in a memorial. The mother of seaman Bruce Hudson spoke for all the bereaved: "Finally, we had our funeral. It is a grave now. Let them rest in peace." The waters of Lake Superior never gave up their secrets, but the compassion of donors and divers and the bonding of mourners finally brought closure to these survivors (Farnquist, 1996).

Inhumane acts and atrocities. Disasters happen by accident or by the vagaries of nature. In contrast, atrocities never just "happen"—other human beings plan and execute them. When trauma arises from deliberate human origin, the need of survivors for answers and eventual closure is still more urgent. In these situations, another dimension is added—justice is an essential part of closure for survivors, and their search for it can be unflagging. As we begin the new millennium, survivors and the descendants of victims are still seeking justice for betrayals and atrocities committed in the first half of the 20th century. Examples of these violations of human rights are the genocide of Jews, disabled people, and gypsies by the Nazis; the abduction and rape of "comfort women" by Japan; and unethical experiments on human beings conducted by agencies in several countries, including the United States.

In situations like these, where basic assumptions about social order and justice have been ruptured, the search for truth often becomes all-consuming, and the vortex of pain that surrounds survivors is likely to threaten potential supporters. A question that was commonly addressed to my respondents was "When will you get over it?" In Chapter 13, I reported the women's responses to this question, as they viewed it about 6 years after their crisis of recall. They generally agreed that, when survivors confront their trauma, its effects do not disappear with time but, rather, diminish and become more manageable. In 1998, I had the opportunity to learn whether another 6 years had brought these women any closer to closure.

CHANGES IN THE SURVIVORS' LIVES

The average age of respondents had progressed from 39 to 51 during the 12-year course of this study, and by 1998, their lives had changed markedly in many ways. In 1986, **Nina** was pregnant, and now her son is preparing for high school. **ILENE** was enduring prison, which today seems to her like someone else's story. **Pamela** was unaware that her children were being sexually abused by their father; in the years since, she has provided them with a safe recovery. **Alison** was convinced that she was a poor student, but in 1998 she was completing a master's degree in education. **NANCY** had just been released from a psychiatric ward, and now she is one of the happiest people I know. **Penny** had given up hope of "any kind of normal life." Today, she enjoys her "close and loving" family, and together they run a home for retarded adults.

For some respondents, their progress has been modest, but in other cases, the change in a survivor's life has been stunning. On sentence completion items in 1986, **Abigail** had called her childhood "hell." She had been most afraid when "father was home or mother was smiling"; her greatest regret was "that I was born"; and her goal for the future was "death." Through the years, she was at the mercy of multiple (dissociated) personalities, and she constantly dreamed of "somebody killing children." As late as 1992, she wrote me, "Fear sits always on my shoulder. I have only to turn and look at him and I am lost." Such deep emotions do not disappear, but the survivor can take charge of them. In 1998, Abigail told me with confidence, "I know myself. I have to take everything a step at a time, stepping over or through or around my many fears." Using skills that she had learned in therapy, she was building a positive life for herself—employed in a position of responsibility, recently married to a nurturing man, and enjoying positive relationships with her children and stepdaughter. She reported that she no longer dissociates to other personalities.

Marital Relationships

Over these 12 years, there were one or more shifts in marital status for a third of the 39 women in the memory groups. (Ten of the survivors were divorced, two were widowed, and these and the other women had entered seven new marriages.) To my knowledge, respondents initiated most of the divorces, and typically, that happened late in the recovery process. It seemed that, as they grew healthier themselves, they were no longer willing to tolerate damaging relationships. The women whose 1998 status was single or divorced were generally not averse to marriage but were unwilling to enter a relationship that would not increase their current level of satisfaction. As for the married women, two thirds of those who remain in a first marriage consider themselves unusually happy, and all of the remarried women do.

Certain qualities characterize the relationships of these happily married women. The key ones are mutual respect, honest communication, commitment to working through any conflicts, companionship, and a loving relationship. The word *appreciate* came up often when the women talked of their husbands. **Natalie**'s comment was typical: "I'm so grateful to my husband for hanging in there through the bad years to get to these good years." So was **Adele**'s observation that "my husband is a wonderful (step)father to my kids." In some marriages, a good relationship was hard won. **PAULA**'s husband had been upset by her survivor status and had resented her intense love of learning. After he remembered his own abuse, they attended a counseling group together, and he became increasingly supportive of her schooling. Today, they are "best friends" and are enjoying joint activities in these less stressful years.

Parenting

The theme here was open communication. In many cases, it seemed that honesty about abuse had opened up family communication. Recently, when I was visiting **Pat**, her teenage daughter walked in with a friend from school, asking, "Mom, can we interview you for my paper on incest?" **Arna** had been anxious about the impact that her abuse might have had on her children:

> I was lost in the past for a while—volatile flashbacks—and felt guilty toward my kids. But amazingly, they were OK with it. Now, they say, "You were up front about it, Mom, and we knew that you wanted to do better for us. You tried to be the mother that you didn't get, and we understood the bumps."

Nedda, whose sadistic rape and battering had lasted for years, recently had an emotional breakdown. She found herself warmly nurtured by her son and his wife, who live next door to her. Apparently, they deeply appreciate the mothering that she had managed to do despite her background: "My children knew how much they were loved, and that I did the best I could for them." Today, they are giving that love back.

Employment

The occupations chosen by the 39 survivors in the memory groups reflect their strong desire to promote healing in the world. Eighteen women were equally distributed in teaching, counseling, and health care professions. Three each were engaged in social work and religion. Four others worked for child protection in the courts, schools, or government. Some of these women were completing course work or internships to increase their competence in these fields. Among the remaining women, there were an artist, a writer, workers in various other occupations, two homemakers, and several retired women.

Three of the respondents have worked (either professionally or as volunteers) for 4 to 6 years with groups of perpetrators in prison or in the community. They stated a belief that helping even *one* abuser to recover could save *several* children. **Noelle** was especially motivated because she and her nine younger siblings had all been sexually abused by relatives and/or other siblings. She stated,

> My goal in life is to bring incest out into the open so that people can know about it, talk about it, and understand it. I was scared to death to work with perpetrators, but it helped me a lot. I realized that they are human too. It's a power and control issue. They had pain inflicted on them and they turned it outward on others. I turned it inward, abusing myself.

However, for Noelle, understanding the dynamics of sexual abuse doesn't excuse the crime. She has sent several relatives to jail to stop the abuse of younger siblings, nieces, and nephews. She is also committed to gaining full emotional health for herself.

MEASURING THE RESULTS OF TRAUMA

Stabilization or Continuing Change?

Astrid's childhood sexual abuse had left her severely traumatized and with dissociated personalities, yet she faced the challenge of recovery with courage:

I can't settle for less than reclaiming *all* of myself, becoming as whole as possible. The task reminds me of how the Russians reconstructed the bombed-out palace in St. Petersburg after World War II from fragments flung into the river and over the surrounding area. That image tells me *it can be done.*

Chapter 13 documented the women's perception of their progress between 1986 and 1992, the first 6 years following their crisis of recall. The 1998 interviews updated many key dimensions of the women's lives for an additional 6 years. Thus, they help us understand the long-term process of recovery, including the question of stabilization versus continuing change. Below is evidence regarding three important results of trauma—the women's self-esteem, PTSD symptoms, and psychosocial development. For each of these topics, findings are presented in two tables. The first shows the process of change over 12 years for the whole final group of 44 women (somewhat like a moving picture). The second compares the current status (like snapshots taken in 1998) for the three memory groups and for the imprisoned women.

Self-Esteem

> *With incest you are powerless. You have no self-worth. My greatest accomplishment is that I took my power back. And I never give it away to bosses, authorities, my own family. No one can make me feel unworthy again.*
>
>   —**Nyla** in 1998

Table 14.1 shows five aspects of self-esteem for the 44 final respondents at three points in time (up to 1986, 1992, and 1998). These dates represent the beginning, middle, and end of this study. Comparisons across that 12-year period can reveal when self-esteem changed and by how much. The general expectation was that problems with self-esteem would diminish with time. Among the memory groups, the amnesic women were expected to show less improvement than the nonamnesics.

Table 14.1 strongly validates the expectation that problems with self-esteem would diminish during the recovery process. To examine the pattern of change, consider the first negative self-perception item ("unworthy, never good enough"). Those four words capture the essence of these women's low self-esteem from childhood on. Over the 12 years, survivors' responses changed from 91% "yes," through "somewhat," and be-

Table 14.1 Percentage of Survivors of Childhood Sexual Abuse Reporting
Symptoms of Low Self-Esteem at Three Points in Time ($N = 44$)

Item	Response	Up to 1986	1992	1998
Unworthy, never good enough	Yes	91	11	7
	Somewhat	9	36	18
	No	0	52	75
Something wrong with me	Yes	86	16	9
	Somewhat	9	18	12
	No	5	66	79
To blame for my problems	Yes	80	5	9
	Somewhat	14	34	25
	No	7	61	66
Excessive need to please	Yes	91	11	21
	Somewhat	7	30	27
	No	2	59	52
Different from others	Yes	73	30	37
	Somewhat	14	50	34
	No	14	20	29

NOTE: Data for all time periods are for the 44 respondents who answered the 1998 questionnaire. The figures for 1986 and 1992 differ slightly from similar tables in Chapter 7 and Chapter 13 because these cases are a subset of those in Chapter 13, and both are subsets of the full original sample. Figures in each cell may not add to 100% due to rounding error.

came 75% "no." I can describe this improvement more specifically by looking at the "yes" and "no" responses separately. The survivors' endorsement of "yes" answers dropped precipitously to 11% and then 7%, suggesting that self-esteem had stabilized by 1992. Interestingly, however, much of the improvement in no responses came during the second 6-year period (1992 to 1998), when a number of the respondents who had given the ambivalent answer "somewhat" changed to an unequivocal "no." That strong denial of unworthiness by 1998 is impressive because it signals that the survivors' self-esteem continued to improve into the present.

A similar pattern of change can be seen for the next symptom of low self-esteem, "something is wrong with me." Growing up, most of the women had felt seriously flawed. Change in this self-perception by 1992 was also remarkable, and the rise in "no" responses by 1998 essentially reversed the 1986 percentages. The third symptom, feeling "to blame for my problems," does not refer to accepting responsibility but rather to inviting trouble, and thus it is a powerful statement of guilt. Strong improvement in it was evident by 1992 ("yes" responses dropped from 80% to 4%, and "no" responses rose from 7% to 61%), and this improvement stabilized through 1998. The fourth measure of low self-esteem, "an excessive need to please," was reported by 91% of the women in 1986. This trait, in earlier years, had won favor from teachers and employers, but it had kept survivors focused on others rather than centered within themselves. As **Adele** expressed it, "I was turned outside in." This symptom proved less amenable to continuing improvement than the preceding ones, and a bare majority said "no" to it in 1998.

The last symptom in Table 14.1, however, had undergone a metamorphosis: "Differentness" from others was increasingly interpreted as a positive sign, reflecting the women's pride in their remarkable achievements. It could no longer be considered a symptom of low self-esteem. Growing up, 73% of the survivors were ashamed of being "different from others." By 1992, however, several women commented that being different had some positive aspects. By 1998, about one third of the women fell in each response category (yes, somewhat, and no). Some wore differentness (yes) as a badge of honor, signifying their own strength and courage. Several even pitied an abuser who was incapable of self-awareness. Those answering "somewhat" tended to recognize, with growing compassion, how many people struggle with life. The rest, answering "no," felt a sense of their common humanity. Whatever their answer, however, respondents were no longer afraid of being different, and their energy, which had previously been drained by keeping up a façade, was freed for positive pursuits.

These findings fulfilled the expectation that problems with self-esteem would drop markedly over time. This was especially true for the two signature symptoms, convictions of unworthiness and of personal defect ("something wrong with me"). For these symptoms, improvement had continued up to 1998.

Continuing with the topic of low self-esteem, I turn from comparing the whole sample of respondents with themselves across time to comparing the four groups with each other during the final survey in 1998. Here, instead of looking at the process of change, I examine the end result. The general expectation was that, because more of the amnesic women had experienced severe abuse (e.g., parental incest and penetration), their low self-esteem would have dissipated less than that of the nonamnesic women. In other words, the percentage of women still saying "yes" to

Table 14.2 Percentage of Survivors of Childhood Sexual Abuse Reporting Symptoms of Low Self-Esteem in 1998, by Group (*N* = 44)

Item	Response	**Amnesic** (N = 14)	Partial Amnesic (N = 11)	**Nonamnesic** (N = 14)	Imprisoned (N = 5)
Unworthy, never good enough	Yes	0	9	13	0
	Somewhat	14	27	23	0
	No	86	64	63	100
Something wrong with me	Yes	0	27	13	0
	Somewhat	14	0	21	0
	No	86	73	66	100
To blame for my problems	Yes	0	18	13	0
	Somewhat	14	36	26	20
	No	86	46	61	80
Excessive need to please	Yes	21	36	7	0
	Somewhat	7	36	50	20
	No	71	27	42	80
Different from others	Yes	14	64	36	40
	Somewhat	36	27	28	60
	No	50	9	36	0

NOTE: Figures in each cell may not add to 100% due to rounding error.

negative self-esteem items would be higher in 1998 for amnesics than for nonamnesics, and the percentage saying "no" would be lower.

The evidence of Table 14.2 is contrary to that expectation. Averaging percentages on the first four items (and omitting the differentness item), less than half as many amnesic as nonamnesic women (5% vs. 12%) said "yes" to symptoms of low self-esteem in 1998. The average group difference on an emphatic "no" was even more marked—82% versus 58%. Moreover, the partially amnesic women did not fall neatly in between (an average of 23% "yes" and 53% "no").[2] These findings give us important information (although not statistically significant because of the small numbers in each group): The amnesic women, who tended to show *lower* self-esteem than nonamnesics in 1992, showed *higher* self-esteem by 1998. Perhaps even more surprising, the women from the imprisoned group expressed the strongest self-esteem of all on the first four items. On the fifth item, although they all felt at least somewhat different, this did not imply a negative self-image. For example, **ILENE** responded "yes," explaining,

Three things make me different from others: a prison experience, appreciation of freedom, and awareness of what is *really* important. I never hassle
the little things in life.

PTSD Symptoms

*As deep as my pain has been, I know that it was an important factor
in making me who I am today. I believe that I am incredibly strong to
have emerged from the dysfunction of my past into a productive and
feeling person.*

—**Nora**, in 1998

Just as symptoms of low self-esteem indicated the personal impact of
child sexual abuse, PTSD symptoms revealed the respondents' level of
traumatic stress. Table 14.3 shows PTSD symptoms for the 44 final respondents at three points in time—the beginning, middle, and end of the
12-year period that began after their crisis of recall. Comparisons across
the columns can reveal when PTSD symptoms began to dissipate and
how much they changed. The general expectation was that PTSD symptoms would diminish over time (i.e., the percentage of women responding "yes" to these symptoms would decrease, and the percentage saying
"no" would increase). Among the memory groups, the (formerly) amnesic women were expected to show less change than the nonamnesics.

Remember that PTSD is typically expressed in cycles between two opposite symptom patterns—avoidance-denial and arousal-repetition. The
first four symptoms listed in Table 14.3 (numbed emotions, depression,
suicidal feelings, and sexual problems) characterized the first pattern.
They were typical of the interim years when, as **Pam** described it, "I was
enduring rather than living." The second set of three symptoms characterized the months following the crisis of recall. When the amnesic
women began to experience memories of abuse, and when the nonamnesic women could no longer thrust such memories aside, the arousal-
intrusive symptoms of PTSD took ascendance. Then, flashbacks, intrusive images, and sleep disturbance tormented them day and night.
Arlene recalled, "It was wild. I've never felt more acutely alive or more
out of control." During the following months and years, the women often
cycled back into powerful denial, when avoidance-denial symptoms put
brakes on their roller-coaster emotions and memories.

Table 14.3 Percentage of Survivors of Childhood Sexual Abuse Reporting Symptoms of PTSD at Three Points in Time (*N* = 44)

Symptom	Response	Up to 1986	1992	1998
Numbed emotions	Yes	68	7	7
	Somewhat	20	32	27
	No	11	61	66
Depression	Yes	59	11	14
	Somewhat	32	43	32
	No	9	45	54
Suicidal feelings	Yes	43	5	9
	Somewhat	20	18	7
	No	36	77	84
Sexual problems	Yes	77	27	17
	Somewhat	5	43	10
	No	18	30	73
Flashbacks[a]	Yes	78	18	19
	Somewhat	12	34	21
	No	10	48	59
Intrusive thoughts[a]	Yes	52	16	12
	Somewhat	27	32	34
	No	20	52	54
Nightmares, troubled sleep	Yes	57	20	23
	Somewhat	20	34	23
	No	23	45	54

NOTE: Data for all time periods are for the 44 respondents who answered the 1998 questionnaire. The figures for 1986 and 1992 differ slightly from similar tables in Chapter 7 and Chapter 13 because these cases are a subset of those in Chapter 13, and both are subsets of the full original sample. Figures in each cell may not add to 100% due to rounding error.

a. These two PTSD symptoms occurred *after* the crisis of recall instead of during the interim period.

As Table 14.3 shows, between 1986 and 1992, there was a marked reduction in the percentage of survivors reporting the symptoms characterizing *both* PTSD patterns. On the avoidance-denial symptoms, "yes" answers were from 3 to 10 times as likely in 1986 as they were 6 years later, and following that, they continued stable to 1998. The reverse pattern—a sharp increase in "no" answers by 1992 and stability on to 1998—was evident for "no" answers. However, one exception to the pattern of stabilization after 1992 was evident in the area of sexual problems, which I discuss shortly.

Nedra, like most other survivors, accepted the continuing challenge of occasional PTSD symptoms, "There's never a done time. It was part of my life. It *will* return, and I'm thrown back again." However, over time, the women found the eruption of a PTSD symptom less frightening because it had a name, it was understood, and it could be managed. Two other factors made PTSD symptoms less threatening. First, they were no longer so personal. **ANNE** explained, "Depression comes from outside of me now. It is no longer 'who I am.' It's not at the core of me." Second, the symptoms gradually diminished in frequency, intensity, and duration. By 1998, the women frequently added phrases like "not for a long while" or "hardly ever now" to their responses. Even the ultimate threat—the temptation to suicide—had, for over 6 years, no longer troubled the vast majority of the women, although 47% of the women had felt the allure of that final escape in their earlier lives.

There was one noteworthy exception to the general pattern of stabilization by 1992. The women were far more likely to say "no" concerning sexual problems in 1998 (73%) than in 1992 (30%). Relatedly, the earlier sharp decrease in women saying "yes" about sexual problems continued, but at a slow pace, from 1992 to 1998; it dropped from 77% to 27% by 1992 and to 17% in 1998. For several women who said "yes," an uninterested spouse was the problem. This question was seldom skipped, and few of those who were celibate by situation or choice reported this fact as a problem. Looking at the women's responses concerning sexual problems across the 12-year period, "yes" answers were in ascendance in 1986, *somewhat* in 1992, and *no* in 1998. Because sexual problems are a hallmark for survivors of childhood abuse, this recovery is a very encouraging finding.

Arousal-repetition symptoms—flashbacks, intrusive thoughts, and sleep disturbances—had first been measured following the crisis of recall rather than during the relatively quiescent interim period. There was good news on these symptoms also over time. On average, they had dropped from 62% "yes" to 18% by 1998. As with the avoidance-denial symptoms, most of this change had occurred by 1992. For these symptoms, also, there were some intriguing qualitative changes. Although flashbacks are typically understood to be sensory-emotional replays of highly negative events, several women surprised themselves (and me) with a novel interpretation of the term. Their flashbacks in 1998 tended to involve the distinct reexperiencing of pleasant emotional or sensory events from childhood or more recent times. For instance, **ANNE**'s little son frequently evoked her own joyful childhood experiences, previously lost to the profound amnesia that had swallowed her early years.

> My child, holding a book, put me in touch with myself in the first grade. That image was a gestalt for love of learning. Before that experience, my past was a story I was hearing about myself.

The women's reports about intrusive thoughts were not similarly metamorphosed, but in 1998, such thoughts typically came from realistic current problems (rather than long-past trauma), and the women reported being more successful at coping with anxiety. Similarly, when asked about sleep disturbances, they usually attributed them to current stresses, and, generally, nightmares were no longer a problem.

Continuing the analysis of PTSD symptoms, Table 14.4 compares the three memory groups and the imprisoned group with each other at the final point in 1998, showing the end result of changes. Within the overall context of low residual PTSD symptoms, the general expectation, as above, was that more amnesic than nonamnesic women would still be experiencing these negative symptoms. As with self-esteem symptoms, the results reversed that expectation, but to a lesser extent. By 1998, 10% fewer (on average) amnesic than nonamnesic women checked "yes," and 12% more (on average) checked "no." As for the prison group, none said "yes" to PTSD symptoms in 1998 (with the understandable exception that one experienced sexual problems). They were the only group reporting no inclination toward depression or suicide, and they reported better sleep than any other group. According to their 1998 responses—both checklists and written commentary—these incarcerated women felt unusually positive about their progress.

Problems in Psychosocial Development

> *Problems can make us wiser and stronger than those who have never faced such adversities. After I put the memory pieces together, this growth took place. All of these areas have improved so much in my life. I feel alive, and happy to be alive. There was a time when I couldn't say that.*
>
> **—Alicia** in 1998

Table 14.4 Percentage of Survivors of Childhood Sexual Abuse Reporting
          Symptoms of PTSD in 1998, by Group (N = 44)

Symptom	Response	Amnesic (N = 14)	Partial Amnesic (N = 11)	Nonamnesic (N = 14)	Imprisoned (N = 5)
Numbed emotions	Yes	0	9	18	0
	Somewhat	14	50	25	20
	No	86	40	57	80
Depression	Yes	14	18	14	0
	Somewhat	29	36	43	0
	No	57	45	43	100
Suicidal feelings	Yes	0	18	14	0
	Somewhat	8	9	7	0
	No	92	73	79	100
Sexual problems	Yes	8	22	17	25
	Somewhat	17	9	8	0
	No	75	69	75	75
Flashbacks	Yes	14	22	29	0
	Somewhat	36	9	18	60
	No	50	69	54	40
Intrusive thoughts	Yes	0	27	14	0
	Somewhat	43	4	40	60
	No	57	69	47	40
Nightmares, troubled sleep	Yes	21	36	21	0
	Somewhat	7	27	33	20
	No	71	36	47	80

NOTE: Figures in each cell may not add to 100% due to rounding error.

In Chapter 5, I summarized Erikson's psychosocial theory, which
views personality as developing through the interaction of self, others,
and society. There, I used it to show the cumulative developmental damage (both personal and interpersonal) experienced by survivors of child
sexual abuse. Here I use the same framework to show how the women
were faring 12 years after their first interview. Unfortunately, in 1986, the
women were not asked questions on this topic that were identical to those
used later in the research, so change by 1998 could only be measured indi-
rectly. In 1992, each woman assessed her own progress toward the goals
of trust, autonomy, spontaneity, competence, and so forth, and evidence
of their progress was presented in Chapter 13. Here, I look just at 1998 in-

Table 14.5 Percentage of Survivors of Childhood Sexual Abuse Reporting Various Levels of Mastery of Erikson's Developmental Stages in 1998 (*N* = 44)

| Stage | Mastery Level | | | | |
	Very Much	Much	Some	Little	None
Trust and hope	25	41	34	0	0
Sense of autonomy	37	38	16	9	0
Initiative	37	45	14	4	0
Goals and achievement	43	35	16	5	0
Identity and belonging	41	30	14	12	2
Intimacy, loving freely	48	20	28	0	5
Caring about others, especially the young	79	16	2	2	0
Seeing life as a whole, and accepting it	61	20	12	5	2

NOTE: Figures in each row may not add to 100% due to rounding error.

formation to learn the current status, in Erikson's terms, of the respondents.

During the period up to 1986, the survivors had experienced problems in every area of psychosocial development, as documented in Chapter 5. By 1998, however, the picture was quite different (Table 14.5). On average, 77% of the women felt that they now possessed these important qualities at a high level ("much" or "very much"), whereas only 6% answered "little" or "none." The remaining 17% fell in between, answering "some." This outcome supports Erikson's optimistic view that developmental damage can later be repaired, and it suggests the hard work done by the survivors during their recovery. Looking at the specific items on the table, we see that caring about others, especially the young (95%) was the most strongly affirmed of these qualities, and that trust (66%) and intimacy (68%) were the most difficult to achieve.

Probably the outstanding developmental accomplishment of these survivors was their response to Erikson's final stage—seeing one's life as a whole and accepting it. A full 81% affirmed this item, offering a remarkable confirmation of their recovery. They had accepted and integrated the painful events of their early sexual betrayal into their life story. Their courage in doing so was impressed on me by **Penelope**. Still dealing with dissociated personalities and living with a full physical disability, she nevertheless felt quite at peace with her situation: "I see my life and my personality as fragmentary rather than whole, but I can accept that fragmentation now."

Table 14.6 Percentage of Survivors of Childhood Sexual Abuse Reporting Various
Levels of Mastery of Erikson's Developmental Stages in 1998, by
Group (N = 44)

Developmental Stage	Mastery Response	Amnesic (N = 14)	Partial Amnesic (N = 11)	Nonamnesic (N = 14)	Imprisoned (N = 5)
Trust and hope	Very or much	75	55	57	60
	Some	25	45	43	40
	Little or none	0	0	0	0
Sense of autonomy	Very or much	90	68	57	80
	Some	11	23	21	20
	Little or none	0	9	21	0
Spontaneity	Very or much	83	73	93	40
	Some	18	27	0	60
	Little or none	0	0	7	0
Goals and achievement	Very or much	97	73	61	100
	Some	4	18	32	0
	Little or none	0	9	7	0
Identity and belonging	Very or much	75	73	57	100
	Some	25	9	14	0
	Little or none	0	18	28	0
Intimacy, loving freely	Very or much	68	64	64	80
	Some	32	18	36	20
	Little or none	0	18	0	0
Caring about others, especially the young	Very or much	100	100	85	100
	Some	0	0	7	0
	Little or none	0	0	7	0
Seeing life as a whole, and accepting it	Very or much	93	73	71	100
	Some	7	9	21	0
	Little or none	0	18	7	0

NOTE: Figures in each cell may not add to 100% due to rounding error.

We can further understand this overall picture of the women's psychosocial development by comparing the four subgroups with each other
(see Table 14.6). The general expectation, as above, was that fewer amnesic women than nonamnesic women would possess these important
qualities (i.e., a lower percentage of amnesic women would give "much"
or "very much" responses). Again, that expectation was overturned, and
emphatically. On the eight items, the amnesic women were, on average,

17% more likely than the nonamnesics to give affirmative answers (*very much* or *much*), and they gave no negative (*little* or *none*) responses at all.

Overview, Conclusions, and Cautions

The consistency in the finding that more amnesic women than nonamnesics showed strong improvement by 1998, and the fact that they did so in all three problem areas—negative self-esteem, PTSD symptoms, and psychosocial development—is impressive.

However, cautionary points should be remembered. First, comparison of the three memory groups involves small subsamples (14, 11, and 14). In 1998, a difference of 14% (for example) between the amnesic and nonamnesic women would represent only two people. Because the subgroups were small, I have made cautious interpretations of descriptive findings. A second caution is that some of the women's responses may reflect a temporary state. In 1992, for example, two amnesic women were experiencing serious setbacks. By 1998, they were both doing amazingly well, whereas some women in other groups were facing current difficulties.

Some of the 11 partially amnesic survivors are currently struggling. Three of them are disabled by fibromyalgia—a debilitating illness involving extreme fatigue, pain that is hard to control, and unpredictable memory lapses. Another three are divorced working mothers of teenage children and consequently have been overburdened for years with educational, employment, and parenting demands. Objectively, they are carrying their heavy responsibilities well, but their 1998 responses indicate that they tend to feel stressed and depressed. Their self-perception does not, at this time, match their evident accomplishments.

In contrast, the responses of the women in the imprisoned group were particularly heartening. (Among the original group of imprisoned respondents, the only ones I was able to remain in contact with were those who were still in prison, plus **ILENE**, who had completed her 5-year sentence.) Four out of five of the final imprisoned respondents now perceive themselves as having autonomy—they feel in charge of their own lives. All of them report having a strong sense of identity and belonging, concern for others, and the ability to achieve their goals. All five now say that they see their life as a whole and accept it. To explore these responses, I looked at all of the surveys that these five women answered in the course of this study, and I found that their changes were increasingly evident over time. None of these women has won release or a shorter prison term because they joined the survivors' therapy group, but they are winners because they have continued their growth into the present. As **Iris** wrote, "I may be in prison, but I am free within myself."

In summary, five findings concerning long-term changes in traumatic reactions stand out in this study. First and most important, the women in all four groups showed dramatic amounts of improvement over the course of the research. Second, the nonamnesic women showed greater improvement in symptoms by 1992 than the amnesic women, but that progress stabilized for some of them and lessened for others thereafter. Third, the formerly amnesic women—most of whom were severely abused as children, as well as more often betrayed by their own natural parents—were more likely than the other memory groups to register an increasing level of well-being over the 12-year period ending in 1998. This outcome echoes Tedeschi and Calhoun's (1995) finding that severely traumatized survivors can display an excellent level of "posttraumatic growth." Fourth, the imprisoned women, who remain in the most difficult circumstances, saw themselves as making the strongest improvement of all, and much of it was already achieved by 1992.

Fifth, the *most* socially privileged survivors (the amnesic women) and the *least* privileged ones (the imprisoned women) have both demonstrated remarkable recovery and have exhibited a stronger sense of closure on trauma symptoms than the other groups. This similarity of the amnesic and imprisoned women is striking and counterintuitive. The amnesic women had been born to parents who were apparently more stable—in terms of marriage, education, and occupation—than those of the imprisoned women, and this divergence in social privilege continued in the women's own lives. As one example, in facing their abuse as adults, the amnesic women could afford continuing private therapy, whereas the imprisoned women were only permitted time-limited access to group therapy. Apparently, however, the imprisoned women, living together through the years and isolated from outside responsibilities, bonded together in mutual support and understanding. Again and again, they spoke of how important this had been to their healing. A possible interpretation of the parallel success of these two groups is that they shared one key characteristic: They both knew that they were in serious trouble when they chose to confront the past. The survivors in the prison group were serving lengthy sentences for major crimes, whereas those in the amnesic group were, for the first time, recalling massive childhood betrayal. Survivors in both groups seem to have been especially motivated to change their lives. They each grabbed for a lifeline and held on until they reached a safer place. That lifeline was a therapeutic alliance that could pull them toward health.

The findings from this study cannot be simplistically generalized to all women suffering from child sexual abuse because respondents in the memory groups were not randomly selected. Because the focus of the study was on amnesia, it was necessary to obtain a purposive sample of women who were amnesic to their early abuse. The respondents were recruited from private therapists and therefore cannot adequately represent survivors who did not have sufficient funds for therapy or who did not choose to undertake it. Moreover, the strong improvement in these women's lives may not be replicated among other groups of survivors. However, although generalizable findings are important research goals, the descriptive findings from studies such as this one are also valuable in filling in the details of new areas of knowledge. That is particularly true for this longitudinal study of amnesia and the process of recovery among sexual abuse survivors.

THE DEBATE OVER RECOVERED MEMORIES

In the 1990s, a backlash developed against the claims of women and men who reported that they had recovered memories of childhood sexual abuse after relatively long periods of amnesia. In some cases, these claims had led to notorious publicity, police reports, and even court cases and imprisonment for the accused offenders. Naturally, people who were accused—either rightly or wrongly—of being perpetrators were eager to avoid such publicity and potential sanctions, and they found that a potent reply was to claim that their accusers suffered from "false memories."

The term *false memory syndrome* was initially coined and then widely popularized through the media by a group composed of accused parents and professionals who were sympathetic to them. In 1992, these individuals founded the False Memory Syndrome Foundation, which since then has been vigorously asserting that the United States is experiencing an "epidemic" of tens of thousands of cases of false memories of sexual abuse and that these memories are being suggested and/or fostered by many therapists (Pope & Brown, 1996). The foundation's literature suggests that therapists who work with sexual abuse survivors are either naive incompetents or greedy zealots. The public conflict between those who support the validity of recovered memories of sexual abuse and those who proclaim their falsity has led to much more heat than light, and rigorous empirical research is badly needed in this area (Pezdek & Banks, 1996).

Allegations that many therapists working with child sexual abuse survivors are misguided or unethical have become a standard litany among critics of recovered memories. Certainly, it must be acknowledged that therapists range, in their training and competence, from excellent to poor and, morally, from highly ethical to unprincipled. But that is true of every profession. A similar range of competence and ethics can be found among doctors, lawyers, researchers, manufacturers, and media professionals. Relevant to the accusation that unethical therapists implant false memories of sexual abuse is the fact that 72% of the amnesic women in this study had started to remember their abuse *prior* to entering therapy.

Sympathizers with the False Memory Syndrome Foundation have made strenuous efforts to identify and control "bad" therapists through education, regulation, legislation, and litigation. A favorite tactic is to single out and threaten leading supporters of survivors. In some countries, such as Colombia, well-known advocates of human rights have been systematically assassinated in their homes or offices, just as some medical personnel have been murdered at family planning clinics in the United States. The threats against therapists involved with survivors of child sexual abuse have been less virulent, but they are still strong enough to convey the message to other advocates for the oppressed that "you are not safe anywhere if you help survivors." In the United States, instead of guns, the weapons of choice are lawsuits, third-party reports, and picketing of offices and homes. The result is an atmosphere of intimidation and fear that threatens *all* supporters.[3]

A prominent target of this intimidation has been David Calof, the articulate editor of *Treating Abuse Today*, a news journal for survivors and therapists, who has been harassed and picketed at his office and at his home for several years. Similarly, there were repeated attacks on the leading self-help book for survivors, Bass and Davis's (1988) *The Courage to Heal*, which was invaluable to survivors at a time when relevant helpful books were rare. Its critics singled out one and one-half pages of poor advice from over 700 pages of useful material. These excerpts were reprinted endlessly for several years, but a suit filed against the authors was eventually thrown out of court. Somewhat similar kinds of harassment have been launched against some of the most vocal advocates of the false memory syndrome by their critics.

The attacks on supporters have made therapy more hazardous as a profession and clients who are survivors more worrisome to conscientious therapists. Not surprisingly, many of my respondents had strong opinions about the debate, the qualifications of therapists, and the welfare of survivors. Most of them had had experience with relatives who insisted that their memories were false.

- **Penny** was surprised that this was an issue: "Of course, there are bad therapists as well as good ones. I've had both, and I knew which was which; but I've also had doctors that gave me wrong diagnoses, a lawyer who was unethical, and teachers who hated kids."
- **Alicia** said, "I can see both sides. And yet, it is *good* therapists who make recovery possible. They are the witnesses to unwitnessed crimes, and they have a lot to teach us."
- **Nell** worried that the public did not know what "real" survivors are like: "The media feature sensation-makers, not *real* survivors who are the 'lifers' in this matter. They struggle for years with repercussions of abuse, trying to make a life after someone betrayed them."
- **Pamela,** herself a therapist, said, "I think the memory debate challenged the therapy profession to a higher level of performance. We needed something to shake us up. Anything less would not have done it."
- **Adele** was introspective: "If I had gone through the remembering during the campaigns against 'false memories,' I think I might have killed myself. But I'm now secure in myself about what happened. I no longer feel threatened, scared, or angry by someone else's skepticism."

Today, it is increasingly evident that recovered memories of childhood abuse are common in our society and that they should neither be dismissed as false memories nor credited as flawless truth. This awareness has resulted from much heated debate as well as conciliatory efforts to find common ground. Several books have laid out both sides of the argument clearly (e.g., Pezdek & Banks, 1996; Williams & Banyard, 1999; Read

& Lindsay, 1997). Other books and articles in this area have developed from collaboration between cognitive and clinical psychologists (e.g., Lindsay & Briere, 1997; Schooler, Ambadar, & Bendikson, 1997). An especially innovative approach, which involves the collaboration of family members in validating or invalidating specific survivors' memories, has been reported by Dalenberg (1997). Over time, many proponents on both sides of the memory debate have softened their stubborn stands in an effort to learn more about traumatic memory.

The heated debate about whether recovered memories are true or false has caused some amnesic and partially amnesic survivors to feel even more distrustful of what they are remembering. However, the percentage of my respondents who had received some external verification of their memories was 67% in the early 1990s and rose to 85% by 1998, and some had a great deal of confirmation. Interestingly, however, the amount of validation did not have much impact on a survivor's certainty. For example, in 1998, there were two respondents (**Annette** and **Polly**) who mentioned that they were no longer sure, after all, whether their fathers had abused them sexually, although, in both cases, the fathers had severely abused them in other ways. Annette has had flashbacks all through the years to her father on top of her, and she knows that her brother remembers extensive sexual abuse at their father's hands. She says that she has found closure through therapy and now feels that it no longer matters whether her abuser was her father, her uncle, or both. Somewhat similarly, Polly has had recent as well as past cognitive memories of two separate rapes in her teens. But she does not now recall her father sexually abusing her as a child. I checked her 1986 questionnaires and reminded her of two memories that she had reported in 1986: She had described flashbacks to her father abusing her and also recalled that a doctor noted, when she was 12 years old, that her hymen was ruptured. Polly replied that fibromyalgia, which has disabled her, may have obscured those memories, and she suggested that her hymen might have been ruptured on the leg of an overturned stool.

Were the earlier or later reports in error? Were these survivors now detached from their abuse experience ("It doesn't matter any more"), or were they forgetting it? Another amnesic respondent processed her returning memories of father-rape and then decided not to keep thinking about them. In her case, her log book has a record of what she remembered, and she hasn't forgotten it (unlike **Amy** on page 94).

Audrey presented the best example of how survivors can be caught between abusive parents and abusive therapists, and her story demonstrates how difficult it is for survivors to find out the truth about past abuse. Audrey's parents had insisted that her 1985 recollections of their sexually abusing her were false memories. Moreover, they protested that she was destroying the family with her demand for information. She eventually moved away, asking her parents for space and time to figure things out in therapy. But her mother tracked her down, insisted on visiting, and pestered her therapist. At that point, her family's denial and intrusiveness made her vulnerable to a psychiatrist who was obsessed with dredging up memories of ritual abuse. She reported,

> If my parents had admitted the truth at *any* point during their 10 years of denial, or even left me alone when I begged them, I would never have gotten into the control of that psychiatrist. Their behavior allowed him to convince me that I was in danger and must make a total break with friends and family. After that, I was a day patient, inpatient, and in hospital for a 5-year period. I was *living* in the past—sometimes *8 hours a day* in individual or group sessions. It took many months of this before I began to believe that I'd had satanic ritual abuse.

When Audrey finally telephoned her parents, they admitted that they themselves had been in therapy (ever since she left town) to deal with the fact that they really had sexually abused her as a child and had encouraged her brother to practice his emerging sexuality on her. No, there had not been satanists involved, but her parents had used rituals and had abused her in front of other people. Their admission brought both anger and relief to Audrey. Realizing that they had finally admitted their guilt to help her, she reunited with them. They promised to give her more information and to do all they could to help her to heal. After some months of this new relationship, Audrey told me,

> I belong again, but I'm aware of the flaws. I really do wish that my parents, when talking to my siblings, would focus less on how "that psychiatrist wrecked my life" and admit that their denial drove me to him. I can *want* that forever, but it will never *happen*. And their full admission of *past* wrongs is less important than what is happening *now*. They are being really supportive of me, in other ways, so I want to center on positives for my own health. Surprisingly, I can relate best to the brother who abused me. He's helped me to sort through the pieces and regain confidence in my own memory of the truth. He's admitted that he had guys over and charged

them money for sex with me. We were new in town, and he wanted to curry their favor. I was angry to hear it but also relieved, because he verified memories that I had totally obliterated. They were true even in key details.

REACHING CLOSURE WITH
THE FAMILY OF ORIGIN

Audrey has provided a clear and poignant example of how desperately survivors will search for closure about their trauma among family members. In her account, she has achieved more verification than any other respondent in this study. In her search for truth, she gained a great deal of information. In demanding accountability, she won admissions of guilt and regret from both of her parents and from her brother. She has received some compensation in terms of emotional and financial support. However, there has been no social recognition of what happened to her. Her abuse is still unknown to people outside her family. She has reconciled herself to this situation, saying, "Today is more important than yesterday, and life is short." In this section, I summarize other examples of attempted closure in a variety of situations.

There is a deep human need to perceive wholeness in one's family—the gestalt of an unbroken circle. Brokenness is hard to accept. But that circle can be a prison, or in other cases, a family member may be abandoned within it. Typically, respondents were blamed for any breach in the family circle, even if they had left it only after repeated efforts to stay within it. At family reunions, relatives tended to see a broken relationship and tried to mend it. They hardly ever saw the abuser as the initial and primary source of family conflict, and they rarely recognized the progress made by a woman who was beginning to feel whole and empowered for the first time. As an example, **Nadia's** father had raped her for years without contrition. Yet his mother took Nadia aside and advised her, "Even if you don't want him as your father, you *could* have him as a friend."

As I interviewed respondents in 1998, each one seemed to have struggled to gain closure on the poignant issue of family. Here are some of the ways that they came to terms with a family, a parent, or a sibling who had supported, abused, or endangered them.

Enjoying a supportive parent. **ANNE's** mother was her strongest support when she was a child, and she continued to sustain her when she remembered child sexual abuse as a young adult. She even asked ANNE if the abuser had been her father, and she combed her own memory to help ANNE ground new memories as they emerged. ANNE still enjoys her "good" mother whenever distance allows a visit between them. This maternal support of her, both as a child and as an adult—and her older brother's willingness to hear her story—may help explain my perception that ANNE began healing notably more quickly than most respondents.

Reassessing nonprotective parents. Several survivors eventually reconnected, at a superficial level, with parents who had not protected them as children. It appeared that they generally did so by reassessing the limitations of those who had raised them. They abandoned their longing for "the good, the understanding, parent," who, they finally recognized, would never materialize. This permitted them a certain generosity of spirit. Over and over, I heard words like **Aurora's**: "I now gauge interaction with my mother as if she were 6 years old. No way could she have handled my problems. I no longer hold any expectations of my parents, but they are relatives—so I let them enjoy their grandchild."

Reconciliation with newly responsive parents. Survivors seemed willing to forgive a history of nonsupport if relatives had a change of heart. **Amy's** parents had been impatient with her hysterical symptoms throughout her childhood and were unsupportive when, as an adult, she sought therapy to deal with emerging memories. Recently, she informed me, "I told my parents that I'd only accept a visit if they came with me to a session with my therapist. They were offended, but they came." During that session, her parents realized that a child rapist who had briefly terrorized their town had abducted her. (Her memory had been "But I didn't get in his car.") Amy's father wept to recognize his daughter's suffering, and her usually impassive mother hugged her and said, "If I failed you, I'm really sorry." Amy told me,

> It was enough—they had acknowledged me. I feel complete with them. I know that, as parents, they did the best they knew how. They feel especially close to me now because I was honest with them, and I don't live in the dark and lonely place anymore.

Amy's words highlight several issues: Family acknowledgment matters greatly to a survivor, and that is why she will push so hard and long for an honest connection and risk so much to attain it. Without that boon, the world can be a "dark and lonely place." Yet one simple, genuine acknowledgment can sometimes bring closure to years of estrangement and open up a close, honest relationship: "It was enough. . . . I feel complete with them. . . . They did the best they knew how." Similar themes are evident in Alison's story, which follows.

Reconciliation with a responsive sibling. When parents are dead or unresponsive, the need for closure extends to a survivor's own generation. In 1984, **Alison** began having flashbacks to incest imposed by her father, and she was desolate when her siblings provided no emotional support. However, both sides soon recognized their inability (rather than unwillingness) to find common ground. This awareness enabled them to maintain a weakened connection until a later time when closure might be possible. Over time, the relationship among the siblings eased, but it seemed to Alison that the family had reunited "as if" the incest had never divided them. When a family reunion took place recently, considerable attention was focused on family archives, primarily displaying the career of her dead father. These described her father's accomplishments but held no record of his dark side.

After the reunion, Alison decided to talk to her sister Sally about her need for closure. They began by each describing her own perception of their parents. This proved really helpful because there was much agreement in their accounts, and the differences were enlightening. Alison told Sally that she wanted to add a statement about the incest to the family archives, and Sally agreed that she had the right to do so. Then, Sally listened, for the first time, to a summation of Alison's childhood trauma, as she had pieced it together over the years. And Sally offered, for the first time, additional insights about their father's distorted sexuality. Sally affirmed her sister's memories; she expressed regret that she had been unable to be supportive earlier and sorrow that Alison had felt so alone as a child and as a remembering adult. In turn, Alison expressed regret that she had pressured her sister to believe that she had also been molested instead of leaving that conclusion up to Sally. When the sisters felt that their sharing was complete, they performed a small ceremony with candles as a symbol of their renewed closeness.

Any family is strengthened when its members bond together by choice instead of obligation. In both of the above stories, we see new truth being revealed, family members acknowledging the survivor's reality and the survivor recognizing the constraints that had kept them from full support of her at an earlier time. These stories are powerful examples of how a family reconciliation can seem simple to achieve. In each story, a small but significant show of support overcame years of tension or estrangement. Of course, these interactions were not really simple but complex, and the effort to gain closure could have deepened estrangement instead. Both parties must truly want to draw closer. I believe that such positive confrontations need as much thoughtful consideration as an accusatory one with an abuser if they are to effective. However, the good outcomes with Amy's parents and Alison's sister suggest that the concept of truth and reconciliation may be more attainable within a family than within a troubled nation that is attempting to heal intergroup conflict.

A superficial relationship. Respondents who chose a superficial relationship with a family member usually did so out of duty or family loyalty. **Nanette** helped care for both her parents prior to their deaths, but she set limits on physical care of her father because he had abused her. **Alicia** says of her 85-year-old mother, "It's sad that she only wants to know her own *image* of me, but I'm past the place of needing anything from her and have no need to shatter her fantasy world." And **Astrid** now understands that her parents could not protect her as a child, nor can they relate to her today:

> My parents disassociate big time. They are incapable of dealing with the past, their own or mine. Mom remembers my "wonderful childhood." Dad remembers nothing. We get together only occasionally.

No relationship. Several of the respondents have broken with their family of origin. There were powerful reasons behind these decisions. Typically, they saw their relatives as highly dysfunctional, and the label was not lightly applied. **Anita** explained, "Both sides of my family are driven by alcohol, depression, and guns," and her two cousins have corroborated that view. At one time or another, most of her relatives sexually abused her (including her mother when she was drunk). When Anita tried to talk to her mother, she responded, "I never drank in my life. Those are false memories." Anita is making healthy choices among family and friends and building a new family. "Older women are my mother, my friends are my sisters. It is they who follow my activities and give me support."

Nell's brothers and mother had sexually abused her, and she doesn't want her children exposed to their pathology and possible danger. Her second husband's warm and healthy family fills her potential emptiness. **Phyllis** was raised by a father who brutalized his children, especially if one showed compassion for another. A brother raped her, regularly and sadistically. All her siblings are scattered to locations unknown, but she says, "My uncle is family to me now. He is caring and aware of our terrible childhood."

THE WOMEN'S REACTIONS TO PARTICIPATION IN THIS STUDY

After their 1998 interviews, many of the respondents had a chance to leaf through the manuscript of this book, and I asked them what participating in the study had meant to them. One theme—a cornerstone for all the others—was that this book gave a voice to silenced children and the survivors that they became. A second theme was expressed by **Pat** (and **NANCY** at the beginning of this chapter). They felt a connection with the other survivors in the book: "We're part of something bigger than any one of us." Other respondents hoped that a similar sense of oneness would envelop the larger community of therapists and survivors as they read the book. **ILENE** said, "I hope that they will see themselves in it." **Nedda** spoke of the satisfaction of reaching and helping others who are hurting: "Bringing good out of evil gives value to a painful experience, and I'm thrilled to be part of anything that helps others." Several other women placed a high priority on educating society. Social denial and ignorance of child sexual abuse frightened them, and they hoped that this book could help readers sort through the complexity.

The feelings that the still-imprisoned women expressed about being part of the study are especially poignant, for they may never enjoy their recovery beyond prison walls. They focused on reaching out to other survivors. **Iris** wrote a message of encouragement: "Please tell them, 'You are not alone. Hang in there and trust the healing process. It will be OK.' " **Isabel** was generous: "Any opportunity to contribute to the healing of others is terrific! I want them to realize the joy, freedom, and healing that I have found." And **Ilsa** was compassionate: "I feel happiness to be in this study. Many victims are scared, as I was, to begin healing. I would do whatever I could to help them. *It feels like love.*"

CONCLUDING REFLECTIONS

During the 12 years of this study, the respondents reviewed their entire lives and determined to relinquish behavior patterns that were no longer productive. Concentrating on building their strength in the present and for the future, they began to live in each day rather than remaining hostage to the past. Almost all of them recognized that they were growing markedly in the range of emotions available to them, in the conviction of their own values, and in the honesty with which they faced themselves and those about them. Perhaps most important, they grew to respect and love themselves.

Of course, the women you have gotten to know through these pages have not reached nirvana. Rebuilding one's life is a continuing challenge —especially for those who fully confront the task. There will be times when they again feel the old pain, but it will not be as deep nor will it last as long. They are no longer victims of trauma or even just survivors. Many are stronger than people who have never come through such pain, and they feel confident that they can deal with whatever life brings. They are facing the responsibilities of a new way of living with sensitivity and compassion, as well as a commitment to justice in the world. They have given voice to their stories in the hope that the children of tomorrow can grow up in an informed and caring society.

THOUGHTS FOR THE NEW MILLENNIUM

As we leave the 20th century, the world is still a place where individuals, groups, and nations can be victimized by those who are more powerful. However, new concepts have entered our vocabulary, and we take them with us to define social reality in the new millennium. Some are highly negative ones, which chasten us and call us to action. We now see long-standing social wrongs that were previously invisible. We recognize evil when it is precisely named—date rape, stalking, elder abuse, war crimes, genocide, and father rape. These concepts arose from enlightened thinking. Only after they were named could we begin to confront them.

There are other new concepts that define social justice, and they lift our spirits and give us hope. None is more fundamental than the concept of human rights. It has already become a powerful social construct for the fulfillment of human needs. Shay (1994) has said that "the understanding of trauma can form a solid basis for a science of human rights" (p. 209).

Wronka (1998) envisions, in the 21st century, a culture grounded in human rights and supported by public commitment.

Certainly, the 20th century has forced us to recognize the many faces of trauma as it arises by human design, and the devastation that follows in its wake. This understanding has been a painful learning experience, but it is the survivors of trauma who have been our greatest teachers. Those who lived through "the final solution" and "ethnic cleansing" told their excruciating stories before international courts of justice. Those whose relatives "disappeared" in South America risked everything to demand answers. "Comfort women," abducted for rape in military brothels, broke through shame and silence 50 years later. Survivors of "fondling" and father "lovers" have spoken out through this book. All of these various survivors have helped us understand the experience and the consequences of trauma. They have done so out of a deep need to be heard at last. They have done so also in the hope that, because they named the wrong, others might be spared.

The 21st century begins with humanity appalled at the evil depths to which it can descend, yet inspired by a vision of what it might attain. It is survivors, like those you have met in these pages, who call us to make the necessary commitments to win social justice for our world.

NOTES

1. Following the original survey in 1986, follow-up surveys had taken place in 1988 and 1992, as well as telephone interviews with most of the women in 1995.

2. Throughout much of the study, the partially amnesic women tended, when the difference between the polar groups was large, to fall between them.

3. This potent mechanism—threatening classes of people through a member of the group—has been described before in other contexts. Susan Brownmiller noted, in 1975, that the rape of individual women threatens *all* women, facilitating their subordination. Her thesis was later corroborated by Bohner and Schwarz (1996). On a similar note, Russell (1995) declared that the incestuous abuse of individual children within the home should be treated as a massive human rights issue.

Bibliography

Abraham, K. (1927). *The experiencing of sexual traumas as a form of sexual activity: 1907 selected papers* (D. Bryon & A. Strahey, Trans.). London: Hogarth.

American Psychiatric Association. (1980). *Diagnostic and statistical manual of mental disorders* (3rd ed.). Washington, DC: Author.

American Psychiatric Association. (1987). *Diagnostic and statistical manual of mental disorders* (3rd ed., rev.). Washington, DC: Author.

American Psychiatric Association. (1994). *Diagnostic and statistical manual of mental disorders* (4th ed.). Washington, DC: Author.

Arrigo, J. M., & Pezdek, K. (1997). Lessons from the study of psychogenic amnesia. *Current Directions in Psychological Science, 6,* 148-152.

Bass, E., & Davis, L. (1988). *Courage to heal.* New York: Harper & Row.

Bender, L., & Blau, A. (1937). The reaction of children to sexual relations with adults. *American Journal of Orthopsychiatry, 7,* 500-518.

Berliner, L., & Briere, J. (1999). Trauma, memory, and clinical practice. In L. M. Williams & V. Banyard (Eds.), *Trauma and memory* (pp. 3-19). Thousand Oaks, CA: Sage.

Betzner, A., & Jensen, B. (1995). Military sexual slavery by Japan. *Whisper, 9*(1),1.

Blank, A. S. (1985). Psychosocial treatment of war veterans: A challenge for mental health professionals. *Medical Hypnoanalysis, 6*(3), 91-96.

Bohner, G., & Schwarz, N. (1996). The threat of rape: Its psychological impact on nonvictimized women. In D. M. Buss & N. M. Malamuth (Eds.), *Sex, power, conflict* (pp. 162-175). New York: Oxford University Press.

Bower, G. (1981). Mood and memory. *American Psychologist, 36,* 129-148.

Bowlby, J. (1980). *Attachment and loss* (Vol. 3). New York: Basic Books.

Breuer, J., & Freud, S. (1955). *Studies on hysteria* (Vol. 2). London: Hogarth. (Original work published 1895)

Briere, J. (1989). *Therapy for adults molested as children.* New York: Springer.

Briere, J. (Ed.). (1991). *Treating child victims of child sexual abuse.* San Francisco: Jossey-Bass.

Briere, J., & Conte, J. (1993). Self-reported amnesia for abuse in adults molested as children. *Journal of Traumatic Stress, 6,* 21-31.

Briere, J. N., & Elliott, D. M. (1994). Immediate and long-term impact of child sexual abuse. *The Future of Children, 4*(2), 54-69.

327

Briere, J., & Runtz, M. (1985, August). *Symptomatology associated with prior sexual abuse in a nonclinical sample.* Paper presented at the annual meeting of the American Psychological Association, Los Angeles.

Briere, J., & Runtz, M. (1987). Post-sexual abuse trauma. *Journal of Interpersonal Violence, 2,* 367-379.

Brody, J. E. (1988). Studies unmask origins of brutal migraine. *New York Times,* pp. B7, B12.

Brown, D., Scheflin, A., & Whitefield, C. L. (1999). Recovered memories: The current weight of evidence in science and the courts. *The Journal of Psychiatry and Law, 26,* 5-56.

Brownmiller, S. (1975). *Against our will: Men, women, and rape.* New York: Simon & Schuster.

Butler, S. (1979). *Conspiracy of silence: The trauma of incest.* New York: Bantam.

Cameron, C. (1994a). Veterans of a secret war: Survivors of childhood sexual abuse compared to Vietnam War veterans with PTSD. *Journal of Interpersonal Violence, 9,* 117-132.

Cameron, C. (1994b). Women survivors confronting their abusers: Issues, decisions, and outcomes. *Journal of Child Sexual Abuse, 3,* 7-35.

Cameron, C. (1996). Comparing amnesic and nonamnesic survivors of childhood sexual abuse: A longitudinal study. In K. Pezdek & W. P. Banks (Eds.), *The recovered memory/false memory debate* (pp. 41-68). San Diego: Academic Press.

Carlson, E. B. (1997). Reported amnesia for childhood abuse and other traumatic events in psychiatric inpatients. In J. D. Read & D. S. Lindsay (Eds.), *Recollections of trauma* (pp. 395-401). New York: Plenum.

Courtois, C. A. (1988). *Healing the incest wound.* New York: Norton.

Courtois, C. (1992). The memory retrieval process in incest survivor therapy. *Journal of Child Sexual Abuse, 1,* 15-31.

Courtois, C. (1999). *Recollections of sexual abuse.* New York: Norton.

Dalenberg, C. (1997). The prediction of accurate recollections of trauma. In J. D. Read & D. S. Lindsay (Eds.), *Recollections of trauma* (pp. 449-453). New York: Plenum.

Donaldson, M. A., & Gardner, R., Jr. (1985). Diagnosis and treatment of traumatic stress among women after childhood incest. In C. R. Figley (Ed.), *Trauma and its wake* (pp. 356-377). New York: Brunner/Mazel.

Elkind, D. (1970, April 5). Erik Erikson's eight stages of man. *New York Times Magazine,* pp. 21-34.

Ellenson, G. S. (1985). Detecting a history of incest. *Social Casework, 66,* 525-531.

Elliott, D., & Briere, J. (1995, November). *Epidemiology of memory and trauma.* Paper presented at the annual meeting of the International Society on Traumatic Stress Studies, Chicago.

Emerson, J. G. (1974). *The dynamics of forgiveness.* Philadelphia: Westminster.

Emerson, J. G. (1986). *Suffering: Its meaning and ministry.* Nashville, TN: Abingdon.

Ensink, B. J. (1992). *Confusing realities.* Amsterdam: Free University Press.

Erikson, E. H. (1963). *Childhood and society* (2nd ed.). New York: Norton.

Erikson, E. H. (1968). *Identity: Youth and crisis.* New York: Norton.

Eth, S., & Pynoos, R. S. (1985). Developmental perspective on psychic trauma in childhood. In C. R. Figley (Ed.), *Trauma and its wake* (Vol. 1). New York: Brunner/Mazel.

Eth, S., & Pynoos, R. S. (Eds.). (1985). *Post-traumatic stress disorder in children.* Washington, DC: American Psychiatric Press.

Farnquist, T. L. (1996), Requiem for the *Edmund Fitzgerald. National Geographic, 189*(1), 36-47.

Felitti, V. J., Anda, R. F., Nordenberg, D., Williamson, D. F., Spitz, A. M., Edwards, V., Koss, M. P., & Marks, J. S. (1998). Relationship of adult health status to child abuse and household dysfunction. *American Journal of Preventative Medicine, 14* (4), 245-258.

Fillmore, R. (1998, Jan. 19-Feb. 1). Sexual trauma main source of PTSD in female Vietnam veterans. *Stars and Stripes,* p. 14.

Finkelhor, D. (1979). *Sexually victimized children.* New York: Free Press.

Finkelhor, D. (1984). *Child sexual abuse: New theory and research.* New York: Free Press.

Finkelhor, D., Araji, S., Baron, L., Browne, A., Peters, S. D., & Wyatt, G. E. (1986). *A sourcebook on child sexual abuse.* Beverly Hills, CA: Sage.

Finkelhor, D. (1997). The victimization of children and youth: Developmental victimization. In R. Davis & A. J. Lurigio (Eds.), *Victims of crime* (2nd ed., pp. 86-107). Thousand Oaks, CA: Sage.

Finkelhor, D., & Browne, A. (1985). The traumatic impact of child sexual abuse. *American Journal of Orthopsychiatry, 55,* 530-541.

Finkelhor, D., & Browne, A. (1986). Initial and long-term effects: A conceptual framework. In D. Finkelhor, S. Araji, L. Baron, A. Browne, S. D. Peters, & G. E. Wyatt, *A sourcebook on child sexual abuse* (pp. 180-198). Beverly Hills, CA: Sage.

Fivush, R., & Hudson, J. A. (Eds.). (1990). *Knowing and remembering in young children.* New York: Cambridge University Press.

Fontana, A., & Rosenheck, R. (1993). DVA Northeast Program Evaluation Center. *PTSD Research Quarterly, 4*(2).

Forward, S., & Buck, C. (1987). *Betrayal of innocence.* Los Angeles: Penguin.

Fredrickson, R. (1992). *Repressed memories.* New York: Simon & Schuster.

Freedman, A. M., Kaplan, H. I., & Sadock, B. J. (1976). *Modern synopsis of comprehensive textbook of psychiatry* (2nd ed.). Baltimore, MD: Williams & Wilkins.

Freud, A. (1981). A psychoanalyst's view of sexual abuse by parents. In P. B. Mrazek & C. H. Kempe (Eds.), *Sexually abused children and their families.* New York: Pergamon.

Freyd, J. (1994). Betrayal-trauma: Traumatic amnesia as an adaptive response to childhood abuse. *Ethics and Behavior, 4,* 307-329.

Freyd, J. J. (1996). *Betrayal trauma.* Cambridge, MA: Harvard University Press.

Friedrich, W. N. (1990). *Psychotherapy of sexually abused children and their families.* New York: Norton.

Garbarino, J., Guttmann, E., & Seeley, J. W. (1987). *The psychologically battered child.* San Francisco: Jossey-Bass.

Gelinas, D. (1983). Persisting negative effects of incest. *Psychiatry, 46,* 312-332.

Glasser, W. (1976). *Positive addiction.* New York: Harper & Row.

Goldberg, J., True, W. R., Eisen, S. A., & Henderson, W. G. (1990). A twin study of the effects of the Vietnam War on post-traumatic stress disorder. *Journal of the American Medical Association, 263,* 1227-1232.

Goleman, D. (1992, January/February). Wounds: How trauma changes your brain. *Psychology Today,* pp. 62-66, 88.

Goodman, J. (Ed.). (1993). *Rediscovering childhood trauma.* Washington, DC: American Psychiatric Press.

Grahlfs, F. L. (1995). *Voices from ground zero.* Unpublished dissertation, University of Michigan, Ann Arbor.

Henderson, J. (1983, February). Is incest harmful? *Canadian Journal of Psychiatry, 28,* 34-39.

Herman, J. L. (1981). *Father-daughter incest.* Cambridge, MA: Harvard University Press.

Herman, J. L. (1992). *Trauma and recovery.* New York: Basic Books.

Herman, J. L., & Harvey, M. (1997). Adult memories of childhood trauma. *Journal of Traumatic Stress, 10,* 557-571.

Herman, J. L., & Schatzow, E. (1987). Recovery and verification of memories of childhood sexual trauma. *Psychoanalytic Psychology, 4,* 1-14.

Hewitt, S. K. (1999). *Assessing allegations of sexual abuse in preschool children.* Thousand Oaks, CA: Sage.

Hilgard, J. R. (1989). The anniversary syndrome as related to late-appearing mental illnesses in hospitalized patients. In A.-L. S. Silver (Ed.), *Psychoanalysis and psychosis* (pp. 221-247). Madison, CT: International Universities Press.

Horney, K. (1950). *Neurosis and human growth.* New York: Norton.

Hunter, M. (1990). *Abused boys: The neglected victims of sexual abuse.* Lexington, MA: Lexington.

Janet, P. (1889). *L'automatism psychologique.* Paris: J. B. Bailliere.

Janoff-Bulman, R. (1990). *Shattered assumptions.* New York: Free Press.

Jones, J. H. (1997, August 25). Annals of sexology: Dr. Yes. *New Yorker,* pp. 99-113.

Kahr, B. (1991). The sexual molestation of children: Historical perspectives. *Journal of Psychhistory, 19,* 191-214.

Kaplan, H. I., & Sadock, B. J. (1988). *Synopsis of psychiatry* (5th ed.). Baltimore, MD: Williams & Wilkins.

Kaylor, J. A., King, D. W., & King, L. A. (1987). Psychosocial effects of military service in Vietnam. *Psychosocial Bulletin, 102,* 257-271.

Kempe, R. S., & Kempe, C. H. (1978). *Child abuse.* Cambridge, MA: Harvard University Press.

Kempe, R. S., & Kempe, C. H. (1984). *The common secret: Sexual abuse of children and adolescents.* New York: Freeman.

Kinsey, A. C., Pomeroy, W. B., & Martin, C. E. (1948). *Sexual behavior in the human male.* Philadelphia: Saunders.

Kinsey, A. C., Pomeroy, W. B., Martin, C. E., & Gebhard, P. H. (1953). *Sexual behavior in the human female.* Philadelphia: Saunders.

Lew, M. (1988). *Victims no longer.* New York: Nevraumont.

Lies, E. (1998, May 11-24). Japan court makes landmark compensation ruling for "comfort women." *Stars and Stripes,* p. 17.

Lindsay, D. S., & Briere, J. (1997). The controversy regarding recovered memories of childhood sexual abuse. *Journal of Interpersonal Violence, 12*(5), 631-647.

Lipstadt, D. E. (1994). *Denying the holocaust.* New York: Free Press.

Loftus, E., & Ketcham, K. (1994). *The myth of repressed memories.* New York: St. Martin's.

Majendie, P. (1998, December 1-14). British military opposes blanket pardon for WWI men shot at dawn. *Stars and Stripes,* p. 20.

Maslow, A. H. (1970). *Motivation and personality* (2nd ed.). New York: Harper & Row.

Maslow, A. H. (1971). *The farther reaches of human nature.* New York: Viking.

Masson, J. (1984). *The assault on truth: Freud's suppression of the seduction theory.* New York: Farrar, Straus, & Giroux.

Meiselman, K. C. (1978). *Incest.* San Francisco: Jossey-Bass.

Meiselman, K. C. (1990). *Resolving the trauma of incest: Reintegration therapy with survivors.* San Francisco: Jossey-Bass.

Melchert, T., & Parker, R. L. (1997). Different forms of childhood abuse and memory. *Child Abuse and Neglect, 21,* 125-135.

Meyer, L., & Romero, J. (1980). *Ten year follow-up of sex offender recidivism.* Philadelphia: Joseph Peters Institute.

Moses, S. (1991, November). Even one adult's help can aid abused youth. *APA Monitor, 22*(11), 30.

National Center on Child Abuse and Neglect. (1978). *Interdisciplinary glossary on child abuse and neglect.* Washington, DC: U.S. Department of Education.

Nethaway, R. (1993, August/September). Whining about abuse as an epidemic. *FMSF Newsletter,* p. 6.

Neuman, D. A., Houskamp, B. M., Pollock, V. E., & Briere, J. (1996). The long-term sequelae of childhood sexual abuse in women: A meta-analytic review. *Child Maltreatment, 1,* 6-16.

Orbach, I. (1988). *Children who don't want to live.* San Francisco: Jossey-Bass.

Osterweis, M., Solomon, F., & Green, M. (Eds.). (1984). *Bereavement.* Washington, DC: National Academy Press.

Pennebaker, J. W. (1990). *Opening up: The healing power of confiding in others.* New York: Morrow.

Pezdek, K., & Banks, W. P. (Eds.). (1996). *The recovered memory/false memory debate.* San Diego: Academic Press.

Pope, K. S., & Brown, L. S. (1996). *Recovered memories of abuse.* Washington, DC: American Psychological Association.

Raphling, D. L., Carpenter, B. L., & Davis, A. (1967). Incest: A genealogical study. *Archives of General Psychiatry, 16*(4), 505-518.

Read, J. D., & Lindsay D. S. (Eds.). (1997). *Recollections of trauma.* New York: Plenum.

Roseman, M. E. (1992). Adult survivors of child sexual abuse litigation. *Western State University Law Review, 20*(1), 81-101.

Rosenquist, C. M. (1932-1933). Differential responses of Texas convicts. *American Journal of Sociology, 38,* 17.

Rowan, A. B., & Foy, D. W. (1993). PTSD in child sexual abuse survivors: A literature review. *Journal of Traumatic Stress, 6*(1), 3-19.

Rush, F. (1980). *The best kept secret.* Englewood Cliffs, NJ: Prentice Hall.

Russell, D. (1986). *The secret trauma.* New York: Basic Books.

Russell, D. E. H. (1995). The prevalence, trauma, and sociocultural causes of incestuous abuse of females: A human rights issue. In R. J. Kleber & C. R. Figley (Eds.). *Beyond trauma* (pp. 171-186). New York: Plenum.

Salter, H. L. (1995). *Transforming trauma.* Thousand Oaks, CA: Sage.

Schooler, J. W., Ambadar, Z., & Bendikson, M. (1997). A cognitive corroborative case study approach for investigating discovered memories of sexual abuse. In J. D. Read & D. S. Lindsay (Eds.), *Recollections of trauma* (pp. 379-387). New York: Plenum.

Schreiber, F. R. (1973). *Sybil.* New York: Warner.

Scott, W. J. (1990). PTSD in DSM-III. *Social Problems, 37,* 294-310.

Seligman, M. E. P. (1975). *Helplessness: On depression, development, and death.* San Francisco: Freeman.

Shatan, C. F. (1973). The grief of soldiers. *American Journal of Orthopsychiatry, 43,* 640-643.

Shay, J. (1994). *Achilles in Vietnam.* New York: Atheneum.

Soothill, K. L., & Gibbons, T. C. N. (1978). Recidivism of sexual offenders: A reappraisal. *British Journal of Criminology, 18,* 267-276.

Sugar, M. (1992). Toddlers' traumatic memories. *Infant Mental Health Journal, 13,* 245-251.

Summit, R. (1983). The child sexual abuse accommodation syndrome. *Child Abuse and Neglect, 7,* 177-193.

Summit, R. C. (1985). Causes, consequences, treatment, and prevention of sexual assault against children. In J. H. Meier (Ed.), *Assault against children* (pp. 47-58). San Diego: College-Hill.

Sveaass, N. (1998). The organized destruction of meaning. In N. J. Lavi, M. Nygard, N. Sveaass, & E. Fannemel (Eds.), *Pain and survival: Human rights violations and mental health* (pp. 44-64). Oslo: Scandinavian University Press.

Tate, T. (Producer, London). (1998). *Secret history.* Los Angeles: KCAL.

Tavris, C. (1993, January 3). Beware the incest-survivor machine. *New York Times Book Review,* pp. 1, 16-17.

Tedeschi, R. G., & Calhoun, L. G. (1995). *Trauma and transformation.* Thousand Oaks, CA: Sage.

Terr, L. C. (1988). What happens to early memories of trauma? *Child and Adolescent Psychiatry, 27,* 96-104.

Terr, L. (1990). *Too scared to cry.* New York: Harper & Row.

Terr, L. (1994). *Unchained memories.* New York: Basic Books.

Vanderbilt, H. (1992, February). Incest: A chilling report. *Lear,* pp. 49-77.

van der Kolk, B. A. (1987). *Psychological trauma.* Washington, DC: American Psychiatric Press.

van der Kolk, B. A., McFarlane, A. C., & Weisaeth, L. (Eds.). (1996). *Traumatic stress.* New York: Guilford.

Van Der Wall (1996, March 11-17). The VA finding sexual assault more than "a minor problem." *Stars and Stripes,* p. 12.

Weinberg, S. K. (1995). *Incest behavior.* New York: Cidadel.

White, S. H., & Pillemer, D. B. (1979). Let's not sweep repression under the rug. In J. F. Kilstrom & F. J. Evans (Eds.), *Functional disorders of memory* (pp. 20-35). Hillsdale, NJ: Erlbaum.

Williams, L. M. (1995). Recovered memories of abuse in women with documented child sexual victimization histories. *Journal of Traumatic Stress, 8,* 649-673.

Williams, L. M., & Banyard, V. L. (1999). Memories for child sexual abuse and mental functioning. In L. M. Williams & V. L. Banyard (Eds.), *Trauma and memory* (pp. 115-125). Thousand Oaks, CA: Sage.

Wilson, J. P. (1977). *Identity, ideology, and crisis.* Cleveland, OH: Cleveland State University Press.

Wilson, J. P., Smith, W. K., & Johnson, S. K. (1985). A comparative analysis of PTSD among various survivor groups. In C. R. Figley (Ed.), *Trauma and its wake* (pp. 142-172). New York: Brunner/Mazel.

Wolff, K. H. (Ed., Trans.). (1950). *The sociology of Georg Simmel.* Glencoe, IL: Free Press.

Wronka, J. (1998). *Human rights and social policy in the 21st century.* New York: University Press of America.

Wyatt, G. E., & Powell, G. J. (1988). *The lasting effects of child sexual abuse.* Newbury Park, CA: Sage.

Author Index

Subject Index